Collins
Tracing your home's history

Anthony Adolph

To Gwen Adolph, wife of my late grandfather Joseph A. S. Adolph. As a schools' librarian she instilled a love of books and reading into countless children – including me.

First published in 2006 by
Collins, an imprint of
HarperCollins Publishers
77–85 Fulham Palace Road
Hammersmith
London W6 8JB

www.collins.co.uk

Anthony Adolph's website is www.anthonyadolph.co.uk

Editorial: Emma Callery, Louise Stanley
Picture research: Mary-Jane Gibson
Design: Richard Marston
Proofreading: Kate Parker

A catalogue record for this book is available from the British Library

ISBN-10 0-00-721140-6
ISBN-13 978-0-00-721140-1

Printed and bound in Great Britain by Butler and Tanner

Contents

PART 3 Digging deeper

PART 4 Broadening the picture

Introduction

For many of us, choices about renting or buying homes are among the biggest financial and emotional decisions we ever make. Yet, as the local historian Arthur Percival points out, our choices are often made on the basis of less information about a building, such as its age and history, than we would demand when buying a car or an antique, hiring an employee or getting married. When it comes to renting or buying homes, we're often content with the flimsiest of explanations. 'It's pre-war/Victorian/Georgian' is usually all we're told.

Our homes make a great impact on our lives, so it's not surprising that some of us want to know a lot more detail about them than a bald and often inaccurate statement about their age. Julie Myerson, whose book *Home: The Story of Everyone Who Ever Lived in Our House* (Harper Perennial, 2005) helped inspire this guide, makes the sensible point that:

> *... most of us live in our homes knowing we're not the only ones to have done so. But we rarely confront those shadows in any significant way. Why should we? This is us and that was them. Their clutter, their smells, their noises, and their way of doing things are long gone. We've painted, decorated, demolished and constructed or converted – a loft, a bigger kitchen, a new power shower in the bathroom. Our moments have blotted out theirs ...*

And yet, as Myerson goes on to say, there are so many parts of homes that time does not erase. Old wallpaper, ancient trees in the garden, the arrival of letters addressed to previous occupants – all these 'shadows' remind us that our homes have their own past, bring our imaginations alive and inspire our desire to know more. When she started her own quest for her home's earlier inhabitants, Julie Myerson found that just seeing her own address in an old record had a strangely moving effect on her:

> *I'm surprised at how just an address can feel like a part of you. In a way, it's hard to believe that those words existed before we lived here. More than a hundred years of letters plopping through the letter box with that precise number and those words on it. Crowds of different people who'd write '34 Lillieshall*

TOP
Buildings can often be judged by their appearance – but they can also be deceptive. Castle Drogo, Devon, was built as a Medieval castle by Sir Edward Lutyens – between 1910 and 1913!

ABOVE
This London square is in fact nothing of the sort – it is part of the purpose-built set of the BBC1 soap opera *EastEnders* in Elstree Studios, Hertfordshire.

Road' each time they had to fill in a form or begin a letter ...

It's a connection with the past you'll feel as well when you start investigating the history of your home.

The traditional term for this sort of research is 'house history'. That's all very well, but it suggests everybody lives in houses. Moreover, it assumes that this is a pastime for homeowners only. However, if you want to find out more about where you live, it doesn't matter whether you own a palatial Tudor farmhouse in a leafy village, lease an apartment in a converted docklands warehouse or rent a council flat. Whatever and wherever it is, home is home. And this book tells you how to trace its history.

By extension, this book also tells you how to trace the history of any home or building. While researching the sources in this book, I often looked up interesting buildings near where I live or homes where ancestors of mine lived in the past. You can use your skills as a home historian to enrich not only your knowledge of your own home, but of ancestral homes, homes of local or national interest, or indeed any building, whether a home, pub, shop, or office, that takes your fancy. Being a 'home historian' is also a transferable skill that can be used to increase your enjoyment of many aspects of history.

Bricks and mortals

Every home, however old or new, has a history. Its bricks and mortar, or thatch or tiles, have stories to tell. Both the era and the area in which a home is built help determine its shape, size, style, use, composition, appearance and feel.

Histories of homes are about change. Homes are almost organic entities in the way they are constantly being altered by redecoration, improvement, embellishment, modification or damage by fire or flood. Equally, their surroundings are in constant flux as roads, trees and buildings appear and disappear and views from the windows expand and contract.

Indeed, home history dovetails neatly into local history. Local history provides the wider context in which the drama of your home's existence is unfolded. It opens grander vistas on the past, too, for even if your home was built the day before yesterday, the land on which it stands has a story dating back millions of years. You can find out how the land below your home was used – factory or farm, field or forest – hundreds of years before the first brick was laid. Going back even earlier, you can learn whether, 10,000 years ago, the ground below your home was

LEFT
'The March of Progress': 1829 Cruickshank cartoon showing the fields of Hampstead being invaded by jerry-built brick houses. The air is polluted with black smoke from the kilns and domestic chimneys, and the landscape is scarred with claypits.

BELOW
Modern houses under construction – this land could have been used for earlier buildings for hundreds of years.

grazed by mammoths or scoured clean beneath a mile-high glacier.

Histories of homes – as Julie Myerson's book illustrates particularly well – are also about family history. The people who lived in your home before you have helped to make it what it is now. Who they were affects what it is now. Your home's history is the story of all the people who lived in it, from the day it was built to the day you woke up in it and decided you wanted to learn more about its past. Within the walls of your home people have been born, grown up, fallen in love, argued, learned, grieved, died. As a home historian, you will also become a historian of the families whose lives have been touched by your – and their – home.

In many cases, in fact, it's curiosity about past inhabitants that inspires people to begin researching. Perhaps an old photograph of an unknown face starts the quest, or even the creaking of a floorboard as a ghost passes. Some people don't believe in ghosts. For others, though, the people who used to live

CAMBRIDGE
9-PM
8 SEP
1933

Mrs Stanislaus. Havers
67. Avondale Road
South Croydon

Descendants of previous occupants of your home may have left all sorts of memorabilia concerning it. This envelope from 1933 has a certain fascination for the present inhabitants of 67 Avondale Road, Croydon.

Derek Acorah, centre, flanked by the author and antiques expert Chris Gower. Taken during the filming of *Antiques Ghostshow*.

in their homes are anything but an historical curiosity – in spirit form, they're still there! In shows such as Living TV's *Most Haunted* series, my friend the psychic Derek Acorah visits buildings all over Britain and uses his paranormal skills to communicate with the spirits of dead inhabitants. It's not to everyone's taste – or credulity – but the fact that the programme has a devoted following of millions worldwide shows how many people are fascinated by the possible ghosts in their attics.

Tracing the history of homes has become really popular in the last couple of decades. This is mainly because, thanks to the opening up of archives, the advent of the internet and the explosion of interest in family history, gaining access to original records has become much easier than it used to be. Yet people's enhanced ability to investigate their home's past has not created the interest, so much as made it a great deal easier to find the answers to questions that have always been there. When you think about it, the history of places lies at the root of a lot of our story telling. From Jane Austen's *Northanger Abbey* to A. A. Milne's *The House at Pooh Corner*, many successful books and films are based around homes and the events that unfold within them. In conjunction with family history, home history is the essence of soap operas, too – there are very few fans who couldn't write brief histories of some of the homes in at least one soap opera, whether it's *Neighbours*' Ramsey Street or *The Archers*' Ambridge; *Coronation Street* or *Emmerdale Farm*. Home history belongs in a much deeper part of our psyche than most of us might realise.

My mother's original family home, 'Old Tiles' in Mark Cross, Sussex, was so called because of the typical local tile cladding of its first floor. The tiles may have been old, but the house was not – it was new when her parents moved in the 1930s.

Whether you live in a block of flats, a palatial Georgian mansion, a 1930s semi, or a half-timbered Medieval town house, there is much to find out about the history of your home.

How to use this book

There is no 'correct' way to trace your home's history. For as long as it's been standing, your home has been appearing on maps, in pictures and generating different sorts of records. It's usually desirable to start research in the present and then work back. One of the fascinating things about home histories, however, is the way different pieces of material can emerge from a wide variety of different sources and from many different decades or even, in the case of older properties, centuries. While dutifully searching for a mention of your home in early-20th-century directories in the local archives, for example, you may spot an old map of the area hanging on the wall, and identify your home on it. If so, good for you! Your home's history is unique, and thus the process you will follow to reconstruct its history cannot conform rigidly to any preconceived models of what it should be.

I can, however, recommend a general approach to tracing your home's history that will enable you to take into account all the complementary sources of information that will feed into each other. First, there are four broad areas to consider:

1. Learning about your home from its architecture; method(s) of construction; special features (such as house name, coats of arms, etc.); and surroundings.
2. Seeking surviving title deeds or abstracts of title, together with details of the building from the Land Registry.
3. Making enquiries of neighbours and tracing past occupants of your home.
4. Beginning archival research.

As the chart opposite shows, each of these steps will then lead you on to more in-depth investigations. There are books on the subject that suggest the history of homes is mainly about tracing past inhabitants; or principally concerned with architecture; or is pretty much complete once the title deeds have been located; or else is solely rooted in archival research (there is one popular guide on the market that focuses on archival research at the National Archives, to the virtual exclusion of all else).

You *can* focus on just one of these areas, but I believe you'll get more out of the subject by making a gentle start on each at about the same time. Judging the rough age of your home by its architectural clues can help focus your research in archives. Title deeds can provide the names of past owners whose descendants you can trace (using archives) to see what information and pictures of the place they might have. Past inhabitants can, in turn, cast light on alterations to the building's fabric you might not otherwise be able to explain, and archival research will also shed fresh light on your home's architectural story.

My suggestion, then, is to plan a steady advance on all four fronts. You could farm out different tasks among different members of the family according to suitability – alloting the

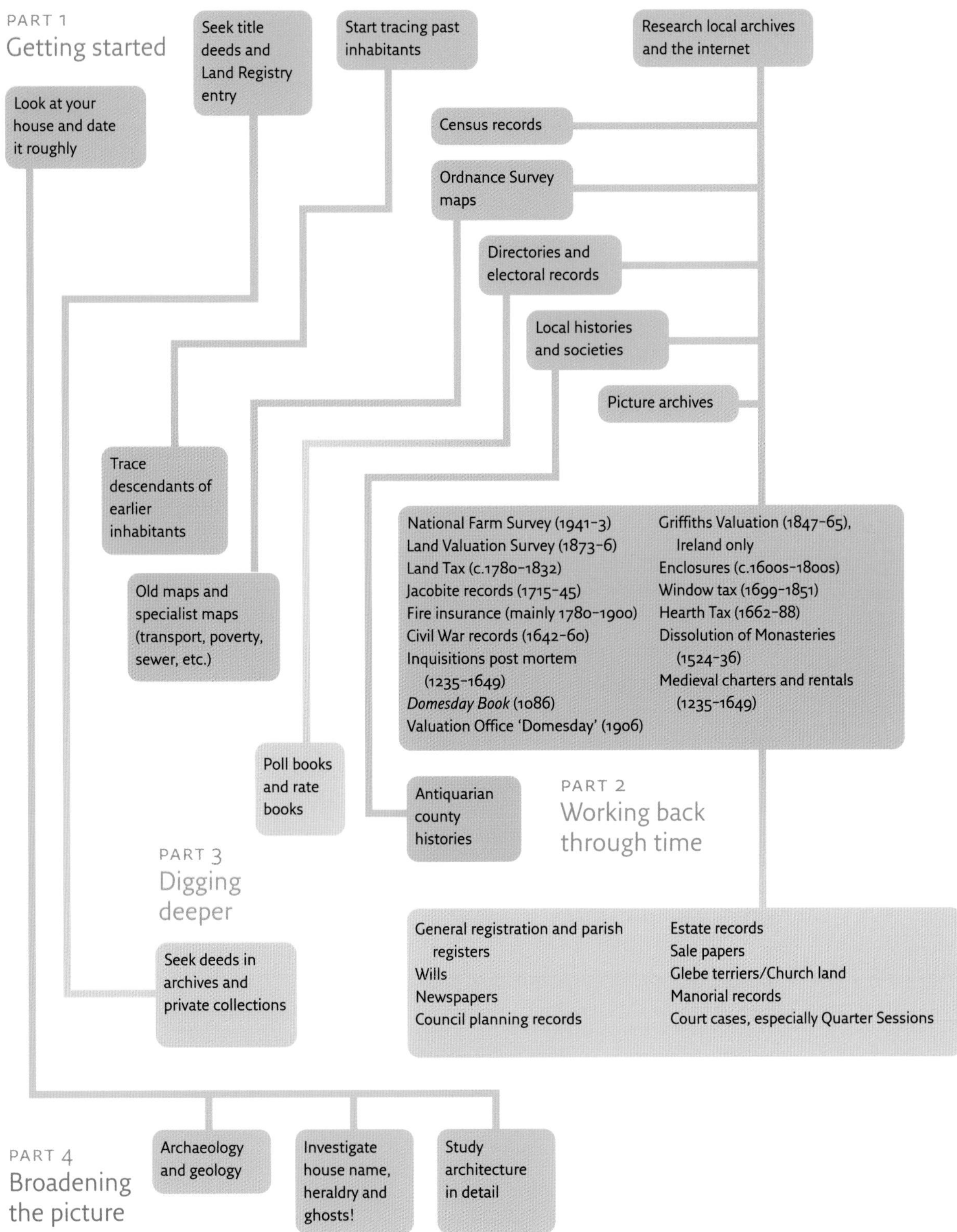
PART 1
Getting started
Look at your house and date it roughly
Seek title deeds and Land Registry entry
Start tracing past inhabitants
Research local archives and the internet
Census records
Ordnance Survey maps
Directories and electoral records
Local histories and societies
Picture archives
Trace descendants of earlier inhabitants
Old maps and specialist maps (transport, poverty, sewer, etc.)
National Farm Survey (1941–3)
Land Valuation Survey (1873–6)
Land Tax (c.1780–1832)
Jacobite records (1715–45)
Fire insurance (mainly 1780–1900)
Civil War records (1642–60)
Inquisitions post mortem (1235–1649)
Domesday Book (1086)
Valuation Office 'Domesday' (1906)
Griffiths Valuation (1847–65), Ireland only
Enclosures (c.1600s–1800s)
Window tax (1699–1851)
Hearth Tax (1662–88)
Dissolution of Monasteries (1524–36)
Medieval charters and rentals (1235–1649)
Poll books and rate books
Antiquarian county histories
PART 2
Working back through time
PART 3
Digging deeper
Seek deeds in archives and private collections
General registration and parish registers
Wills
Newspapers
Council planning records
Estate records
Sale papers
Glebe terriers/Church land
Manorial records
Court cases, especially Quarter Sessions
PART 4
Broadening the picture
Archaeology and geology
Investigate house name, heraldry and ghosts!
Study architecture in detail

tracing of past occupants to the most gregarious and archival research to the more scholarly-minded, for example. However, if you're doing this on your own, that's fine – it's certainly a project one person can take on knowing that while it may be time-consuming, it will certainly be enjoyable.

Getting started

(pages 18-83)

In the 'Getting started' section, I have identified a number of documentary sources: censuses; Ordnance Survey maps; directories; newspapers; electoral registers and poll books; local histories; pictures and records concerning the naming and numbering of homes and streets that are easy to find in local archives, and in some cases online too.

Working back through time

(pages 84-145)

The wealth of written records available in Britain is explored in this and the next section. In 'Working back through time', I look at types of records that were made at specific times in the past, from the National Farm Survey during the Second World War – this includes many buildings that are now homes, and much land later used for post-war building – right back to William the Conqueror's *Domesday Book* of 1086. The latter provides what is often the earliest record we have of England's settlements, and identifies a few buildings, such as mills, that have been homes to people for almost 1,000 years.

A detailed look at the records is presented in chronological order. Many will be useful to you, while you will quickly realise that others won't be. For example, if your home is in an inner city, the National Farm Survey is unlikely to help you, whereas the records of Second World War bombing could well be appropriate. Having read about each type of record, you will quickly be able to decide which are likely to tell you more about your own home. You can then explore them to add flesh to the bones of your home's story: in many cases you may find that they will help solve problems or queries that arose elsewhere in your research.

The sources are arranged chronologically so that you can work back in time. This is usually the best way of researching a home and avoids problems such as a new building built on an old site being mistaken for the original one. By working back from what you know for sure, you will have greater confidence that your research is accurate. However, once you reach the point where your home was built, you needn't necessarily stop research – it is still fascinating to know what the site of your home was before the present building was erected.

Digging deeper

(pages 146-99)

This section is concerned with records that cover broad periods of history, such as parish registers, which chronicle the inhabitants of homes back to the 16th century, to manorial records, which chart the history of homes into the Middle Ages. Just because this section comes after the previous one, 'Working back through time', it needn't necessarily follow that you will want to use the records it describes only after you have exhausted those in the foregoing section. Quite the contrary: the two sets of records are mutually complementary.

The chronological chart on page 16 shows how all the main records described in this book relate to each other in terms of time. Once you know how old your home is, you can use the chart to identify all the different records that might mention your home. Ideally, you will be able to find your home in most of them. If you experience problems finding your home in one type of record (in either section), you will hopefully find that positive results from other records in both sections will help you to overcome such difficulties.

Broadening the picture

(pages 200–57)

This final section returns to the fabric of your home – the history of its 'bricks and mortar'. Again, please don't think of the topics here as things to do after investigating everything else.

Understanding something of Britain's architectural history will increase your knowledge of your own home and its surroundings. This section also explores some of the odder types of building that have been turned into homes; explains how to use any heraldry that may be associated with your home; how to make the best of having a ghost in the attic; and also explains the thorny issue of chancel repairs. Finally (but again this is something you can do anytime) I tell you how take a peek below your walls, at the archaeological remains, flints, fossils and ancient bedrock that may be lying down there now – right beneath your home's foundations.

Useful sources

The chart on page 16 shows the main records you can use. These are as follows:

Land registries (1660–present)

2003 compulsory in Northern Ireland
1990 compulsory in England and Wales
1979 Scottish registry opens
1899 registration compulsory in London
1862 National Registry begins with foundation of the Land Registry
1736 opening of North Riding deeds registry
1709 Middlesex
1708 East Riding, Yorkshire and Ireland
1660 Bedford Level

Deeds and charters (1086–present)

Censuses (1911, Ireland only; 1801–1901)

1911 Ireland only
1901 mainly available each decade from 1841 to 1901
1801–31 a few available

Maps, Ordnance Survey (1086–present)

1854 first Ordnance Survey 25 inch = 1 mile
1850 first Ordnance Survey 10 inch = 1 mile
1843 first Ordnance Survey 5 inch = 1 mile
1801 first Ordnance Survey 1 inch = 1 mile
1700–99 many town, estate and country maps
1683 Ogilby and Morgans, London
1574–9 Saxton's county maps
1560 Agas, London
1479 first map of Bristol

Directories (1677–1960s)

1800–99 most appear in the 19th century
1677 first London directory

Electoral registers (1832–present)

1971 all aged over 17 years
1928 street numbers included
1918 Universal suffrage

Poll books (1699–1872)

1832 lists made annually
1711 most records date from here, as enrolled within Quarter Sessions records
1696 first poll books

Local and family histories (c.1550–present)

Telephone directories (1880s–present)

1950s–present = increasing coverage

Photographs, postcards and paintings (c.1100–present)

1879 Alphons Adolph's first postcard
1839 first daguerreotype
1600–1800 mainly drawings and paintings
c.1100–1599 buildings pictured in old plans and maps

Timeline of useful sources

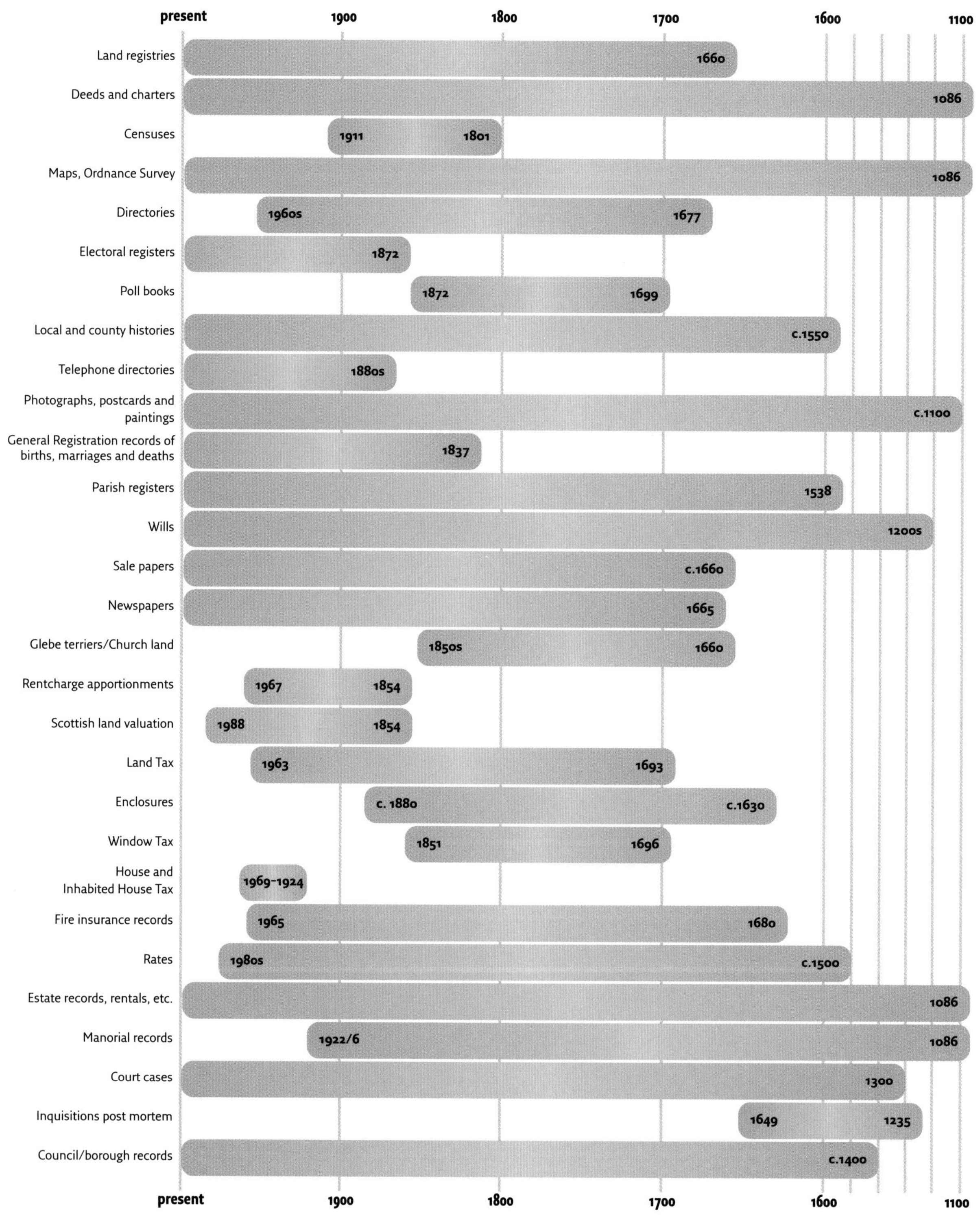
present
1900
1800
1700
1600
1100
Land registries
1660
Deeds and charters
1086
Censuses
1911
1801
Maps, Ordnance Survey
1086
Directories
1960s
1677
Electoral registers
1872
Poll books
1872
1699
Local and county histories
c.1550
Telephone directories
1880s
Photographs, postcards and paintings
c.1100
General Registration records of births, marriages and deaths
1837
Parish registers
1538
Wills
1200s
Sale papers
c.1660
Newspapers
1665
Glebe terriers/Church land
1850s
1660
Rentcharge apportionments
1967
1854
Scottish land valuation
1988
1854
Land Tax
1963
1693
Enclosures
c. 1880
c.1630
Window Tax
1851
1696
House and Inhabited House Tax
1969–1924
Fire insurance records
1965
1680
Rates
1980s
c.1500
Estate records, rentals, etc.
1086
Manorial records
1922/6
1086
Court cases
1300
Inquisitions post mortem
1649
1235
Council/borough records
c.1400
present
1900
1800
1700
1600
1100

General Registration records of births, marriages and deaths (1837–present)

From 1864 full Irish
From 1855 Scottish
From 1845 Irish Protestant marriages
From 1837 England and Wales

Parish registers (1538–present)

From 1820s most Irish survive
From 1745 most Scottish survive
From 1660 most English and Welsh survive

Wills (1200s–present)

1922 start for Irish wills, most pre-1922 Irish wills are lost
1858 principal probate registry begins (England and Wales)
Some wills dated as early as c.1200

Sale papers (c.1660–present)

Newspapers (1665–present)

1855–present many local newspapers
1785 *The Times*
1702 first national daily newspaper, the *Daily Courant*
1701 first local newspaper (Norwich)
1665 first national newspaper, the *Oxford Gazette*

Glebe terriers/Church land (1660–1850s)

Rentcharge apportionments (1854–1967)

Scottish land valuation (1854–1988)

Land Tax (1693–1963)

1780–1832 main period for useful records

Enclosures (1600s–1960)

Window Tax (1696–1851)

1747–1851 poor survival of records
1747 tax re-enforced

House and Inhabited House Tax (1924–1969)

Very poor survival of records overall

Fire insurance records (1680–1968)

1885–1965 Goad fire insurance plans
1865 Metropolitan Fire Brigade
1716 Sun Fire Office
1680 Phoenix Co.

Rates (c.1500s–1980s)

Poll Tax from the 1980s
Most rate books survive from the mid-1700s

Estate records, rentals, etc. (1086–present)

1086 *Domesday Book*

Manorial records (c.1300–1920s)

1732 general adoption of English instead of Latin

Court cases (c.1300–present)

1361–1971 Quarter Sessions records

Inquisitions post mortem (1235–1649)

Council/borough records (c.1400–present)

1800–1910 Records of planning, street names, sewers, etc.
c.1400–1750 older borough records

One-off records

1941–3 National Farm Survey
1909–1920 Valuation Office Survey
1903 Booth's Survey of London Poverty
1873–6 Land Valuation Survey
1847–65 Griffith's Valuation (Ireland only)
1836–56 Tithe apportionments
1823–38 Irish tithe applotments
1715–45 Jacobite Records
1662–88 Hearth Tax
1534–mid 1500s Records of Dissolution of the Monasteries
1086 *Domesday Book*

When they are first mentioned in the text address details are given for the organisation or person concerned, otherwise please see 'Useful addresses' section starting on page 262.

PART 1

Getting started

It's time to start tracing your home's history. This section contains all the basics, which should be applicable to you regardless of whether you live in a modern maisonette or an ancient stately pile. We'll look at the general methodology of keeping records and how to undertake research. We'll take a tour of your home, inside and out, and find out what the building's fabric can tell you. We will explore the records that are likeliest to start you on your quest, in the form of written documents, and maps and pictures. And, all being well, we'll start getting in touch with some of the many people whose own lives – or those of their parents and grandparents – were affected by your home in the past.

CHAPTER 1

Keeping records and writing up the results

How you keep records is a matter of personal preference. You may wish to keep paper files, or transcribe and scan documents into a computer. Whatever you chose to do, the keeping of records is essential. So often in tracing the history of a home, you are faced with lists of people – rate payers, Land Tax payers, people in census returns, and so on – and are left wondering which of them inhabited your home. Evidence that you previously thought unimportant, such as who was enumerated on either side of your home in a census, or whose property abutted yours on an estate map, could suddenly turn out to be the clue to cracking the location of your home in a new set of documents.

I strongly recommend taking the fullest notes you can of all references to your home, and also those surrounding it. In the case of lists of people, it is often best to note half a dozen or more entries on either side. In all cases, make very careful notes of archive reference numbers, dates, locations and anything else that could be useful if – or indeed *when* – you need to refer back to them in the future.

Incidentally, do keep an eye to the future and include in your home history details of your own arrival, changes you have made and important events that have taken place in your life while living there – not least deciding to start the project of tracing your home's history!

Writing up the results

It's usually best to take this in a two-stage process.

1 Compile an 'everything but the kitchen sink' account of your home's records while you are undertaking the research, working your way through each record you have discovered, describing what it is, quoting the pertinent information it contains, and interpreting this in the light of other evidence. This approach will help you place your new finds in their proper context, and helps highlight the almost inevitable inconsistencies or mistakes you may inadvertently have made.

You'll also need to decide whether to compile your results working from the past forwards to the present, or from the present working back into the past. An account working back is likely to be closest to the path you actually followed, and often the evidence for what the house was like is highly dependent on connecting older records with newer ones. Therefore the 'kitchen sink' approach is often most easily tackled by working back in chronological order from the present, and this is why this book has been ordered in that way.

2 Move on to the final narrative. Much of this book is about records. Most research is done through records, and they are tremendously important. The amount that has survived in

Britain is truly staggering. It's salutary to think that we can usually research vastly more about a single British home than about an entire village in the Third World, where there are generally far fewer records.

When writing up the finished results, however, try not to let the records confuse you, or assume too great an importance. Ultimately, they are only various pieces of paper that happen to mention details about your home. It is the place itself that is of primary interest – what it was like in the past, and who inhabited it.

Once you have undertaken the research, therefore, it's healthy to step back from all the documents you have found and ask yourself, 'So what do these records actually tell me about my home?' Now is the time to write your home's history. Consider, for example, the story of 'Little Red Riding Hood'. You could, for clarity's sake, present the story as a series of events:

1 Little Red Riding Hood decides to visit her granny.
2 She puts on her red cloak and leaves the house.
3 She is spotted by a wolf.

... and so on. It's factually accurate – but it is also boring. When told properly, 'Little Red Riding Hood' is a dramatic story that keeps people gripped with excitement, full of tragedy and joy, peril and triumph. If you want people to take more than a passing interest in the hard work you have put in to discovering the history of your home, you will need to tell its story in such as way as to really engage them. And in doing so, you will also realise that the history of your home was a dramatic one. Those wills and death certificates relate to real deaths. Records of people being forced to move out, or triumphantly achieving their ambition of moving in, relate to genuinely emotional events. I am not inviting you to invent dramas that did not exist. I am, however, advising you to recognise and describe those that really took place, for which you have documentary evidence from your researches.

Several times in this book I have quoted from Julie Myerson's *Home: The Story of Everyone Who Ever Lived in Our House*. This is certainly worth reading if you want a good example of how to bring the story of your home alive. However, do bear in mind that while Myerson's approach makes an excellent and inspiring book, it covers far more than you'd expect in a normal home history. At its best, however, the completed history of a home is a biography of a building, full of the texture and colour of the lives of the people who have lived there before you.

Your finished result could take the form of a series of printed pages, which can be kept in a binder, or more elaborately produced using a desktop publishing package. You could turn them into a website, if you were so minded.

Finally, there are also many examples, on view especially in pubs, of histories of buildings presented in a poster style. These don't attempt to tell the whole story by any means. Rather, they are a summary of the highlights, often incorporating a brief narrative or a timeline along with portraits, maps and attractive or particularly interesting documents relating to the place.

Whatever approach you choose, make sure it is clear, concise – and interesting!

CHAPTER 2

Dating your home

Some homes come already labelled with dates of construction. Inset stones carved with the date of building were a continental fashion brought to Britain by immigrants, such as 17th-century Huguenots. It later became more widespread, so now quite a few homes are neatly dated.

Most homes, however, are not ready-labelled in this way, although some have added features, such as coats of arms (see pages 244-7) or fire insurance plaques (see page 123), which can themselves be dated.

The home in its local context

Most homes were not built in isolation, but were part of larger developments. If your home is in an area that saw sudden growth – a city suburb that was rapidly built up by developers, for example, or a village that was suddenly swamped by the Industrial Revolution – then you can work out the period in which your

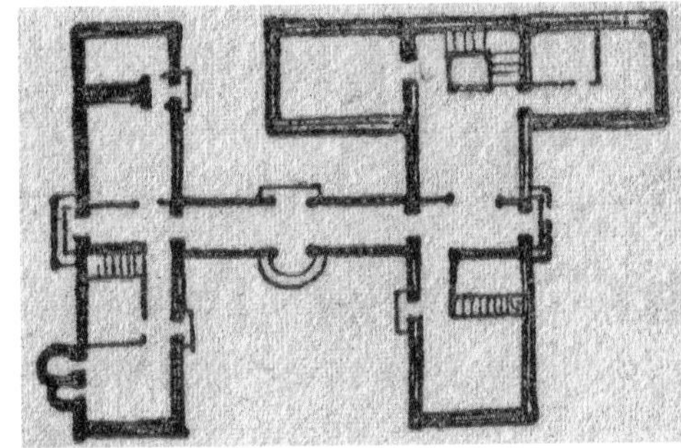

LEFT

Carolean Cottage. Ivy Lane, Canterbury, still has its date of construction carved into the wall. Canterbury was one of the main places of refuge for Huguenot migrants from the continent.

ABOVE

Few homes' designs can so clearly identify their builders as they can here: one John Thorpe, dated about 1600, with the accompanying rhyme:

'These 2 letters I and T
Joined together as you can see
Is ment for a dwelling howse for mee.'

In Tudor times, of course, J was usually written as an I.

building was *likeliest* to have been erected. Bear in mind that your home will therefore share much of its history with those of your neighbours, so it's worth knocking on their doors and finding out if any of their homes' stories have been researched already.

Also consider whether your home has been rebuilt. This is more likely for homes in the middle of old cities, or in the countryside – those in suburbs are more likely to be original. Rebuilding on old foundations may not be immediately noticeable. It can cause pitfalls, fooling you, for example, into thinking that a building shown on your site in an old map is the same building that stands there now. Close examination of your home's architecture should reveal the truth.

A fine jettied box-frame home with a ground-floor shop in Palace Street, Canterbury. If Conquest House looks a bit too perfect, that's because it is. It was built from scratch in the 1930s.

A similar jettied box-frame home with a ground-floor shop in Palace Street, Canterbury. Sir John Boy's House is genuinely old, however, and has adopted a much-photographed tilt, requiring specially angled doors and windows.

Broad styles

The next step is to consider your home's general features and style, and try to assign it to an historical period. Styles such as Tudor, Jacobean, Georgian, Victorian and Arts and Crafts are fairly easy to recognise and give you a broad range of dates in which to look up more particular features. A closer look at architectural styles is on pages 202–37.

|| Breckon, Parker and Andrew's book is highly recommended (see page 31). You can also explore *The Builder*, a journal published from 1842 to 1966, and fully indexed for the 19th century. This contains much contemporary evidence on building styles, social housing projects and much else that could be relevant to your home. The first ten volumes are online at **www.bodley.ox.ac.uk/ilej/**.

The 'comparison' approach contains pitfalls, however. Especially in cheaper housing, architectural styles, or mutated versions of them, continued to be used long after they had dropped out of mainstream fashion. Your home, for example, may *look* Tudor, but it could date

A 20th-century mock-Tudor home in Canterbury.

from a later period. This is true, for example, in the Cotswolds, where a great deal of stone building took place in the Tudor period. Economic decline followed and styles became ossified: Tudor features such as stone-mullioned windows and gabled dormers that rose straight up from the house fronts were still being built in the 18th century, and are thus so typical of local style they are being copied to this day. Equally, the revival of interest in Tudor styles resulted in the building of many mock-Tudor homes in suburbs in the period between the two world wars. So 'Tudor' can apply not just to a particular period.

The solution, therefore, is to examine the building in more detail. Smaller features will tie the building more accurately into its true period. Do the roof timbers or bricks of your 'Tudor' house, for example, look more like 70 than 470 years old?

Another problem is that many houses are hybrids. The original structure may have been added to many times. Many chimneys were added to older houses in the 16th century, for instance. Old hearths and staircases, roof tiles and window frames may very well have been replaced several times. Old farmhouses in villages may have been divided into cottages and then reconverted to single dwellings. And, just as older homes may now contain more recent features, so too have old items, from period fireplaces to antique timbers, been inserted into much more modern buildings.

If you suspect this is the case for your home, look at the list below and then, once you have carried out your mini-architectural survey, you can start the analysis. The Bricks and Brass website (**www.bricksandbrass.co.uk/desroom/bedroom/bedsochist.htm**) includes a useful online questionnaire or 'dating tool'. You can

Features to examine

windows Shapes (whether the tops are straight or arched, for example, and if arched, whether they have a keystone in the middle); what sort of frames were used.

doors Shapes and styles and features such as knockers, letter boxes and so on.

porches Whether original or added later.

roofs Especially the details of the eaves and ridge and the material used; the style of the tiles; the position and style of the chimneys and the steepness of the slope.

the material used to build the walls and, if bricks, what colour.

how the house was laid out and how it looks in cross section.

location of baths and loos Especially whether they are in purpose-built rooms, or added later to substitute an outside loo and portable tin bath.

how the stairs fit into the overall layout Are they original or were they added later?

layout of the garden and the presence of old trees.

use this to seek a rough date for your home, though you may need to mug up on architectural terms first (the **www.lookingatbuildings.org** website contains a useful glossary).

Types of building

There are many books on different types of buildings that will help you date your own. Purpose-built flats, for example, only really appeared in the late 19th century: Perks's book outlines the styles and floor plans popular in 1905, and can therefore be used for comparison purposes. Muthesius discusses terraced homes and Cooper's book is one of the many works on the homes of the Tudor, Georgian and Regency gentry (see page 31).

|| The Shire Books series includes many very useful books on types of building, such as those by Harris, Peters and Powell on timber-framed buildings, farms and cottages respectively (Shire Books, Cromwell House, Church Street, Princes Risborough, Buckinghamshire HP27 9AA; tel: 01844 344301; **www.shirebooks.co.uk**). For all publishing details and other useful books, see page 31.

Pevsner

|| The Pevsner architectural guides (**www.pevsner.co.uk**) are an extraordinary resource for British architecture. Started in 1951 by the architectural historian Sir Nikolaus Pevsner (1902–1983), the series provides an up-to-date guide to the most significant buildings in every part of the British Isles. Each volume starts with a general overview of the architectural history of the area covered, followed by a gazetteer of each place describing all buildings of note and interest. These include everything from great country houses and cathedrals down to interesting terraces and blocks of flats. Your home may not be

TOP
Purpose-built flats. 1930s style.

ABOVE
A pair of front covers for Pevsner's *Buildings of England* books.

Pevsner's architectural guides

These are a couple of extracts from the section on Stoke Newington, North London, from Pevsner's *The Buildings of England: London 4: North* (Bridget Cherry and Nikolaus Pevsner, eds), to show you the sort of detail and information available:

Stoke Newington Church Street

The centre of the old village is still recalled by Church Street's informal character and scatter of older houses, although the big mansions which stood in their own grounds on the N side have all gone. The Manor House, which lay close to the church, on the site of the municipal buildings, disappeared already in the C18 ...

Nos. 81–87, built 1733–5; exuberant eared doorcases with carved friezes. Nos. 89–93, of 1792–3, typical of the greater restraint of the 1790s; nice Doric porches to Nos. 89 and 91. Nos. 109–111 was built as a single house c. 1700; above the later shopfront is a projecting centre with rubbed brickwork ... No. 129 is decent C19, with end pilasters and cornice.

On the N side, at the corner with Lordship Road, the magpie and stump, early C20, with a forceful cranked gable, and original ground- and first-floor interiors. Behind is a stuccoed early C19 house with a N-facing bow, and the former parish lock-up ...

This is what Pevsner described as one of the 'exuberant eared doorcases with carved friezes', dated to about 1733–5, in Stoke Newington Church Street.

included, but you will nevertheless learn a great deal about the buildings of your area. More pertinently, you're likely to learn a lot about buildings similar to your own.

Architectural historians

|| Experts to consult on your home's architecture can be found in the *Institution of Historic Building Conservation Yearbook* (copies in most good libraries or from IHBC, Jubilee House, High Street, Tisbury, Wiltshire SP3 6HA; tel: 01747 871717; **www.buildingconservation.com/books/ihbc.htm**) and on websites such as **www.periodproperty.co.uk/information.shtm**, under the 'suppliers' section.

Kent historic buildings

Kent is unique in having an Historic Buildings Committee, which has produced a series of volumes called the Kent Historic Buildings Index, covering 17 districts from Thanet right up to Greenwich. These provide notes on listed buildings, ancient monuments and other buildings of interest and can be used to help date many buildings and streets.

|| A list of what is available can be obtained from Michael H. Peters, Hon. Secretary, CPRE Kent, 24 Evegate Park Barn, Station Road, Smeeth, Ashford, Kent TN25 6SX; info@cprekent.org.uk.

Historic buildings preservation

The first attempt to preserve old or interesting buildings by law was the Ancient Monuments Protection Act of 1882. After several subsequent acts, the 1944 Town and Country Planning Act empowered the Ministry of Town and Country Planning to draw up lists of historic buildings and constructions, from graves to pillar boxes, for local authorities, and to classify them in grades of importance. These are shown in the box below.

Grade listings

Grade 1 Preserved from demolition under all circumstances.

Grade 2 Can only be demolished under exceptional circumstances.

Grade 3 More modest buildings.

All buildings constructed up to 1700 and most up to 1840, provided they are in anything like their original condition, are listed. Those built after 1840 are included only if they are particularly interesting.

You will already know if your home is listed. The records have a wider use, however, for they allow you to trace buildings similar to your own home, enabling you to learn more by comparison.

- All listed structures – from stately homes to terraced cottages – are included on **www.imagesofengland.org.uk**, which also contains pictures of many of them. The site provides the century (not the year) of construction and very useful technical details: it sometimes gives details of past owners. Saxon's short article provides more details (see page 31).
- You can go into more details on older buildings via the National Monuments Record Centre (Great Western Village, Kemble Drive, Swindon SN2 2GZ; tel: 01793 414600; **www.swindon.gov.uk.nmro**).
- For Wales, see also the Comisiwn Brenhinol Henebion Cymru – the Royal Commission on the Ancient and Historical Monuments of Wales (Plâs Crug, Aberystwyth, Ceredigion SY23 1NJ; tel: 01970 621200; chc.cymru@cbhc.gov.uk).

These bodies hold detailed information on listed buildings (and other items, such as old telephone kiosks), down to reports on their architectural history and state of preservation, and accompanying photographs.

Architects

Knowing who designed your home may help you learn more about it. We are used to the idea of architects being specially trained men working in the grand tradition of Inigo Jones and Sir Christopher Wren. In fact, trained professional architects only emerged in any significant number in the late 19th century. In the Middle Ages, architectural work was undertaken by master masons – masons trained in building techniques, geometry, Gothic design and so on,

An engraving of Inigo Jones, the great 17th-century innovator of Classical architecture in Britain.

Useful websites

www.bbc.co.uk/history/society_culture/architecture/architecture_01.shtml The BBC History website's 'Concise History of British Architecture': it's *very* concise, but interesting nonetheless.

www.bricksandbrass.co.uk/desroom/bedroom/bedsochist.htm The Bricks and Brass website provides considerable information on how social history has affected homes. Under Victorian bedrooms, for example, we learn that, even in moderately affluent homes, a four-bedroom house might contain the parents in one room; elderly relatives in the second; servants in the third; and all the children - however many there were - in the fourth. It was only from the 1850s onwards that families thought it a good idea to give boys and girls separate rooms. The little back-to-back houses of the industrial north generally only had one bedroom for everyone - and, of course, the outside loo and washhouse would be shared between several families. Because bedrooms received no formal visitors they tended to be sparsely decorated, usually lacking picture rails. By the late Victorian period, though, even the poorest houses would have fireplaces in the bedrooms, generally painted white, but they would usually only be lit if one of the occupants was ill.

www.building-history.pwp.blueyonder.co.uk Material on the history of building.

www.georgiangroup.org.uk Very useful material on Georgian homes, especially on restoring them.

www.lookingatbuildings.org This is a joint venture by the Pevsner Architectural Guides and the Buildings Books Trust. It describes regional variations in buildings and building materials and includes an excellent glossary and pictures of architectural features. This fascinating site is broken down into three areas:

1. 'Understanding buildings', giving an introduction to architecture, architectural styles, traditions, building materials and methods of construction.
2. 'Tools and study aids', including a glossary, links to related sites, an index of architects and their works, and a guide to further reading on all aspects of English archiecture.
3. 'Exploring buildings', a continually expanding guide to specific buildings.

www.nationaltrust.org.uk While this is mainly a directory of the Trust's properties, there is much to be learned about the periods and styles of the buildings featured. Bear in mind that besides its stately homes, the Trust also maintains many smaller historical buildings, such as a row of workers' back-to-back houses in Birmingham (see pictures below).

www.periodproperty.co.uk/information.shtml Period Property is mainly concerned with buying, selling, insuring and maintaining old buildings, but the site has a number of useful sections for researchers. There are essays on different sorts of building, such as mud-built houses and wattle and daub. The suppliers section includes a useful list of architectural historians.

www.spab.org.uk The Society for the Protection of Ancient Buildings has much useful general information, especially on its technical Q&A pages.

www.victorian-society.org.uk Provides a brief guide to researching Victorian homes.

Interior of a bedroom of a restored back-to-back house in Birmingham maintained by the National Trust.

usually working under the aegis of Freemasonic Lodges. The 17th century saw the appearance of Jones, Wren and their successors, who devoted much of their polymath careers to architecture. In the 18th century, architecture was routinely taught to upper-class boys as one of the 'polite arts', and many a gentleman was known to dabble in it, while mainstream architects tended to learn by a form of apprenticeship. The majority of men who actually planned and designed buildings continued to be builders, along with surveyors and dilettante gentlemen with varying degrees of competence and imagination. Most Georgian and Victorian housing developments, therefore, were the work of builders who knew about architecture, not professional architects.

When architecture started being taught in universities in the 19th century, it moved towards becoming a true profession in its own right. This was reinforced by the foundation of the Royal Institute of Architects in 1834 and the appearance of two architectural journals, *The Builder*, in 1842, and the *Architectural Review*, at the end of the century.

- Colvin's book (see page 31) is a biographical dictionary of identified architects in the period 1600–1840. The website **www.lookingatbuildings.org** contains an online section on architects as well.
- It's always worth checking your local record office to see if any local builder-architects left records that have been deposited. You may find the records of local authority surveyors deposited in local authority archives. These can include reports on the building of streets, naming their builders/ architects.
- Pevsner (see page 31) identifies, wherever possible, the architects of notable buildings: many of these would have been active elsewhere in the area as well, so may have designed, or otherwise influenced, the design of your home.

This house in Ivy Lane, Canterbury, now part of the Chaucer Hotel, will always be cherished by fans of Rupert the Bear.

Here, a blue plaque marks the one-time home of Virginia Woolf.

Additional dating tools

Commemorative plaques: Many places have schemes to erect plaques to commemorate famous people who lived in local buildings. If your home has a blue plaque on it, that's a great bonus. If you discover that someone well known lived in your home, you can apply to have a

TOP
Early Georgian period room, 1720–60, at the Geffreye Museum.

BOTTOM
Mid-Victorian period room, 1840–70, also at the Geffreye Museum.

plaque erected. Perhaps the best known are the Blue Plaques, which require the building to be the one in which the person lived rather than one erected later on the same site. Originally confined to London, the scheme is now being broadened out to cover the whole country. See **www.english-heritage.org.uk/blueplaques** or contact Blue Plaques Team, English Heritage, 23 Saville Row, London W1S 2ET; tel: 020 7973 3794. Many London boroughs maintain their own plaque schemes as well, with less restrictive rules.

Fixtures and fittings: Old fixtures and fittings – presupposing they were installed at the time they were popular, and not as antiques – can be additional dating tools. They also enable to you reconstruct what life would have been like in your home in the past. There are many books on the way people lived, such as *Enquire Within upon Everything 1890* (see box opposite). This was a compendium of contemporary advice on lifestyle, decorating, gadgets and so on, to which we can now refer to try to date Victorian relics in homes.

For in-depth research, you can examine original patents at the British Library Science Reference Library (British Library, 96 Euston Road, London NW1 2DB; tel: 020 7412 7873; **www.bl.uk**). The National Archives holds a huge collection of samples and designs, for such things as wallpaper, registered with the Board of Trade between 1839 and 1964. The National Art Library of the Victoria and Albert Museum has a substantial collection of furnishings and fixtures (V&A, South Kensington, Cromwell Road, London SW7 2RL; tel: 020 7942 2000; **www.vam.ac.uk/nal/** with its catalogue at **http://ipac.nal.vam.ac.uk** – look especially under 'architecture, domestic – British Isles' and 'interiors and interior decoration').

Also, if you're in London, a much smaller but absolutely fascinating museum of furnishings is the Geffreye Museum, Kingsland Road, London E2 8EA; tel: 020 7739 9893; **www.geffrye-museum.org.uk/**. Besides some splendid reconstructions of rooms from different historical periods, the museum holds a body of both published and physical material, including an archive of visual images of domestic interiors.

Rubbish: What is or was tantamount to rubbish can also prove fascinating. When friends of ours decorated their newly bought home in Clapton, London, they peeled up a layer of unwanted lino in the hall floor and found layers of old newspaper underneath. When they had been placed there as a cheap underlay, they were of no interest whatsoever: now, framed, they provide a ghostly record of the day, 50 years ago, when the lino was laid. Julie Myerson writes of a similar experience in her book *Home*:

It was three o'clock, almost dark. It felt strangely moving and intimate, scraping the layers off – history unpeeling itself. There was a smell of dissolving paper, of oldness – the hiss of the steamer in the silence, the sight of naked walls ... the layers of paper curled and rolled off and dropped onto the floor – and, quite perfectly preserved, half a dozen different patterns were revealed: imitation wood grain (the sixties?), brown zigzags (the fifties?) – then a bold Art Deco style in cobalt and scarlet (the twenties?). Under that, large Morris-style chocolate ferns and flowers, and beneath that a solid layer of thick custard-coloured paint, then a fuzzy snatch of long-ago roses, then another more satiny paper with tiny gold and mauve squares. Each layer – imperfectly glued, faded, merged – revealed another.

BOOKS

- **T. D. Atkinson, *English Architecture* (Methuen & Co. Ltd, 1918)**
- **M. W. Barley, *The Buildings of the Countryside 1500–1750* (Cambridge University Press, 1990)**
- **M. W. Barley, *The English Farmhouse and Cottage* (Sutton, 1987)**
- **B. Breckon, J. Parker and M. Andrew, *Tracing the History of Houses* (Countryside Books, 2003)**
- **R. W. Brunskill, *Illustrated Handbook of Vernacular Architecture* (Faber & Faber, 2000)**
- **R. W. Brunskill, *Traditional Buildings of Britain: An Introduction to Vernacular Architecture* (Gollancz in association with Peter Crawley, 1981)**
- **H. M. Colvin, *A Biographical Dictionary of British Architects 1600–1840* (Yale University Press, 1995)**
- **N. Cooper, *Houses of the Gentry 1480–1680* (Yale University Press, 1999)**
- **D. Cruickshank, *A Guide to the Georgian Buildings of Britain and Ireland* (Weidenfeld & Nicholson, 1995)**
- **P. Cunnington, *How Old is your House?* (Alpha Books and A. & C. Black, 1982)**
- **E. Gray, *The British House: A Concise Architectural History* (Barrie & Jenkins, 1994)**
- **R. Harris, *Discovering Timber-Framed Buildings* (Shire, 2004)**
- **D. Iredale and J. Barrett, *Discovering Your Old House* (Shire, 2002)**
- **A. Jackson and D. Day, *Collins Period House: An Owner's Guide* (Collins, 2002)**
- **E. Mercer, *English Vernacular Houses* (HMSO, 1995)**
- **S. Muthesius, *The English Terraced House* (Yale Univrsity Press, 1982)**
- **J. Myerson, *Home: The Story of Everyone Who Ever Lived in Our House* (Harper Perennial, 2005)**
- **S. Perks, *Residential Flats* (Batsford, 1905)**
- **J. E. C. Peters, *Discovering Traditional Farm Buildings* (Shire, 2003)**
- **Pevsner Architectural Guides (Buildings of England, Ireland, Scotland and Wales) (Penguin and Yale University Press, 1951–present)**
- **C. Powell, *Discovering Cottage Architecture* (Shire, 2003)**
- **H. Pragnell, *Britain: A Guide to Architectural Styles from 1066 to the Present Day* (Batsford, 2002)**
- **A. Saxon, 'Building up Images of England' (*Ancestors*, January 2005, pages 62–3)**
- **J. Summerson, *Architecture in Britain 1530–1830* (Penguin, 1993)**
- **A. Quiney, *House and Home: A History of the Small English House* (BBC, 1986)**
- **T. W. West, *Discovering English Architecture* (Shire, 2000)**
- ***Enquire Within upon Everything 1890* (Old House Books, Old Police Station, Pound Street, Moretonhampstead, Devon TQ13 8PA; tel: 01647 440707; www.OldHouseBooks.co.uk)**

CHAPTER 3

Land registries and title deeds

This chapter looks at two ways in which ownership of homes is recorded – through the Land Registry and in title deeds. Whether you own your home or not, these records of ownership provide the structure onto which you can pin the rest of your investigations into your home's history.

The Land Registry in the UK

The English and Welsh Land Registry is at HM Land Registry, 32 Lincoln's Inn Fields, London WC2A 3PH; tel: 020 7917 8888; **www.landreg.gov.uk**.

The Land Registry's website has a new service whereby, for £2, you can find out the sale price of any house sold since 2000, and also who owns it and details of the title. The service is designed for house buyers, but will also be useful for anyone interested in buildings.

The Scottish Land Registry is at the Registers of Scotland Executive Agency, Meadowbank House, 153 London Road, Edinburgh EH8 7AU; tel: 0845 607 0161; **www.ros.gov.uk**. It started in 1979 as a register of title as opposed to older deeds and sasines (see pages 196–9).

The Northern Irish Land Registry, called Land Registers of Northern Ireland, is at Lincoln Building, 27–45 Great Victoria Street, Belfast BT2 7SL; tel: 02890 251515; **www.lrni.gov.uk/**. It was established in 1898 and was, until recently, concerned mainly with rural land.

National Land Registry

(1862–present)

The Land Registry records present-day owners and, to some extent, past owners of many homes and other properties. The records are easily accessible and provide a good first port of call when starting to research the history of your home.

Until 1862, most property transactions were not officially recorded. In that year, the government established the Land Registry at which transfers could be recorded. Initially, the system was voluntary, and was little used. In 1899, registration became compulsory for London, thus providing nearly four decades of information for many properties in the metropolis. Compulsory registration spread slowly through other towns and cities, covering most counties only by the 1970s. It became compulsory everywhere in England and Wales in 1990, (1979 for Scotland), and in Northern Ireland in 2003. In most cases, only properties that have changed hands since compulsory registration will appear: about 30 per cent of properties do not yet appear.

You can apply for a copy of the registration records for your home – if it has been registered – for a small fee, from one of the land registries. The register records details of:

- Sales.
- The current owner.
- Details of current mortgages.

- Historical information that has been computerised (not all of it has been).
- Older deeds containing clauses, such as restrictive covenants, that still affect the property.
- Plans showing boundaries.

When applying, it is worth specifically asking for any historical information on record, as well as current details.

Title deeds

Most of the records you will encounter in your research will be in archives, arranged by village, parish or county, or by type, such as census or tithe records. To begin with, however, you may be lucky enough to find a group of records, all relating to your home, called the title deeds.

For our purposes, a deed is a record of property transfer. If someone wanted to sell a property, or the lease of one, they had to prove they were entitled to do so by possessing the title deeds to the property, the 'paper trail' showing the different transactions by which the property and the land on which it stood had changed hands and come into their ownership.

Originally, land was transferred by 'livery of seisin' (or sasine). This was the handing over of a lump of turf (or similar) from the original owner to the purchaser – who thus became literally the 'holder' of the land. During the course of the Middle Ages, these transactions started being recorded in deeds. Title deeds – also called 'muniments of title' – were a bundle of deeds, usually recorded in ink on vellum or parchment (animal skin), latterly on paper, all bound together. They were compiled by solicitors, so were usually quite verbose. They were also very detailed, and might include copies of wills that affected the property's descent, or affidavits, in which people swore to facts not fully elucidated by the other documents.

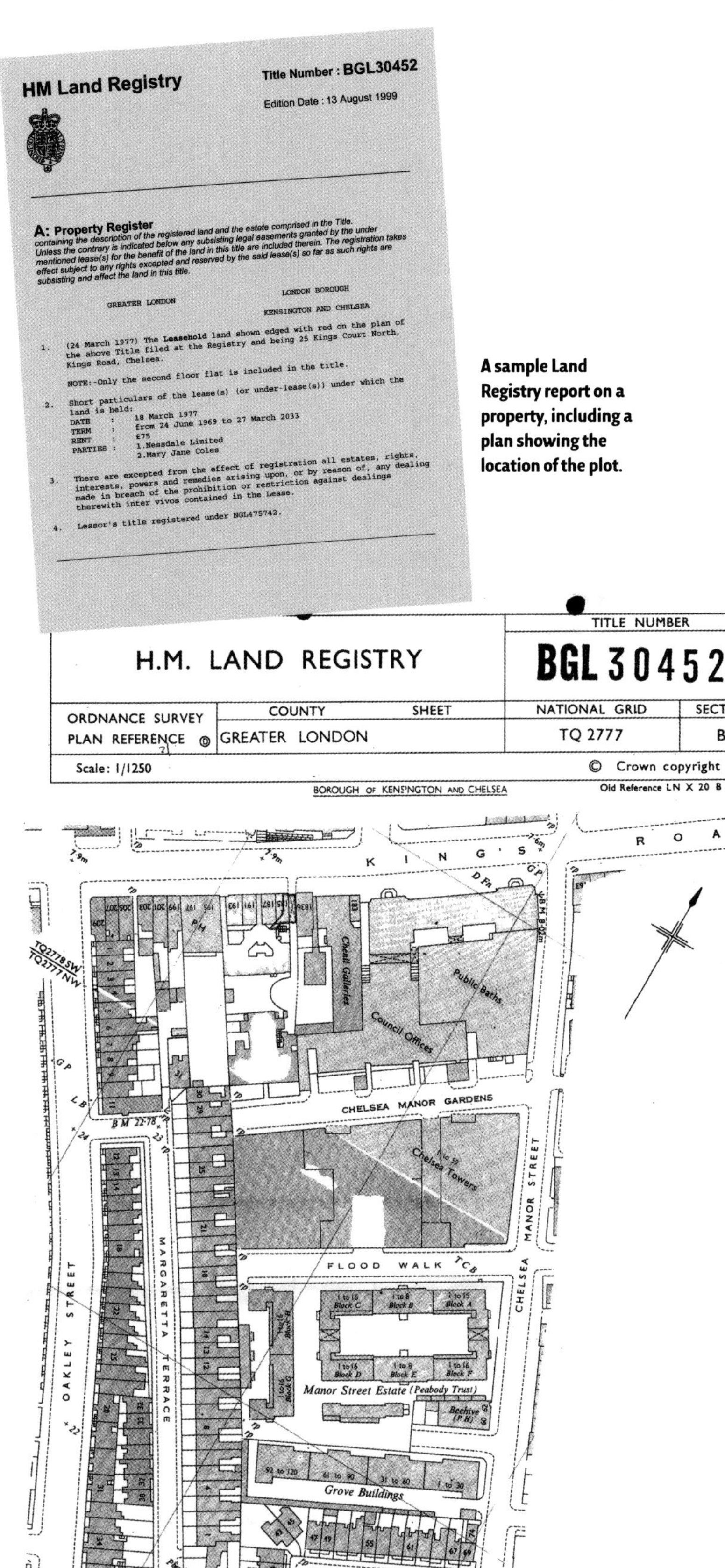

HM Land Registry

Title Number : BGL30452

Edition Date : 13 August 1999

A: Property Register

containing the description of the registered land and the estate comprised in the Title.
Unless the contrary is indicated below any subsisting legal easements granted by the under mentioned lease(s) for the benefit of the land in this title are included therein. The registration takes effect subject to any rights excepted and reserved by the said lease(s) so far as such rights are subsisting and affect the land in this title.

GREATER LONDON — LONDON BOROUGH KENSINGTON AND CHELSEA

1. (24 March 1977) The **Leasehold** land shown edged with red on the plan of the above Title filed at the Registry and being 25 Kings Court North, Kings Road, Chelsea.

   NOTE:-Only the second floor flat is included in the title.

2. Short particulars of the lease(s) (or under-lease(s)) under which the land is held:
   DATE : 18 March 1977
   TERM : from 24 June 1969 to 27 March 2033
   RENT : £75
   PARTIES : 1.Nessdale Limited
   2.Mary Jane Coles

3. There are excepted from the effect of registration all estates, rights, interests, powers and remedies arising upon, or by reason of, any dealing made in breach of the prohibition or restriction against dealings therewith inter vivos contained in the Lease.

4. Lessor's title registered under NGL475742.

A sample Land Registry report on a property, including a plan showing the location of the plot.

A handing-over ceremony takes place in April 1970 – the symbols of sasine (title) are being given to the Chairman of the Corstorphine Trust ... for the Corstorphine sycamore tree!

Especially after 1840, maps might be included. In some cases, original deeds were replaced, or augmented, by an 'abstract of title', which was a summary of their contents.

Deeds will seldom state when a property was built. They may well refer, however, to building or alterations obliquely, in terms of 'new built' or 'late[ly] built', and so give you clues for working out more exact dates. However, such phrases sometimes ended up being repeated in successive deeds, and could therefore still be in use quite a long time – sometimes many decades – after the place had been built. If the deed states by whom a place was built, you can then check other sources to see when that person was alive.

- Title deeds can be the backbone of your home's history. They will most likely be held by the owner of your home (which could be you) or the owner's solicitor.
- If the property is mortgaged, the title deeds will be held by the bank or building society, quite possibly without your knowledge. Therefore, ask the solicitor and mortgage provider where they are. Most organisations charge for the privilege of letting you see the documents, which is somewhat scandalous, but worth the price.
- Once a mortgage is paid off, the deeds should be handed to the property's owner. This does not always happen, however, so if you're entitled to the deeds but haven't been offered them, some chasing-up may be required.
- You may be disappointed to find that any older title deeds have been thrown away. Up to 1925, they all had to be kept safe. Unfortunately, the 1925 Law of Property Act decreed that deeds were only needed to prove changes in ownership over the preceding 30 years: in 1970 the law reduced this period to a paltry 15 years. As a result, older ones could be thrown away with impunity, and sadly many were. They were either thrown in the bin, or sold to antiquarian document sellers or people who made trendy lampshades for pubs. Luckily, however, many old deeds have survived even so.

Abstracts of title

Even if your home's title deeds have been destroyed, you may yet find that they were substituted with an abstract of title, summarising previous transactions. Abstracts can sometimes be as useful as the original deeds themselves. Most of the words in deeds are pure verbiage – so the abstracts could well contain all the salient details you actually need. Equally, many deeds may themselves recite the substance of earlier (and now lost) ones.

Nonetheless, if the older deeds have been separated from the current ones, it's still worth trying to track them down using the methods suggested above. If you own the property, you may also technically own the earlier deeds

Deeds can tell us when a building was built, by and for whom, what its floor plan was, who lived next door and also some details of external features.

This indenture, dated 30 April 1845, was made between Elizabeth Baroness von Zandt 'of Ovington Park, Hampshire and Clarges Street, Piccadilly', the lessor, and William Willmer Pocock 'of Mallin Terrace, Belgrave Square, Middlesex, architect', the lessee. 'In consideration to the expense to which the said William Willmer Pocock hath been at in erecting the messuage hereinafter demised pursuant to an agreement of 18 November last', the Baroness leased Mr Pocock a piece of land in Kensington 'on the west side of a certain new road leading from Lower Grove Brompton to a certain new intended Square and more particularly described in the plan drawn in the margin hereof and also all that messuage or tenement lately erected on the said ground and distinguished as Number 7 Ovington Square'.

The lease was set to run for 80 years, at a rent of £10 a year, together with £2 a year, payable at Christmas, for the maintenance of 'the road pavement gates enclosure railing and plantation of Ovington Terrace' and the lighting, cleaning and watching of the same. The lessee was also to repaint the 'outside cement work and wood and iron work' once every four years.

The plan drawn in the margin shows the house's layout: there is also a note that its rear abutted some 'livery stables leased to Mr Green'.

Background research using *Burke's Peerage* and other sources outlined on pages 72–5 showed that Elizabeth was left Ovington Park by her father, James Standerwick, a London merchant who happened to be a great grandson of Daniel Defoe, author of *Robinson Crusoe*. She married first Sir Thomas Dyer, and then the romantically named Baron von Zandt. Through her first husband she had the use for life of the Dyer family's land in Brompton, which included Ovington Square, named after her Hampshire home.

This Indenture

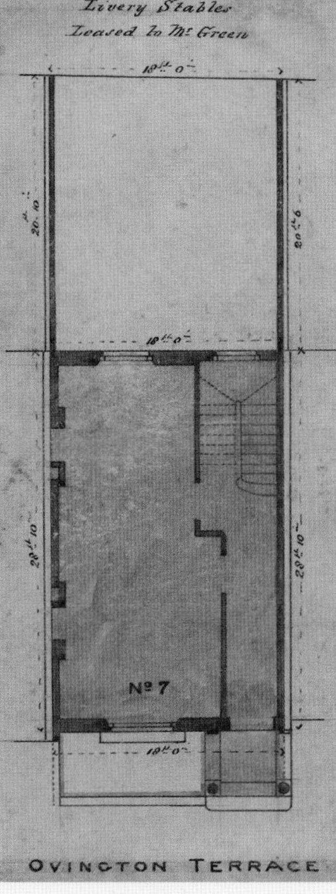

The lease for 7 Ovington Square, showing its floor plan.

relating to it, wherever they are, so you could have a go at claiming them back.

It's worth considering the title deeds of neighbouring properties as a potential source of information too. Deeds often described property boundaries in terms of what was next door – the properties that 'abutted' the one concerned. Equally, your home may have been built on land detached from a neighbouring property, whose previous ownership is therefore as much a part of your home's history as theirs. Sometimes, when one person owned a group of properties (that may or may not all have adjoined one another), the deeds may all have been kept by the 'head' property, which could be the one next door, or simply another property owned by the same person elsewhere, whose identity you will hopefully discover during your research. You may find yourself knocking on some surprising doors in the course of researching the history of your home!

Dealing with deeds

The different types of deeds and the types of land holding to which they relate are a fairly complex topic, covering hundreds of years of legal history. Rather than provide a summary here, I have written a separate chapter explaining them in full, on pages 184–91. You don't need to learn it inside out – just use the bits you need to interpret any deeds you find relating to your home.

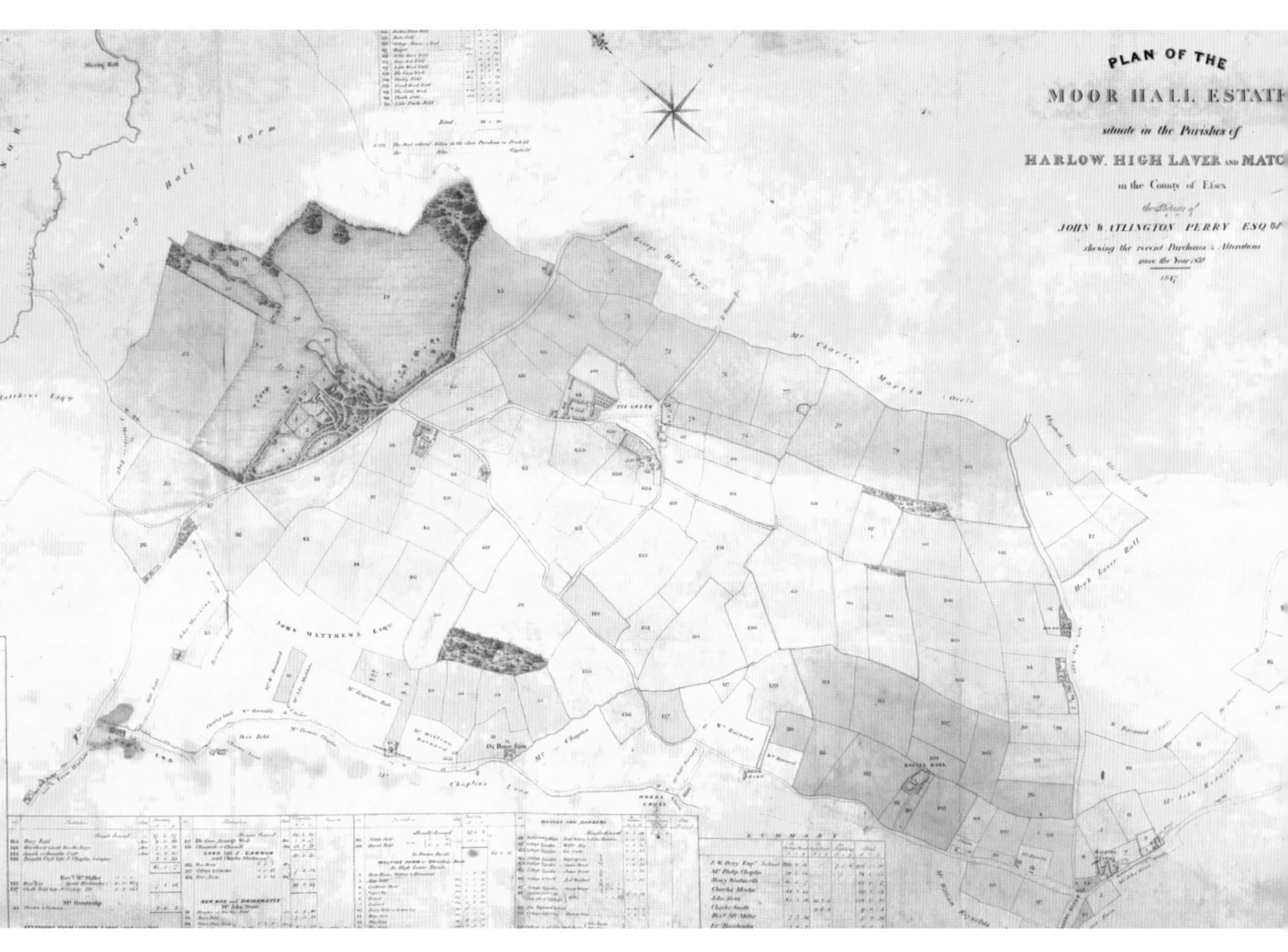

Plan of the Moor Hall Estate, the property of John Watlington Perry, drawn in 1847.

Home Information Packs

Home Information Packs (HIPs) are a new feature of buying and selling homes. Available voluntarily from June 2006 and compulsorily (under the Housing Act, 2004) from 1 June 2007, they exist primarily online and comprise mandatory and voluntary information.

The compulsory element of the pack, which will cost between £500 and £1,000, will contain information formerly provided later in the sale process, including terms of sale; evidence of title; details on planning applications, building regulation and listed status; and a home condition report, based on a professional survey of the property. Packs for leasehold properties will include information on regulations made by the landlord or management company, and the memorandum and articles of the landlord or management company. In Scotland, HIPs will be known as Purchasers' Information Packs (PIPs): at the time of writing, the date of their introduction has not been set, and there are no immediate plans to introduce the scheme to Northern Ireland.

The compulsory element of HIPs does not contain any historical information besides a bare estimate of the property's age. For home historians of the future, however, HIPs will be an important and interesting element of research. Let's hope they will be preserved, both by home owners, and perhaps as part of the archives of the 21st century.

The voluntary element of HIPs can contain any information that sellers may want to include, over and above what's compulsory. Here, the possibilities for including further details of the home's history are immense. HIPs may indeed become one obvious place to keep copies of finished home histories. They will certainly be a place where hopeful sellers can put forward historical information on the home and its surroundings which they hope will interest and attract potential buyers. It could actually lead to home histories becoming a normal element of the voluntary part of your home's HIP, adding a financial incentive to this already thoroughly fascinating pastime.

(It may also lead to a little selectivity in what's included and left out: even as a researcher dedicated to the truth at all costs I'd have to admit that, unless you were legally required to do so, if you found your home was built on a former graveyard it would probably best to keep quiet about it in your HIP's home history section!)

Contacts

www.hip-inspection.co.uk/
House Information Packs

www.hipsdirect.com/
HIPs Direct Ltd, 7 Grosvenor Street, Chester, Cheshire CH1 2DD; tel. 01244 340 159; mail@hipsdirect.com. One of several suppliers of HIPs (others are Easier 2 Move, Live, LMS, Open Book HIPs, Pack Provider).

CHAPTER 4

Tracing past inhabitants

Tracing people who used to live in your home would not, perhaps, be as important an exercise as it is, if we weren't such a transitory lot. However, most people move an average of four times during their lifetime – some a lot more. As a result, the history of the average British home over even just the last 40 or 50 years is likely to cover several completely separate families. It also means many disparate people will have memories, stories, pictures or documents that are of direct relevance to the history of your home.

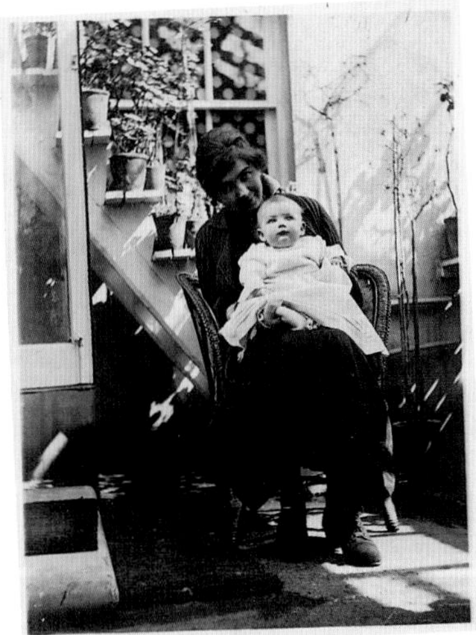

Julie Myerson's book *Home* provides many examples of her efforts to contact past inhabitants, or their descendants, of her home. Some were evasive and others extremely helpful. In one case, she was rather embarrassed to find that, thanks to her research, she actually knew more solid facts about someone's childhood sojourn at her house than that person did themselves.

Contacting people for this sort of research can be seen as nosey or intrusive, so it's important to be extremely polite. While you're obviously burning to know as much as you can about your home's history, the person to whom you have just written, e-mailed or telephoned is likely to have other more pressing matters on their mind. They may be thoroughly flattered that you want to talk to them, or they may not want to dredge up old memories. So, while avoiding being so deferential as not to make any progress, do try not to be pushy. If treated gently, people will often end up being co-operative.

- You can trace people using several of the records described in later chapters, especially General Registration and wills (see pages 148–50 and 154–61). In particular, a death certificate (see page 150) will provide the name and address of an informant, often a child of the deceased. Wills provide names and addresses of beneficiaries – both excellent ways of tracing backwards to the present.
- Genealogy contact websites are also useful for tracing people or their descendants. **www.genesreuninted.com** has well over a million members, all of whom are interested in historical research. Even if the person you want isn't a member, there is an ever-increasing chance that you will find a relation of theirs on the site.

Telephone directories

Telephone directories are the best tool of all for tracing past inhabitants of your home. They date from the 1880s, but only really become useful for research after the Second World War, because only then did many people have telephones: this also coincides with the period

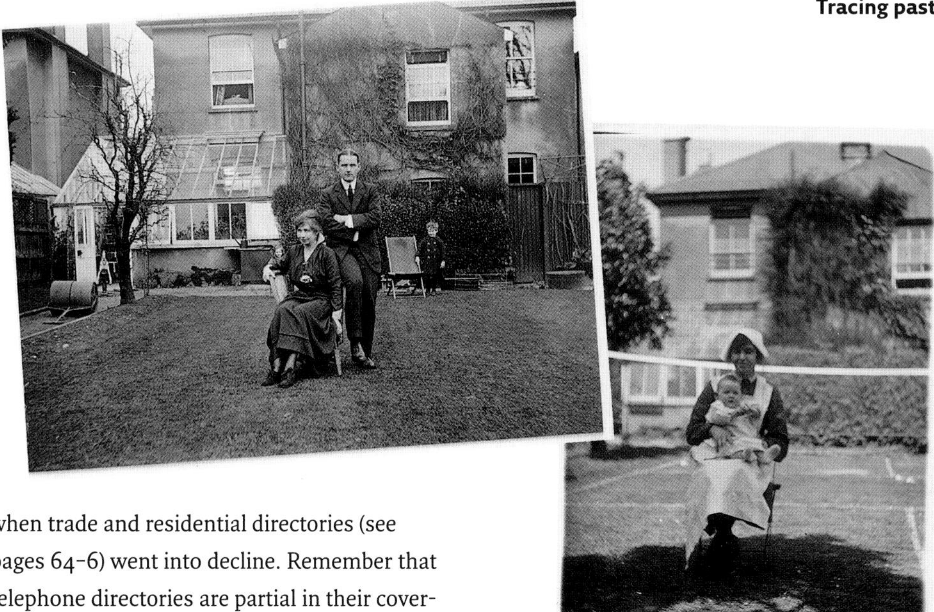

This sequence of pictures shows life at 'Homefield', Park Road, Wallington, Surrey, about 1915, when it was occupied by my great-grandfather Joseph Adolph and his young family. Before he died, my grandfather (who can be seen as a small boy, standing next to a deckchair) confirmed the location and who was who. The pictures are special because they show both the front and the back of the house. The family's maid, Edith Robb, appears in three of the pictures, always seated. In one she appears in front of a tennis net (in another, a roller can be seen – the tennis lawn was obviously important to Joseph). In another (see opposite page), she is seated inside the conservatory, so we can see a little of what the interior was like.

when trade and residential directories (see pages 64–6) went into decline. Remember that telephone directories are partial in their coverage. Even before mobile phones arrived, only about 70 per cent of households had landlines, and some of those were ex-directory.

You cannot look up your address in an old telephone directory. However, once you know the name of a former inhabitant – from random post arriving for them, or from title deeds or other sources – you can use a run of old directories to establish the span of years during which they lived in your home. Bear in mind, when calculating this, that telephone directories tend to contain information gathered the year before, so are generally a year out of date.

- Most local libraries have collections of old local telephone directories. There are also substantial collections held nationally at the British Telecom Archives, 3rd Floor, Holborn Telephone Exchange, 268–270 High Holborn, London WC1V 7EE; tel: 020 7492 8792; **www.btplc.com/archives**.
- You can search current directories, and those for several past years at **www.infobel.com** and **www.192.com**. The latter also has electoral registers from 2002 to last year, and plans to add more material for home history research.
- Also worth considering purchasing, unless you can get access to one in a local library or archive (you often can), is a UK Info Disk. The latest at the time of writing is the *UK Info Disk V10.0 Standard: People Finder 2005*, but they are updated annually. They are available from CD and software suppliers – key 'UK Info Disk' into an internet search engine to find many suppliers. These research tools contain data from British electoral registers, telephone directories and company listings. The addresses are also linked to a road map.

CHAPTER 5

Archives and the internet

The reason why archival research is often regarded as the backbone of home history is that British archives and libraries are literally jammed full of really useful documentation on buildings. That's why a large proportion of this book is devoted to different sorts of written records.

Getting hold of many records is relatively straightforward. In other pursuits, such as tracing your family history, most archival research entails long journeys to the places where relevant records are held, for people seldom live near the archive that happens to contain the material they need. In the case of your home, however, most of the records you need are unlikely to have travelled far. In some cases, in fact, modern technology means you can start your archival research simply by switching on your computer.

The internet

The following few chapters identify some types of record, especially census returns, directories and Ordnance Survey maps, which you will find in local archives. Increasingly these – and many of the other records identified later on in this book – are becoming available on the internet. The sites containing them are usually aimed at either local or family history – but they're perfect for home history as well. On the web, you will either find indexes to records or indexes combined with actual images of the records themselves, some free, others available for a small payment using a credit card.

Using the websites identified in the following chapters, you can start tracing your home's history at home! If you don't have internet access, you can see all the records concerned in archives. Equally, internet users should not think that what's online is a substitute for visiting local archives. You will get a lot out of actually going to the places where the records are kept and seeing records in the flesh.

Levels of archives

Local archives and study libraries: On the closest geographical level are local archives and study libraries, which are often one and the same thing – and which should be reasonably close to your home. Local archives may be housed in libraries, museums or larger record offices. Enquiries at any of these places will point you in the right direction, or you can discover their whereabouts on your local authority's website:

|| Key in 'www.' followed by the authority's name, and then '.gov.uk'. Their website should indicate whether they have published any special advice for tracing the history of homes in your area.

Before visiting any archives, check in advance for opening times and find out whether you need to book a time or take any identification with you. Always remember to take some paper and a pencil – pens usually aren't allowed, as they can damage the records. Once in the local archive, you will see for yourself how much potential there is for discovering a great deal about your home.

It is worth visiting your local archive as soon as you can. You can spend the journey comparing the different styles of buildings you pass with your own, and so become more experienced in placing your home in its local context. When in the archive, besides looking up the specific types of record you will have identified from reading the next few chapters of this book, you will also discover special local sources. Most archives have a rack of local history books, magazines and newsletters, and shelves of books on local subjects. Many archives also have leaflets on sources for tracing the history of local homes. Many have special collections, too – the archives of deceased local historians, for example – which could turn out to be unexpected treasure troves.

County record offices: Since the Second World War, every county in the British Isles has acquired a county record office – or, in some cases, several. These tend to hold material deposited from parish churches, from the courts of bishops and the courts where local justice was administered – the Quarter Sessions. They also have a great deal more material, some of which partly duplicates what is in local archives, some of which doesn't.

- You can find your county record office(s) in your local telephone directory or at **www.a2a.org.uk**, which also allows you to browse county record office catalogues.
- For Scottish archives see **www.scan.org.uk** and for Irish county heritage centres inspect **www.scripts.ireland.com/ancestor/browse/addresses/major.htm**.
- Some county record offices have produced leaflets on how to trace the histories of homes in their counties. Essex's, to give but one example, is online at **www.essexcc.gov.uk/vip8/ecc/ECCWebsite/display/guideContents/index.jsp?oid=14818**.

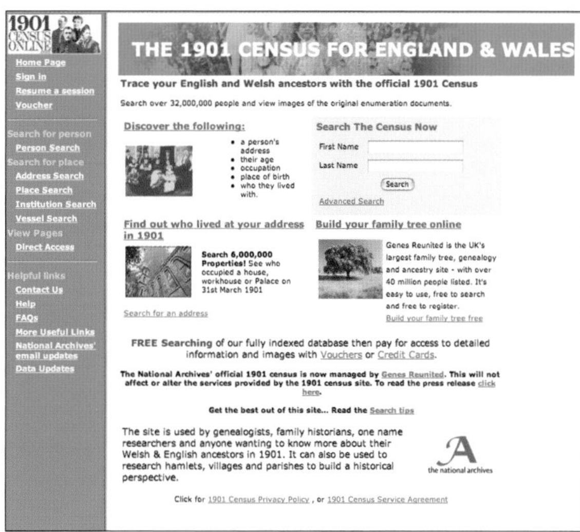

The internet has become a major resource for home historians.

National libraries, museums and archives: Useful material held in these archives is identified later in this book. The main national archives are as follows:

- National Archives (formerly Public Record Office), Ruskin Avenue, Kew, Richmond, Surrey TW9 4DU; tel: 020 8876 3555; **www.nationalarchives.gov.uk**. These are the national archives for the whole of Great Britain, with an emphasis on England. Records are identified by reference codes and numbers: HLG 45, WORK 7, C 87/345 are all National Archive references.
- National Archives of Scotland (formerly Scottish Record Office), General Register House, 2 Princes Street, Edinburgh EH1 3YY; tel: 0131 535 1334; **www.nas.gov.uk**.
- National Library of Wales (Llyfrgell Genedlaethol Cymru), Penglais, Aberystwyth, Dyfed SY23 3BU; tel: 01970 623816/7; **www.llgc.org.uk**.

- Public Record Office of Northern Ireland (PRONI), 66 Balmoral Avenue, Belfast BT9 6NY; tel: 028 9025 5905; **http://proni.nics.gov.uk**. In 1922, southern Ireland became the Republic of Eire, gaining full independence from Britain in 1949. Thus, many records for Northern Ireland before these dates are in Dublin. However, much of that is accessible in Belfast on microfilm.
- National Archives of Ireland, Bishop Street, Dublin 8; tel: 00 353 1407 2300; **www.nationalarchives.ie**.

You should be prepared for a few long(ish) trips to national repositories, but if that doesn't suit, you can also pay record searchers at the archives to look things up for you. Almost all archives (local and national) have an in-house research service or a list of independent researchers, or sometimes both – ask for details to be posted to you, or look them up on their websites.

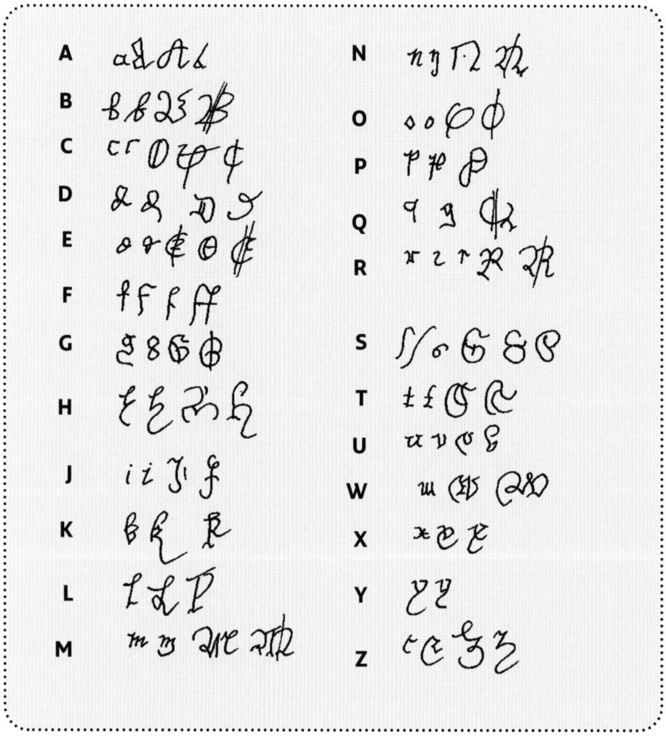

How the letters of the alphabet might look in old handwriting.

Using old records

As you start using old records in archives or online, you will begin to come across handwriting, terminology and forms of dating that are unfamiliar. A brief guide follows about the main oddities you are likely to encounter.

To get the best out of old records it is necessary to understand why and how they were set up. In almost all cases, they were created in a hurry, for specific purposes and with no eye to posterity – it's luck, not judgement that has given Britain one of the finest collections of historical records in the world.

Spelling: The idea of 'correct' and 'incorrect' spelling is a modern phenomenon: it was not an issue until well into the 18th century. Your home's name, its surroundings and its inhabitants will be spelled in many different ways in original records. Never reject anything because the spelling is 'wrong'. Always think of variant spellings under which places and people may have been recorded if you do not find them under what you initially expected.

Old handwriting: The deciphering of old handwriting is called palaeography. Handwriting presents two types of problem. First, in the past, some letters were written differently to the way they are now, so look extremely unfamiliar. For example, 'e' was often written as ɵ, 'c' as ɼ, 's' as ʃ and so on. Excellent guides to old scripts are given by Grieve, Marshall, Mumby and Thoyts (see page 45). A free course in English palaeography, 1500–1700, is available at **www.english.cam.ac.uk/ceres/ehoc.index.html**.

The second problem is simply bad handwriting! Like cracking codes, though, you can often work out what an incomprehensible letter is by studying its companions (for example, if you can read 'Ed-ard' then you can surmise the missing letter is a 'w'). Once you have identified a letter in an easily recognisable word, you can look out for it in an incomprehensible one. Many wills, for example, will start, 'In the name of God Amen', so you can see how the scribe wrote his 'I's, 'n's, 't's and so on before tackling the rest of the text.

Don't be daunted by age – sometimes a 16th-century document can be in handwriting much neater and clearer, say, than your own!

Be aware that writers often abbreviated words, sometimes using apostrophes, sometimes not. 'Tenement' was often written 'ten't' or 'tent'; 'William' as 'Will'm' or 'Wm' and so on – after a while you will get used to this.

Old words: You will encounter many old-fashioned expressions and phrases – that's half the fun of exploring the past.

|| There are some specialist dictionaries, such as Milward's (see page 45). A stalwart source, however, remains the *Oxford English Dictionary* – the older the edition, the better.

Money: L.S.D. was the acronym for pre-decimal currency of pounds (livres), shillings and pence (denarii). Amounts were recorded in a number of different ways; for example, four pounds, two shillings and three pence ('thruppence') could

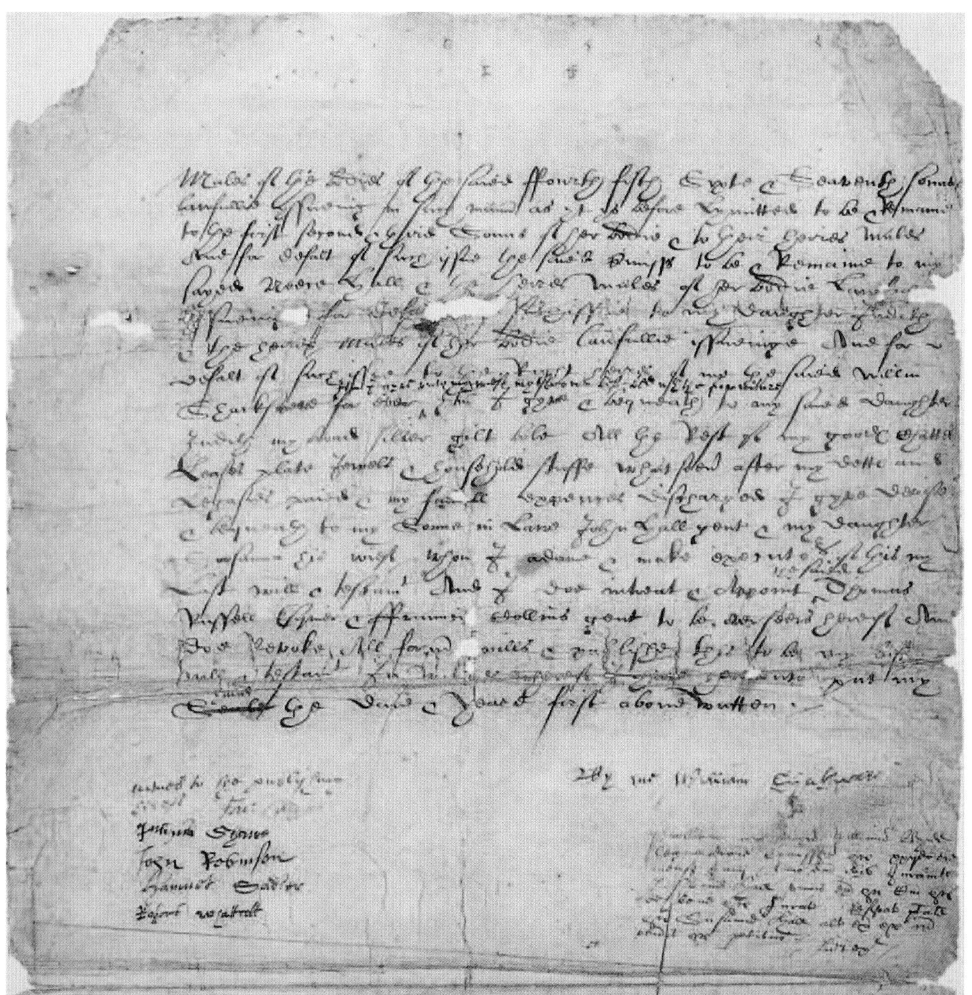

Wills can be tremendous sources for home history as they often name and describe people's homes and their contents. They also present many challenges in terms of old handwriting, as this example of a famous writer shows. This is the will of William Shakespeare himself.

Pre-decimalisation UK money from 1969 including pound notes and shillings.

be written £4-2-3 or £4 2s 3d or 4^{l} 2^{s} 3^{d} or using Roman numerals: iv^{l} ii^{s} iii^{d} or even $iiij^{l}$ ij^{s} iij^{d}.

It's difficult to find out what old money was worth relative to what it is today. Everything is relative and house prices are especially volatile. What we pay for an orange, posting a letter and buying a house now is completely out of proportion to what people paid for those things 300 years ago, when oranges were luxuries, the postal system very expensive but property relatively much less costly.

|| The Bank of England (**www.bankofengland.co.uk**) has a 'ready reckoner', and you could also study Chapman or Mumby (see box opposite).

Dates: Years and days have not always been recorded in the same way in every country. Cheney (see box opposite) lists all old forms of dating, including by saints' days (e.g. St George's Day 1660 was 23 April 1660) and popes' and kings' regnal years. Years were often counted from the date of a sovereign's accession, so, for example, 1 Elizabeth II, the first day of the first year of the reign of Elizabeth II, started on 6 February 1952, the day she succeeded her father, and 53 Elizabeth II starts on 6 February 2004 and ends on 5 February 2005.

|| Cheney also provides a calendar for looking up which day of the week fell in what date in a given year; for instance, if someone wrote a letter dated 25 May 1657 saying their father died 'last Monday' you can find out that 25 May 1657 was a Friday, so 'last Monday' was 20 May.

New-style and old-style calendars: Britain and Europe used to use the Julian calendar, whereby the year began on Lady Day, 25 March, not the Gregorian calendar, which starts the year on 1 January. The Julian calendar started to die out among lay people in the Tudor period, and by the 18th century it is often hard to tell whether a date is being given in old or new style. Different countries changed to the Gregorian calendar at different times. Most of Western Europe changed in 1582, Scotland in 1600, England and Wales in 1752 and Russia and the Balkans in the 20th century. Therefore, a letter written in France on 1 February 1610 was most likely to have been written just under a year before one dated 25 January 1610 in England.

This means that dates appearing in old records need adjusting to make sense in modern terms. A property sale recorded in an old deed on 24 January 1722 would, in modern terms, have taken place on 24 January 1723 because, under the old calendar, New Year's Day (25 March) had not yet arrived. To avoid confusion – and as you will probably appreciate confusion often arises – researchers tend to record the date using 'double dating', recording the old-style year followed by the new-style year, i.e. 24 January 1722/3. Never, when you see this, strip out the 'old' date and just write 24 January 1723, because someone else may come along, realise that 23 January is before 25 March, not know that you've already adjusted for double dating and write 24 January 1724 instead. Be aware too that non-conformist registers were using new-style dating well in advance of 1752.

Another difference between the old-style Julian and new-style Gregorian calendars was that the latter used leap years and the former didn't. By the time Pope Gregory introduced the new calendar in 1582, the lack of leap years had already caused the old-style date to lapse ten days behind the solar year, so he simply ordered ten days to be cut out off 1582, between 4 and 15 October. Because England persisted with the old calendar, it sunk increasingly behind Europe, and was 11 days behind by the 17th century. Therefore events that share the same dates in different countries, such as the deaths of Shakespeare and Cervantes on 23 April 1616 in England and Spain respectively, actually took place 11 days apart in real life. England and Wales lost the days between 2 and 14 September 1752 in order to catch up with Europe.

Latin: Working back to and before the 18th century, you may start to encounter documents written in Latin. Don't be too scared of this. Often you should be able to manage using basic word lists, however poor or non-existent your school-taught Latin may be. Many of the compilers of the records, after all, had only the most tenuous grasp of Latin. They therefore used it very basically, often with English rather than Latin word orders, plenty of stock phrases and not much in the way of complicated declensions.

|| Useful guides to Latin include Gooder, Latham, Stuart and Trice Martin (see box right). There is a very good Latin word list on **www.genuki.org.uk**. And, failing that, there are some very good, modestly priced translators about.

Land measurements

Acre This started as the area a team of oxen could plough in a morning but became fixed at 4,480 square yards in England, 6,100 square yards in Scotland and 7,840 in Ireland.

English mile 8 furlongs or 1,760 yards.

Furlong 40 rods or 220 yards.

Hide/carucate/ploughland The area a team of oxen could plough in a year, which varied from 60 to 180 acres depending on the soil.

Rod/pole/perch 16½ square feet or 5½ square yards.

Rood 40 square rods.

Square mile 640 acres.

BOOKS

- **C. R. Chapman, *How Heavy, How Much and How Long? Weights, Money and other Measures used by our Ancestors* (Lochin Publishing, 1995)**
- **C. R. Cheney (ed.), *Handbook of Dates for Students of English History* (London, 1955); rev. ed. M. Jones (CUP, 2000)**
- **E. A. Gooder, *Latin for Local History: An Introduction* (Longman, 1978)**
- **H. E. P. Grieve, *Examples of English Handwriting 1150–1750* (Essex Record Office, 1949)**
- **R. A. Latham, *Revised Medieval Latin Word-list from British and Irish Sources* (OUP, 1965)**
- **H. Marshall, *Palaeography for Family and Local Historians* (Phillimore, 2004)**
- **R. Milward, *A Glossary of Household, Farming and Trade Terms from Probate Inventories* (Derbyshire Record Society, occasional paper 1, various edns)**
- **L. Mumby, *How Much is that Worth?* (Phillimore for BALH, 1996)**
- **L. Mumby, *Reading Tudor and Stuart Handwriting* (Phillimore for BALH, 1988)**
- **D. Stuart, *Latin for Local and Family Historians* (Phillimore, 1995)**
- **E. E. Thoyts, *How to Read Old Documents* (Phillimore, 2001)**
- **C. Trice Martin, *The Record Interpreter* (Phillimore, 2002)**

CHAPTER 6

Census returns

1801–1901, but mainly 1841–1901

One of the most accessible and rewarding records to use in the early stages of tracing the history of your home are census returns. They are becoming increasingly easy to obtain on the internet and microfilms of relevant local sections are in archives. Censuses also provide a graphic picture of who inhabited your home throughout the second half of the 19th century and shed some light on the physical nature of the building at the time.

Census returns do not record property ownership. Instead, they record who was physically present in each building on the Sunday nights when the returns were made. These will normally be the usual occupants. However, if visitors were present and regular members of the family were away, this will be reflected in the returns. You may, for example, find a big house occupied by only a couple of servants, while their employer and his family were elsewhere or, on the other extreme, a boarding house full of transient residents. Whatever you find, however, you will have vivid, interesting records about real Victorians to add to your home's history.

Sometimes, censuses can indicate when a property was built. The returns for 1841 to 1891 include a column where the enumerator could indicate if a house was inhabited, and another to note 'uninhabited or building [being built]'. Those for 1901 have columns to indicate inhabited buildings; those uninhabited but normally occupied, or uninhabited but usually unoccupied; whether being built; and, finally, the number of rooms occupied if these numbered under five. Sometimes, then, you can find a street actually in the process of being built – excellent for dating your home.

Censuses started to be taken in 1801. Their initial purpose was to assess the population, particularly to establish how many men could be mobilised should Napoleon invade these shores. There was also considerable interest in population growth and its possible impact on available food supplies. The 1801 census comprised a headcount of all those attending Church of England services in England and Wales on Easter Sunday. As this excluded all non-Anglicans, a second census was taken in 1811,

Dates of censuses

with National Archive reference numbers from 1841

10 March 1801	(no records at National Archives)
27 May 1811	(no records at National Archives)
28 May 1821	(no records at National Archives)
30 May 1831	HO 71 (a few give names of heads of households)
6 June 1841	HO 107
30 March 1851	HO 107
7 April 1861	RG 9
2 April 1871	RG 10
3 April 1881	RG 11
5 April 1891	RG 12
31 March 1901	RG 13
2 April 1911	RG 14 (not yet open to public searching)

this time including every household in the land. The results, of course, were wildly different – 10,164,000 in 1811, compared to 8,893,000 ten years earlier. Unaware of the different criteria used to achieve these figures, the economist Thomas Malthus deduced that the population must be exploding and that it was not long before we would everyone starve!

Censuses have continued to be taken every ten years, except for 1941, when the Second World War was raging. Those after 1901 are held under a 100-year secrecy rule; those for 1911, therefore, will be released for public inspection in 2012, though there is pressure for this date to be brought forward.

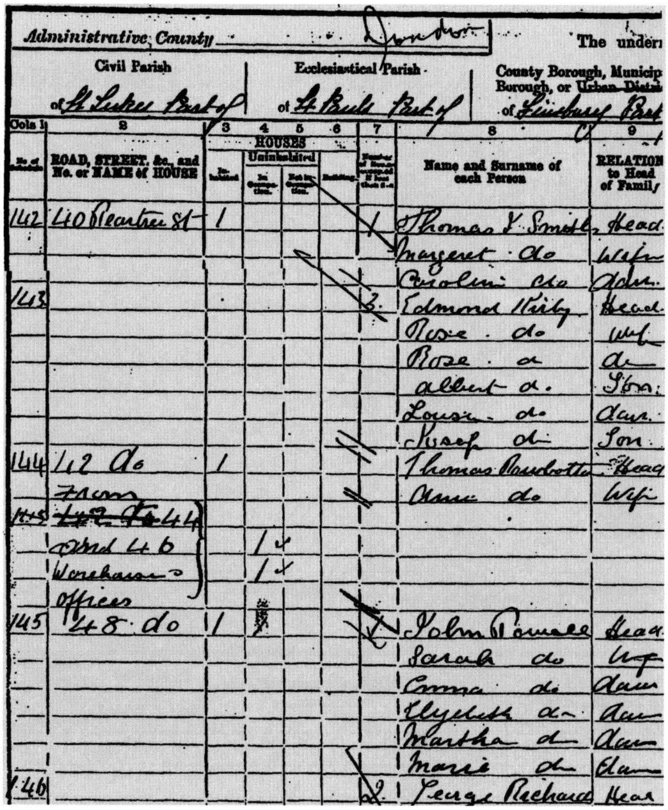
Administrative County ... London ... The under...
Civil Parish of St Lukes Part of | Ecclesiastical Parish of St Pauls Part of | County Borough, Municipal Borough, or Urban District of Finsbury Part

Cols 1	2	3	4	5	6	7	8	9
No. of Schedule	ROAD, STREET, &c., and No. or NAME of HOUSE	Inhabited	HOUSES Uninhabited In Occupation	Not in Occupation	Building	Number of Rooms occupied if less than five	Name and Surname of each Person	RELATION to Head of Family
142	40 Peartree St	1				1	Thomas T. Smith	Head
							Margaret do	Wife
							Caroline do	Dau.
143						3	Edmond Kirby	Head
							Rose do	Wife
							Rose do	dau
							Albert do	Son
							Louise do	Dau.
							Joseph do	Son
144	42 do	1					Thomas Rowbottom	Head
							Anne do	Wife
145	From 42 to 44 and 46 Warehouses offices		1 1					
145	48 do	1					John Powell	Head
							Sarah do	Wife
							Emma do	Dau
							Elizabeth do	Dau
							Martha do	Dau
							Marie do	Dau
146						2	George Richards	Head

Part of the 1901 census returns for Peartree Street, Finsbury. Number 40 Peartree Street was occupied by Thomas Smith, his wife and daughter, who had one room, and Edmond Kirby, his wife and four children, with three rooms; then came Thomas Rowbottom and wife at number 42. Numbers 44 and 46 were occupied (as opposed to vacant) warehouses and offices, but nobody was sleeping there on census night.

Censuses: 1841–1901

- From 1841 to 1901, almost complete sets of returns survive for the whole of England and Wales. The main set is at the Family Records Centre, a London search room open to the public (1 Myddleton Street, London EC1R 1UW; tel: 020 8392 5300; **www.familyrecords.gov.uk/frc**).
- The sections for your local area can be found on microfilm or occasionally microfiche at most local archives and study libraries. Gibson and Hampson have written a full guide to local holdings (see page 53).
- Census returns can also be searched at Mormon Family History Centres – your nearest can be located using **www.familysearch.org** or your local telephone directory. It should be explained that the Mormon Church is a religious organisation, whose beliefs include tracing ancestors in order to baptise them posthumously into their faith. As a result, they have collected a huge amount of copies of records. They make these freely available to all researchers – with absolutely no element of proselytising involved.
- Many census returns are also being indexed on the internet – see the box on page 49.
- Many other sections of the returns, especially for 1851, are indexed by printed or CD indexes: copies are usually kept with the relevant returns in local repositories and are listed in Gibson and Hampson's book on census indexes (see page 53).
- The National Archives' 1901 census (**www.1901censusonline.com/**) has a special address search facility. Unfortunately, though, as the target users are mainly family historians, most of the other on- and off-line indexes are only searchable by the surnames of occupants. If you know or can guess the name of the occupant of your home in the relevant year, then these indexes will be very useful, because they provide the precise reference for the original entry.

Work in progress

Comeragh Road in Barons Court, London, was developed by Major Sir William Palliser, inventor of such unusual artefacts as railway chairs and the Palliser missile. All the streets in his development had names reflecting aspects of his family history: Comeragh in Waterford was the residence of his brother Captain Wray Gladstone Palliser. The road's name was approved by London County Council in 1877 and confirmed three years later, as is shown in the 1955 London County Council official list of streets.

When the next census was taken, on Sunday 4 April 1881, the enumerator, Walter Barry Harvey, had to pick his way through the building site. His census page, therefore, is a vivid snapshot of the street in the process of construction.

On the page shown, you can see the end of the enumeration for number 27, giving details of two school children and two family servants – the previous page listed the parents and older children. Normally, names were written properly, but our enumerator just dashed down initials – rather slapdash of him. Number 27 was the last inhabited house on that side of the street. Numbers 29, 31, 33, 35 and 37 were uninhabited. For some reason, the enumerator then broke the sequence by listing the inhabitants of number 15, before moving on to Castletown Road. You'd think from this that number 39 was yet to be built. Actually, it had already been listed on its own, some pages back, and very revealingly showed it being inhabited by the Winfield family. And Mr Winfield's job? He was the builder's manager!

Page 42] The undermentioned Houses are situate within the Boundaries of the

Civil Parish [or Township] of	City or Municipal Borough of	Municipal Ward of	Parliamentary Borough of	Town or Village or Hamlet of	Urban Sanitary District of	Rural Sanitary District of
Fulham			Chelsea			

No. of Schedule	ROAD, STREET, &c., and No. or NAME of HOUSE	HOUSES: Inhabited	HOUSES: Uninhabited (U.), or Building (B.)	NAME and Surname of each Person	RELATION to Head of Family	CONDITION as to Marriage	AGE last Birthday of Males	AGE last Birthday of Females	Rank, Profession, or OCCUPATION	WHERE BORN
201	Comeragh Rd 27	1		E. A. Skelton	Dau	Un		9	Scholar	Lincolnsh
	do			J. C. "	Son	"	6			
				M. Curle	Serv	"		[illegible]	Dom: Servt	Norfolk
				J. E. Abbott	"	"		[illegible]	"	"
	29		1U							
	31		1U							
	33		1U							
	35		1U							
	37		1U							
202	15	1		E. B. Craig	Head	M	49		Solicitor	Essex
				M. "	Wife	"		41		Ireland
				H. J. Clifford	Visitor	Widow		67		Mauritius
203	Castletown Road 6	1		Geo: Elliott Bart.	Head	M	48		Retired Admiral R.N.	Calcutta
				H. do	Wife	"		63		Switzerland
				I. McMillan	Serv	Un		48	House Keeper	Aberdeen
				L. Taylor	"	"		[illegible]	Cook	Somerset
				O. Butler	"	"		[illegible]	Housemaid	Christchurch
204	" 8	1		A. M. Beaumont	Head	Widow		43		Middlesex
				M. E. do	Dau			11	Scholar	Scotland
				E. A. "	"			10	"	"
				A. H. "	"			9	"	"
				H. D. "	Son		8		"	Wales
				E. G. "	"		6		"	Middlesex

|| On some websites, you can even download an image of the original census return. Be cautious, though, for many houses are poorly identified. If you rely solely on surname indexes, you may successfully find a family who had lived in your home at one time or another, but you may still need to check through the original returns to be absolutely sure they were in your home at the time.

|| Census indexes will also help you track down the whereabouts of people who were missing from your home on census night – children away at boarding school, fathers away working, and so on.

|| In many cases, the online censuses do not give you the facility for searching by addresses, or for scrolling through the returns for whole streets or neighbourhoods – an enjoyable exercise best undertaken with the microfilms of the original returns in your local archives.

|| Many sections of census returns are now available on CD-Rom and are advertised in family history magazines (see also Useful addresses, page 265). These may be worth buying if you want to make a concerted study of your home and its surroundings in a particular year.

Enumerator conventions

A very important point to note here is that enumerators often found several families, called 'households', living in the same building. Each building is separated from each other one by a set of double dashes: //. Within each building, households are separated by single dashes: /. Knowing this will save you from thinking that a series of households in one building in fact represents several houses in a street.

Main internet sites for census returns

A summary of the main sites at the time of writing is as follows:

1841–1901 **www.ancestry.com** All censuses for these years are indexed here. Other sites have their own indexes to these censuses, particularly:

1861 **www.1837online.com**

1881 **www.familysearch.org**

1901 **www.genesreunited.com**

Registration districts

Where census surname indexes do not help you locate your home, you will need to undertake a longer search. Census returns are arranged by registration districts. These were created in 1837; there were initially 619 of them, reorganised into 623 in 1851. They corresponded to the old poor law unions.

|| Directories (see pags 64–6) state the registration district or poor law union for each parish.

|| Alternatively, you can key your parish into **www.visionofbritain.org.uk** and it will tell you both, with additional details from *Bartholemew's Gazeteer of the British Isles* (1887).

|| You can also consult Youngs' book for further details on local administrative divisions (see page 53).

Registration districts were broken down into subdistricts, and these were, in turn, split into enumeration districts. A census enumerator would then make a circuit of his allotted patch on census night, delivering forms to each household and filling them in himself if the inhabitants were illiterate. He then copied all the results into his enumeration book. The forms have been lost, but the books were sent to the Registrar General for statistical analysis. This was done by clerks with blue pencils, ticking or crossing off entries as they were counted – don't be put off when you see entries marked in this way.

Page numbers and folio numbers

Confusion is sometimes caused by these numbers. Each enumerator's book page has a page number, 'Page 1', Page 2' and so on. Each sheet of paper, front and back, also has a folio number, stamped in slightly bigger print on the front surface of each, but not on the back. Pages 1–2, therefore, are one folio, pages 3–4 the next. The pages are specifically identified by the Latin terms 'recto' and verso': the front surface (i.e. page 1) is 'r[ecto]', and the back of the page (i.e. page 2) is 'v[erso]'. The street indexes use folio numbers, not page numbers.

To find your home in a census return

- First find the correct reference or 'piece number' to your village or town. You can do this by typing the place name into **www.catalogue.nationalarchives.gov.uk**, together with the National Archives reference to the census year (HO 107 for 1851, for example), given in the table on page 46.
- Alternatively, use the Place Name Indexes that accompany the local and national holdings of census returns. These will provide you with a page number for the corresponding Reference Book, where you can learn the 'piece number' covering the place you want. This will correspond to the roll of microfilm you require.
- Each 'piece number' contains a group of numbered enumeration books (in the returns for 1851 these are referred to as 'enumeration districts'). The Reference Book will tell you which enumeration book you need, and you can scroll through the microfilm looking for it.
- Small villages are often covered by just one enumeration book. Bigger ones will be covered by several. You may have to scroll through these looking for the house you want.
- Towns and cities are covered by many enumeration books, and indeed may sprawl over several 'piece numbers' and hence rolls of microfilm. For these, in almost all cases, there are additional street indexes provided. Enumerators covered geographically compact patches, and did not always march up and down the entire length of a single street. Parts of your street may therefore have been covered by several enumerators: this should be indicated by the street indexes.
- When you find your home, note down *all* the details provided, and also note carefully who occupied the homes on either side. In fact – and this applies to many other records you will encounter later, such as rate books (see page 162–4) – it's often sensible to note down all the households in the street.
- If you are lucky, your home will be clearly identified by a distinctive name. Alternatively, it may have been occupied by the same family for a lengthy period, or have been used for a consistent purpose, such as a butcher's shop.
- House numbering can be helpful, but this was not used particularly widely or consistently. Don't rely solely on house numbers. If the street was lengthened or otherwise added to between censuses, the house numbers may have been altered.
- Sometimes, what appear to be house numbers are actually just numbers assigned to each property by the enumerator himself as he walked along: they may have no validity in any other records.
- Occupants, uses and even house names, however, can change rapidly. To overcome such problems, and to double-check you're right when you think you've found the correct building, look carefully at the surroundings. At the start of each enumerator's book is a sheet on which he recorded the precise route taken. This, used in

A census enumerator collects a completed census form.

conjunction with the returns and a map, will help you check that you have identified the right section of road. In the enumerated sheets, look carefully at several houses on each side. See how many households lay between your home (or what you suspect was your home) and fixed points, such as other streets, churches, shops and so on. Using such techniques – or a combination of several – you should be able to pin down the right place.

What the records tell you

In general terms, people are resistant to giving personal details on forms. Enumerators recording what illiterate householders told them could make mistakes. Be prepared, therefore, to find vague or ambiguous information. Ages were often stated slightly inaccurately, and sometimes places of birth might be generalised ('London' instead of a specific place within the metropolis) or just plain wrong (many Irish immigrants, fearing repatriation, didn't want to

What the records tell you

Address The 1841 returns did not usually record street numbers, even if they existed. Those from 1851 will, but, as stated above, they may not be consistent between census years, or tie in with house numbers given in other contemporary records. Remember, a double dash separates buildings; single dashes separate households within the same building. Street numbers and names were often subject to change, especially in urban areas. If you encounter problems finding the correct address, or suspect that what appears to be the right address is really the wrong building, see also pages 81–3.

Status of the building Those from 1861 state whether uninhabited or being built. The returns for 1901 also include whether buildings uninhabited on census night were normally occupied or not. For occupied buildings of under five rooms, the number of rooms occupied by the family was stated.

Name of each person in the household Middle names could be reduced to initials, or (especially in 1841) left out altogether.

Relationship to the head of household In 1841, relationships were not stated, and should not be assumed: two 50-year-olds of opposite sex and a 20-year-old could be husband, wife and child, but they could equally be brother, sister and a young child. From 1851 onwards, relationships are stated: these include stepchildren, in-laws, servants, elderly parents or grandparents and so on.

Marital condition Not given in 1841: from 1851, the returns indicate whether the person was married, single or widowed.

Age In 1841, ages of those under 16 were recorded precisely, and the ages of those over 16 were rounded down to the nearest five years. Thus, people aged from 50 to 54 were recorded as 50. Luckily, some enumerators failed to heed this and wrote down the exact ages. In 1851 and subsequent censuses, ages were recorded precisely.

Occupation In 1891 and 1901, the census notes whether the person was an employee or employer and, if the latter, how many people, if any, they employed. The acreage of farms was also noted.

If working at home This was a new and very interesting column, added in 1901.

Place of birth The 1841 census asked whether people had been born in the same county: 'Y' was for 'yes', 'N' for 'no' and 'NK' for 'not known'. If the birth was outside England and Wales, the abbreviations were 'S' for Scotland, 'I' for Ireland or 'F' for 'foreign parts' – the rest of the world! From 1851, the place of birth was recorded by parish and county. If the person was born outside England and Wales, usually only the country would be given.

Physical and mental condition This column was for those who were blind, or deaf and dumb. Further categories, 'imbecile or idiot; lunatic' were added in 1871 and changed to 'lunatic, imbecile, feeble-minded' in 1901.

TOP
In this 1851 cartoon by Cruickshank entitled 'Taking the Census' the head of an over-sized, extended family has difficulty remembering the names of his kin and servants, let alone how many there are.

BOTTOM
Engraving from the *Illustrated Times* showing the census enumerator in a Gray's Inn Lane tenement, 1861.

admit they had been born somewhere other than where they were then living). However, if you are aware of such potential problems, you will not be misled by them. What the records tell you are outlined in the box on page 51.

Censuses: 1801–31

Censuses for 1801–31 were mainly headcounts – quite interesting to assess the population and implied spread of housing in your area, but generally useless for home histories *per se*. In some cases, the headcounters exceeded their briefs and recorded a few details of the people and places they were enumerating.

|| The whereabouts of these exceptions are detailed in Gibson and Medlycott's book (see box opposite). Shropshire Record Office, for example, has partial 1821 returns for Shrewsbury, listing occupiers street by street.

|| The 1821 Hackney returns, found in a cupboard in St John's church, Hackney, have been published by the East of London Family History Society, whose online shop is at **www.eolfhs.org.uk/eolstore/default.asp**. These list the heads of households, or, if several families lived in one building, just the head of the first family encountered. Two sample entries show the sort of information available:

Rossomond, Joseph, Aldermans Walk, tailor, 5 males, 2 females, total 7, p. 30.
Rothschild, Mr [Nathan Mayer], Stamford Hill, gent, 3 males, 7 females, total 10, p. 162.

|| Similar returns survive for Hackney for 1831, as does (for example) an enumerator's notebook for Saxmundham, Suffolk.

Even earlier censuses

|| Gibson and Medlycott's guide covers local census listings from 1522. These are usually just lists of names and are unlikely to give details of houses. However, as people were often listed by someone walking the streets, you may be able to tie in some of these with other similar listings, such as rate books (see pages 162–4).

Scotland

|| Scottish census returns for 1841–1901 are searchable online at **www.scotlandspeople.gov.uk**.

|| The original returns are on microfilm in local archives, and a complete set is at New Register House (Charlotte Square, Edinburgh, EH1 3YT; tel: 0131 334 0380; **www.gro-scotland.gov.uk**).

The returns give the same information as those for England and Wales, but with a very important addition for home historians. From 1861 onwards, they state the number of rooms in the building that had more than one window, or in the case of multiple occupancy, the number of rooms with more than one window occupied by each household. Beware, though, that if one part of a multiple-occupancy building was temporarily uninhabited, this will not be recorded, giving a skewed view of how many more-than-one-window rooms there were.

Ireland

Sadly, virtually all the returns are lost - some thrown away, others blown up by the IRA - except those for 1901 and 1911.

- The surviving fragments are at the National Archives in Dublin and PRONI in Belfast.
- Details are given by Ryan (see box right). Returns can be searched freely. They are arranged by poor law union, and within that by district, parish and townland. They include religious denomination, but are rather vague on places of birth. Those for 1911 include details of how long couples had been married. Some local archives, especially the county heritage centres, have indexes to households.
- Other census entries survive as individual extracts submitted as proof of age in pension applications made between 1908 and 1921. These are indexed by applicant, not place, and can be searched at the National Archives in Dublin, the Public Record Office of Northern Ireland, and the Society of Genealogists in London (14 Charterhouse Buildings, Goswell Road, London EC1M 7BA; tel: 020 7251 8799; **www.sog.org.uk**).

Isle of Man

- Manx returns are at the Manx Museum, Kingswood Grove, Douglas, Isle of Man; tel: 01624 648 000; **www.gov.im/mnh/heritage/museums/manxmuseum.xml**. The 1851, 1881, 1891 and 1901 returns are fully indexed.

Channel Islands

- Copies for Guernsey are with HM Greffier at the General Register Office, Royal Court House, St Peter Port, Guernsey GY1 2PD; tel: 01481 725277.
- All returns for Jersey from 1841 to 1891 have been indexed by Jersey Library, Halkett Place, St Helier, Jersey JE2 4WH; tel: 01534 759991; **www.jsylib.gov.je/**. There are also (indexed) censuses for 1806 and 1815, called 'General Don's muster rolls'. Those for 1806 list some 4,000 heads of households with the numbers of people in their families, while those for 1816 list all men aged 17 to 80, with the numbers of women, boys and girls in their households.

BOOKS

- **J. Chaudhuri, *Hackney Street Directory 1831* (East of London FHS, 2001)**
- **J. Gibson and E. Hampson, *Census Returns 1841–1891 in Microform: A Directory to Local Holdings in Great Britain, Channel Islands, Isle of Man* (FFHS, 1994)**
- **J. Gibson and E. Hampson, *Marriage and Census Indexes for Family Historians* (FFHS, 2000)**
- **J. Gibson and M. Medlycott, *Local Census Listings 1522–1930: Holdings in the British Isles* (FFHS, 1994)**
- **J. G. Ryan, *Irish Records: Sources for Family and Local History* (Ancestry, 1997)**
- **F. A. Youngs, *A Guide to the Administrative Units of England*, 2 vols (RHS, 1991)**
- ***The Parish of Hendon, 1801, 1811 & 1821* (CD-Rom, www.archivecdbooks.co.uk)**
- ***Parish Returns Series no. 2 part 1, Hackney 1821* (East of London FHS, n.d.)**

A bust of James Paterson, imaginatively photographed by his great-grandson Tinka Paterson. It would probably have spent part of its life at 'Melrose'.

FACING PAGE
Two views of Stamford Hill in the 1860s; the left house is very near James Paterson's, and very similar to how it would have looked.

When the 1881 census was taken, 'Melrose', Stamford Hill, was occupied by James Paterson, of the haulage firm Carter, Paterson & Co., and his family, as follows:

James Paterson, head, married, 50, carrier employing 470 men and 280 horses, born in Scotland.
Isabella Lorraine Paterson, wife, married, 47, born St Pancras, Middlesex.
John James Paterson, son, unmarried, 26, commercial clerk, born in Alnwick, Northumberland.
Harry Lorraine Paterson, son, unmarried, 15, scholar, born Islington, Middlesex.
Thomas Paterson, son, unmarried, 13, scholar, born New Cross, Kent.
Edith Isabella Paterson, daughter, unmarried, 12, scholar, born New Cross, Kent.
Janet Louise Paterson, daughter, unmarried, 10, scholar, born Stoke Newington, Middlesex.
Nellie Paterson, daughter, unmarried, 6, scholar, born Stoke Newington, Middlesex.
Mary Sutton, visitor, unmarried, 31, governess, born New Cross, Kent.
Jane Wilkin, grandmother, 78, born Holy Island, Northumberland.
Catherine Quinn, servant, unmarried, 24, housemaid, domestic, born in Embleton.
Alice Aubery, servant, unmarried, 17, housemaid, domestic, born in English Bicknor, Gloucestershire.

The census paints a vivid picture of 'Melrose' on the night of 4 April that year – we even know that James's mother-in-law was staying, no doubt talking to everyone with her strong north-eastern accent.

There would probably have been a schoolroom, complete with text books, a blackboard and no doubt a map of the world, with the British Empire marked boldly in red. The two domestic servants probably slept in very cramped conditions in the attic, but Miss Sutton the governess would have had a comfortable bedroom of her own (actually, there's cause for speculation as to where she really slept – after James's second wife Isabella died, Mary Sutton became the third Mrs Paterson!).

We can work out a bit more from the next entry in the census. It follows straight on from 'Melrose', and is separated by a single dash, indicating a separate household in the same building. It has a different schedule number, because each head of household had his or her own one to fill in – this underlines the fact that the numbers in the left-hand column are not house numbers. This second household at 'Melrose' comprised John Hauke, 44, domestic gardener, and his wife Christian, 43, both born in St Columb, Cornwall.

A similar pattern is repeated for the houses on either side:

Schedule 224, Amhurst Road, household forming part of 'Stadarona', Stephen Catt, coachman.
Schedule 225, Main Road [i.e. Stamford Hill], 'Lion House', Ann Baker, aged 66, widow.
Schedule 226, 'Highfield House', Eliza Gray Munday, independent means.
Schedule 227, 'Avenue House', Fanny Everitt, parlour-

Total of Houses... 4

Total of Males and Females... 9 | 16

NOTE.—*Draw the pen through such of the words of the headings as are inappropriate.*

maid [she was with a cook, the two women clearly looking after the house in their employer's absence].

Schedule 228, George Pymm, domestic gardener.
Schedule 229, 'Melrose', Stamford Hill, James Paterson.
Schedule 230, John Hauke, gardener.
Schedule 231, 'The Hall', John Brockett, solicitor.
Schedule 232, Frederick Howard, domestic coachman.
Schedule 233, 'The Hall, the Cott[age]', John Powell, gardener.
Schedule 234, George Thompson, 41, [meat] salesman, with a household including three servants and a governess.
Schedule 235, Joseph Higgins, domestic coachman.
Schedule 236, William [?] Coles, gentleman.
Schedule 237, Alfred Collier, merchant.

Stamford Hill was clearly lined with substantial houses, each with plenty of accommodation for live-in unmarried indoor servants, and a semi-independent family of outdoor servants.

The census returns also enable one to work out exactly where buildings were. At the start of the enumerator's book that includes 'Melrose' is an explanation of the route the compiler took. This includes the following:

Cross the road [the Main Road, i.e. Stamford Hill] *opposite Bailey Lane taking Amhurst Park Road, right & left to Stamford Hill Railway Station, return & continue on to the Railway Bridge which crosses Stamford Hill Road which finishes the District.*

This enables us to work out on a modern map where 'Melrose' would have been had it still be standing – sadly, it's not there anymore – and to pinpoint it precisely on old Ordnance Survey maps (see pages 58–63).

Further research into 'Melrose' in Hackney Archives' splendid collection of local pictures turned up two surviving pictures taken in the 1860s, not of the house itself, but of 69 Stamford Hill. A directory of 1884 helpfully lists 'Melrose' as 77 Stamford Hill, thus confirming that it was only four villas up from number 69 and must have been very similar to it. The pictures show a substantial house set in spacious, well-groomed lawns, in which we can see a group of ladies in sombre Victorian attire enjoying their tranquil garden, and even a gardener, just like John Hauke, hard at work.

Research at the archives also revealed a quote from Charles Dickens' *Sketches of Boz*. Dickens knew Stoke Newington well – a picture survives of him with fellow author Wilkie Collins attending a garden party nearby in Church Row, Stoke Newington, only a few years before the Patersons had lived there (see page 111) prior to their own move up to Stamford Hill. Of Stamford Hill's residents, Dickens wrote, 'If they ever had any recreation beyond their dinner, it was their extensive gardens. They always took a walk round before starting for town in the morning and were particularly anxious that the fishponds should be kept specially neat.'

I hope the above will show you how a census return and a visit to the local archives help establish a great deal of background on what was before a mere name and address.

CHAPTER 7

Ordnance Survey and other modern maps

1801–present

Ordnance Survey maps are an absolute lynch-pin for home histories. Whatever your home is, and wherever it is, few records will be as singularly useful to you as these maps. Besides finding out all the great things they can tell you, however, it's also important to appreciate the small pitfalls they can sometimes contain for the unwary.

Maps – Ordnance Survey and others – serve three main purposes for home historians:

- They identify your home in the context of its wider area, showing how its location relates to other buildings, roads, railways and geographical features.
- They show what your own home looked like at the time the map was made, albeit often in a simplified form.
- A series of maps made at different points in the past illustrates how the area, and maybe even your home itself, developed through time.

Maps are one of the sources you will encounter in your research. They give us the almost godlike ability to look down from the clouds at our home, from different times in the past, and see what it was like.

Before I extol any more of their virtues, however, you need to bear in mind that:

- While maps may show a building standing where your home is now, that doesn't necessarily mean that it is actually the same building. Your home might have been rebuilt on the site of an older one: an old map will not tell you this.
- Before the Montgolfier brothers' first successful balloon flight in 1783, nobody had ever got up high enough to know what the country really looked like from above. Only in the last few decades have satellites been able to beam down truly accurate, flat pictures. Most maps, therefore, are inherently flawed by being, to some degree or another, made up. They are attempts to represent on paper what people think the country looked like, rather than what is actually there.

The accuracy of maps

Mapmakers can generalise. A map may represent every street in a town, but not every house. It may be more detailed, and show every house in the street, but not show the houses accurately. The map may give a highly accurate outline of each house, but the mapmaker will still leave out the flowerbeds in the garden, or the dormer windows in the roof. At some point, the mapmaker you're relying on to give you information about your home decided there were things he was *not* going to show.

Even the highly accurate Ordnance Survey maps were subject, albeit to a lesser degree, to the same failings as the maps of earlier eras. Especially on the original one-inch to the mile Ordnance Survey maps, roads were necessarily drawn much wider than they really were, while the need to squeeze so much information onto small sheets of paper led to generalising: a small L-shaped building, for example, might be shown as square. Maps produced before the Ordnance Survey came on the scene were subject to even greater inaccuracies and – very significantly – omissions.

So, when approaching a map, it's always sensible to consider why it was made. Many were produced by book- and print-sellers for purely commercial purposes, and in some cases the main aim was simply to be decorative. Others were produced with a single purpose in mind. On a road map, for example, you can expect the roads to be shown larger than they really were, yet probably quite accurately. But other features, such as woods, fields and – yes – buildings, were of only secondary importance to the surveyor. They are likely to be shown with less accuracy or, if they got in the way of showing the roads clearly, not shown at all. So, when studying maps, always remember – if the building's not shown, that doesn't mean it wasn't actually there.

Dates of maps

Time is another factor to bear in mind. Maps are a fantastic way of observing how areas changed over the years. Yet, sadly, when it comes to dates, most maps are works of fiction. It is unlikely, even with a modern Ordnance Survey map, that you could walk through any of the landscapes depicted on paper and recognise the two as being exactly the same – a tree will have been cut down here, a new building erected there. And there's always a time lag between an area being surveyed and the map being printed. Maps generally bear the date of the latter, not the former. So a map claiming to show the area around your home in 1875 is probably actually truer of the situation in 1874, or 1873, or perhaps even 1860, depending on how long it took to produce the map.

In an effort to overcome this problem, mapmakers often anticipated things that never actually happened. If a road was due to be built, the mapmaker might decide to include it, causing problems for later researchers if it was never actually built. Many maps were produced specifically to show proposed developments, such as slum clearances and railway lines, which never took place: they are indeed works of fiction.

These aren't terrible problems. As long as you bear these points in mind, you won't be misled into saying, 'The 1875 maps shows this building existing, so it must have been there', despite the cartographic evidence contradicting other sources that suggested, say, that a building had been demolished three years earlier. It probably had been, for the map may have been surveyed over three years before the publication date. And if a map shows a railway line ploughing through your back garden, but there's no physical evidence it ever did, then you can add it to your home's history as a development that was planned but never happened.

Cataloguing of maps

Because maps can be large and unwieldy, they are often treated differently to books and documents. Libraries and archives might catalogue maps separately from other collections. Often, the map catalogues – sometimes referred to as 'deposited plans' – will not be particularly detailed, either.

The Ordnance Survey

One of the finest graphic sources for the history of your home – and one in which your home is certain to feature – are Ordnance Survey maps. You will find collections of local Ordnance Survey maps, both current and dating back over the last 200 years, at your local archives, and some can also be inspected online (see page 62).

In 1744–5, Prince Charles Edward Stuart landed in Scotland and marched south into England. Although he only reached Derby before he was defeated, there is a fairly plausible 'What if?' scenario suggesting that he could

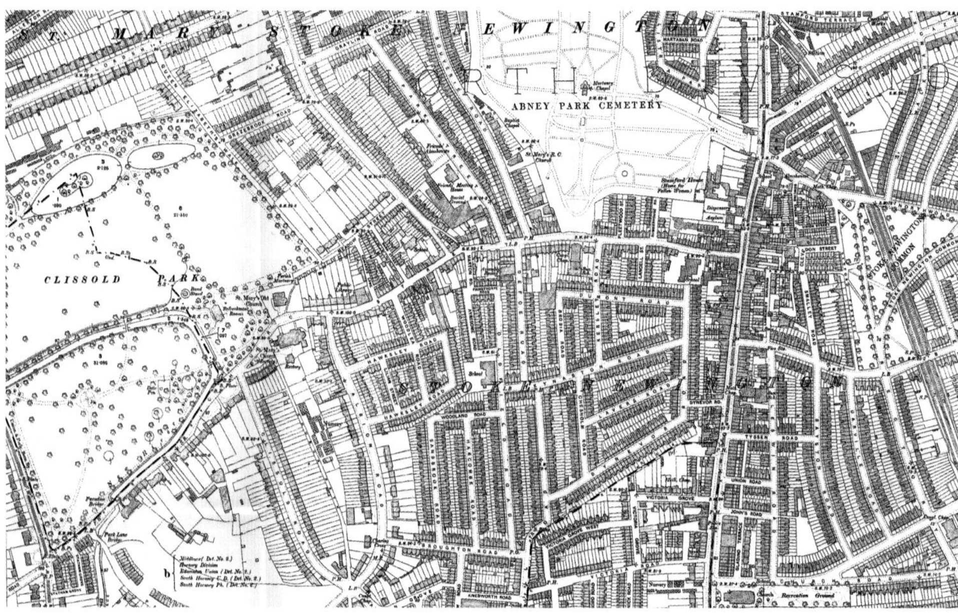

Looking at change over time – these maps of Stoke Newington of 1868 (top) and 1894 show the urbanisation of the area, including the advent of the railway which you can see on the right-hand end of the 1894 map.

quite easily have taken London and displaced George II. Trying to prevent an armed enemy rampaging through the country highlighted the government's need for accurate maps showing the precise routes of roads and rivers and the lie of the land, not least for selecting suitable battle sites – maps, moreover, that covered the whole country and did not abruptly terminate, as so many contemporary ones did, at county borders.

George II's government reacted by commissioning the Board of Ordnance to start surveying the realm. Between 1747 and 1755, William Roy of the Royal Engineers – it was to officers of the Royal Engineers and Royal Artillery that most surveying work was entrusted – organised a survey of Scotland. The results, the first reasonably accurate topographic survey of Scotland, are in the British Library. It was not until 1791 – and due in no small part to renewed fears of invasion, this time from Revolutionary France – that formal work started to create accurate topographical maps of England and Wales. Originally called the Trigonometrical Survey, the project soon adopted the name by which it is now best known – the Ordnance Survey. In 1841, after 50 years of mapmaking, the Ordnance Survey became a separate institution in its own right.

The Valuation Office used to use OS maps for their record sheets. This one dates from 1910 and covers the St Albans District, Hertfordshire.

One-inch maps

The country was initially surveyed to create maps showing each square mile of land on one square inch of paper – one inch to a mile.

The first Ordnance Survey map, covering Kent, was produced in 1801 (a re-surveyed version was issued in 1819), followed by Essex in 1805. By 1824, most of the country had been surveyed: the original papers are in the British Library's map section. Most resulting maps were published by 1844, though it took until 1874 to publish the map for the Isle of Man. Many of the original maps have been printed in book form by Harry Margary (see page 63).

The original maps were subsequently updated with those containing rapidly growing urban areas being re-surveyed much more frequently than rural ones. Railways were engraved onto the printing plates of existing maps as the rail network spread.

A series of reproductions of old Ordnance Survey maps has been produced by David & Charles (see page 62). Although termed 'first editions', these are, in fact, maps from various dates, to which railways had been added. They therefore give a generally true picture, but there must be many instances of buildings that had been extended or demolished before the railways they are shown to be standing near had been built. Equally, many homes were built before the arrival of the railways but are not shown on yet older maps to which railway lines have been added. This does not render the maps useless – far from it – it's just that they may be unreliable evidence for precise dating.

Indeed, fantastic as all the old one-inch maps were at the time, the drawback now is that they were undated. Clues to when they may have appeared come from small details:

- Adjacent sheet numbering started in 1837.
- The phrase 'printed from an electrotype' was used from 1847.
- Latitude and longitude were included from 1856.
- An 'electrotype' date was included from 1862.
- Maps showing the date of railway insertions cannot date from before 1882.

Even when dates of publication did appear (mainly from 1891, but not between 1935 and 1945), you need to bear in mind that they may be based on surveys made several years earlier.

25-inch maps in the Ordnance Survey's library

Buckinghamshire:	Ballaugh, 1870	Patrick, 1869
Fawley, 1876	Bradden, 1869	Rushden, 1869
	Bride, 1870	Stanton, 1868
Co. Durham:	German,1869	
Aycliffe, 1864	Jurby, 1870	**Isle of Wight**:
	Lezayre, 1870	Brading, 1875
Hampshire:	Lonan, 1869	Chale, 1862
Freshwater, 1862	Malew, 1869	Gatcombe, 1864
	Marown, 1869	Godshill, 1863
Isle of Man:	Maughold, 1870	
Andreas, 1870	Michael, 1870	**Oxfordshire**:
Arbory, 1869	Onchan, 1869	Bix, 1878

Six- and 25-inch maps

In 1824, surveying work started to produce a much more detailed series of maps, depicting the British Isles at the greater scale of six inches of paper to every actual mile. Ireland was surveyed first, and by 1846 its emerald hills, complete with its peppering of homes, had been fully mapped on 1,875 sheets. Similar work started in England and Wales in 1841. Pretty soon, however, it was realised that this scale was not as detailed as was really required. Starting with Durham in 1854, therefore, a vastly increased scale of 25 inches to the mile (1:2500 in metric) was adopted. The six-inch survey, however, was retained for the more desolate regions of Scotland, where the larger scale would have been of little use – and probably would have driven its bored surveyors to desperation. The new 25-inch survey was completed by 1888. A first revision resulted in a second series, produced between 1891 and 1914, followed by a second revision for a third series from 1904 to 1939.

|| A table of the resulting different series of six-inch and 25-inch maps is given in Hindle's book on pages 126–7 (see page 63).

|| A more detailed account is in the Ordnance Survey's own catalogue of maps, covering the period 1862 to 1924 (see page 62).

|| Alan Godfrey (Alan Godfrey Maps, Prospect Business Park, Leadgate, Consett, Durham DH8 7PW; tel: 01207 583388; **www.alangodfreymaps.co.uk**) has reproduced many original series 25-inch and one-inch maps. Most also have historical essays and reproductions of sections from directories printed on the back, making them extremely handy little documents. However, beware: the directory sections printed on the back of the maps are not always from the same year as the map itself, and this is not always stated. The 1868 map of Stoke Newington,

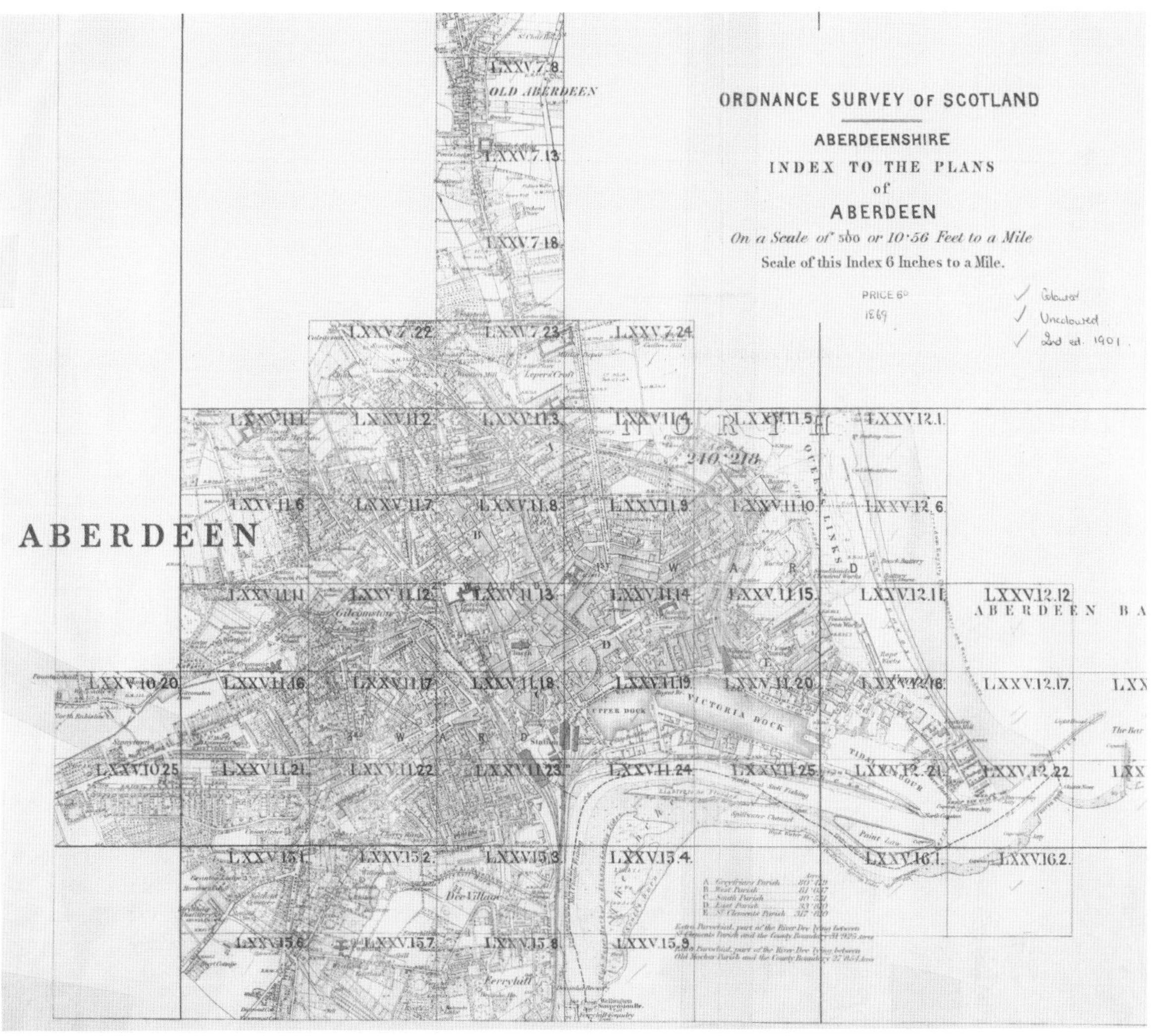

Index to the Ordnance Survey maps of Aberdeen of 1866/7.

for example, carries pages from 'Ellis's Directory': in fact, the directory concerned was not published until 1876.

In 1928, a rolling system of revisions of Ordnance Survey maps was commenced, resulting in ongoing updates.

While the one-inch maps show many houses, especially in rural areas, the detail is obviously very poor, and for urban areas it is impossible. The 25-inch maps are much better, showing the rough shapes of buildings, with roads to actual scale, the presence of trees, and much other fascinating detail. Although printed in black and white, the original editions could be hand coloured: where they were, brick and stone buildings were coloured red and wood and iron ones were grey.

Some of the 25-inch maps were accompanied by reference books. Those produced between 1855 and 1872 were called *Parish Area Books*; those produced from 1873 to 1886 were termed *Books of Reference*. These outlined the size and use of each unit of land. They exist mainly for parishes in Cheshire, Cumberland, Essex, Gloucestershire, the Isle of Man,

Where to find Ordnance Survey maps

Archives and libraries Most have collections of local Ordnance Survey maps, of varying scales and ages. It is also worth enquiring at local university libraries. There are excellent national collections at the Royal Geographic Society, 1 Kensington Gore, London SW7 2AR; tel: 020 7591 3000; **www.rgs.org**; Oxford and Cambridge Universities (see **www.ox.ac.uk** and **www.cam.ac.uk**); the National Archives and the map library of the British Museum, **www.thebritishmuseum.co.uk**.

www.collectbritain.co.uk/collections/osd The British Library's 'Collect Britain' site includes this selection of 410 Ordnance Survey drawings from the late 18th to the early 19th centuries, made in preparation for the original one-inch maps. The site includes many older maps too. Sadly, the resolution is not desperately good.

www.multimap.com A useful map resource, the maps do not show individual houses, but the site offers excellent aerial photographic views. These, too, tend to show individual homes as a blur, but they are splendid for getting a feel for the layout of the area.

www.nationalarchives.ie/cgi-bin/naigenform02?index=OS+Parish+List The National Archives of Ireland's Ordnance Survey parish index.

www.nls.uk/digitallibrary/map Scottish Ordnance Survey town plans 1847–95.

www.nls.uk/digitallibrary/map/townplans Large-scale Ordnance Survey maps for 63 Scottish towns.

www.old-maps.co.uk This includes an almost complete set of the First Series six-inch to the mile Ordnance Survey maps of England, Wales and Scotland (not Ireland). The site enables you to search by place name or National Grid grid reference. Once you have found your home, you can compare it with a modern Ordnance Survey map. You can also purchase copies of maps online.

The Ordnance Survey Romsey Road, Southampton, Hampshire SO16 4GU; tel: 08456 050505; customerservice@ordnancesurvey.co.uk; **www.ordnancesurvey.co.uk**. The library is in Room C454 and it is now possible to see many Ordnance Survey maps, modern and historical, online.

www.ordnancesurvey.co.uk/oswebsite/freefun/didyouknow This section of the Ordnance Survey's site contains a gazetteer of some 250,000 place names – from towns and villages to individual farms. The search results state the county or unitary authority, grid reference, latitude and longitude, and have a link to the Ordnance Survey's Get-a-Map facility, showing a 2km square area around the chosen place from the relevant 1:25000 map.

www.sites.scran.ac.uk/townplans/index/html Part of the National Library of Scotland's collection of old Ordnance Survey maps.

www.streetmap.co.uk A useful map resource, though not detailed enough to show houses.

See also the list of websites on pages 138–9 which mainly include older maps.

Many old OS maps are reproduced by David & Charles Ltd, Brunel House, Forde Close, Newton Abbott, Devon TQ12 4PU; tel: 01626 323200; fax 01626 323319; postmaster@davidandcharles.co.uk; email: **www.davidandcharles.co.uk**.

Kent, Middlesex, Northumberland, Surrey, Westmoreland, Flint, Glamorgan, Monmouth and Pembroke.

|| The books were published (variously by Eyre & Spottiswoode for HMSO and the Ordnance Survey Office itself) and described in detail in Harley's *The Ordnance Survey and Land-Use Mapping*, and are best sought through local archives.

Ordnance Survey town maps

For urban areas, maps more detailed than 25 inches to the mile were needed. These were surveyed to two scales, five feet to the mile from 1843, and ten feet to the mile from 1850. The latter was altered slightly to 1:500 from 1855 (10ft 7in to the mile), thus bringing the maps in line with metric standards. These maps were so detailed that they showed buildings in perfect outline, down to bay windows jutting out onto pavements. Public buildings such as churches were even shown with interior ground plans. By 1891, the Ordnance Survey could report with justifiable pride that they had surveyed the English and Welsh towns 'sufficiently large to show detail down to the size of a doorstep' and subsequent revisions have kept these wonderful resources up to date.

Boundary records

|| The National Archives holds a series of records relating to changes in public boundaries, in its Ordnance Survey series. These will be useful only if your home is situated on a boundary (or a former one). If it is (or was), then you may find useful information in OS 26 (record books); OS 31 and 33 (mainly property on parish boundaries); OS 23 (parish name books); OS 32 (boundary disputes); OS 27 (sketch maps); OS 29 (journals of inspection); OS 38 and 39 (deposited newly issued six-inch Ordnance Survey maps for England and Wales, and Scotland, respectively, showing the agreed boundary changes).

|| The maps produced in 1885 by the Boundary Commission, covering the whole British Isles including Ireland, but with only partial coverage of Wales and Scotland, are online at **www.londonancestor.com**.

Google Earth

http://earth.google.com/index.html

This extraordinary freely downloadable program enables you to zoom in on any part of the planet you wish. The quality of close-up you get seems to depend on the area you choose, but for some towns and cities you can see individual homes in considerable detail. You may therefore be able to see your home, or any other building you want to study, from above and can certainly get a good idea of its surroundings.

BOOKS AND MAPS

- **P. Christian, 'Finding Places' (*Ancestors*, August 2004, pp 38–9)**
- **J. B. Harley, *The Ordnance Survey and Land-Use Mapping* (Historical Geography Research Series, no. 2, 1979)**
- **P. Hindle, *Maps for Historians* (Phillimore, 2002)**
- **H. Margary, Ordnance Survey Old Series One-Inch (1975–87, Lympne Castle, Kent)**
  1. **Kent, East Sussex, Essex and Suffolk**
  2. **Devon, Cornwall and West Somerset**
  3. **South Central England**
  4. **Central Wales**
  5. **Lincolnshire, Rutland and East Anglia**
  6. **Wales**
  7. **North Central England**
  8. **North England and Isle of Man**
- **R. Oliver, *Ordnance Survey Maps: A Concise Guide for Historians* (Charles Close Society, 1993)**

CHAPTER 8

Directories and newspapers

Directories: 1677–1960s, but mainly mid-late 19th and early 20th centuries
Newspapers: from 1665, but mainly 1855 onwards

When you visit your local archives, you will see their collection of directories. Directories are published lists of people's addresses and occupations. They fulfilled broadly the same role in the past as domestic and commercial telephone directories do today. They are essential tools for historians of homes, both in their own right and as a means of finding your way around other records, such as census returns (see pages 46–55). Increasingly, directories are also appearing online.

Early directories date from the late 17th and 18th centuries, but they tend to be very sparse on addresses, usually just listing people's names and their streets where they lived. The assumption was that once you or the deliverer of your letter found the right street, there would be no trouble asking for the correct house. They are useful for looking up people you already know existed, but not much else.

In the 19th century and right up to the decades just after the Second World War, however, detailed directories were produced for the whole country. Some covered counties, listing each town and village; others focused on specific towns and cities, or (as in London) cities and their suburbs. As they were created by competing firms, there could be anything between no and several directories produced for a given place each year.

Exploring directories

Directories provide useful, contemporary and evocative descriptions of parishes, towns and cities, together with practical details of population and geography; soil types; roads, railways

Where to search

- Directories for your local area can best be sought in your local archives, study library and county record offices.
- Shaw and Tipper's book (see page 69) may alert you to directories for useful years you have not already found in archives, and there are also large national collections at the Society of Genealogists and Guildhall Library, Aldermanbury, London EC2P 2EJ; tel: 020 7332 1868; **www.cityoflondon.gov.uk**.
- You can buy originals at local antiquarian booksellers and car boot sales.
- Many are also now available on CD-Rom (see page 265), and use word searches for quick access to relevant information.
- A new and rapidly growing website from Leicester University containing much material from directories between 1750 and 1920, including maps, is at **www.historicaldirectories.org**.

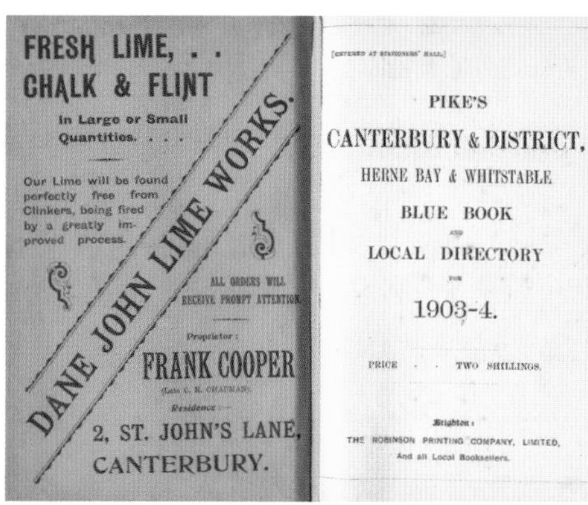
FRESH LIME, . .
CHALK & FLINT
In Large or Small Quantities. . . .

Our Lime will be found perfectly free from Clinkers, being fired by a greatly improved process.

DANE JOHN LIME WORKS.

ALL ORDERS WILL RECEIVE PROMPT ATTENTION.

Proprietor:
FRANK COOPER
Residence:
2, ST. JOHN'S LANE,
CANTERBURY.

PIKE'S
CANTERBURY & DISTRICT,
HERNE BAY & WHITSTABLE
BLUE BOOK
AND
LOCAL DIRECTORY
FOR
1903-4.

PRICE . . TWO SHILLINGS.

Brighton:
THE ROBINSON PRINTING COMPANY, LIMITED,
And all Local Booksellers.

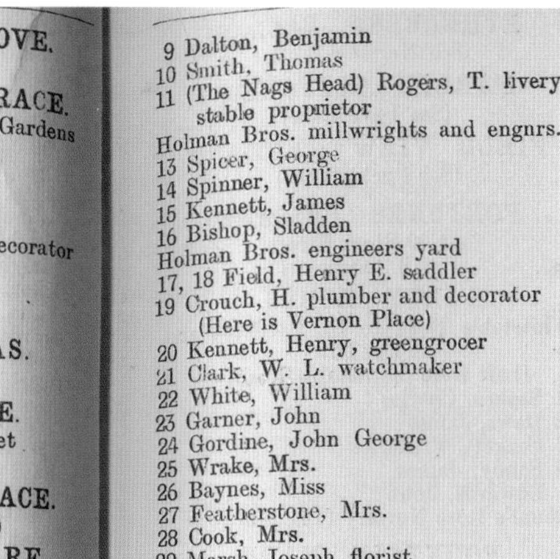
9 Dalton, Benjamin
10 Smith, Thomas
11 (The Nags Head) Rogers, T. livery stable proprietor
Holman Bros. millwrights and engnrs.
13 Spicer, George
14 Spinner, William
15 Kennett, James
16 Bishop, Sladden
Holman Bros. engineers yard
17, 18 Field, Henry E. saddler
19 Crouch, H. plumber and decorator
(Here is Vernon Place)
20 Kennett, Henry, greengrocer
21 Clark, W. L. watchmaker
22 White, William
23 Garner, John
24 Gordine, John George
25 Wrake, Mrs.
26 Baynes, Miss
27 Featherstone, Mrs.
28 Cook, Mrs.
29 Marsh, Joseph, florist

Some homes' histories are hard to research; others are astonishingly simple. In Dover Street, Kent, two homes still retain old adverts for the shops they once were. Pike's *Canterbury & District, Herne Bay & Whitstable Blue Book & Local Directory* for 1903–4, shows Henry E. Field, saddler, at 17 and 18 Dover Street, followed by Henry Kennett, greengrocer, at number 20. A later directory for 1914 shows that Kennett had been replaced by W. L. Clark, watchmaker, who had moved over the road to number 49, where he and his son ran a dairy. Presumably he had opened the dairy at number 20 sometime after 1903 and just before the First World War. Number 20 (pictured left) then had a varied history: until very recently it was a launderette, and has now become a private home, with its old Kennett signboard lovingly restored.

and canals; the main forms of agriculture and industry; schools; charities; hospitals; almshouses and antiquarian information on local history. They also identify parishes within their counties; poor law unions (and thus general registration districts); hundreds (units of land comprising several parishes); and, to a limited extent, manors (see page 179).

Directories generally listed people whom literate or reasonably well-off people would want to find – tradesmen; craftsmen; merchants; professionals; farmers; clergy; gentry and nobility. The poor generally were not listed, though the closer you come to the future, the more inclusive directories tend to become. As the 19th century progressed, directories –

Maps in directories

Directories can also contain local maps, though many were subsequently torn out for separate use. Although directories could be updated every year, maps often were not, so an 1840 directory may contain a map that's actually accurate for 1830. Some, such as Pigot's 1824 directory for Manchester, anticipate changes (in this case, improvements to Market Street and Cannon Street) that never actually transpired. But these are small caveats set against their immense overall usefulness.

especially for towns and cities – started giving ever more precise addresses for both commercial and private residents. They often divided their lists into several sections:

- 'Court' listed private residents alphabetically.
- 'Commercial' gave an alphabetical list of those in trade or business (the two lists were not mutually exclusive).
- 'Trade' broke the 'Commercial' list down into the different trades and professions.

In all cases, you can look up the occupiers and owners of your home. Most usefully for home historians, however, are the 'Street' sections found in directories for larger conurbations. These listed each street alphabetically and, within that, gave the occupiers and street numbers of each house. Again, these lists tended to leave out the poor, but they can still be extremely useful, sometimes being so detailed as to indicate where other roads ran into the street in question.

Due to the delay between collating information and publication, directories can show information that was a year or more out of date. Taking that into account, however, you can use directories to follow your home through year by year, noting any alterations in occupants. They can also be useful in indicating whether your home was used for commercial purposes.

Another potential use of directories is that they can give exact street numbers where census returns do not. They are very effective when used in conjunction with census returns (see pages 46–55).

Newspapers and where to search

Newspapers are a rich source of information on homes. Sales of property and goods were reported and advertised extensively in local newspapers. You may even find references to prominent sales in national papers.

Newspapers may also provide you with

Where to search

- National papers and an extensive collection of local newspapers from all over the country (and some from abroad) are held at the British Library Newspaper Library, Colindale Avenue, Colindale, London NW9 5HE; tel: 020 7412 7353; **www.bl.uk/collections/newspapers.html**.
- *The Times* Digital Archive – including all the adverts – can be searched by word from 1785 onwards. It is a marvellous resource for seeking details on larger and sometimes not-so-large homes, and the people who owned or occupied them. The index can be searched in many large libraries and archives. **www.galeuk.com/times**.
- You will find local newspapers in archives and libraries. Some local archives, such as the Suffolk Record Office at Ipswich, are compiling indexes to their newspaper collections, but most are not. If you do not have a specific date or event in mind, they are quite a lucky dip – though seldom an entirely unrewarding place to search.
- You can also see whether the offices of your local newspaper has its own archive, which may, in turn, include some form of indexing.

much additional information about your home: advertisements for rented rooms; incidents that took place there, including deaths (see page 125); and so on.

Most local newspapers date from the mid-19th century, especially after stamp duty on newspapers was abolished in 1855. Some go back further – the oldest is the *Norwich Post*, founded in 1701. National newspapers started in 1665 with the *Oxford Gazette*, later to become the *London Gazette*. The first national daily was the *Daily Courant*, started in 1702. It's no longer being published, but *The Times*, founded in 1785, is.

Cambridgeshire. CAMBRIDGE, &c. Pigot & Co.'s

BAKERS &c.—*Continued*
Crawley William, Trumpington st
Crisp William, Green st
Dearle John, St. Mary st
*Diver John, Sun st. Barnwell st
Dockrell John, Wellington row, Barnwell
Driver Henry, Coronation st
Elborne Sarah, jun. Trumpington st
Emmerson Mary, Warwick st
Fortin John, Castle st
*Garner John, George st. Barnwell
Goode Sarah, 9 Crescent
Greenwood Thomas, Butcher row
Harris Mary, Bridge st
*Hovell James, George st. Barnwell
Hunt John, Northampton st
Johnson Ann, St. Andrew's hill
Knightly Wm. Trumpington st
Lawrence Thomas, Magdalen st
Lewis William, Market st
Livermore Thomas, Trumpington st
Livermore William, Union st
Lusher Wm. King st [Barnwell
Marfleet Frances, Staffordshire place,
Moyse John, King st
Muggleton Jas. George Fourth st
Mustill William, Sidney st
Parker Thos. St. Sepulchre passage
Parsley John, King st
Rayment Elizabeth, Butcher row
*Roberts Michl. East road, Barnwell
Rolfe Thos. (biscuit only) St. John st
Rushbrook Jeremiah, Bridge st
Rutherford Walter, Union road
Squires William, Green st
*Stearn Joseph, King st
Stratton Wm. Willow place, Barnwel
Swann Thomas, King st
Thompson William, Blucher row, Barnwell
Tuffil and Purchas, Chesterton
Tunwell John, Trumpington st
Vaughan William, jun. St. Peter st
*Wallis Richard, Castle st
Walters Hen. Market st [Barnwell
Ward James, Adam and Eve row,
Ward Richard, Abbey st. Barnwell
Watson John, Castle st
Wilderspin Thomas, Green st
Young Andrew, Occupation road, Barnwell

BANKERS.
Barker Field D. Trinity st,—(draws on Sir Wm. Lubbock & Co. London)
Fisher Thos. & Sons, Petty cury—(draw on Curries, Raikes & Co.)
Foster Ebenezer and Chas. Finch, Trinity st—(draw on Grote, Prescott & Co. London)
Humfrey Chas. Trinity st—(draws on Grote, Prescott & Co. London)
Mortlock John & Sons, Ben'et st—(draw on Smith, Payne & Smiths)
SAVINGS' BANK, Green st. (open on Saturdays) Mr. Js. Brown, actuary

BASKET MAKERS.
Campion Robert, Magdalen st
Freeman Wm. Blucher row, Barnwel
Graves William, Butcher row
Wheeler Saml. & Geo. K. Wheeler st

BIRD STUFFERS.
Brett Wm. (& modeller) Jesus place
Denny Thos. (& practical ornithologist & entomologist) 4 Sidney pl

BLACKSMITHS.
Brunton John, Emanuel st
Fromont Samuel, Sun st. Barnwell
Fromont Saml. East road, Barnwell
Frost Robert, Cook's yard
Howard Henry (& drill maker) Abbey street, Barnwell
Langton John, Bridge st
Mallerson John, Union road
Meeks William, Chesterton

Muncy David, Newnham
Paxman Thos. George st. Barnwell
Pryke Benjamin, Hyde park corner
Whitehead Edward, Chesterton
Wonfor William, Castle st

BOAT BUILDERS.
Cross John, Chesterton
King Charles (from London) Brunswick walk, Barnwell

BOOKBINDERS.
(*See also Booksellers & Stationers.*)
Allen Charles, Green st
Bowtell John, All Saints' passage
Lawrance William Henry, St. Edward's passage
Nichols William, Blackbear yard
Wiseman Henry Richard, Trinity st
Wootton William, Pembroke st

BOOKSELLERS & STATIONRS.
Marked thus * are also Circulating Libraries.
Barraclough George, Trinity st
Barrett Mary Ann & Son, Trinity st
Deighton J. & J. J. (& publishers & agents to the University) Trinity st
*Gee & Bridges (& bindrs) Market hill
Grant Wm. Peter, Trinity st [ton st
*Hall Jno. (& publisher) Trumping-
Hankin Jas. (& binder) Petty cury
*Hatt John (and binder) Peas hill
Hutt Richd. (& binder) 18 Crescent
Johnson Elijah (and publisher) Sidney st [Trinity st
Newby Richard (and publisher)
Page Martha (& binder) Market st
Sandifer Mary, Free School lane
Smith Wm. Haddon, 7 Crescent
*Stevenson Ths. (& binder) Trinity st
Wallis Henry, Sidney st [Barnwell
Waters Elijah, Adam and Eve row,
Wright Edward, Market st

BOOT AND SHOE MAKERS.
Atkins Thomas, Chesterton
Benstead John, Trumpington st
Bentley John, Trinity st
Bond John, Market hill
Brett Francis, Magdalen st
Butterfield William, St. Mary st
Butteriss Joseph, Sidney st
Currie William, Sussex st
Feaks John Shallow, Trinity st
Gray Ward, Sussex st
Harvey John, Bridge st
Hayles John (wholesale and retail) Warwick st
Ison John, St. Andrew st
Kirkup Robert, St. Andrew st
Langley Charles, New st. Barnwell
Lutt Edward (gent.'s slipper dealer only) Trumpington st
Peters Robert, Magdalen st
Phillips James, Bridge st
Phillips John, Bridge st
Pratt James, Jesus lane [st
Pratts Mary (shoe dealer only) Green
Shedd James B. Pembroke st
Swan Simpson, Trumpington st
Thrift John, Chesterton
Uffindell Jno. Peas hill [Barnwell
Waters Elijah, Adam and Eve row,
White James Day, Peas hill
White John, Maid's causeway
White William & Son, Warwick st

BRAWN MAKERS & DEALERS.
Marked thus * are dealers only.
Hopkins and Broadbelt, Slaughter-house lane
*Marshall Henry & Son, Peas hill
*Rutledge John, Trumpington st

BRAZIERS AND TIN-PLATE WORKERS.
Armstrong John, Market hill
M'Intosh William, Market st
Miller George, Union st
Press Robert, Sussex st
Pryor Stephen, Petty cury

Smith Richard Jas. Trumpington st
Spalding James, 3 Crescent

BREECHES MAKERS.
(*See also Tailors.*)
Brown Thomas, Sun st. Barnwell
Davies John, St. John st
Ransom George, Trinity st
Stuart Joseph, Trinity st

BREWERS & MALTSTERS.
(*See also Maltsters, Inns & Taverns*)
Berry & Beales, (brewers) Magdalen street
Bullen Mark, Chesterton road
Casburn William, Quay side
Foster Richd. & Son, Thompson's la
Gotobed Jas. & Son, Trumpington st
Hopkins and Broadbelt, Slaughter-house lane [Chesterton
Meadows Edwd. (victualler) Sluice,
Nash Thos. & Co. St. Andrew st
Nutter Jas. & Ths. St. Andrew's hill
Steward, Cotton & Co. Trumpingtn st
Twiss James, East road

BREWERS—RETAIL.
Green Robert, King st
Ind Sarah, Warwick st
Jackson Henry, Gold st, Barnwell
King Thomas, Castle st
Mason Henry, East road, Barnwell
Riddel Thomas, Magdalen st
Theobalds Wm. Burleigh st, Barnwl
Wagg Robert, Eden walk, Barnwell
White Thomas, Green st

BRICKLAYRS & PLASTERERS
(*See also Builders.*)
Bradwell David, New square
Burbage George, St. Andrew st
Hall Pell, Pound lane
Harris John, Sussex st
Turner John, Maid's causeway
Turner William, Thompson's lane

BRICK MAKERS.
Asby Wm. & Chas. Trumpington st
Clabbon Sarah, Trumpington st
Mason Henry, East road, Barnwell
Thurston Thomas, Paradise cottage, Barnwell

BRUSH MANUFACTURERS.
Cooke Simon, Sun st, Barnwell
Driver William, Princess st

BUILDERS.
Marked thus * are also Bricklayers, &c. and thus † are also Joiners & Carpenters.
*Asby Wm. & Chas. Trumpington st
†Barber Richard, New square
†Bell William, Castle st
*Bradwell David, sen. St. Andrew st
†Crowe Wm. Gonville lodge, Hill's r
*Culledge Richard, Northampton st
†Frohock Thos. St. Andrew's hill
*Fromant John, King st
Hillman James, Downing st
†Hoppett Thomas, Union road
*Howell Jas. Downing terr [well
†Papworth Wm. Brunswck pl, Barn-
†Peck William, Coronation st
†Quinsee William, Hobson st
†Rickard James, St. Andrew st
†Taylor James, Tennis court lane
†Webster James, Trumpington st
†Whittaker Richd. Tennis court la
†Woods Richard, Union road

BUTCHERS.
Brown Wm. Magdalen st [well
Carpenter Geo. Occupation rd, Brn-
Chiddenton George, Chesterton
Crabb John, Bene't st
Cross George, Sidney st
Dennis Wm. East road, Barnwell
Gifford Edward, Coronation st
Gunton John, Eden walk, Barnwell
Haslop John, Chesterton
Haslop Peter, Bene't st
Hill Ann, Trumpington st
Hill Thomas, Trumpington st

104

Pigot's Commercial Directory of Cambridgeshire, 1830.

RIGHT

One side of this newspaper page from 1926 shows Barley Down House, Ovington, Hampshire, being sold with 'about 203 acres', along with other parts of the Ovington Park Estate (here spelled 'Avington'), and two further houses, 'Harefield' and 'Woodlands' in Itchen Abbas. The reverse shows advertisements for less exalted houses, though sadly their precise addresses are generally not given – though for the house in Sussex there is a giveaway clue – 'write [to the] owner, Stricklands, Robertsbridge'.

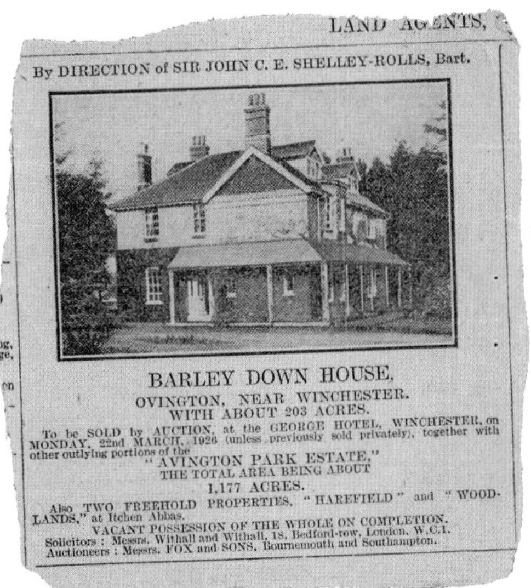
LAND AGENTS.

By DIRECTION of SIR JOHN C. E. SHELLEY-ROLLS, Bart.

BARLEY DOWN HOUSE,
OVINGTON, NEAR WINCHESTER.
WITH ABOUT 203 ACRES.

To be SOLD by AUCTION, at the GEORGE HOTEL, WINCHESTER, on MONDAY, 22nd MARCH, 1926 (unless previously sold privately), together with other outlying portions of the

"AVINGTON PARK ESTATE,"
THE TOTAL AREA BEING ABOUT
1,177 ACRES.

Also TWO FREEHOLD PROPERTIES, "HAREFIELD" and "WOODLANDS," at Itchen Abbas.

VACANT POSSESSION OF THE WHOLE ON COMPLETION.

Solicitors: Messrs. Withall and Withall, 18, Bedford-row, London, W.C.1.
Auctioneers: Messrs. FOX and SONS, Bournemouth and Southampton.

BELOW RIGHT

Newspapers are full of advertisements relating to property. This one, from 1965, concerns Little Park House, Brimpton, and confirms that it had been converted into nine flats by that year. The current owner, David Courtier-Dutton, tells me that the house, built in 1869, was once occupied by Lady Delia Spencer, a great-aunt of the late Princess of Wales, and, during the Second World War, by the exiled King of Norway. Thanks to this newspaper advert, the house was bought from its then owner, Miss Betty Paget-Clark, by one Mike Bissel, who ran it as a nursing home. It is now a private residence again.

X.1,725, The Times,

FOR SALE. BY ORDER OF EXECUTORS.
TUNBRIDGE WELLS.—Attractive detached FREEHOLD RESIDENCE, occupying a delightful situation near to the Common; four reception rooms, six bed rooms, two bath rooms, kitchen, and good offices; conservatory; passenger lift; electric light; pretty garden.—Apply to Messrs. VENTOM, COOPER and Co., Surveyors, 35, Old Jewry, London, E.C.2.

VENTNOR.—Well-built LABOUR-SAVING BUNGALOW, brick and tile, with garage; gas, electric; glorious sea views, pretty terrace gardens; about ¼-acre. Only £1,250 FREEHOLD.—WELCH, Wroxall, I.W.

WATFORD. BUSHEY. NORTHWOOD. PINNER. | STIMPSON, LOCK, AND VINCE are agents for most of the available properties. State requirements.—Offices adjoining Railway Stations.

OVERLOOKING NOTED GOLF LINKS.
WOODBRIDGE, SUFFOLK (one mile station).—Attractive COUNTRY RESIDENCE; lounge hall, two reception, six bed, two bath; excellent water, gas; double garage; grounds two acres. For Sale, with possession.—COBBE and WINCER, Arcade-street, Ipswich, and at Chelmsford.

XVIIth CENTURY PAIR of COTTAGES in favourite Thames-side village, HENLEY, MAIDENHEAD district, overlooking a well-known golf course, for SALE. VACANT POSSESSION, £1,000. FREEHOLD. Contains four living and four bed rooms. Requires some adaptation.—Apply C. W. BRIGHTEN, F.S.I., 3, High-street, Maidenhead.

10 MILES COLCHESTER.—An ideal RESIDENCE in red brick, bungalow style, with cottage and sunken drive; draughtsman-built 1908 for own occupation; S. aspect; two-three reception, four beds, bath, lavatory, &c.; garage; main water; heating and drainage systems; secluded, convenient P.O., &c.; ¼-mile station; exceptional gardens, shrubberies, orchard, lawn, &c., paddock of two acres and poultry appliances, in all 3¾ acres. A very charming property, in excellent order. POSSESSION. FREEHOLD £1,800, with less land, £1,250.—Particulars and photo, TYLER and OWERS, Estate Agents, Halstead, Essex.

£2,175.—SUSSEX, lovely South views; three reception, six bed, bath, box rooms, conservatory, walled garden; gas, main drains; near station.—Write Owner, Stricklands, Robertsbridge.

£1,250.—SOUTH HANTS, between SOUTHAMPTON and WINCHESTER.—Detached FREEHOLD RESIDENCE; two reception, four bed rooms amongst the pines, on high ground. Grounds about ONE ACRE

HOUSE AGENTS.
E. BARTON, Ltd.,
'Phones, 63 and 1017.

PRE-WAR COST.
SSEX BORDERS.
TIAL DISTRICT; high,
—Attractive COUNTRY
billiard room, eight bed

WANTED Very large properties suitable FLATLET HOUSES or HOTELS (20-100 rooms) required for active cash purchasers.

MARLIN, MEDLICOTT & ROBERTS
14 Motcomb Street, Belgrave Square, S.W.1. BEL. 6557/8 and 6559.

FREEHOLD RESIDENTIAL INVESTMENT
Little Park House, Brimpton, Nr. Newbury, Berkshire

Attractive country house, converted into nine flats with magnificent views and standing in extensive grounds. Suitable for school, nursing home, etc. Full Central Heating. Convenient for Newbury, Reading, Basingstoke and Aldermaston. Vacant possession on completion

TO BE SOLD BY PUBLIC AUCTION (if not previously sold) on WEDNESDAY, 21st JULY, 1965

Further particulars apply: TUFNELL & PARTNERS, Station Parade, Sunningdale, Berkshire. Ascot 2555.

Perry Nursey (1771–1840) was a country surgeon turned Suffolk landscape painter who married an heiress but unfortunately forgot, until it was too late, about the need to earn money. His bankruptcy was reported in detail in the *Ipswich Journal*, particularly the auctions of his possessions, which were held locally to raise money to pay back his creditors. Under the bankruptcy rules, everything he owned, save personal clothes, had to be sold – ghastly for him, but resulting in a marvellous historical record for everyone else and helping, ironically, to ensure he survived in memory.

The first auction, at the Crown Inn, Woodbridge, at noon on 14 February 1834, saw the disposal of the remaining ten years of Perry's lease of Foxboro' Hall, near Melton, Suffolk, and its associated lands. The Hall was described so meticulously you could almost imagine walking around it:

... all that Modern built, elegant Family Mansion, Plantations and Gardens, partly walled in, Stable and Coach House, Lawn and Arable Land, The whole containing about Forty-Eight Acres.

The Mansion is stuccoed, and faced with stone – comprising a handsome, circular Vestibule, 17 feet diameter; Library; Dressing-Room, adjoining; Breakfast Room, 22 feet by 17 feet; Dining Room and Drawing Room, the same size, all 11 half feet high, a Hall 17 feet diameter; Stone Geometrical Staircase, leading to 6 Best Bedrooms, one 22 feet by 17 feet, also others 17 feet square, dressing room, water closet all 10 feet high; a second Staircase, and two servants' sleeping-rooms; Kitchen (in which there is a lifting pump, with excellent water); servants' halls, butler's pantry, cooks' ditto, store room, china closet, butler's bedroom, Brew and wash-house, good dry cellerage, with wine and beer vaults, and also fitted up for a larder and store-room; paved yard, containing Stabling, hay-lofts, chaise-house, and all the usual domestic offices.

The mansion is bounded by thriving Plantations, placed on a cheerful lawn, selected for its picturesque beauties, and commanding extensive and diversified views of hills and a fertile vale, beyond which is a rich and varied scenery.

The next three auctions were held at Foxboro' Hall itself, on Monday, Tuesday and Wednesday – 3, 4 and 5 March – the latter finishing punctually at noon, we are told, in time for the Woodbridge market. The newspaper details exactly what was sold off, from household goods, books, farm stock, livestock and wheeled transport – we know, for example, that Perry Nursey had 30 sacks of potatoes and 19 dusters. In the 'Drawing Room and Hall' he had:

Set polished fire irons, fender &c, 12 black and gold ornamented cane bottomed chairs, mahogany framed sofa, ditto table, ditto table, Pembroke and card ditto, fire screens, pair printed window curtains 3 and a half yards long, 3 breadths; new Kidderminster carpet, 7 yards by 5 and a half yards; hearth rug, painted floor cloths, piano forte, with the additional keys, by Stoddart, 8 day spring clock &c.

The creditors decided that his art collection should be auctioned separately and the sale was arranged for 10 and 11 April, at 11am each day at Foxboro' Hall. A catalogue was distributed throughout East Anglia and London and a detailed notice listing Perry's lovingly assembled collection appeared in the *Ipswich Journal*, addressed 'To lovers and admirers of the Fine Arts'. From the newspaper report, again, we know exactly what original pictures and

... on Friday, the 7th of February, 1834, at Six o'clock in the Evening, when a full statement of the affairs of the deceased will be laid before them.
Ipswich, Jan. 24th, 1834.

FOXBURROW HILL HOUSE,
MELTON, near WOODBRIDGE.

To be SOLD by AUCTION,
By Mr. CANA,
At the Crown Inn, Woodbridge,
On FRIDAY, the 14th of February, at Twelve o'clock,
BY ORDER OF THE ASSIGNEES OF
MR. PERRY NURSEY, A BANKRUPT,

ALL the Beneficial Interest of the said Bankrupt in the Unexpired Term of the Lease for Ten Years from the 11th October last, of all that MODERN built, elegant

FAMILY MANSION,
Plantations and Gardens, partly walled in,
STABLE & COACH-HOUSE,
LAWN, & ARABLE LAND,
The whole containing about FORTY-EIGHT ACRES.

THE MANSION

Is stuccoed, and faced with stone—comprising a handsome, circular VESTIBULE, 17 feet diameter; LIBRARY; DRESSING-ROOM, adjoining; BREAKFAST-ROOM, 22 feet by 17 feet; DINING-ROOM and DRAWING-ROOM the same size, all 11½ feet high; a HALL, 17 feet diameter; *Stone Geometrical Staircase*, leading to 6 BEST BED-ROOMS—one 22 feet by 17 feet, the others 17 feet square; DRESSING-ROOM, WATER CLOSET, all 10 feet high; a second Staircase, & 2 servants' Sleeping-Rooms; KITCHEN, (in which there is a lifting pump, with excellent water); SERVANTS' HALLS, BUTLER'S PANTRY, COOKS' DITTO, STORE-ROOM, CHINA CLOSET, BUTLER'S BED-ROOM, BREW and WASH-HOUSE, good dry CELLARAGE, with Wine and Beer VAULTS, and also fitted up for a Larder and Store-Room; paved Yard, containing Stabling, Hay Lofts, Chaise-House, and all the usual Domestic Offices.

The Mansion is bounded by thriving Plantations, placed on a cheerful Lawn, selected for its picturesque beauties, and commanding extensive and diversified views of hills and a fertile vale, beyond which is rich & varied scenery.

The Premises are *Leased* at a very low Rent, and with advantageous Covenants to the Lessee.

☞ About 13 Acres are Lawn and Pasture; the remainder fine Arable Land, which would readily let at a good rent, should the purchaser of the lease object to occupy it.——Immediate possession may be had.

The Lease may be seen, and further particulars had on applying to Mr. Giles, Mr. Brooke, and Mr. Manby (the ... Rouse, their Solicitor, and the Auc-

LEFT
Column from the *Ipswich Journal* describing 'Foxburrow'.

prints Perry owned: these included '100 prints of English scenery, from drawings and sketches by Gainsborough; 50 prints and etchings, after Gasper Poussin & Claude, extra size, and extremely fine. The Resurrection; from Rubens, by Monachie, very scarce and fine ...' . This gives a very rounded picture of Perry's artistic tastes, and more than hint at how magnificently decorated Foxboro' Hall must have been in its heyday.

LEFT
Foxboro' Hall was put on sale again in 1998, as shown from this page from the *East Anglian Daily Times*. Much has been added since Perry Nursey's time, including the double-dormer projecting from the roof. The 'original' house was created by Nursey as a neo-classical mansion incorporating an Elizabethan farm-house.

It is always worth considering what local magazines and other similar publications might have included a reference to your home. The *Gentleman's Magazine* was published monthly from 1731 to 1868, and included some designs and plans of prominent new buildings. On a more local level, in mid-19th-century Suffolk, for example, engravings of local buildings appeared regularly in *Pawsey's Pocket Book and Ladies' Fashionable Repository*. This engraving of a painting by Perry Nursey of Edwarton Rectory appeared in the 1844 *Pocket Book*.

BOOKS

- **A. Adolph, *Tracing Your Family History* (Collins, 2004)**
- **Archive CD Books, 5 Commercial Street, Cinderford, Gloucester GL14 2RP; tel: 01594 829870;** www.archivecdbooks.org
- **Back To Roots (UK) Ltd, 16 Arrowsmith Drive, Stonehouse, Gloucestershire GL10 2QR; tel: 0800 298 5894;** www.backtoroots.co.uk
- **Cyrene Publications, West Surrey Family History Society, Beverly, 17 Lane End Drive, Knaphill, Woking, Surrey GU21 2QQ;** www.wsfhs.org
- **Colin Hinson, 119 High Street, Blunham, Bedfordshire MK44 3NW; tel: 01767 640503;** www.blunham.demon.co.uk/cdroms
- **Direct Resources, 33a Ruskin Avenue, Wakefield WF1 2BG; tel: 0797 467 2648;** www.direct-resources.uk.com
- **Fitzmartyn Publications, 10 Fitzwilliam Street, Wath-upon-Dearne, Rotherham, South Yorkshire S63 7HF;** www.fitzmartyn.co.uk
- **JiGraH Resources, 85 Heythrop Drive, Acklam, Middlesborough TS5 8QX; tel: 01642 288937;** www.jigrah.co.uk
- **Original Indexes, 113 East View, Wideopen, Tyne & Wear NE13 6EF; tel: 0191 236 6416;** www.original-indexes.demon.co.uk
- **G. Shaw and A. Tipper, *British Directories, A Bibliography and Guide to Directories Published in England & Wales (1850–1950) and Scotland (1773–1950)* (Leicester University Press, 1997)**
- **S&N Genealogy Supplies, Manor Farm, Chilmark, Salisbury SP3 5AF; tel: 01722 716121;** www.sandn.net
- **Stepping Stones, PO Box 295, York YO32 9WQ; tel: 01904 400503;** www.stepping-stones.co.uk
- **Your Old Books & Maps, 2 Temple Road, Dewsbury WF13 3QE; tel: 01924 452987; Sales@youroldbooksandmaps.co.uk**

In addition, many local history and family history societies produce useful publications on CD (see page 265).

CHAPTER 9

Electoral registers and poll books

Electoral registers: 1832–present
Poll books: 1696–1872

Records of people entitled to vote have been produced continuously from the 18th century to the present day. They are an incomplete source, for until recently not all adults were entitled to vote. Especially for the 20th century, however, they have the advantage of being arranged geographically. Because of this, they constitute useful additional records for the history of your home. Your local electoral registers and poll books will be held between your local archives and libraries, and the county record office.

BELOW
Lincolnshire Poll Book, 1818.

FACING PAGE
Bristol Poll Book, 1812.

Besides the fun of seeing whether pre-1872 inhabitants of your home were true-blue Tories or reforming Whigs, the records have two main uses. Modern lists can be used to track down the current addresses of living people who used to occupy your home, who will undoubtedly have memories and older photographs of it. Using a run of annual lists, you can track your home and its occupants back through time. The appearance of new people of the same surname in a certain year usually means they were children who had reached voting age. The disappearance of one family member can mean they moved or died – when John and Mary Smith changes to just Mary Smith, John had probably died. Working back you will discover when one family moved into your home and another moved out. You will also pick up some interesting snippets of information. The letter 'S' against a name in an electoral register, for example, indicates someone serving in the armed forces.

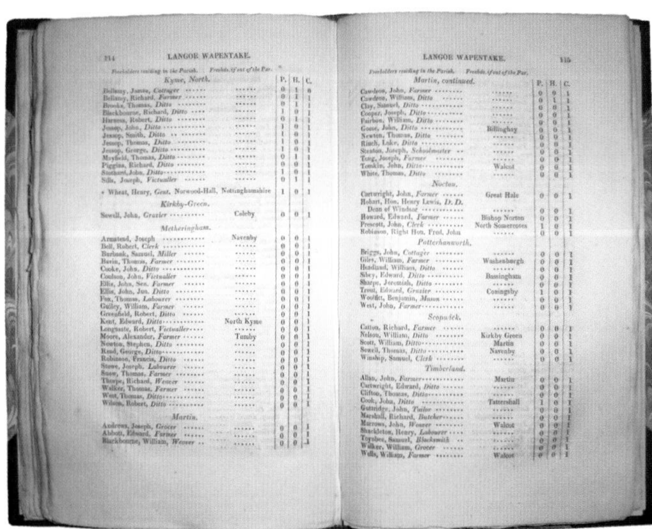

114 LANGOE WAPENTAKE.

Freeholders residing in the Parish.	*Freehds. if out of the Par.*	P.	H.	C.
Kyme, North.				
Bellamy, James, *Cottager*		0	1	0
Bellamy, Richard, *Farmer*		0	1	1
Brooks, Thomas, *Ditto*		0	1	1
Blackbourne, Richard, *Ditto*		1	0	1
Harness, Robert, *Ditto*		0	1	1
Jessop, John, *Ditto*		1	0	1
Jessop, Smith, *Ditto*		1	0	1
Jessop, Thomas, *Ditto*		1	0	1
Jessop, George, *Ditto*		1	0	1
Mayfield, Thomas, *Ditto*		0	1	1
Piggins, Richard, *Ditto*		0	0	1
Stothard, John, *Ditto*		1	0	1
Sills, Joseph, *Victualler*		0	1	1
* Wheat, Henry, *Gent.* Norwood-Hall, Nottinghamshire		1	0	1
Kirkby-Green.				
Sewell, John, *Grazier*	Coleby	0	0	1
Metheringham.				
Armstead, Joseph	Navenby	0	0	1
Bell, Robert, *Clerk*		0	0	1
Burbank, Samuel, *Miller*		0	0	1
Bavin, Thomas, *Farmer*		0	0	1
Cooke, John, *Ditto*		0	0	1
Coulson, John, *Victualler*		0	0	1
Ellis, John, Sen. *Farmer*		0	0	1
Ellis, John, Jun. *Ditto*		0	0	1
Fox, Thomas, *Labourer*		0	0	1
Gulley, William, *Farmer*		0	0	1
Greenfield, Robert, *Ditto*		0	0	1
Kent, Edward, *Ditto*	North Kyme	0	0	1
Longnate, Robert, *Victualler*		0	0	1
Moore, Alexander, *Farmer*	Tumby	0	0	1
Newton, Stephen, *Ditto*		0	0	1
Read, George, *Ditto*		0	0	1
Robinson, Francis, *Ditto*		0	0	1
Stowe, Joseph, *Labourer*		0	0	1
Snow, Thomas, *Farmer*		0	0	1
Thorpe, Richard, *Weaver*		0	0	1
Walker, Thomas, *Farmer*		0	0	1
West, Thomas, *Ditto*		0	0	1
Wilson, Robert, *Ditto*		0	0	1
Martin.				
Andrews, Joseph, *Grocer*		0	0	1
Abbott, Edward, *Farmer*		0	0	1
Blackbourne, William, *Weaver*		0	0	1

LANGOE WAPENTAKE. 115

Freeholders residing in the Parish.	*Freehds. if out of the Par.*	P.	H.	C.
Martin, continued.				
Cawdron, John, *Farmer*		0	0	1
Cawdron, William, *Ditto*		0	1	1
Clay, Samuel, *Ditto*		0	0	1
Cooper, Joseph, *Ditto*		0	0	1
Fairbon, William, *Ditto*		0	0	1
Goose, John, *Ditto*	Billinghay	0	0	1
Newton, Thomas, *Ditto*		0	0	1
Rinch, Luke, *Ditto*		0	0	1
Stenton, Joseph, *Schoolmaster*		0	0	1
Tong, Joseph, *Farmer*		0	0	1
Tomkin, John, *Ditto*	Walcot	0	0	1
White, Thomas, *Ditto*		0	0	1
Nocton.				
Cartwright, John, *Farmer*	Great Hale	0	0	1
Hobart, Hon. Henry Lewis, *D. D.* Dean of Windsor		0	0	1
Howard, Edward, *Farmer*	Bishop Norton	0	0	1
Prescott, John, *Clerk*	North Somercotes	1	0	1
Robinson, Right Hon. Fred. John		0	0	1
Potterhanworth.				
Briggs, John, *Cottager*		0	0	1
Giles, William, *Farmer*	Washenborgh	0	0	1
Headland, William, *Ditto*		0	0	1
Sibey, Edward, *Ditto*	Bassingham	0	0	1
Sharpe, Jeremiah, *Ditto*		0	0	1
Trout, Edward, *Grazier*	Coningsby	1	0	1
Woolfitt, Benjamin, *Mason*		0	0	1
West, John, *Farmer*		0	0	1
Scopwick.				
Catton, Richard, *Farmer*		0	0	1
Nelson, William, *Ditto*	Kirkby Green	0	0	1
Scott, William, *Ditto*	Martin	0	0	1
Sewell, Thomas, *Ditto*	Navenby	0	0	1
Winship, Samuel, *Clerk*		0	0	1
Timberland.				
Allan, John, *Farmer*	Martin	0	0	1
Cartwright, Edward, *Ditto*		0	0	1
Clifton, Thomas, *Ditto*		0	0	1
Cook, John, *Ditto*	Tattershall	1	0	1
Guttridge, John, *Tailor*		0	0	1
Marshall, Richard, *Butcher*		0	0	1
Marrows, John, *Weaver*	Walcot	0	0	1
Shackleton, Henry, *Labourer*		0	0	1
Toynbee, Samuel, *Blacksmith*		0	0	1
Walker, William, *Grocer*		0	0	1
Wells, William, *Farmer*	Walcot	0	0	1

Electoral registers

These list those people who were entitled to vote, and have been kept annually from 1832, with the exception of parts of the war periods, 1916–17 and 1940–4. Electoral registers were originally arranged alphabetically by voter, but changed gradually in the 19th century to a street-by-street arrangement within electoral wards.

From 1928 onwards, you can be certain of finding street names and house numbers. Bear in mind that they were usually printed about half a year after the information had been collected, so may include people who had died before the date of publication.

Poll books

Produced in the days before secret ballots, poll books listed those who had voted in elections, giving their parish of residence and which candidate they had chosen. Although the earliest date from 1696, few survive before 1711, the year in which they started to be enrolled in the Quarter Sessions. They ceased to be produced in 1872, the year in which voting became secret.

Where to search

- Current electoral registers are held at District Council offices and those for previous years in local libraries.
- Electoral registers can be searched online at **www.192.com**.
- A national collection for the current year is at the Office for National Statistics, Segesworth Road, Titchfield, Fareham, Hampshire PO15 5RR; tel: 0845 601 3034; **www.statistics.gov.uk/**. That for the previous year is kept at the Family Records Centre and the earlier ones are at the British Library.
- You can seek poll books in record offices. There are also substantial collections at the Society of Genealogists, the British Library and the Institute of Historical Research (**www.ihrinfo.co.uk**).
- Gibson and Rogers' book (see box below) is a guide to their whereabouts. For more detail on Scottish records see Cheffins's book (also see box below).

Who could vote?

Originally, only certain men aged over 20 could vote in Parliamentary elections. Those who owned a freehold worth 40 shillings of more could, unless they lived in towns and cities. Here, qualifications varied - in some cases, only freemen could vote, while in others all householders, known as 'potwallopers', could have their say. From 1832, all men owning land worth £10 or over, and townsmen leasing land worth £10 or over, could vote. In 1867, the countryside qualification value was dropped to £5 and the franchise was extended to those paying £50 or more in rent, while in the towns all householders were allowed to vote. In 1884, this latter qualification was extended to the countryside. Votes for all men over 20 and female householders over 30 came in 1918, with the vote extended to all women aged over 20 in 1928. Up to 1970, those over 20 were listed, and in the year someone reached the age of 21 the letter 'Y' may appear. From 1971, everyone of 18 and above appears.

Qualifications to vote in local elections were different. From 1835, voting in local elections was generally open to a broader number of people than were eligible for Parliamentary elections. All men who paid poor rates could vote from 1835. Women who owned property of the requisite value and paid poor rates could vote from 1869, making local poll books of more use than those for national elections.

Scotland: The Scottish franchise was extremely restricted. A mere 2,662 men - a tiny percentage of the population - could vote in the 1788 Parliamentary election. The number grew rapidly thanks to the reforms of 1832. Poll books can be found at the National Archives of Scotland and the National Library of Scotland (George IV Bridge, Edinburgh EH1 1EW; tel: 0131 466 2812; **www.nls.uk**).

Ireland: Most Irish poll books for before 1922 were blown up at the Four Courts. Those that survive are listed in Ryan's book (see box below).

BOOKS

- **R. H. A. Cheffins, *Parliamentary Constituencies and their Registers Since 1832* (British Library, 1998)**
- **J. Gibson and C. Rogers, *Electoral Registers Since 1832 and Burgess Rolls* (FFHS, 1990)**
- **J. G. Ryan, *Irish Records - Sources for Family and Local History* (Ancestry, 1997)**

CHAPTER 10

Local and family histories

Your local archives will have a collection of local history books, including copies of recently published histories for sale. Local histories take a number of different forms. All can be incredibly useful for your research by providing the background story of your community. You may be lucky and find your home is actually mentioned or featured.

A magnificent 16th-century heraldic pedigree of the Lucys of Charlcote, Warwickshire, also serves as a fine illustration of the history of their home, Charlcote Park – in whose grounds the young William Shakespeare was said to have been caught poaching.

Local histories

- Many parishes already have excellent published histories. They may mention your home specifically or just give useful background information. They will also cover and identify many local sources (including maps), which you can then search for your own home.
- A prolific publisher of local history is Sutton Publishing (Phoenix Mill, Thrupp, Stroud, Gloucestershire GL5 2BU; tel: 01453 731114; **www.suttonpublishing.co.uk**). Their website shows the local histories they have produced both of specific places, from Cirencester to Wallingford, and also on local themes, such as 'Literary Cambridge' and 'Brontë Country'.
- Phillimore produces many local histories both in their own right, and as publishers of the Darwen County History Series (Phillimore & Co. Ltd, Shopwyke Manor Barn, Chichester, West Sussex PO20 2BG; tel: 01243 787636; **www.phillimore.co.uk**).
- For Scotland, a good place to start searching is the Grimsay Press (57 St Vincent Crescent, Glasgow G3 8NQ; **www.thegrimsaypress.co.uk**).
- Most counties have a record or archaeological society, or similar. The old archaeological societies were, in fact, as interested in the 17th century and the Middle Ages as in the dim and distant past: their publications contain much useful information for home historians.

Victoria County Histories

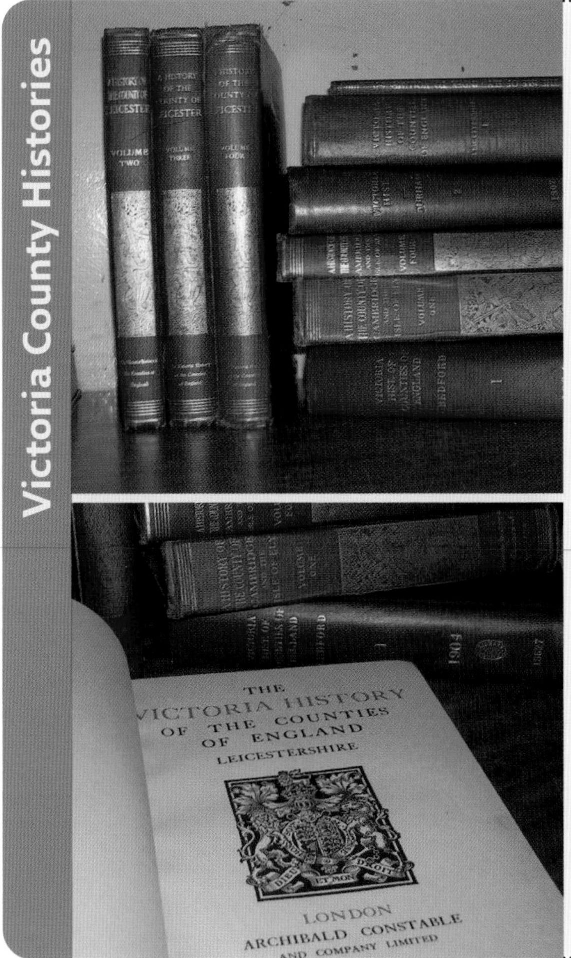

There's nothing Victorian about the Victoria County History series (Institute of Historical Research, University of London, Senate House, Malet Street, London WC1E 7HU; tel: 020 7862 8770; and see **www.englandpast.net/**). It is a project that is very much alive, still producing volumes to this day.

For each county, there will eventually be two complete sets of books: many have already been published and are in local libraries. Others are still being researched. The 'general' series looks at broad topics, from geology, natural and ancient history through to such matters as *Domesday Book* coverage (see pages 143–5), political history and modern institutions.

The second, topographic, series covers each parish, giving as rounded a picture of each place as possible, looking into everything from archaeology to modern architectural history. Interesting buildings are mentioned in each parish chapter. Even if your home is not mentioned, you cannot fail to learn a great deal of relevance to your investigations. The chapters draw on a wide variety of sources – including much field work – and relate to records such as old deeds and manorial records. Examining the footnotes for the relevant chapter is often a good place to start seeking sources that may mention your home.

|| Pevsner's series on buildings (see pages 25–6) covers all of Britain and provides much useful detail on local history.

Antiquarian histories

Most counties are covered by at least one antiquarian county history. These were compiled mainly between the 17th and 19th centuries and concern themselves with archaeological remains, important buildings, such as mansions and churches, histories of prominent local families, and much else. Although rather dated, they record what was known, and visible, several hundred years ago, so are now in themselves historical documents of the first order. Some, such as Ormerod's *Cheshire* include many engravings, not just of the main buildings, but of villages, and whole streets in Chester, so their use and appeal are very broad.

An example of the use of a local antiquarian history, Oliver's *Ecclesiastical Antiquities in Devon*, appears on page 238.

Local history online

|| Some parishes now have online histories. The best portal is **www.localhistories.org/**. Tim Lambert's **www.localhistories.org/gosport.html**, for example, examines the

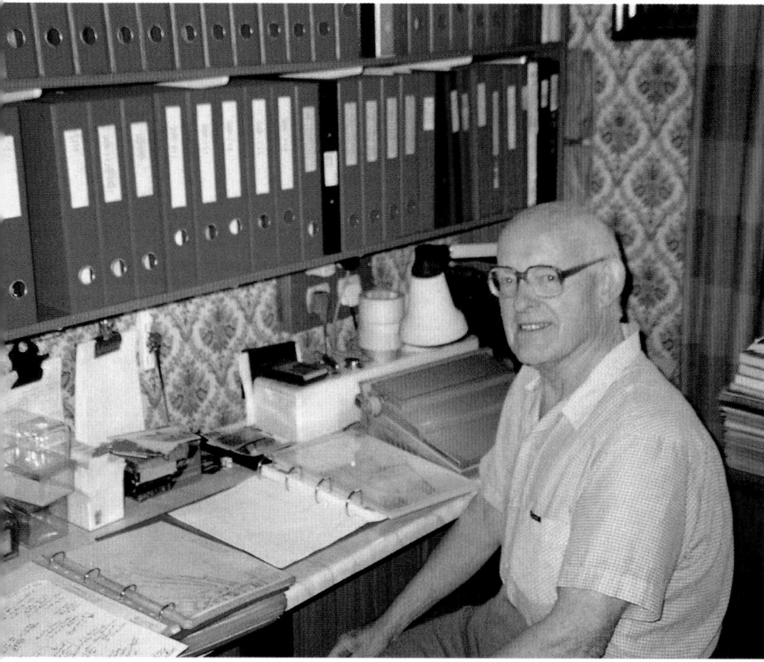

Don't spare any effort making contact with local historians. You might do this through a local history society, but there are other ways. I heard about local historian Derek Baker (pictured here), simply because he does odd jobs for my neighbour. Although not a member of any local history organisation, he knows more about the Stoke Newington area than any of the authors of local history books.

history of Gosport, part of the great naval conurbation of Portsmouth, Hampshire. Besides all the useful content that such sites contain, you can also contact their authors with contributions and enquiries.

|| There are many local history websites that you can find using search engines. One that stands out is **www.victorianlondon.org/**, compiled by Lee Jackson, an extremely detailed website covering many aspects of Victorian London and its inhabitants, with much useful information on buildings and the expansion of the suburbs.

|| The site **www.visionofbritain.org.uk**, produced by the Great Britain Historical Geographical Information System, enables you to search for your locality by postcode and find details on such matters as local population and industry, collated from the 19th-century census returns. It also contains a growing library of historical travellers' accounts, which may mention your locality in the past.

Place names

|| Ekwall's dictionary (see box opposite) is excellent for finding out what the names of towns and villages mean.

|| For place names within parishes, you can consult the English Place Names series, published county by county (although not all have been published (see also box opposite)).

|| Gelling's book (see also box opposite) remains the foremost popular modern study of the historical significance of English place names, some of which date back to pre-Roman times, indicating how settlements with ancient names would have originated.

Prominent families

Members of prominent landowning families occupied homes and owned many more as part of their estates. In both cases, you may be helped by a detailed printed account of the family concerned.

|| Many appear in *Burke's Peerage* and *Burke's Landed Gentry*. Old editions are in most good libraries. The most recent editions are on **www.burkes-peerage.net**.

|| Other printed sources can be found through the genealogical bibliographies of Barrow, Marshall, Raymond, Thompson, and Whitmore; Ferguson and Stuart for Scotland; and Clare for Ireland (see box opposite). Of these, Whitmore and Marshall include bibliographical references to the heraldic pedigrees made in the 16th and 17th centuries and which provide the backbones for older English manorial family trees.

Researching local history

|| As someone researching the history of your home, you are effectively a micro local historian. Fowler, Hey, and – in a less direct way – Tate, all provide excellent introductions to this field (see box opposite).

BOOKS

- G. B. Barrow, *The Genealogists' Guide: An Index to Printed British Pedigrees and Family Histories 1950–75* (Research Publishing Co., 1977)
- R. Blatchford (ed.), *The Local and Family History Handbook* (33 Nursery Road, Nether Poppleton, York YO26 6NN, www.genealogical.co.uk)
- W. Clare, *A Simple Guide to Irish Genealogy*, first compiled by the Rev. Wallace Clare (Irish Genealogical Research Society, rev. edn., R. Folliott, 1966)
- D. Dymond, *Researching and Writing History: A Practical Guide for Local Historians* (British Association for Local History, n.d.)
- E. Ekwall, *The Concise Oxford Dictionary of English Place-names* (Clarendon Press, 1960)
- English Place-Names series, (county by county) (Leopard's Head Press, n.d)
- P. S. Ferguson (compiler), *Scottish Family Histories* (National Library of Scotland, 1986)
- S. Fowler, *Starting Out in Local History* (Countryside Books, 2001)
- M. Gelling, *Signposts to the Past: Place Names and the History of England* (Phillimore, 2000)
- D. Hey, *The Oxford Companion to Local and Family History* (OUP, 1996)
- G. W. Marshall, *The Genealogists' Guide* (1903, repr. GPC, 1973)
- C. Mosley (ed.), *Burke's Peerage, Baronetage and Knightage* (Burke's Peerage & Gentry, 2003)
- G. Ormerod, *The History of the County Palatine of Chester*, 3 vols (George Routledge & Sons, 1882)
- S. Raymond, *County Bibliographies* (county by county) (S. A. and M. J. Raymond, 6 Russet Avenue, Exeter, Devon EX1 3QB)
- M. Stuart, *Scottish Family History* (1930, repr. GPC, 1978)
- W. E. Tate, *The Parish Chest* (Phillimore, 1983)
- T. R. Thompson, *A Catalogue of British Family Histories* (Research Publishing Co. and SoG, 1980)
- J. B. Whitmore, *A Genealogical Guide; An Index to British Pedigrees in Continuation of Marshall's Genealogists' Guide* (repr. J. B. Whitmore, 1953)

|| You will find many useful contacts in Robert Blatchford's annually updated *The Family and Local History Handbook* (see box above). This contains detailed listings of local history societies along with museums, family history societies, archives and record offices.

|| You might also consider joining the British Association for Local History (BALH), PO Box 6549, Somersal Herbert, Ashbourne, Derbyshire DE6 5WH; tel: 01283 585947; mail@balh.co.uk; **www.balh.co.uk**. The annual membership fee is £25 and BALH produces two quarterly publications, *The Local Historian* and *Local History News*, along with one-off publications such as Dymond's book (see box above).

CHAPTER 11

Pictures of your home

And here's Leon yet again, sitting in the kitchen – our kitchen! – patting a dog, a birthday cake on the table. How many birthday cakes of ours have we had in that kitchen?… how many birthday cakes has the house seen in that kitchen? Hundreds? How many candles? Thousands?

Julie Myerson's *Home: The Story of Everyone Who Ever Lived in Our House*

SECOND EDITION.

Thelton Hall, Norfolk.

For Sale by

Messrs. NORTON, HOGGART, & TRIST,

62, OLD BROAD STREET,

E. C.

Thelveton Hall (here called 'Thelton Hall'), Norfolk, illustrated in the catalogue produced by Messrs Norton, Hoggart & Trist for its sale in 1864. This copy was found in the papers of the Mann family, who bought the estate.

Old pictures of your home can add wonderfully to a finished home history. More importantly, they provide valuable evidence of what your home used to look like, and therefore how it has changed. Local archives and libraries often have collections of old pictures of their area that may, if you are fortunate, include some of your home. Local histories (see pages 72–5) are usually well illustrated with old pictures. Past inhabitants (or their descendants) may also have old pictures of your home from the time when they lived in it.

Private 'archives'

The most direct way of tracking down old pictures is to ask neighbours who have been in their homes longer than you have been in yours, or to trace the people who used to live in your home, using the techniques described on pages 38–9. Often your home will only appear incidentally, as the backdrop of family photographs – but what a rich source such almost accidental records can be.

Going further back, you may find people with photographs, or even painted portraits, of ancestors of theirs who lived in your home. These can be wonderful, but potentially misleading too. Interiors, especially those involving pillars and drapes, were more often than not created in studios. In fact, the bodies and clothes in portraits were often pre-painted in bulk by apprentices, with only the heads and hands of sitters added later by the master.

Photographic collections

The first photographs were taken by L. J. M. Daguerre in Paris in 1839, followed rapidly by W. H. Fox Talbot's invention of the modern 'calotype' process, using negatives. The first photographic studio in Britain was opened in London in 1841, taking off sharply after new technical innovations in 1851.

- Most local archives have collections of photographs dating back to the 19th century. Some of these appear online, such as the Mitchell Library's archive of some 9,000 pictures of old Glasgow at **www.glasgow.gov.uk/en/Residents/Leisure_Culture/Libraries/Librarylocations/themitchell.htm**. An impressive collection for London is at **www.photolondon.org.uk**.
- Some local archives hold the collections of early photographers. For example, the National Library of Wales holds the collection of John Thomas, who travelled around Wales in the late 19th century, recording streets and villages and their inhabitants. The National Archives has a number of large collections, to which there is a catalogue in the Reading Room: these include the Dixon-Scott archive of town and village scenes, taken between 1925 and 1948 (in INF 9).
- The largest photographic collection in Europe – with a vast 12 million pictures – is the Hulton Getty Collection at Unique House, 21–31 Woodfield Road, London W9 2BA; tel: 0800 376 7977; **www.gettyimages.com**.
- The National Monuments Record Centre (Great Western Village, Kemble Drive, Swindon SN2 2GZ; tel: 01793 414600; **www.Swindon.gov.uk.nmrc**) has 6.5 million pictures, mostly of buildings around the time of the Second World War, indexed by parish.
- There are also many commercial outlets for old photographs and reprints from old

ABOVE
Steeple Claydon c. 1955.

LEFT
Midhurst, North Street, 1906.

LEFT
Homes often appear in pictures accidentally. Here is part of the Barry family's cottage in Ballyin, near Lismore, Ireland, used as the background for a family photograph in 1926. The thatched roof shows it only had one storey. Living conditions inside, with six boys to accommodate, must have been extremely cramped!

A beautifully hand-coloured 1906 postcard of Church Row, Stoke Newington, looking down towards Whithorn House (former home of James Paterson (see page 54)) and Old St Mary's (courtesy of Derek Baker).

LEFT
Alphons Adolph, whose invention, the picture postcard, is a major source of old pictures of many houses.

negatives, such as the Francis Frith Collection at Charlton Road, Andover, Hampshire SP10 3LE; tel: 01722 716376; **www.francisfrith.co.uk**. Impressive though their collection is, however, the chances of your home appearing in their collection is still very low, unless it is in a village, town or city centre.

Old postcards

Many pictures of places found in local history books and elsewhere are, in fact, old postcards. Picture postcards were invented in Germany in the 1870s or 1880s. Five people each claimed to have invented them: Ludwig Zrenner, Heinrich Lange, Cesare Bertanza, Alphons Adolph and Pastor Ludolph Parisius. Naturally, as Alphons Adolph (1853–1934) was my great-great-grandfather's first cousin, my money's on him. His first picture postcard was produced at Löbau, Saxony, in 1879. The idea was such a good one that it spread rapidly, and soon there were cards depicting practically every village and town in Britain – and many of these include people's homes.

You might be lucky enough to find your own home pictured in an old picture postcard. Even if not, you might be able to find some that show parts of your area in the late 19th and through the 20th century, and which will give a lovely flavour to the history of your own home.

|| Old postcards can be acquired relatively easily and cheaply at specialist postcard collectors' sales. These are held all over the country. A major one is held monthly at the Royal National Hotel, Bedford Way, near Euston Station in London – see **www.memoriespostcards.co.uk** for more details.

Old paintings

Sometimes, research into your locality may lead you to landscapes and other paintings showing the area in the past – and which may even include your home. From the 17th century, there is increasing evidence that many painters of buildings used camera obscuras – darkened chambers into which the real world was projected using a lens. The results were highly accurate pictures, in terms both of perspective and architectural detail, so works produced in such a manner are certainly not to be sniffed at. The paintings of Jan Siberechts in the late 17th century, for example, contain wonderful details of houses, grand and humble. The chances of your home appearing in such a picture are, of course, small – but always remain alert to the possibility.

Archives, galleries and private homes are also full of many much more ordinary paintings of buildings. The Rev. Richard Cobbold (1797–1877), for example, made detailed sketches – and accompanying notes – of most of the buildings and inhabitants of his parish of Wortham, Suffolk, in about 1860. The originals are at the Suffolk Record Office, and some have been published in Fletcher's book (see box below). Of Spinks Cottages, for example, Cobbold wrote, 'These are so called from the fact that they did once belong to a man who was a miller of that name in this parish. Poor Spink bore the character of an honest-hearted man but he was too confiding in others and was therefore treacherously deceived into suretyship and was reduced to poverty...'

BOOKS

- **R. Fletcher (ed.), *Biography of a Victorian Village* (printed version of Cobbold's notes and paintings) (B. T. Batsford, 1977)**

ABOVE AND TOP
Jan Siberechts' 17th-century painting of Henley, at the River and Rowing Museum, showing the entire painting and two close-up views of homes.

ABOVE
'Old Maria's' cottage, one of the many watercolours of ordinary homes in Rev. Richard Cobbold's collection.

CHAPTER 12

Names and numbers of houses and streets

House and street names can provide major clues for home historians as they often have some bearing on their history. Why a house is so named will often emerge from your research and can usually be discovered using local archives and local histories. At the archives you can also discover whether your home's number has ever changed – something you definitely need to know to ensure you identify the right building in older records.

Sometimes, rows of homes erected by a developer were each given their own name. The aim was presumably to make standardly produced homes seem more individual. The names usually followed themes. A terrace in Wincheap, Canterbury, for example, has names derived from Cornish beauty spots, while this row in south Canterbury includes a home named after Vitznau in Switzerland.

House names

The naming of streets and houses is usually a fairly random process. House names often recall places where the original (or subsequent) owners had lived before. Many houses in England, for example, have Irish or Scottish – and latterly Caribbean and Indian – names recalling the birthplaces of their occupants.

Other house names may hark back to the building's past. Names such as the 'Old School House' are pretty obvious and can send you looking for records of the building when it was a school. Others will have their old uses disguised behind rather arcane words, such as 'Glebe Cottage': this indicates that the building was once part of the church glebe lands, and it can be investigated through glebe terriers (see page 239).

|| The English Place-Names series published county by county (see page 83) can be useful if your home is a particularly old or notable one, for the derivation of its own name may be discussed. If not, you can study the way the name was recorded in old records and try to work it out yourself, based on the many similar examples you may find in these books.

Street names

Names of old streets may have their roots in the area's ancient past. Streets that were purpose-built were given names either by the developers or local authorities. These often recalled the land's earlier history – the names of previous landowners, for example (see page 168), or buildings, such as farms, and natural features that were destroyed to make way for the new homes.

Other street names were chosen to commemorate contemporary events: Coronation and Jubilee Streets, for example, or Mafeking Avenue to celebrate a military victory of the Boer War in 1900 – handy, incidentally, for dating when the street and its homes were built. Names might also reflect the identity of the developer and his own family – the example on page 35 shows how Ovington Square was named after Ovington Park in Hampshire. Jermyn Street in Westminster, to give another example, was named by its developer, Henry Jermyn, Earl of St Albans, after himself (see pages 222–3). Street names might also be chosen in groups to give an historical or cultural feel to a newly developed area: Hatch Warren in Basingstoke, for example, which is full of thoroughly anodyne modern houses, has a series of roads named – apparently without intentional irony – after some of Britain's greatest architects. Poets are also a popular source for street names, though not in Great Yarmouth – a bye-law was passed there forbidding this very thing, on the grounds that many wordsmiths led immoral lives and were therefore unworthy of having streets named after them!

Street names in modern developments were usually chosen by the developer: the reasons were seldom stated, and indeed the authorities' concern was usually not that streets should have appropriate names, but simply that they were distinctive and did not create confusion

This unprepossessing office block in Canterbury was named Salthill House after I researched the history of its site. Although I found virtually nothing of interest for the site itself, I discovered that it was opposite the site of a great mound that stood in the middle of the old road around the city walls, on which Medieval merchants traded salt.

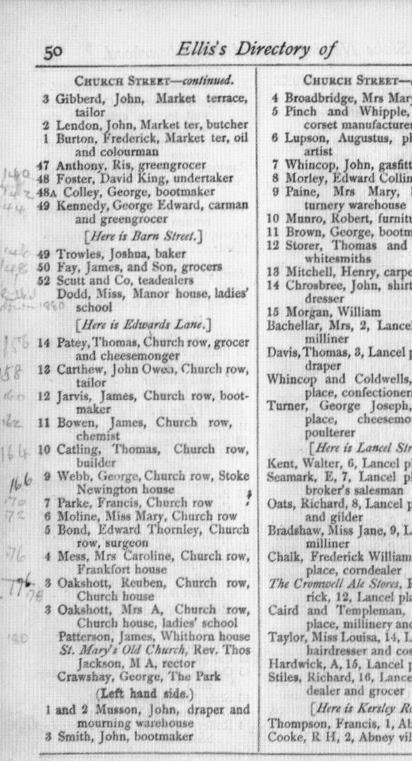

50 *Ellis's Directory of*

CHURCH STREET—*continued.*

3 Gibberd, John, Market terrace, tailor
2 Lendon, John, Market ter, butcher
1 Burton, Frederick, Market ter, oil and colourman
47 Anthony, Ris, greengrocer
48 Foster, David King, undertaker
48A Colley, George, bootmaker
49 Kennedy, George Edward, carman and greengrocer

[*Here is Barn Street.*]

49 Trowles, Joshua, baker
50 Fay, James, and Son, grocers
52 Scutt and Co, teadealers
Dodd, Miss, Manor house, ladies' school

[*Here is Edwards Lane.*]

14 Patey, Thomas, Church row, grocer and cheesemonger
13 Carthew, John Owen, Church row, tailor
12 Jarvis, James, Church row, bootmaker
11 Bowen, James, Church row, chemist
10 Catling, Thomas, Church row, builder
9 Webb, George, Church row, Stoke Newington house
7 Parke, Francis, Church row
6 Moline, Miss Mary, Church row
5 Bond, Edward Thornley, Church row, surgeon
4 Mess, Mrs Caroline, Church row, Frankfort house
3 Oakshott, Reuben, Church row, Church house
3 Oakshott, Mrs A, Church row, Church house, ladies' school
Patterson, James, Whithorn house
St. Mary's Old Church, Rev. Thos Jackson, M A, rector
Crawshay, George, The Park

(Left hand side.)

1 and 2 Musson, John, draper and mourning warehouse
3 Smith, John, bootmaker

CHURCH STREET—*continued.*

4 Broadbridge, Mrs Mary, stationer
5 Pinch and Whipple, belt and corset manufacturers
6 Lupson, Augustus, photographic artist
7 Whincop, John, gasfitter
8 Morley, Edward Collins, sadler
9 Paine, Mrs Mary, basket and turnery warehouse
10 Munro, Robert, furniture dealer
11 Brown, George, bootmaker
12 Storer, Thomas and William, whitesmiths
13 Mitchell, Henry, carpenter
14 Chrosbree, John, shirt and collar dresser
15 Morgan, William
Bachellar, Mrs, 2, Lancel place, milliner
Davis, Thomas, 3, Lancel place, linen-draper
Whincop and Coldwells, 4, Lancel place, confectioners
Turner, George Joseph, 5, Lancel place, cheesemonger and poulterer

[*Here is Lancel Street.*]

Kent, Walter, 6, Lancel place, grocer
Seamark, E, 7, Lancel place, pawnbroker's salesman
Oats, Richard, 8, Lancel place, carver and gilder
Bradshaw, Miss Jane, 9, Lancel place, milliner
Chalk, Frederick William, 10, Lancel place, corndealer
The Cromwell Ale Stores, Richard Patrick, 12, Lancel place
Caird and Templeman, 13, Lancel place, millinery and baby linen
Taylor, Miss Louisa, 14, Lancel place, hairdresser and costumier
Hardwick, A, 15, Lancel place, hosier
Stiles, Richard, 16, Lancel place, teadealer and grocer

[*Here is Kersley Road.*]

Thompson, Francis, 1, Abney villas
Cooke, R H, 2, Abney villas, surgeon

W. A. HIGGS & Compy., Wine Importers, 80, Kingsland High St., E.

RIGHT
This page from *Ellis's Directory of Stoke Newington and Neighbourhood* (1879) lists the occupants of Church Street, including James Paterson at Whithorn House. This edition, at Hackney Archives, shows the original numbering of the houses within Church Row, but an anonymous hand has also pencilled in the new numbering of the houses within Church Street.

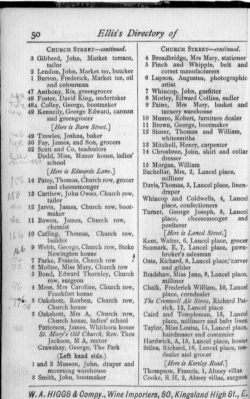

with existing streets. For this reason, more Victoria and Albert Roads were strictly off limits. The London County Council and later Greater London Council street naming and numbering files are indexed through files on the open shelves of relevant local archives.

At Hackney Archives, I examined the files (referenced LBH/7/7/) from the 1930s concerning Stoke Newington. These contained notes on well-known(ish) people in the local cemeteries whose names had not yet been used in street names, and a similar list of members of the Royal Academy, though none that I checked against a modern street atlas ever seem to have been used.

Finding out why homes and streets were so called is often a matter of researching the historical associations that probably led to their names being chosen. Some localities' street names have been studied, some are held in manuscript form in local archives and a few have been published. Some are very accurate; others contain what must, ultimately, be regarded as complete guesses. A local manuscript account of Stoke Newington place names (F. W. Baxter, 'Stoke Newington Street Names', now in Hackney Archives), for example, states for Boleyn Road that Henry VIII had a hunting lodge nearby, so 'it does not take much imagination to work out why Boleyn Road is so-called'. Plausible, yes, but not exactly substantiated (in that secondary source) by much evidence.

The re-numbering of houses shown in action on this 1936 map of Stoke Newington's Church Street.

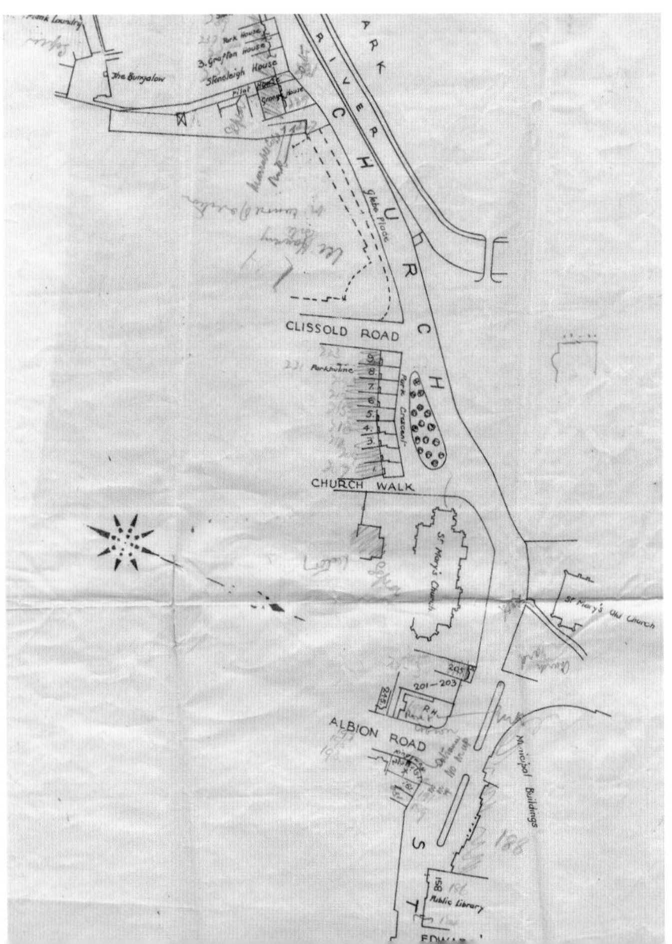

Changed identities

Street numbering can be liable to change, partly due to the incorporation of rows of houses into the general street numbering system, and also, of course, because new houses tend to be added to streets as time passes.

|| Records of street re-numbering may also be found in local archives. The general street file for Stoke Newington at Hackney Archives (LBH/7/7/6,228) includes a map showing one effort at re-numbering Church Street (see left). The original map and numbers are in black, and the new numbering system is written over in red crayon. 1–9 Park Crescent, for example, are here re-numbered 207–223 Church Street, in red.

A surprising number of streets have had their names changed too. You will find this out in the course of your researches – after, no doubt, being initially thrown by such alterations. Changes were sometimes made to give an old street a more fashionable name – I suspect this was the case with Dover Street, Canterbury, renamed thus from its Medieval name, Rithercheap. Rithercheap meant 'cattle market', reflecting the original use of the street that led down to the city's eastern gate. Attitudes have changed again, however, and people obviously thought it was rather a shame to have disposed of such an interesting old name, so now the street is labelled 'Dover Street (formerly Rithercheap)'.

New street names were often chosen by the Post Office to end confusion. Too many Victoria and Albert Streets in one area frequently caused havoc, so many have had their names altered to something less ubiquitous. In 1936, no less than 36 streets in Stoke Newington had their names altered: Meadow Street, the narrow lane running behind the gardens of Church Row, for example, was given the grander but much less picturesque name of Lordship Terrace. Rows of houses or distinctive sections of long streets often used to have their own names, but many of these were abolished and the houses given new addresses under the main street name. For example, Church Row was officially re-named and numbered as part of Church Street.

The records of these activities reveal the extent to which street re-naming became a focus for local identity. Original proposals handed down from London County Council included re-naming Church Street as 'this name is very much repeated in the County, and the London Fire Brigade has drawn particular attention to the confusion caused by this repetition'. An article appearing in the local paper – and duly included in the file – argued that, because the church in Church Street dated back to AD 960, this street had more right to keep its original name than any other similarly named street in London. A compromise was reached and the street was re-named Stoke Newington Church Street. When it came to changing Defoe Road so as not to cause confusion with Defoe Road in Tooting, however, the locals were more vociferous: Defoe had lived there for some 20 years, they argued, and was there when *Robinson Crusoe* was published in 1719. Now, Daniel Close and Defoe Close lead off Tooting's rather piqued looking Robinson Road!

A Canterbury street sign that provides the current and also the original street name 'Dover Street (formerly Rithercheap)'. It is attached to a jettied boxframe house with a Georgian front door and sash windows, an exposed first-floor front of timber infilled with brick and a steep-sloping roof, once thatched, no doubt, but now covered with a decorative pattern of tiles and sporting dormer windows.

|| You may find a surprising amount of detail on street naming and numbering in local council records, and local archives sometimes contain records of street re-naming. London County Council, for example, published periodic lists of changed names – alphabetically listed, frustratingly, under the old rather than the new name. In some cases, the date of the 'abolition order' is given, in others not.

|| Some local archives – especially those in the London area – have card indexes on streets. These can include such wonders as records of the apportionment of costs for paving streets, allocation of street numbers and references to the naming and re-naming of streets.

BOOKS

- **English Place-Names Series (county by county) (Leopard's Head Press, n.d.)**

PART 2

Working back through time

Part 1 covered the basic records generally useful to all home historians. There are many more records, however, that may be helpful to you depending on where your home is and when it was built. This section is arranged in chronological order working back through time and should contain much material that will be of use to you. The records will either reveal specific details of your home or provide you with more background information on your home's site and its surroundings.

CHAPTER 13

The 20th century

The best place to look for records concerning your home in the 20th century are your local archives, where you may find information on planning, road naming and numbering and much else dealt with in other chapters. Here, I look at some of the categories of documentation that may help you.

RIGHT
Bidder Street, Borough of Newham.

OVERCROWDING AT PELSALL.

To the EDITOR *of the* WALSALL OBSERVER.

SIR,—With reference to your report, under the heading "Disease and Overcrowding," of statements made at the last meeting of the Walsall Rural District Council, may I be allowed to say that I fully realise the danger to my wife, three children and myself in having to live and sleep in one front room, and it stands to reason that we should not do so if we could get elsewhere. Shortly after Dr. Fox visited us I heard of a house which was likely to become vacant, and my wife saw the owner, explaining that the Medical Officer had ordered us to get other accommodation; but she was told that we could go on to the Common for all that person cared. That is the sort of treatment we get from some of those for whom we fought. I may say that that person has had a house standing vacant for months. I also resent as an insult the remark of the Medical Officer that we should be better off in the Infirmary. Is the Workhouse the fitting home for heroes and their families that we hear so much about? Up to last week I have had the magnificent pension of 12s. 8d. a week, but now our prospects are brighter. We still need a new home, but not in the Workhouse.

W. H. WOOLLEY
(Disabled Ex-Serviceman).

New Street, Pelsall.

Post-war developments

The years following the Second World War saw much urban redevelopment that may have affected your home's surroundings – or even caused it to be built. The Town and Country Planning Act of 1947 dealt with bomb damage, post-war slum clearance, town planning and regulating the way new homes were built.

- Resulting records generated by local authorities will be in your local archives or county record office.
- Much documentation was created too by the Department of Housing and Local Government, whose records are in series HLG at the National Archives. If you think your home may have been affected, consult the National Archives catalogue or the series lists for HLG at the National Archives. In particular, you may find relevant local surveys and development plans in HLG 79 and HLG 119 with further material in HLG 47, 49, 101 and 118, that could also be useful.
- Post-war new towns are well documented in their local archives and HLG 90 and HLG 91 (the records of the New Towns Development Council) and HLG 115 (plans and maps for new towns).

Modern planning permission

Applications for planning permission and approval under the Building Regulations may include plans of properties before and after alteration. Modern planning permission dates from 1947, but files have only had to be retained since 1974, so their survival before that date is very patchy. Copyright on such plans rest with the compiler of the plans, not the house owner.

|| Very few records have been deposited at archives, but many local authorities retain theirs. When authorities have changed their boundaries, or been split, there may be confusion as to where the relevant records are – but it is worth persisting to find out if there are any records for your home.

Post-war renting

|| If your home was rented after the Second World War, it would have been affected by the 1946 Furnished Houses (Rent Control) Act. This generated records of disputes between tenants and landlords that survive for Cornwall, Devon and South Middlesex, in National Archives class HLG 97.

|| The subsequent 1965 Rent Act covered unfurnished property. Selected records of disputes survive in HLG 121 and HLG 122.

Rentcharge apportionments

When a block of rented land was divided, the rent payable was divided between the new holders. Division sometimes took place due to the enclosures (see pages 114–15) but most usually due to random divisions of land or buildings. From 1854 onwards, the division of rent was handled by Parliamentary commissioners.

|| If you suspect your home was split off from a larger unit, you can search for details in the National Archives in MAF 17 (1854–1964) and HLG 61 (1965–7), with certificates in MAF 19 (1854–1965) and HLG 62 (1965–7) and certificates of redemption of rentcharge in MAF 21 (1843–1965) and HLG 63 (1965–7). The records are arranged by district or street and should name the landlords and many of the tenants directly affected.

RIGHT
Labourers working on trenches which will serve as air-raid shelters, on land recently cleared of slums, Wigan, Lancashire, 11 November 1939.

BELOW RIGHT
Bermondsey Borough Council carried out slum clearance and council house and flat building in the 1920s and 30s. Although bleak by modern standards, the facilities provided in local authority housing in the years before the Second World War were significantly in advance of anything provided by private landlords, as shown by this kitchen.

The two world wars

It is impossible – and highly undesirable – to separate the history of your home from that of the people who lived in it. There is no greater case in point than the men (and sometimes women) who left virtually every home in Britain to play their parts in the First and Second World Wars.

|| My book, *Tracing your Family History* (see page 91) provides an outline for tracing the records of all servicemen and women throughout the past.

|| Specific places to look, however, are on local war memorials or on the Commonwealth War

Graves Commission's website **www.cwgc.org**. In both places you may recognise names of people who lived in your home; the latter often includes the parents' names and address.

- There are also several published rolls of honour, such as the *National Roll of the Great War 1914–1918*, and *Ruvigny's Roll*, which includes many photographs of the dead heroes (see also page 91).
- Second World War service records can only be accessed by next-of-kin, but the medal rolls can be searched by anyone at the National Archives and these will give an outline of a Second World War soldier's service.
- Service Records can be searched for First World War soldiers at the National Archives, and indeed for servicemen right back into the 18th century.
- The National Archives also has an excellent set of *Army Lists*, outlining the careers of officers.

TOP
15 August 1914 – a soldier sets off for the war from Nine Elms station.

MIDDLE
Inspecting the damage. Suburban house in south-east London after it had been hit by a bomb in 1940.

BOTTOM
Detail of a map showing the air raids on Birmingham. Every red and blue dot shows where bombs were dropped in the city centre. Forty-nine maps showing bomb damage in Birmingham were commissioned by Birmingham City Council after the Second World War.

Bomb damage and other physical impacts of war

Soldiers' records will have an emotional effect on the home historian, but the war may have had a direct physical impact on your home. Bombing damage to many older properties is still being revealed – coming as a nasty shock to current owners – in building surveys to this day. Bombs also destroyed many homes: Prince Charles famously said that while the Luftwaffe can be blamed for reducing many fine old buildings to rubble, what he termed the ghastly post-war buildings that arose in their place were entirely our own fault.

In areas affected by Second World War bombing it's not hard to find people who have extremely vivid memories of seeing the bombs drop. In Canterbury, I heard some first-hand accounts so vivid that I could really imagine the sound of doodlebugs exploding around me.

- Invaluable local knowledge is sometimes recorded in local history books and on tape in local archives and the Imperial War Museum, Lambeth Road, London SE1 6HZ; tel: 020 7416 5320; **www.iwm.org.uk**. The latter also has an extensive collection of aerial photographs of bomb damage.
- The National Archives has a collection of maps (HO 193) showing where bombs fell, and various categories of Department of Housing and local government records, particularly HLG 79; HLG 7 (details of consequent homelessness and of repairs to damaged properties); HLG 99 (case files) and HLG 112 (appeal files). The War Damage Commission's records are in IR 33-9.
- Some homes were requisitioned by the army or other official bodies. National Archives class WORK 50/23-9 covers requisitioned properties, but only in parts of the Home Counties. HO 101-2 concerns what happened to requisitioned property after the war. Further material can be sought in HO 7, 186-7, 205 and 207, and LT 6-7.

The National Farm Survey (1941-3)

If your home was a farm, or has been built on land used during the Second World War for any form of agriculture - from water meadows to bulb fields - then these records should prove very enlightening.

During the war, German U-boats cut off Britain from many sources of food and fertiliser abroad. Churchill encouraged Britain to 'dig for victory', but his government engaged in more than just rhetoric. The Ministry of Agriculture and Fisheries established County War Agricultural Committees to survey all land in agricultural use, to enforce greater efficiency or even take over badly run farms altogether.

In 1940, a survey was undertaken of all 'farms' in England and Wales - some 300,000 in all - and productivity was rated on a scale from A to C. Only statistics from this survive.

In 1941-3, however, a much more detailed survey was undertaken. All agricultural plots of five acres or more were surveyed. Plans were drawn up of the land and its boundaries. Records were made of conditions of land holding; who owned and occupied the land; the state of the farm; how well it was managed; how many people worked there; the fertility of the soil; what equipment, such as tractors, was being used; what sort of and how many animals lived there; and what food was being produced. The survey even included details of water and electricity supplies, and the numbers of rats scurrying about.

Although theoretically for office use, the maps seem sometimes to have been used in the

A poster encouraging people to grow their own vegetables for the war effort.

Lake Street Manor in Mark Cross, Sussex, is a converted oast-house. Oasthouses were used for drying hops used in the brewing process: the white cap was for ventilation, and was free to revolve to catch the best breezes. Records of the building's history are to be found in those relating to the farm to which it belonged. The National Farm Survey would be a sensible place to start. The two images left and below left show the type of record generated by the survey and a map depicting farmsteads.

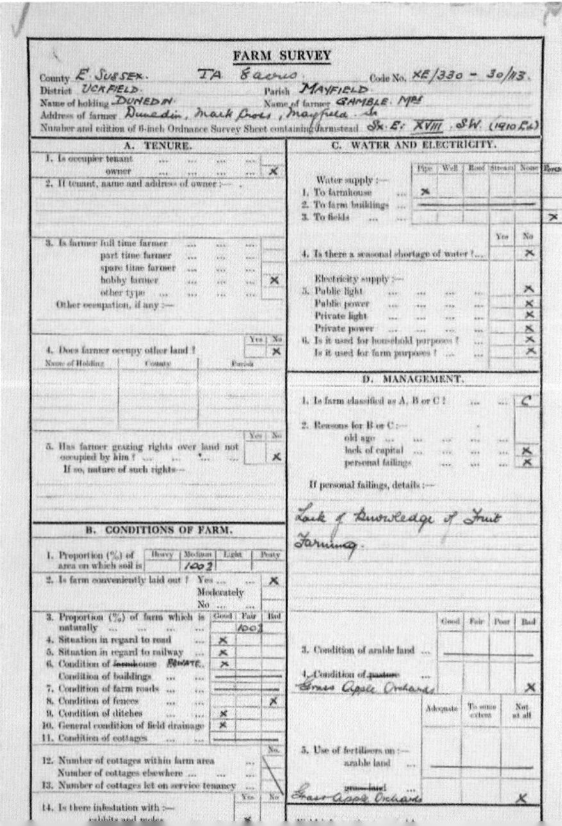

FARM SURVEY

County E. SUSSEX. TA 8 acres Code No. XE/330 – 30/113.
District UCKFIELD. Parish MAYFIELD.
Name of holding DUNEDIN. Name of farmer GAMBLE. Mrs
Address of farmer Dunedin, Mark Cross, Mayfield. Sx
Number and edition of 6-inch Ordnance Survey Sheet containing farmstead Sx. E: XVIII. SW. (1910 Ed)

A. TENURE.

1. Is occupier tenant ... owner ... X
2. If tenant, name and address of owner :—
3. Is farmer full time farmer ... part time farmer ... spare time farmer ... hobby farmer ... X other type ...
Other occupation, if any :—
4. Does farmer occupy other land ? Yes / No X
Name of Holding | County | Parish
5. Has farmer grazing rights over land not occupied by him ? Yes / No X
If so, nature of such rights—

B. CONDITIONS OF FARM.

1. Proportion (%) of area on which soil is — Heavy / Medium 100% / Light / Peaty
2. Is farm conveniently laid out ? Yes ... X Moderately No ...
3. Proportion (%) of farm which is naturally — Good / Fair 100% / Bad
4. Situation in regard to road ... Good X
5. Situation in regard to railway ... Good X
6. Condition of ~~farm~~house PRIVATE ... Good X
Condition of buildings ... —
7. Condition of farm roads ... —
8. Condition of fences ... Bad X
9. Condition of ditches ... Good X
10. General condition of field drainage Good X
11. Condition of cottages ... —
12. Number of cottages within farm area ... Number of cottages elsewhere ...
13. Number of cottages let on service tenancy ...
14. Is there infestation with :— rabbits and moles ... X

C. WATER AND ELECTRICITY.

Water supply :— (Pipe / Well / Roof / Stream / None / Bores)
1. To farmhouse ... Pipe X
2. To farm buildings ... —
3. To fields ... X
4. Is there a seasonal shortage of water ? ... No X
Electricity supply :—
5. Public light ... No X
Public power ... No X
Private light ... No X
Private power ... No X
6. Is it used for household purposes ? ... No X
Is it used for farm purposes ? ... No X

D. MANAGEMENT.

1. Is farm classified as A, B or C ? ... C
2. Reasons for B or C :— old age ... lack of capital ... X personal failings ... X
If personal failings, details :—
Lack of knowledge of Fruit Farming.
3. Condition of arable land ... (Good / Fair / Poor / Bad) —
4. Condition of ~~pasture~~ Grass Apple Orchards ... Bad X
5. Use of fertilisers on :— (Adequate / To some extent / Not at all) arable land ... —
~~grass land~~ Grass Apple Orchards ... Not at all X

field, and thus contain additional pencil notes on such matters as changes in farmers or land use.

Four forms were filled in for each farm, the first three being completed by the farmer on 4 June 1941. These were:

1 Amount and nature of vegetables, fruit, bulbs, flowers, hay and straw.
2 Land use, including acreage, and also the numbers of animals and workers.
3 Rent paid; how many years the farmer had been there; what machinery and working horses there were; additional information on labour used. Because this form asked some rather probing and delicate questions, such as which members of the family were working on the farm, many were not completed.

A fourth form, the Primary Farm Record, was completed by an inspector. The information here repeated or corrected much of the foregoing. This is where you will find out about infestations of mice and other 'pests'; a grade for how well or badly the farm was being run; and comments on the farm or workers, such as 'rather dilatory – spends too much time running about'. One female farmer was criticised for lacking 'the strength of a man'. The forms bear two dates – that of the inspection and when the form was completed in the office.

From these records, which are held at the National Archives (see the box opposite), you may learn much about the nature and state of repair of the farmhouse and its associated buildings.

Irish soldiers and sailors' trust

Various trusts were established to provide affordable homes for servicemen who had survived the First World War. One such was established in 1924 for Irish soldiers and sailors.

|| Records are in the National Archives of

Ireland in AP 1–8, including details and photographs of the houses themselves. Related records are in T 233/145, 146 (sales to tenants); HO 351/199; CAB 27/85; and papers on allocation of houses in Northern Ireland 1921–4 in HO 45/11708.

Building plans

From the mid-19th century onwards, local councils could require builders to submit plans for new developments to them for approval.

- Some plans survive at local councils or with their engineering departments, and many more – especially for built-up areas – are in local archives. The Mitchell Library in Glasgow (201 North Street, Glasgow G3 7DN; tel: 0141 287 2999; **www.glasgow.gov.uk/en/Residents/Leisure_Culture/Libraries/Librarylocations/themitchell.htm**), for example, has plans and warrants for Govan (1870–1912); Hillhead (1873–91); Partick (1873–1912); Pollockshaws (1893–1912) and Pollockshaws East (1880–7).

BOOKS

- **A. Adolph, *Tracing Your Family History* (Collins, 2004)**
- **G. Beech and R. Mitchell, *Maps for Family and Local History* (National Archives, 2004)**
- **A. J. H. Jackson, 'The 1941–1943 National Farm Survey: Investigating the Powderham Estate' (*Devon and Cornwall Notes and Queries*, Spring 2001, XXXVIII, part IX)**
- **R. Mitchell, 'The National Farm Survey' (*Ancestors*, 7, April/May 2002)**
- **Marquis de Ruvigny, *The Roll of Honour: A Biographical Record of Members of His Majesty's Naval and Military Forces who Fell in the Great War 1914–1918* (Standard Art Book Co., 1917, repr. LSE, 1987)**
- ***National Roll of the Great War 1914–1918*, 14 vols (National Publishing Company, 1918–21)**

Where to search

Finding records of your farm at the National Archives

- Start by inspecting the county maps (called 'index' or key sheets') on open access in the Map and Large Document Reading Room (note that maps for London come under Middlesex, and there are separate maps for the Isle of Ely, the Soke of Peterborough and Isle of Wight. Lincolnshire, Suffolk, Sussex and Yorkshire are subdivided).
- Armed with the appropriate grid reference, order the relevant map from MAF 73 using the reference MAF 73/county number (as stamped on the lower right-hand corner of the key sheet)/grid number (the number in the large rectangle containing your home).
- You will receive a number of maps, one of which will contain the right spot. Each farm or other block of agricultural land is coloured distinctively and assigned a farm number. If the farm extended onto other maps, this will be indicated by Ordnance Survey grid references.
- The written records are in MAF 32. You can order the records for the parish by keying its name into the online catalogue at **www.catalogue.nationalarchives.gov.uk** and putting 'MAF 32' in the catalogue's reference field. You will receive a folder of forms covering the parish.
- The four different forms for each farm are arranged by type of form, not by farm, but using the farm number you found on the map you should not have too much trouble finding the right ones.

  Unfortunately, some maps, especially for parts of Co. Durham, Monmouthshire and the Scilly Isles, are missing. In these cases you can still search manually through the forms for the area for your farm. Of course, some urban areas had no agricultural land, so there are no records for them.
- The National Farm Survey for Scotland was more limited in its scope. The National Archives of Scotland hold maps showing farm boundaries in RHP 75001–285.
- A far less detailed survey of farms was conducted during the First World War. You may find some of its records surviving in your local county record office.

CHAPTER 14

The Valuation Office

1909–1920

The great improvements in the country's infrastructure in the late 19th and early 20th centuries caused substantial increases in property values. In 1909, David Lloyd George, Liberal Chancellor of the Exchequer, decided to tax these increases. In order to establish a baseline against which to measure all future growth in land value, his Finance Act (1909–10) sought to establish the rateable value of all properties in the land as it stood on 30 April 1909.

The project, dubbed the 'New' or '20th-century Domesday', was undertaken by the Board of Inland Revenue's Valuation Office. The survey never recouped its cost of £20m and was repealed in 1920. It left, however, a splendid snapshot of the country just before the huge upheaval of the First World War, and a fabulous set of records of homes.

The National Archives series of Valuation Office maps

These are grouped into regions:

London, IR 121
South East, IR 124
Wessex, IR 125
Central, IR 126
East Anglian, IR 127
Western, IR 128
West Midlands, IR 129
East Midlands, IR 130
Wales, IR 131
Liverpool, IR 132
Manchester, IR 133
Yorkshire, IR 134
Northern, IR 135

The records

Each property appears in three records – two maps and a field book.

The maps: Ordnance Survey plans were annotated in ink and coloured washes to show how the land and buildings were divided among individual owners. Your home may stand alone, or you may find it coloured as part of a large block or patchwork of land owned by a single person. Whether it comprised one cottage or a whole estate, each block of ownership was called an hereditament.

The field books: In these, four pages are devoted to each hereditament. From these records you will learn the names of the owners and occupiers. If you find names crossed out and substituted by others, this indicates a change of personnel. Sometimes, the 'owner' will be the estate of a dead person, in which case you can look for their will.

The field books also tell you how the land was held (freehold or leasehold); whether the land was subject to payment of tithes; details of insurance; and who had to pay for repairs. They state the gross value of the property; the value of the site minus buildings; the gross value minus any fixed charges; rights of way, or common rights; and finally the assessable site value – the total value minus work and expenditure by the owner to improve the land.

These records tell you about amenities – for

this was the point of the government's desire to increase its taxes – i.e. whether the property had gas, electricity and running water. Further architectural descriptions – how the building was constructed; how many rooms it had; what the windows were like; and so on – may be included. You may find plans, and the date when the place was built. You can sometimes even learn what general condition your home was in, and how it was furnished. Occasionally, you may find a home under construction. All buildings were included, so if your home used to be something else, such as a factory or church, you can still look it up here.

Using the maps

Finding your home in the maps can be slightly complicated, but entirely worthwhile.

- The first map on which your home will appear is a working map. These were copies of Ordnance Survey maps carried by the surveyors in the field and annotated as they went.
- Each unit of land (the 'hereditament'), which could consist of anything from a vegetable patch to a whole estate, was marked and annotated. These maps, some of which continued to be used by the Inland Revenue until the 1970s, are now largely deposited in county record offices.
- The second maps, the official Record Sheet Plans, were compiled from the foregoing working maps. They are at the National Archives (see box opposite). On the maps, each hereditament was marked by coloured washes and numbered in red. If you find yourself examining a map on which the property you want is not numbered, you will probably find there is a larger-scale map available, on which the number does appear. Detached parts of hereditaments were denoted 'Part or Pt [of hereditament number]'. The whole country was divided into Income Tax Parishes: their boundaries are usually shown on the maps in yellow ink with their names written in the margins.

A Valuation Office map, c. 1910 for northeast Peterborough.

The maps are arranged into valuation districts within the regions, each covered by separate sub districts. In these, the maps are arranged by county, then by scale, and finally by Ordnance Survey sheet number. The Valuation Office used the largest-scale maps available wherever possible, especially in towns. You may therefore find there are a couple of maps of different scales covering your home. More additional detail will usually be on the larger-scale one.

How to find the relevant map

If you already know the hereditament number of your home, you can look in the relevant field book (see right), which will provide the Ordnance Survey sheet number. Usually, however, you will need to start from scratch by finding this sheet number from the key maps available in the Map and Large Document Reading Room at the National Archives. The map reference will be a Roman numeral followed by an Arabic number, e.g. 'VII, 5'.

To locate the National Archives document reference for the map, you need to perform a two-stage search, using the online catalogue, **www.catalogue.nationalarchives.gov.uk**, available in the search room.

- Enter the county where your home is situated, the date 1910 and the series 'IR' in the relevant fields. This will give a list of Board of Inland Revenue record sheet plans for the county, with a series of reference numbers. If you keyed in Yorkshire, for example, the reference numbers will start IR 135/.
- Then perform a second search. Use the reference IR again, but this time in the search field type in the Ordnance Survey sheet reference for the map you want, leaving the date blank. This will also produce a list of results and reference numbers. Only one of these, however, will correspond to one of the reference numbers from the previous search. That is the one you want: you can now order your map.

BOOKS

- **N. W. Alcock, *Documenting the History of Houses* (British Records Association, 2003)**
- **G. Beech, 'The 20th-century Domesday Book' (*Ancestors*, February 2005, p. 36)**
- **G. Beech and R. Mitchell, *Maps for Family and Local History* (National Archives, 2004)**

Field books

Armed with the hereditament number obtained from the map, you can now seek your home in the relevant field book. These are in series IR 58. They are arranged alphabetically by valuation district. A list of these is available at the National Archives and also in Beech and Mitchell's book (see below).

- The field books are arranged by Income Tax Parish. These did not always correspond to normal parishes. You may already have found the name of the Income Tax Parish for your home written on the map. If not, look up the regular parish in the *Board of Inland Revenue's Alphabetical List of Parishes and Places in England and Wales* in the Map and Large Document Reading Room.
- Once you know the name of the Income Tax Parish, you can look it up in the online catalogue, **www.catalogue.nationalarchives.gov.uk**, keying in IR 58 as the series number, and order your field book.

Less detailed but still interesting – and useful if the field book has not survived – are the valuation books. These were compiled by sending out forms at the beginning of the Inland Revenue's survey. Those for towns and cities can help by having detailed street and house name indexes. Where they survive they are in county record offices, but those for the City of London and Westsminster are at the National Archives, in IR 91.

These records were very accurate, largely because there was a £50 fine – some £3,000 today – for anyone who failed to return their forms.

Omissions

There are some gaps in the records, for most Crown land and also Basildon; Birkenhead; Chelmsford; Coventry; the Isle of Wight; Liverpool; Portsmouth; Southampton; Winchester, and most of the Wirral and Chichester. However, if what you want is not at the National Archives, check for surviving copies at your county record office.

- If a field book ran out of space, information was continued on sheets called 'Form 4'. Sadly, most have been thrown away, save those for admiralty property (in ADM 116/1279), Forestry Commission land (in F 6/16) and land owned by the Rhymney Railway Company (in RAIL 1057/1714).
- Some Form 4 sheets for individual estates, however, turn up in archives and may be found through **www.a2a.org.uk**. Alcock (see box opposite) points out that the Form 4 sheets for the London estate of the Pell family, for example, are in Cambridge University Library, **www.lib.cam.ac.uk**.

Other countries

The '20th-century Domesday' covered the whole British Isles.

- Those for Scotland are at the National Archives of Scotland in IRS 51–88 (field books) and IRS 101–133 (maps), covering the period 1909–15. They contain many fascinating descriptions of buildings; sadly, the extended descriptions in 'supplementary books' appear to have been destroyed.
- The corresponding records for Northern Ireland are at PRONI and those for the Republic of Ireland are in the National Archives in Dublin, where they are currently being catalogued.

This field book page (1910–15) show the entry for the Temperance Hall at Merthyr Tydfil.

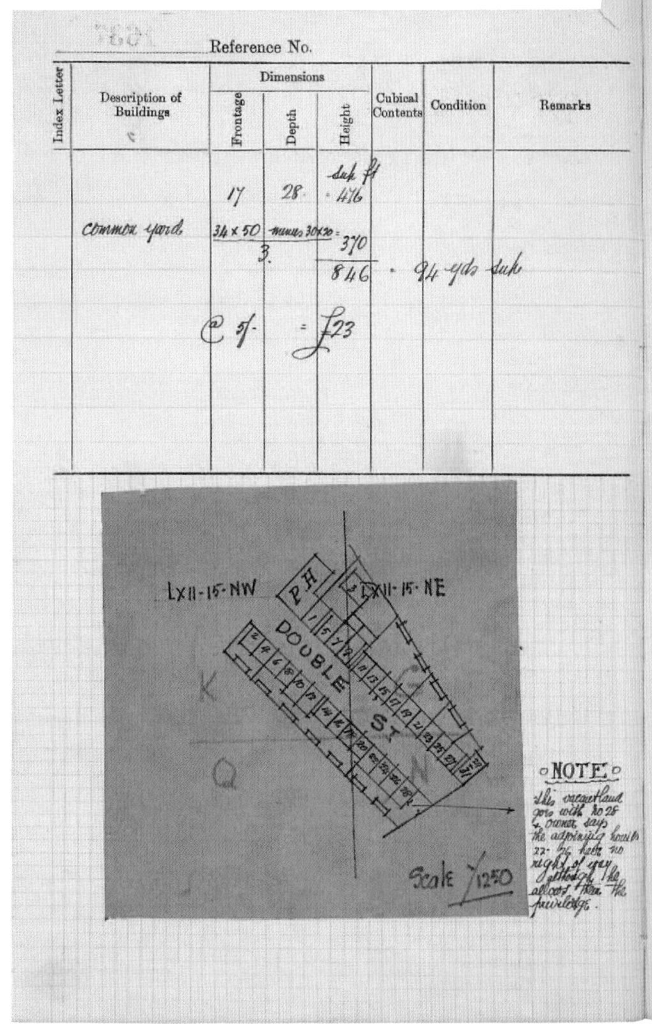

Reference No.

Index Letter	Description of Buildings	Dimensions: Frontage	Depth	Height	Cubical Contents	Condition	Remarks
		17	28	sup ft 476			
	common yard	34 x 50 minus 30x30 = 370					
				846	94 yds sup		
		@ 5/-		= £23			

This field book entry, for a house in Lambeth, is dated 1910.

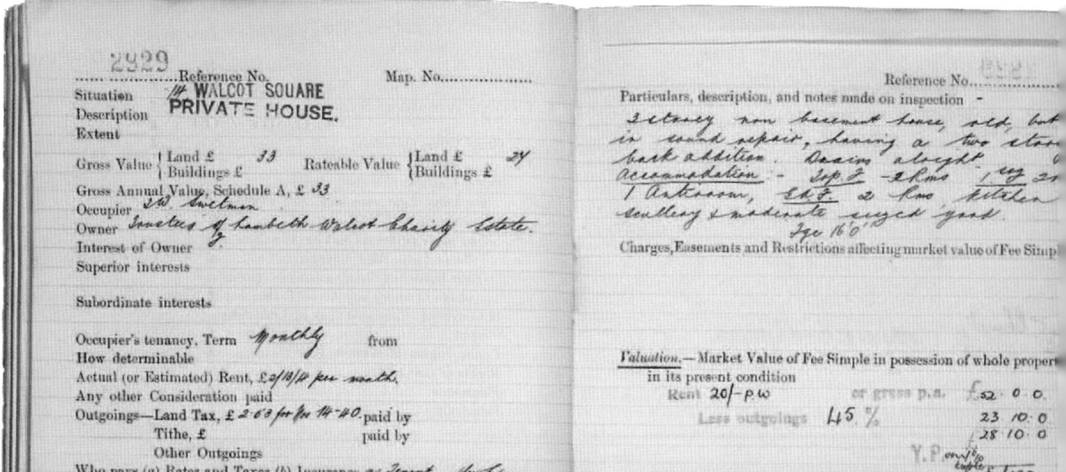

2929 Reference No. Map. No.

Situation 14 WALCOT SQUARE

Description PRIVATE HOUSE.

Extent

Gross Value { Land £ 33 / Buildings £ } Rateable Value { Land £ 24 / Buildings £ }

Gross Annual Value, Schedule A, £ 33

Occupier

Owner Trustees of Lambeth Walcot Charity Estate.

Interest of Owner

Superior interests

Subordinate interests

Occupier's tenancy. Term Monthly from

How determinable

Actual (or Estimated) Rent, £2/18/4 per month.

Any other Consideration paid

Outgoings—Land Tax, £ 2·6·3 paid by

Tithe, £ paid by

Other Outgoings

Who pays (a) Rates and Taxes (b) Insurance

Reference No.

Particulars, description, and notes made on inspection -

3 storey non basement house, old, but in sound repair, having a two storey back addition. Drains alright.
Accommodation - Top F - 2 Rms 1st F 2 ... 1 Bathroom, Gd F. 2 Rms kitchen scullery & moderate sized yard.

Charges, Easements and Restrictions affecting market value of Fee Simple

Valuation.—Market Value of Fee Simple in possession of whole property in its present condition

Rent 20/- p.w. or gross p.a. £52 0 0

Less outgoings 45 % 23 10 0

28 10 0

Y.P. £400

CHAPTER 15

19th-century developments

The 19th century saw huge developments in transport, amenities and social housing. These great innovations generated vast numbers of records that are often relevant, one way or another, to the histories of our homes.

Railways

Although mainly a 19th-century development, railways have actually existed from the mid-17th century as waggonways and plateways, whereby carriages were pulled along sets of rails by horses. These usually covered very short distances in industrial areas, such as coalmines. The first 'long-distance' railway line of this sort ran between Middleton and Leeds from 1758. Steam locomotives were developed at the start of the 19th century and the first railway line for steam trains was built in 1812.

Railways had a vast impact on the country. Country stations led to the growth of new villages and the decline of established ones that were not on railway lines. The routes they followed out of towns in turn stimulated the growth of new suburbs.

As it was easier to coerce the poor than the rich into making way for new lines running into towns, railways tended to plough through

Railway construction, c. 1840. Railways have had a massive impact on our landscape, especially by encouraging the growth of suburbs and commuter towns.

poorer urban districts. This is why, as Paul Hindle points out in *Roads and Tracks for Historians* (see page 105), none of the London terminals of the northern railways come within one and a half miles of Charing Cross. Cutting through the remaining areas would have been vigorously opposed by the upper-class interest in Parliament, and would have been prohibitively expensive.

Until their post-war nationalisation, the railways were run by a plethora of small companies. Local directories and local histories should tell you which operated in your area - there may have been several. The companies amalgamated into the 'big four' - London, Midland and Scottish Railway Company (1923–47); London and North Eastern Railway Company (1923–47); Great Western Railway Company (1835–1947); and the Southern Railway Company (1923–47).

Railway company records include detailed maps not just of railway lines, but also of the great deal of property they owned, including stations and warehouses - at that stage most goods were transported by train. From 1853, railway companies had to produce detailed 'demolition statements' with associated large-scale plans for any projects that involved knocking down more than 30 houses in any one parish. Unless the plans were cancelled, such homes will obviously no longer be there, but if your home stands near a railway line, it may be shown as one of those that weren't destroyed.

Home on the rails

Your home may even be a converted railway station. When Horsebridge Station, near Romsey, Hampshire, was sold recently, the *Telegraph* described it as 'a three-bedroom, converted railway station with further accommodation in separate parcel office, signal box and [railway] carriage ... unusual extras including original lamp and cycle sheds ... would suit stranded commuters who feel most at home waiting for a train to arrive'.

Another converted station, Old Droxford Station House, Soberton, was advertised with an extraordinary piece of history attached to it: on 2 June 1944, Winston Churchill and his War Cabinet arrived there, boarded a train and were steamed away to a siding near a tunnel, to protect them from bombing in the days leading up to the D-Day landings.

How to find railway records

- Private acts of Parliament concerned with railways are at the House of Lords Record Office, Palace of Westminster, London SW1A 0PW; tel: 020 7219 3074; **www.parliament.uk**. Although many were produced earlier, Parliament first required maps of proposed railway developments to be submitted in 1837. The resulting plans are in the House of Lords Record Office with copies, called 'deposited plans', in Quarter Session records and now to be found at county record offices.
- Further records relating to railway building are in the British Transport section in the National Archives. Specifically, you can search in RAIL 1029–37 and 1071 (maps and plans with private acts of Parliament for railway building) and MT 54.

RAIL 1062–79, 1014–19, 1038–60 and 1147–57 contain much concerning the impact of railways on existing buildings and the creation of new ones.

Associated photographs are in AN 14 and 31 and RAIL 1057 and 1157. You can also key the name of the relevant railway company into the online catalogue, **www.catalogue.nationalarchives.gov.uk**, and see what appears.

Amenities: water, sewers, gas and electricity

The creation and extension of sewers, underground drains, gas and electricity supply lines, all generated maps, and are mainly to be found in local archives. Once the Ordnance Survey town plans had been created (see page 63), they were generally used as the basis of such amenity maps, but before then special surveys were sometimes undertaken. An amusing optional addition to the sewerage plans created for public inspection, noted by Paul Hindle in *Maps for Historians* (see page 105), was the labelling of 'those places where noxious vapours are emitted'!

Water supplies: Until comparatively recently, streams, springs and wells provided people's water. If there was not a well in your garden, you walked to the nearest one with a bucket, or paid a water-carrier to deliver some.

Some towns have had piped water for a very long time, starting with Southampton, whose pipe network originated in 1420, followed by Hull 27 years later. Most water pipelines, however, date from the 19th century. Pipes were installed by combinations of local authority and private ventures, often established by acts of Parliament. These projects became particularly widespread after the realisation in the 1840s that epidemic diseases and plain bad health were in many cases due to contaminated water supplies.

Under the Public Health Act of 1848, sewerage and drainage became the responsibility of new local Boards of Health, who also generated their own local maps, some usefully pre-dating

Detail of the plans of the sewers for Canterbury in the 19th century.

Loo clues

Applications to connect new homes to the sewers can help date buildings. The house in Evering Road, Stoke Newington, where I wrote this book, is part of a Victorian street that was clearly all developed at once. In the Hackney Archives street card index I found an application made by the developer of Evering Road to the Metropolitan Board of Works. He was asking for permission to build sewers for the road and connect them to the general London system, the application dated 1874 (ref: cxxxviii, vol. 595) - thus accurately dating the street's construction.

the first town plans of the Ordnance Survey. It was the Public Health (Water) Act of 1878 which insisted that new houses in rural areas must be built near a good water supply.

After 1855, records were kept when houses were connected to London's rapidly expanding system of drainage pipes. Some local authorities keep these records as working documents, while others have deposited theirs in local archives. Arranged annually by street, they can be quite detailed, including the applicant's name, whether they were the owner or builder, and details of the pipes needed to connect the property to the drainage system. Sometimes, you may also find architectural plans and even architectural elevations of the building. Records will also include subsequent changes, such as if the building was divided into flats.

If you cannot find any records of drainage, a useful substitute are Local Authority Minutes, usually to be found at local archives, which are mostly bound and indexed and date from the 1890s onwards.

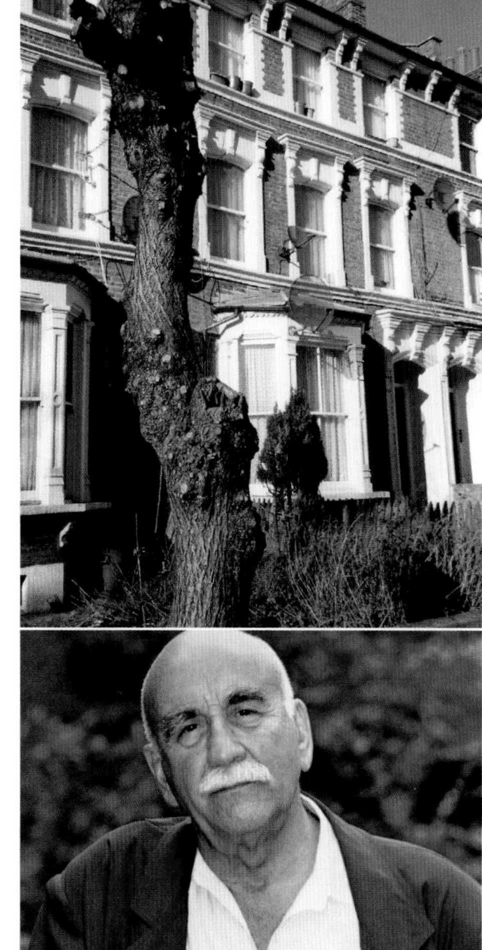

Evering Road, Stoke Newington – a typical late-Victorian terrace. Number 149 was the birthplace of actor Warren Mitchell, best known for his portrayal of the xenophobic Alf Garnett. In real life, Warren's family, the Misels, were Jewish immigrants from Eastern Europe.

Gas supplies: These date back to the formation of the Chartered Gas Light and Coke Co., in 1812. It supplied gas to light homes in Westminster, the City of London and Southwark. By 1815, some 4,000 gaslights twinkled all over London, growing to an enormous 51,000 four years later. Demand burgeoned, both in London and all over Britain. By 1819, people from Glasgow to Exeter stayed up reading by gaslight.

|| Richardson's encyclopaedia (see page 105) provides dates for the formation of gas companies all over Britain. Many date from the mid-19th century, though the majority were focused on towns, not the countryside.

Electric lighting: This started to be introduced by private companies from the late 1870s but from the Electric Lighting Act of 1882 it was generally in the hands of local authorities.

|| Local directories, local newspapers and authority archives should enable you to chart this in your area.

Social maps

The growing concern of the Victorian upper class for the health and welfare of the poor generated a number of very interesting and often relevant records for home historians.

These records often took the form of 'social maps', produced to study and try to explain

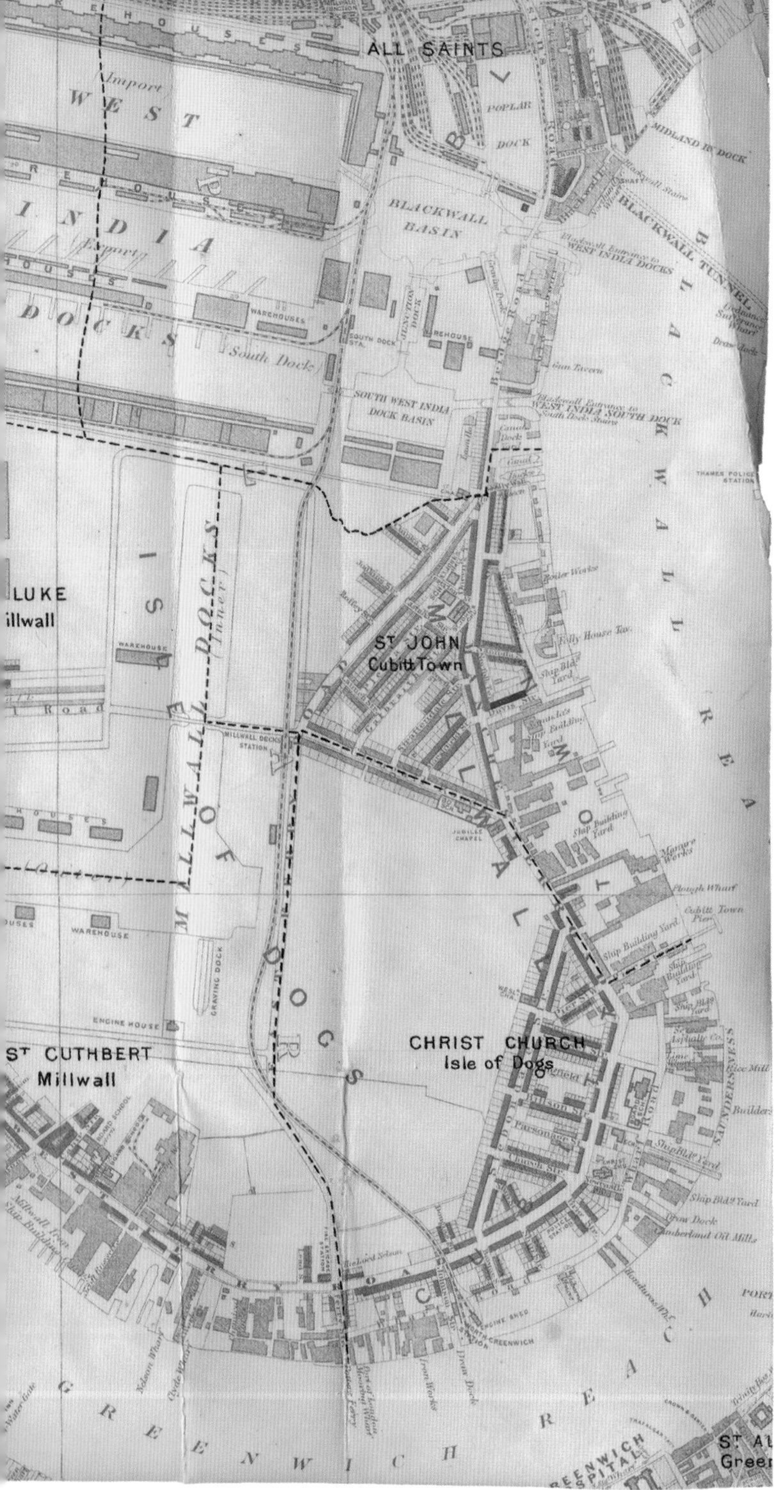

One of Booth's maps of London.

social issues. You can use these not only to find out some surprisingly graphic details about your area at the time, but you may even learn about the general health, economic and social status of the inhabitants of your home at a fixed point in the past.

The first maps of this sort plotted deaths caused by the flu and cholera epidemics of the 1830s, 40s and 50s. Charles Fowler's map of Leeds (1833) is a good example, as is Dr John Snow's 1855 map of London's Soho, which successfully linked the spread of the epidemic to the whereabouts of water pumps.

In 1857, Henry Mayhew used criminal statistics to produce crude maps of London showing the distribution of crimes such as rape, bigamy, prostitution, abduction and back-street abortion. In 1858, Rev. Abraham Hume used maps to study the distribution of poverty and crime – and their relationship to one another – in Liverpool. Hume carefully studied the city, identifying the 'pauper streets', 'semi-pauper streets' and 'streets of crime and immorality'. From 1859, the National Temperance League started producing 'drink maps', showing the whereabouts of pubs in towns such as Oxford, York and King's Lynn. At that stage, many pubs were run out of the front rooms of people's houses. The aim was to alarm the public by showing how many drinking dens there were – but presumably many people fancying a tipple in a strange town would have found them quite useful as well.

A major social study of London was launched in 1886 by Charles Booth, a prominent social reformer, and several of his friends. These included Octavia Hill, a pioneer of social housing (and a co-founder of the National Trust), and the children's writer Beatrice Potter. A keen promoter of social welfare, Miss Potter recorded in her diary for 17 April 1886, 'Object of the Committee: to get a fair picture of the whole of London Society, the four millions! By district and by employment.'

After 17 years' exhausting work, Booth's *Life and Labour of the People in London* was published in 1903. With it were 12 'Maps Descriptive of London Poverty'. Every street of the metropolis was colour-coded from black to yellow, ranging from the 'lowest class, vicious, semi-criminal' and 'very poor, casual. Chronic want' right up to 'Upper-middle and Upper classes. Wealthy'.

The main data for the maps was supplied by the School Board visitors. They noted street numbers; rent; the occupations of the adults; how many children they had; and the number of rooms occupied by each family – several poor families often shared even the smallest house. To save time, however, details of only one house in each street were used when deciding how to colour it on the map. The maps were later revised as a result of walks made by committee members who joined Metropolitan policemen on their beats. The accompanying notebooks contain a wealth of information on the areas covered.

For Rupert Place, Mayfair, for example, we have this entry, describing both the building and its occupants:

No. 18. A high house with railings in front. In the kitchens lives Verney, a market porter of fifty. His wife does mangling. They have three children, one of whom, a young woman, goes to work, and a boy has just begun to go.

On the ground floor, in one room, there is Mrs. Watson, a widow with one daughter, who goes to work and earns 8s a week by gilding the edges of picture mounts. She is a cripple and humpbacked.

In the back room another widow, Mrs. Casson, lives with two grown-up daughters who go to work. She has some sons; one, a soldier, comes home sometimes. Mrs. Casson dresses well and is probably comfortably off. She is not very friendly to the visitor.

On the first floor there is a young man called Bernard, a leather dresser, whose wife is a daughter of Mrs. Watson, and does the same work as her unmarried sister. The Bernards have a little girl which the grandmother minds, being paid 2s 6d a week for this.

On the top floor in front live Quaritch and his wife and two children, one an infant. The man, age thirty-four, is a costermonger. His wife used also to go out, and they would attend race meetings, &c., and earn about 9s a day. Now she has regular work at a laundry.

The surveys concern the wider landscape too. Writing about them in *Ancestors* magazine (see page 105), Sue Donnelly quotes Sergeant Hearns in Hammersmith:

The Uxbridge Road once west of the station, there is a feeling of being out of London, though London does not technically end before the Askew Road is reached. Tramlines begin here. The houses fronting

Old Cottages, Wood Lane, London, c.1889. These cottages stood in a turning near the Shepherds Bush end of Wood Lane. A drawing appeared in the *West London Sketcher*, 16 July 1889, suggesting that they were ripe for improvement. Wood Lane is now famous as the home of the BBC.

on the road are still irregular, some standing back in their own grounds, others mere cottages and poor. Others, new shops built on what were formerly the gardens of homes. The neighbourhood is filling up very quickly.

When I battle through the crowds and traffic to see the publishers of this book in Hammersmith, I think of this quote with a wry smile!

A further survey, *The New Survey of London Life and Labour* (LSE, 1930), was made in 1928. Its maps included a revised colour-coding system, as follows:

- Black: 'the lowest class of degraded or semi-criminal population'.
- Blue: 'making a living below Charles Booth's poverty line'.
- Purple: 'the mass of unskilled labourers (and other of similar incomes) who are above the poverty line'.
- Pink: 'the skilled workers and others of similar grades of income'.
- Red: 'the "Middle Class" and wealthy'.

The project included a survey of 12,000 working-class families in London. Each was recorded in terms of the number of people in the house; number of rooms; rent; occupations; how much it cost people to get to work; and other interesting details. One house in Stepney, for example, is described thus: 'front room used as small bird shop. Sell linnets & bird seed. Open only evenings & Saturday afternoons. Says earns about 2/6 per week from it,'

|| Copies of the published maps and surveys are in local archives and libraries. The original records are at the London School of Economics, Archives and Rare Books Department, 10 Portugal Street, London

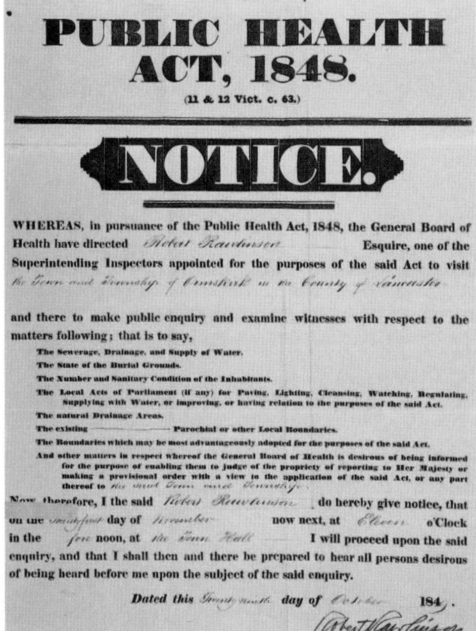

PUBLIC HEALTH ACT, 1848.

(11 & 12 Vict. c. 63.)

NOTICE.

WHEREAS, in pursuance of the Public Health Act, 1848, the General Board of Health have directed Robert Rawlinson Esquire, one of the Superintending Inspectors appointed for the purposes of the said Act to visit the Town and Township of Ormskirk in the County of Lancaster

and there to make public enquiry and examine witnesses with respect to the matters following; that is to say,

The Sewerage, Drainage, and Supply of Water.

The State of the Burial Grounds.

The Number and Sanitary Condition of the Inhabitants.

The Local Acts of Parliament (if any) for Paving, Lighting, Cleansing, Watching, Regulating, Supplying with Water, or improving, or having relation to the purposes of the said Act.

The natural Drainage Areas.

The existing ———— Parochial or other Local Boundaries.

The Boundaries which may be most advantageously adopted for the purposes of the said Act.

And other matters in respect whereof the General Board of Health is desirous of being informed for the purpose of enabling them to judge of the propriety of reporting to Her Majesty or making a provisional order with a view to the application of the said Act, or any part thereof to the said Town and Township.

Now therefore, I the said Robert Rawlinson do hereby give notice, that on the twenty-first day of November now next, at Eleven o'Clock in the fore noon, at the Town Hall I will proceed upon the said enquiry, and that I shall then and there be prepared to hear all persons desirous of being heard before me upon the subject of the said enquiry.

Dated this Twenty-ninth *day of* October 184 .

Robert Rawlinson

Poster showing the details of the Public Health Act, 1848.

Stuffing mattresses in an East End slum, late 19th century.

Denniestown

The development of housing around factories was often a matter of direct concern to industrialists. Background to the houses can be sought in material, such as newspaper obituaries and references in biographical dictionaries, of the founders. One such industrialist was Peter Denny (1821–95), owner and leading light of the Denny Shipyard in Dumbarton. He and his brothers founded a small shipyard just at the time when iron- and steel-framed ships were coming to the fore. Peter was a great planner and innovator, and turned the yard into one of the greatest in the world, even having a hand in the building of the famous *Cutty Sark*.

Due to his success, Dumbarton grew from a small burgh on the banks of the Clyde to a bustling conurbation. Families migrated there from all over Scotland to seek work, and housing was at a premium. Consequently, Peter Denny and his brother William planned an entirely new suburb, Denniestown. Peter's obituary in the *North British Daily Mail* for 23 August 1895 tells us that he laid the foundation stone 'with suitable Masonic honours' on 20 May 1853, and that the development cost almost £3,300. Peter also made money available for his employees to build their own houses, with easy methods for repayment, again encouraging the area's growth.

The slums of London, engraving by Gustave Doré, published in 1872. Doré chronicled all aspects of London's buildings and their occupants, rich and poor alike. Here, we see the dwellings of the poor crammed below towering arched bridges as new steam trains pound along overhead.

WC2A 2HD; tel: 020 7995 7223; documents @lse.ac.uk.

- They are also searchable via the Charles Booth Online Archive at **www.lse.ac.uk/booth**. Among the exciting features of this excellent site is the facility to search by modern postcode and compare the maps with modern ones.

Other surveys were undertaken of cities, but sadly only the published results, not the original notes, survive. Starting in 1888, Frank Banfield created maps to identify the large estates of private landlords in London. Other notable social studies are Bowley and Bennett-Hurst's work in Northampton, Warrington, Stanley and Reading, and Seebohm Rowntree's surveys of York (see box opposite).

Wherever such surveys and maps survive, there is a lot you can learn from them about your home and its inhabitants in the context of previously very different social conditions.

Records of housing the poor

Concern over the housing of the poor, before and after Booth and his colleagues, led to much government effort to address the problems.

- Early housing policy records can be found in the National Archives in the Poor Law Commission papers (MH files 1, 12 and 15), with plans of buildings and land used for the poor by local authorities in MH 14, HLG 6 and MH 48.
- In 1843, a Royal Commission on the Health of Towns and Populous Places was established as a direct response to the perceived spread of diseases. Their records are in MH 13 and HLG 1 and 46. These are more useful as background material, though, than sources for specific detail on your home.

In 1871, the Local Government Board succeeded the local Poor Law Commission in responsibility for local housing issues, especially slum clearance. Its Sanitary Board was responsible for housing until 1910, when it was superseded by the Board's Town Planning Department. Responsibility for housing was transferred to the Ministry of Health after the First World War.

In 1875, Disraeli's Artisans and Labourer's Dwellings Act empowered local authorities to make compulsory purchases of slums. Wide powers in this field were granted to the Ministry of Health's Housing Department too.

- Much material generated by these bodies, including maps and plans, is at the National Archives, especially in HLG 4, 5, 13, 23, 26, 41, 44, 47, 49, 95, 96, 111 and 118.
- Many plans for re-housing people displaced by public works (including railways, road building and so on) are in HLG 24. Much slum clearance stems from this time.
- Subsequent developments in public housing for London are covered by Cox's guide (see also box opposite).

The Chartist Lands Purchase Scheme (1845–51)

In 1845, the great reformer and Chartist Feargus O'Connor organised a Utopian scheme, finally entitled the National Land Company, to enable workers to buy their own land and homes – and thus to give them the property entitlement then required to allow them to vote (see page 71). The scheme encouraged workers to buy small shares. The resulting money was used to buy land, which was then allocated to some lucky shareholders by ballot.

The first land purchased was at Heronsgate near Rickmansworth, Hertfordshire. Further land was acquired at Lowbands and Snig's End, Gloucestershire; near Minister Lovell, Oxfordshire; Dodford in Worcestershire; and Mathon in Herefordshire, although the latter was never developed.

The scheme was not very practical – most winners had no idea how to manage land, and due to this, and some very bad financial management, the scheme was wound up in 1851.

- Surviving records are at the National Archives in BT 41.

Workers' houses

The Industrial Revolution created a great demand for a high concentration of workers in areas with little pre-existing housing. Industrialists were thus obliged to create new suburbs, or even whole new towns, for their employees.

- Archives of the firms may contain records to do with this.
- Records of housing schemes run by nationalised industries are at the National Archives, particularly those of the Coal Board, in COAL 48 and 66, while Ministry of Housing files (HLG 40) relate to housing and tied housing built by other firms.

Engraving of Feargus O'Connor.

BOOKS

- **C. Booth, *Life and Labour of the People in London* (MacMillan and Co., 1903)**
- **A. L. Bowley and A. R. Bennett-Hurst, *Livelihood and Poverty: A Study in the Economic Conditions of Working-class Households in Northampton, Warrington, Stanley and Reading* (G. Bell and Sons Ltd, 1915)**
- **K. Chater, 'A Charter for Disillusion' (*Ancestors*, February 2005, pp 25–7)**
- **A. Cox, *Public Housing: A London Archives Guide* (Guildhall Library and the London Archive Users' Forum, 1993)**
- **S. Donnelly, 'Mapping London's Rich and Poor' (*Ancestors*, August/September 2003, pp 45–50)**
- **S. Donnelly, 'Mapping the Working Class' (*Ancestors*, October 2004, pp 40–6)**
- **P. Hindle, *Maps for Historians* (Phillimore, 2002)**
- **P. Hindle, *Roads and Tracks for Historians* (Phillimore, 2001)**
- **J. Richardson, *The Local Historian's Encyclopaedia* (Phillimore, 2003)**
- **B. Seebohm Rowntree, *Poverty and Progress: A Second Social Survey of York* (Longmans, Green and Co., 1941)**
- **B. Seebohm Rowntree, *Poverty and the Welfare State: A Third Social Survey of York Dealing only with Economic Questions* (Longmans, Green and Co., 1951)**
- ***The New Survey of London Life and Labour* (LSE, 1930)**

CHAPTER 16

Tithe apportionments and other 19th-century land records

c.1836–56

Tithe apportionments can provide both maps and written records of your home in the early-mid-19th century. The payment of a tenth of all agricultural produce to the Church was a fixed event by the 9th century, and continued pretty much unaltered for the next thousand years. By the 19th century it had accrued a vast number of anachronisms, not least because relatively few people actually worshipped in the Church of England, and manufactured goods were not tithable.

Initially, people actually handed over a tenth of all their mangelwurzels, or whatever else they had succeeded in growing, to the local priest. The 18th-century enclosures (see pages 14–17) changed or 'commuted' payment in kind to a tenth of the produce's monetary value instead. Land that had been owned by monasteries was usually tithe-free, and remained so after the dissolution of the monasteries. In many towns and cities, where there was usually no agricultural production, most tithes had long since been commuted. Yet in some cases, the Church's fiscal claws remained dug into even domestic gardens. In the early 19th century, many parishioners, mainly in the country but some in built-up areas too, were still burdened with having to sort through their plums and gooseberries to work out how many were due to the vicar. Note that areas that were then extra-parochial (those outside the jurisdiction of the adjoining civil or ecclesiastical parish) usually paid neither poor or church rates, nor tithes.

In 1836, Parliament passed the Tithe Commutation Act, which set up a commission to translate all remaining payments in kind into an agreed cash payment, basing its assessments on a seven-year average of the price of oats, wheat and barley. After local negotiations, the Tithe Commission produced a document called a Tithe Agreement (or a Tithe Award, if they had to enforce their decision), resulting in a tithe apportionment that fixed the amount due to be paid by the owner of each piece of land liable for tithes. The records are arranged by owners, but they still shed considerable light on the homes concerned.

The records consist of maps showing the properties liable to pay tithes, and apportionment schedules showing the landowners' liabilities. While most parishes that had been enclosed had already had their tithes commuted, some had not, so in moderately rare cases you will find tithe records for an enclosed parish. Some counties, like Sussex, have tithe maps for virtually every parish, regardless of its enclosure status. Wales and the south west, too, are almost completely covered.

The payment of monetary tithes continued until 1936, when the Tithe Act drew a line under the system. Payments called 'redemption annuities' were agreed, to run for 60 years, but in 1977, an abrupt termination came about to this ancient system of tithes.

How to find tithe apportionments

- The Tithe Commissions' records and maps are in the National Archives in IR 29 and IR 30 respectively, with copies in county record offices. Both collections contain gaps: if the record you want is not in the record office, try the National Archives, and vice versa.
- Most record office catalogues will lead you to their tithe records. Those for Kent have been computerised and can be inspected on CD-Rom at the record offices at Maidstone and Canterbury. Those in the National Library of Wales are described in Davies' book (see page 111).
- You can find the references to the maps and apportionment documents you want at the National Archives, using the online catalogue, **www.catalogue.nationalarchives.gov.uk**. Type the name of the tithe district into the search field, leave the dates blank and key 'IR 29' or 'IR 30' into the department code's field (if what you want does not appear at once, and the parish name consists of more than one word, try just entering the main one, e.g. Neots instead of St Neots).
- Usually, the tithe district was the same as the parish. Sometimes, however, your home may come under a tithe district that was not the immediate parish. This will usually be indicated by the online search. If not, you can consult the paper series list of tithe districts at the National Archives.
- Kain and Oliver's book (see also page 111) provides a complete catalogue of surviving maps, giving the date of the apportionment, when known, and stating whether maps cover whole parishes or just the tithable parts of them. It also provides the National Archives reference number.
- Maps for the counties in alphabetical order, up to and including Middlesex, are available on microfiche open access in the Map and Large Document Reading Room. Those after Middlesex need to be ordered (and take three working days to arrive).
- Some original maps are in very poor condition. If you cannot use the one you have been given, there may be a substitute, especially for Essex, Kent, Middlesex and Surrey, in IR 77 – these too are noted in Kain and Oliver.
- The apportionment records are on microfilm in the Map and Large Document Reading Room.
- On the maps, each piece of tithable land is assigned a plot number. You can look this up in the key at the start of the parish apportionment, which will tell you the page on which it appears. A shortcut to finding people in the records is by using the summary of the schedule at the end.

The vicar of a parish receiving tithes from a woman and a small boy, 1793.

The most frequently encountered abbreviations on appointment schedules:

AA (altered apportionment) Attached to the original ones.

CR (compulsory redemption) Generated by the 1836 Act, a few records relating to this are in IR 900.

CRA (corn rent annuity) These were usually created by enclosures. Certificates of redemption are in IR 108; some records relating to the rents are in IR 900. Altered apportionments of these are in IR 107.

KA (voluntary redemption of tithe redemption annuities) See IR 94, though the redeemers' names are not given.

M (declarations of merger) See TITH 3, especially found when the landowner was also the recipient of the tithes.

OA (order for apportionment of the tithe redemption annuity) Orders for this are in IR 94; maps are either with them or in IR 90.

R (redemption of tithe rentcharge by a one-off payment) Certificates are in IR 90 but names are not stated.

RA (redemption of tithe rentcharge by setting up an annuity) Certificates are in IR 102 but again names are not stated.

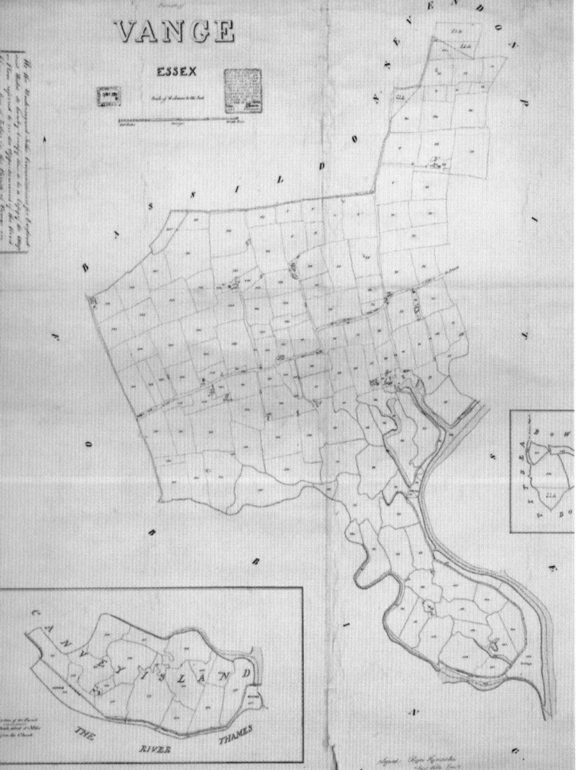

Tithe map of Vange, Essex. 1831–51.

Some record offices have made searching even easier. Essex Record Office, for example, has transcribed many of its apportionments into plot-number order for many of the parishes covered by its collection.

Tithe maps

Despite attempts to impose uniformity, the tithe maps for each parish were drawn up on an ad hoc basis, to different scales and standards, over a 20-year period. Beech and Mitchell (see page 111) state that some Welsh maps were simply surveyed from the top of the nearest mountain, with the effect that the closest fields were shown being bigger than those further away.

The maps are detailed enough to show individual buildings. Sometimes, you will find domestic houses coloured red, and public ones like churches and pubs painted grey. Each tithable plot was numbered.

Later changes and amendments were usually noted on the maps now in the record offices, but they were not marked on the National Archives' set.

Tithe apportionment schedules

These were completed much more quickly than the maps, mostly by the 1840s. Some, it must be said, took decades longer to be agreed – the last was Hemingstone, Suffolk, where arguments over who should pay what dragged on until 1883!

The apportionment schedules will tell you the names of the landowner and occupier; name and description of the land and buildings; state of cultivation – whether the land grew grass, arable and so on; the 'quantities in statute measure' – the acreage, both tithable and non-tithable (non-tithable land included commons and land owned by the Crown); and miscellaneous remarks. The schedules also include details of events that happened subsequently. They may lead on to further records. The most frequently encountered abbreviations are listed in the box opposite.

The records are extremely useful for discovering the names of fields – some of which were later converted into road names when areas were developed.

Although the apportionments were concerned with land and not buildings, the column 'name and description of lands and premises' will state the sort of building(s) standing on the plot, such as 'cottage building and yard' or 'house and garden'. The more unusual the building, the more useful will be its description.

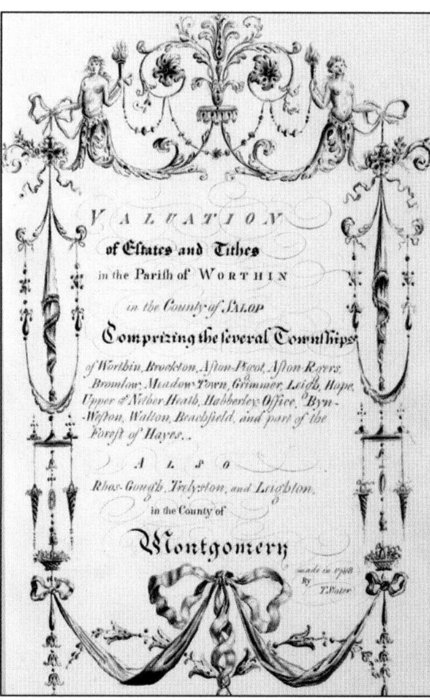

VALUATION
of Estates and Tithes
in the Parish of WORTHIN
in the County of SALOP
Comprizing the several Townships
of Worthin, Brookton, Aston Pigot, Aston Rogers, Bromlow, Meadow Town, Grimmer, Leigh, Hope, Upper & Nether Heath, Hubberley Office, Bynweston, Walton, Beachfield, and part of the Forest of Hayes.
ALSO
Rhos-Goch, Trelystan, and Leighton,
in the County of
Montgomery
made in 1783
By
T. Slater

LEFT
Valuation of Estates and Tithes in the Parish of Worthen, Shropshire, by T. Slater, title page, 1783.

BELOW
Tithe Award for the parish of Glanton, Northumberland, from 1842.

Tithe files

‖ Although by no means all tithe files have survived, you may chance upon more information on your home in IR 18, especially if the apportionment was later altered. Key in the tithe district and the code 'IR 18' into the online catalogue at **www.catalogue.nationalarchives.gov.uk** and see what appears. The files can provide information on the general state of the land, how far it was from roads and rivers, and other interesting local information.

Scottish tithe records

The Scottish equivalents of tithes, called 'teinds', were paid by owners of heritable property in the parish. There was no equivalent of the apportionments, and the system ended relatively quietly in 1925. However, when disputes arose, they were referred to the Teinds Court and Commissioners.

‖ Their records are at the National Archives of Scotland in TE 1–6 (pre-1700) and TE 7–32 (post-1700).

Tithe records online

An online index to Devonshire tithe records is at **www.devon.gov.uk/index/community/the_county/record_office/family_history_3/tithe_records/indexing_the_tithe_apportionments.htm**.

There are also some locally produced transcriptions that you can find through search engines. For example, the records for Luppitt, Devon, are at **www.luppitt.net/text/res/tithemap/tithemap.htm**. Details on the tithes of Little Dunmow, Essex; Guiseley, West Yorkshire; and north Hampshire are at **www.digital-documents.co.uk/archi/tithlist.htm**.

Irish tithe records

In Ireland, tithe applotment books were compiled a little earlier, between 1823 and 1838.

- They are in the National Archives of Ireland, with copies of the Northern Irish ones in FIN/5A at PRONI. Arranged parish by parish, they list the occupiers of all agricultural land, the name of the land, the landlord and the amount of tithes deemed to be payable.
- They are indexed on CD-Rom by occupier with Griffith's Valuation (see below).

An interesting addition to these are the 1831 records of Irish Tithe Defaulters, compiled by the Church of Ireland clergy. That year, there was a widespread protest against the iniquity of Catholic tenants having to pay ten per cent of the value of their produce to Protestant clergymen, many of whom didn't even live in their parishes.

- The records are easily searchable (by defaulter) on a CD-Rom produced by Eneclann (Eneclann Ltd, Unit 1b, Trinity College Enterprise Centre, Pearse Street, Dublin 2; tel: 03531 671 0338; info@eneclann.ie). They include the incumbents' accounts of how the protests affected their parishes.

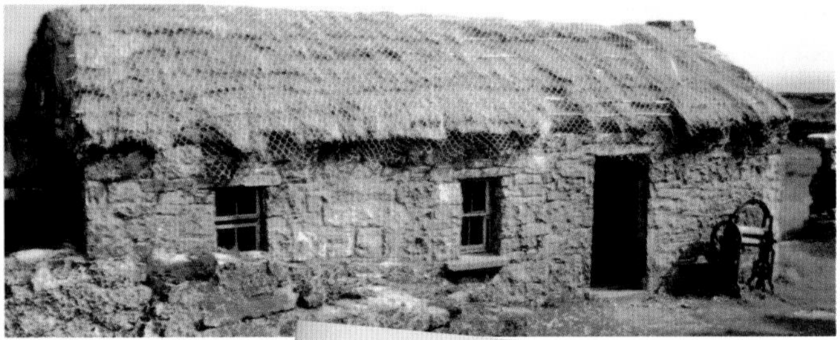

ABOVE

This is an Irish cottage on the island of Innishmore, restored to its original condition (though they wouldn't have had wire netting to keep the thatch on).

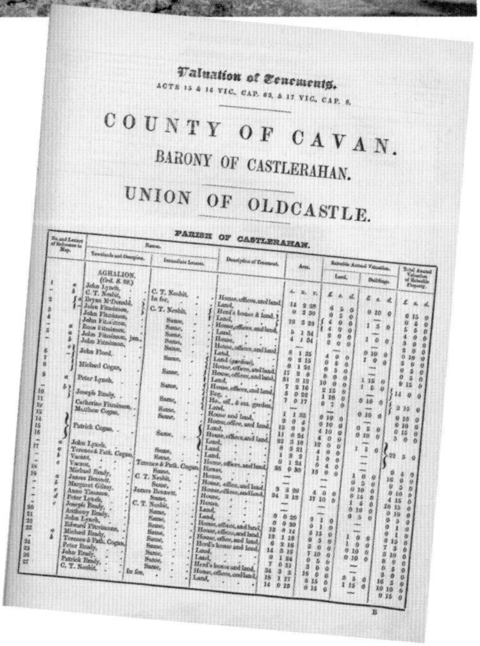

Valuation of Tenements.

ACTS 15 & 16 VIC., CAP. 63, & 17 VIC., CAP. 8.

COUNTY OF CAVAN.

BARONY OF CASTLERAHAN.

UNION OF OLDCASTLE.

PARISH OF CASTLERAHAN.

No. and Letters of Reference to Map.	Names: Townlands and Occupiers.	Names: Immediate Lessors.	Description of Tenement.	Area.	Rateable Annual Valuation: Land.	Rateable Annual Valuation: Buildings.	Total Annual Valuation of Rateable Property.
	AGHALION. (Ord. S. 39.)						

RIGHT

A page from Griffith's Valuation for Co. Cavan.

Land valuations: Griffith's Valuation (mainly 1847–65: Ireland only)

The best Irish land valuation was Griffith's Primary Valuation. This was a project overseen by Sir Richard Griffith, a civil engineer who served as Commissioner of Valuation in Ireland from 1828 to 1868. Griffith set out to record all those liable to pay the poor rate and assess how much they should each contribute. To this end, Griffith's team worked through the Irish counties from 1847 to 1865, recording all buildings and land, noting the nature of the holding, with precise size and rateable value within each poor law union, and details of who tenanted and owned each plot.

- The original records are at the National Archives, Dublin.
- Maps showing the location of the properties in Griffith's Valuation are at the Valuation Office, Irish Life Centre, Abbey Street Lower, Dublin 1; tel: 353 1817 1000; **www.valoff.ie**. The Valuation Office also has the surveyors' notebooks. These may provide additional information about the valuation; later valuations, made between 1865 and 1968; and records of changes in ownership and occupation since the original valuation was made.
- Those for Northern Ireland are in PRONI, in the VAL series. These include the earlier land valuation survey of 1830 (VAL 1B) and its

associated maps (VAL 1A), and Griffith's survey of 1848–64 (VAL 2B) with its maps (VAL 2A). Subsequent valuations from 1864 until the 1930s are in VAL 12B. There was a general revision in 1935 (VAL 3B), with maps in VAL 3A.

|| If you know (or can guess) who the occupier of the land where your home stood was, you can take a short cut by searching the records on CD-Roms produced by Heritage World and the Genealogical Publishing Co. Inc. This information is also searchable online at **www.otherdays.com** and **www.irish origins. com**.

Land registration (1873–6)

A valuation survey was conducted throughout the British Isles between 1873 and 1876, including everyone who owned an acre or more. The records were intended to help the Poor Law Board assess rates. Now they can add an extra bit of information to the history of your home. The returns state the owner's name, the amount of land and its gross estimated value. Sadly, addresses are stated rather imprecisely, so you'll usually need to know who owned the land before using these records.

The returns cover everywhere except Middlesex and Yorkshire (the counties that had deeds registries, see page 186) and were published on a county-by-county basis for England, and single volumes for Scotland and Ireland, as *A Return of Owners of Land of One Acre and Upwards*. Copies are in good local libraries, and they have also been reproduced for sale by S&N Genealogy Supplies (see page 265), **www.genealogysupplies.com**.

Whithorn House, Stoke Newington

Church Row, Stoke Newington, home of the Patersons in the 1870s (see also page 54), was built in 1695 and appears in Stoke Newington's two tithe assessments, of 1813 and 1848. Whithorn House, later the Patersons' home, appears in the 1813 tithe assessment as being occupied by James Thomas. He had a house, chaise house, stable and garden, all comprising 23 poles.

Five doors away in Church Row lived an interesting character – Benjamin D'Israeli, grandfather and namesake of the famous Victorian prime minister. The second tithe assessment, of 1848, shows a William Muskett in residence in Whithorn House, with a slightly increased plot of 26 poles. The accompanying map shows the house, with a service wing jutting out from the eastern half of the rear, and a building at the end of the garden, clearly the chaise house and stables.

Oddly enough, the 1868 Ordnance Survey map shows a similar arrangement but with the service wing jutting out from the eastern half of the rear. Unless extensive rebuilding had gone on, this suggests the 1848 mapmaker had been somewhat inaccurate.

Both tithe assessments indicate that the land was owned by the Prebendary of St Paul's Cathedral and sublet *en masse* to the Eade family, from whom the individual houses in Church Row and elsewhere in Stoke Newington were leased.

BOOKS

- **G. Beech and R. Mitchell, *Maps for Family and Local History* (National Archives, 2004)**
- **R. Davies, *The Tithe Maps of Wales* (National Library of Wales, 1999)**
- **E. J. Evans, *The Contentious Tithe: The Tithe Problem and English Agriculture, 1750–1850* (Routledge and Kegan Paul, 1976)**
- **R. J. P. Kain and R. R. Oliver, *The Tithe Maps of England and Wales: A Cartographic Analysis and County-by-County Catalogue* (CUP, 1995)**
- **R. J. P. Kain and H. C. Prince, *Tithe Surveys for Historians* (Phillimore, 2000)**

CHAPTER 17

Land Tax

1692–1963, but mainly 1780–1832

Land Tax records are a fantastic source for the names of the owners and occupiers of your home. They generally survive for the period just before tithe records (see pages 106–11), and usually carry your home's history back to at least the late 18th century.

Land Tax replaced many earlier, random taxes, particularly the Hearth Tax and Lay Subsidies. It was raised from 1693 to 1963, but most surviving records date from the period 1780–1832. Returns survive mainly for countryside areas. In 1780, the right to vote was extended to people who paid Land Tax on property valued at £2 a year and upwards. Therefore, Land Tax returns took on a new importance, being enrolled henceforth in the Quarter Sessions, and so are to be found in county record offices. Before 1780, some returns survive in parish chest material – the records kept by parishes aside from parish registers, and usually kept safe in an iron-bound chest in the vestry – which will also be at the county record office.

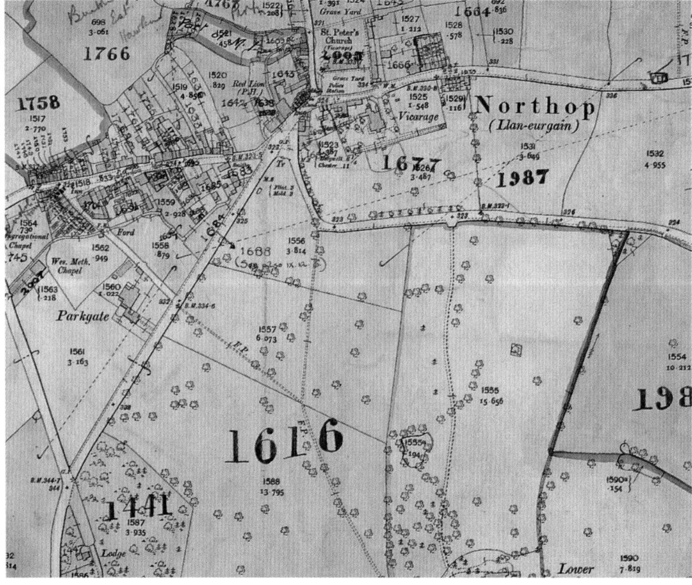

A Land Tax map for Flintshire, Wrexham, 1910.

- The precise whereabouts and survival of these records is in Gibson, Medlycott and Mills' book (see box opposite). An almost complete record for England and Wales for 1798 is in National Archives class IR 23.
- The records are arranged parish by parish within hundreds (units of land comprising several parishes; see page 120 for how to find a hundred). The records sometimes provide brief descriptions of the property itself, but are mainly focused on people. The returns list all properties worth 20 shillings or more – thus, annoyingly, leaving out the smallest cottages.
- Originally, properties were identified by the owners' names. 'Owners' could be freeholders, copyholders or holders of long leases – these were not always, by any means, the same as the tenants who actually lived in the property.
- Tenants were also given from 1772 onwards and from 1782 you should find both landlord and occupier listed. However, if several tenants lived in a building, only one is likely to have been listed, so in this respect the records can be misleading: the absence of a

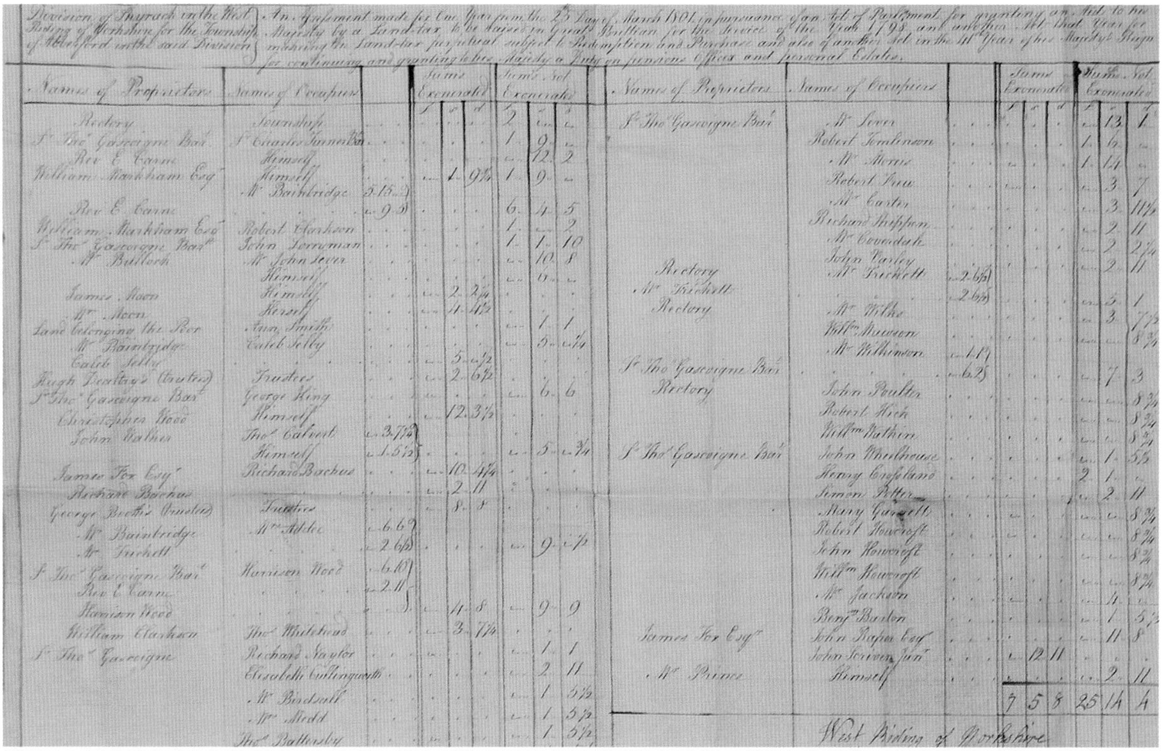

Land Tax records for the year 1801 for Aberford, Yorkshire.

tenant's name does not mean they he or she was not there!

- After 1798, the tax could be commuted by a lump-sum payment, equivalent to 16 years' payment of tax. Records of those 'exonerated' are in IR 22 (books of redemptions) and IR 24 (redemption certificates). Copies may be found in country record offices and a list, complete for all of England and Wales except Flintshire, is in IR 23. These returns can be slightly more detailed than usual – the returns for Bristol, for example, include street names (but not all – see James Mottley's story on page 126).
- In 1832, voting rights extended, and keeping the Land Tax returns became far less important, so many weren't kept.

Land Tax returns seldom give explicit details about properties – 'house and land' was the usual stock phrase, though farm names are sometimes stated. The returns were not always kept up to date. Sometimes people were still being listed several years after they had died. Nor are returns always reliable indicators of personal fortune. The amount each parish had to pay was fixed in 1698, and this sum was then parcelled out proportionately to the rateable values of the houses. The amount payable then usually stayed the same. If you find it rising suddenly, though, this may provide good indirect evidence of the building of an extension, or indeed complete renovation of an old home.

BOOKS

- **J. Gibson, M. Medlycott and D. Mills, *Land and Window Tax Assessments* (FFHS, 1998)**
- **D. T. Hawkins 'Listing the Landowners' (*Ancestors*, December 2004, pp 22–3)**

CHAPTER 18

18th century: enclosures and other matters

1600s–1900, but mainly 1760–1820

In the Middle Ages, most agricultural land was divided into large, communal fields – in which villagers had the right to farm their own strips – and areas of meadow and common land, which were also shared.

Mainly from the 17th century onwards, and particularly in the mid-late 18th and early 19th centuries, landowners started enclosing their lands. This entailed scrapping the old communal system, either so the landowner could create his own deer parks and pleasure grounds, or to create consolidated areas of agricultural production – large-scale sheep pastures or more efficient farms. Sometimes, enclosures were undertaken at the behest of the villagers, who wanted to consolidate their strips of land into single farms. More usually, enclosures were foisted on country people and their protests ignored.

Enclosure maps were mainly concerned with land, but some go into detail about buildings, and indeed tenants. The absence of a building from an enclosure map certainly should not be

Around the mid-late 18th century many landowners started enclosing their lands to create their own deer parks or pleasure grounds. Anthony Devis's painting of about 1767 depicts the results of enclosures in the form of the graceful parkland of Tabley House, Cheshire.

taken as evidence that it wasn't there: it may simply not have been very important to the surveyor. The maps can, however, be a treasure trove of historical information on the area around your home, particularly making it clear who owned what at the time.

- Tate and Kain's books provide essential guides to the present location and date of English and Welsh enclosure awards and maps; see also the website: **www.ahds.ac.uk/history/collections/hpew.htm**
- Some early enclosures were agreed or imposed privately and records do not survive. Others were recorded as enclosure awards and enrolled in the records of a law court, to create an official copy. These could be in a number of places at the National Archives (see box on page 116).

A very modern building in Castle Street, Cambridge, considerately retains a relic of turnpike days – an original plaque reading: 'GODMANCHESTER TURNPIKE ROAD ENDS HERE. To Horse-shoe Corner GODMANCHESTER 14 Miles 4 Furlongs'.

From 1760 onwards, enclosures were usually undertaken by obtaining an Act of Parliament. This happened almost without fail after the Enclosure Acts of 1801, 1836, 1840 and 1845.

The procedure was usually for a surveyor to draw up copies of an enclosure award, comprising a book with attached plans. The original was given to the parish priest for the parishioners to inspect. These copies usually ended up in the parish chest and hence, now, in county record offices. A second copy was sent to Parliament and will now be found in the House of Lords Record Office. From the 1830s, most enclosures were overseen by Parliamentary commissioners, whose own records are at the National Archives in MAF 1.

In the end, almost 21 per cent of England was enclosed. Proportions differ among the counties. The figure rises to over 50 per cent for Oxfordshire, Cambridgeshire, Northamptonshire and Huntingdonshire.

In most cases of enclosure, some land was allocated to the parish church in lieu of tithes (see pages 106–10). Tithes were thus usually – but not always – extinguished in such parishes, making it unlikely you will find tithe records for these.

Roads

The 18th century was one of wholesale improvement everywhere. As progress was made in farming, so it was in transport. Many new roads were built or improved, and from 1773 plans for these had to be deposited with the local Quarter Sessions (now at county record offices). Hindle's book on roads (see page 105) has much to say that will interest you if your home is situated on an old thoroughfare.

Turnpike roads are especially well recorded. These roads were built by private trusts between 1663 and 1888, but mostly between 1750 and 1770. Users had to pay tolls at toll houses, usually of a farthing per cow or 6d per horse. The toll houses were built specially to house the collector or 'pikeman', and usually stuck out into the road. Records of disputes relating to turnpikes – and often concerning the occupiers and owners of the homes they passed by – can be found in local Quarter Session records.

- At the National Archives, Ministry of Transport files (in series MT) contain maps relating to royal commissions examining roads maintained by turnpike trusts.
- Control of turnpikes was assumed by the Ministry of Housing and Local Government in

Enclosure records at the National Archives

Private enclosures

Commissions of enquiry C 47/7, 205; E 134, 178; DL 44 (for the Duchy of Lancaster)
Petitions to the Privy Council PC 1, 2
Licences to enclose C 66

Enclosure by enrolled decree

Chancery C 78
Exchequer E 159, 368; E 123–31
Duchy of Lancaster DL 5
Palantine of Durham DURH 26

Non-enrolled awards CRES 2, 6

Enclosure maps

Can be found through the online catalogue, **www.catalogue.nationalarchives.gov.uk**

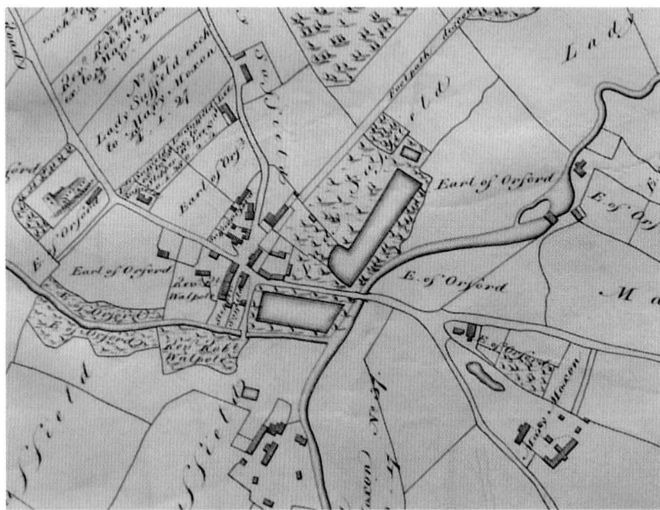

Itteringham, Norfolk, enclosure map, 1823. The houses are marked in red and other buildings in grey.

1888, whose records are in series HLG and contain details of road building and improvement schemes, again including much information about homes on the routes.

- Further information may be found in MH 28 and MT 149.
- Maps from Cary's *Traveller's Companion* (1790), showing main roads and noting distances, can be found at **www.maproom.org.maps/britain/cary/turnpikes**.

Canals

Rivers were canalised by widening their banks and creating locks, and many new canals were cut from the 17th century onwards, but it was the 1790s that saw true 'canal mania'. Parliament first required maps to be made for proposed canal developments in 1792, so many may be found in the House of Lords Record Office. These maps may show buildings along the route of the proposed new canals. The canals' main impact on homes was the ease with which building materials, such as Welsh slate, could now be moved to any part of the country, thus making substantial inroads into regional diversity in building styles.

Registration of Papists' estates and forfeited estate papers (1715 and 1745)

In 1688, Catholic James II was overthrown by his Protestant nephew, William of Orange. In 1715, some of the dwindling number of English Catholics joined the Anglican Jacobites in a rebellion against George I in favour of James's son, James the 'Old Pretender'. The rising had little effect, except in the north, and was put down.

In the aftermath, the government forced all Catholic landowners to register their estates with the local Justices of the Peace. The resulting records can be searched in their records, and also in Payne, and Estcourt and Payne (see box opposite).

The records are very useful for home historians. For example, Thomas Havers of Thelveton Hall, near Diss, Norfolk, was obliged to register his manor of Thelveton, which was entailed (i.e. the succession was fixed and could not be altered by his own will) and apparently only worth £151-18-11. His widowed mother Mary,

Trundleys Road, Deptford. View of the Greenwich Railway viaduct from the Surrey Canal showing the towpath, barges and horses and a steam train, 1836. Lithograph by G. F. Bragg.

as the senior trustee of the family's other lands, registered an annuity of £140, which she received from the revenues of Thelveton, payable by her son Thomas. Mary also held the leasehold of Shelfhanger Hall, which was in trust for her younger children Mary, William and John. The total annual income from these was £361-8-6, including her annuity. The daughter Mary was at this time living as a spinster in Suffolk, where she registered her one-third share of the lease of Shelfhanger Hall, held in trust by her mother and worth £73-2-10 per year. Another family holding, Roydon Hall, was *not* mentioned in the 1717 Registration, indicating that it had been sold by then.

The year 1745 saw another uprising in favour of the exiled James, lead this time by his son Charles – 'Bonnie Prince Charlie'. This came close to being a success, but the Jacobites were defeated at Derby and retreated back into Scotland, to be finally decimated at Culloden.

Both the 1715 and 1745 rebellions were punished by seizures of lands by the Forfeited Estates Commission. While some English land was taken, the majority of reprisals were in Scotland.

|| Records are at the National Archives and National Archives of Scotland. Besides being interesting in terms of the details they provide of estates, they also link the story of homes affected to these two dramatic historical events.

BOOKS

- **J. Chapman, *Guide to Parliamentary Enclosures in Wales* (University of Wales Press, 1992)**
- **E. E. Estcourt and J. O. Payne, *The English Catholic Nonjurors of 1715* (Burns & Oates, 1885)**
- **P. Hindle, *Roads and Tracks for Historians* (Phillimore, 2000)**
- **S. Hollowell, *Enclosure Records for Historians* (Phillimore, 2000)**
- **R. Kain, J. Chapman and R. Oliver, *The Enclosure Maps of England and Wales, 1595–1918* (CUP, 2004)**
- **J. O. Payne, *Records of the English Catholics of 1715* (Burns & Oates, 1889)**
- **W. E. Tate, *A Domesday of Enclosure Acts and Awards***

CHAPTER 19

Window Tax

1696–1851

Window Tax was introduced in 1696 by the new, Protestant government of William and Mary. It replaced the earlier Hearth Tax (see pages 128–33), a tax on the number of hearths in each building. If the Justices of the Peace did not believe a householders' accounts of how many hearths they had, they could enter the property and look for themselves.

Many windows were bricked up to avoid paying so much tax. This is a cross window, at the Old House, Blandford Forum, Dorset.

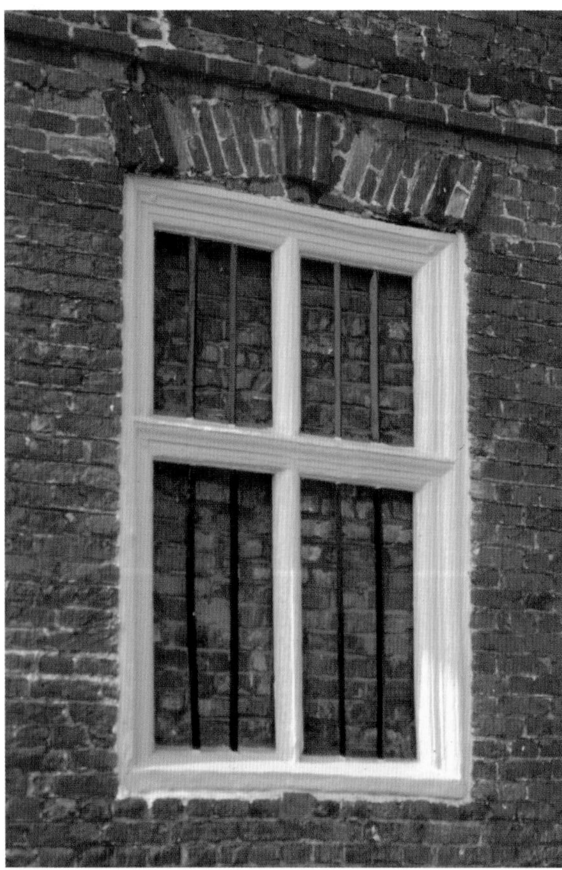

Such invasion of Englishmen's 'castles', great and small, aroused enormous antipathy. In London and Bristol it even led to rioting. Window Tax, William and Mary felt, would be far less unpopular, because all the assessors had to do was walk around the outside of people's homes, counting the number of windows.

Window Tax returns provide the address; the number of windows (either specifically or the bracket into which the number of windows fell); the amount payable; and the name of the occupier. Occasionally the owner's name may appear too.

These records are fairly unusual, because they combine the relatively useful information you would normally find in a tax list with some information specific to each home's architectural history. They quite literally shed light on your home's past.

The initial rate of tax was 2 shillings per house, paid by all occupiers except those on poor relief (not all paupers' cottages had windows, in any case). Non-resident owners did not have to pay either but were subject to Land Tax instead. Houses that had more than ten windows paid 8 shillings. In 1709, the rate for those with more than 20 windows went up too. For brief periods during the tax's existence, windows in houses that provided light in workplaces were exempt.

If the Crown thought it would be thanked for getting rid of Hearth Tax, it was mistaken. Now the king and queen were accused of taxing daylight itself. The tax was unusual in that it had a long-lasting effect on the appearance of our buildings. To get below the 10- or 20-window thresholds, people resorted to blocking up windows they either didn't use or, sadly, couldn't afford. However, be aware that from the 17th century onwards, blind windows were also deliberately built into Classically styled homes to maintain proportion and balance in walls behind which no light was required, such as the underside of a stairwell.

Despite the population rising, the bricking-up of windows led to a reduction in the tax's yield. In 1747, the tax was re-introduced, with the same basic rate for fewer than ten windows, but a graduated scale of 6 pence per window for houses with 10–14 windows, 9 pence per window for those with 15–19, and an additional shilling per window for 20 or over. You would think that would make things better, and it did, for a while. Yet where the judicious application of a few bricks and a bit of mortar could save a few shillings, people did so. The government got less money, and people had less light but more cash – though presumably some of the money saved then had to be spent on extra candles. From Sussex comes the story of a man so determined to avoid paying Window Tax that he had *all* his windows bricked up, forcing his servants to keep the doors open summer and winter to let in any light at all.

In 1766, the number of windows covered by the basic rate was reduced to seven (out came the trowels again) and then increased to a generous eight in 1825. In 1834, the lower rate was removed but, by now, non-payment was increasingly going unpunished. In 1851, Window Tax was abolished.

Many windows were unblocked but, as we know, not all. In many cases, people had just got used to things the way they were. One of

TOP
17th-century house in Trowbridge, Wiltshire, with some windows sealed up to avoid window tax.

ABOVE
Blank windows give a pleasant sense of proportion to these ersatz Georgian homes in Canterbury. The whole street, with its varying styles, was built from scratch in the late 1990s.

A VISION OF THE REPEAL OF THE WINDOW-TAX.
"Hollo! Old Fellow; we're glad to see You here."

The 'tax on light' was a tax which directly affected living conditions.

the most extreme examples I have encountered is a beautiful Georgian sandstone house in the Derbyshire village of Stanton in the Peak. Of the 14 windows of its three storeys facing the street, no less than eight were – and remain (as it is a listed building) – blocked, giving it a most unusual and slightly lopsided appearance. As it has six still unblocked, the owners were perhaps trying to save some money after the rules changed in 1766, with an extra window blocked out to maintain some semblance of symmetry.

Where to search

- Gibson, Medlycott and Mills' book (see box opposite) is a complete guide to what has survived.
- Window Tax records are usually to be found in your local county record office, and in the Exchequer Records at the National Archives in class E 181; the National Library of Wales and the National Archives of Scotland. The Scottish returns, mainly for 1748 and 1798, are well preserved in NAS 326. They provide occupiers' names and also list those properties that were not liable.
- Sadly, the records' survival rate is relatively poor. Staffordshire Record Office, just to give an example, holds returns for the following hundreds: Brewood (1801–6); Cuttlestone (1711); Fradswell (1785–7); Leek Frith (1704); Patshull (1738–59); and Stowe (thought to be 1750). However, if the records do survive, be sure to consult them.

House Tax and Inhabited House Duty (1696–1924)

You would think House Tax should occupy a key position in this book. It cannot, sadly, largely because the returns are very patchy in their survival. In fact, the survival rate is so poor it would make no sense to set off in specific search of such records for your home.

- The tax was paid by those occupants of houses who were responsible for paying poor and church rates. The assessments were usually written at the end of Window Tax records and are thus filed with them in county record offices, though some material is in the National Archives in E 182, but in a very disorganised state.
- There are also precedent books of composition cases (1718–1834) in IR 68, recording those who ended their ongoing liability by paying a lump sum over a three-year period.
- You may occasionally encounter records of assessment or payment of duty on inhabited houses (1834–1924) or even uninhabited houses (1851–1924) in archives or family papers. Barratt (see box opposite) quotes the example (in IR 40/1157) of Brighton Aquarium, which was assessed for Inhabited House Duty because a party of Zulus slept there during an exhibition in 1880.

Holly House, Stanton in the Peak, Derbyshire. As glass was costly, and generally the more windows the bigger the house, windows were indicative of a house owner's wealth. It was deemed the more windows the richer the owner, and so he could be taxed more. Many owners still resented the tax and bricked up some of their windows.

BOOKS

- N. Barratt, *Tracing the History of your House* (Public Record Office, 2002)
- J. Gibson, M. Medlycott and D. Mills, *Land and Window Tax Assessments* (FFHS, 1998).

CHAPTER 20

Fire insurance records

1680–19th century (but mainly 18th century)

The records of fire insurance companies are a copious and informative source for home historians. They can include plans of buildings and details of what they contained.

Fire insurance started in a 17th-century London still traumatised by the ravages of the Great Fire of 1666, in which many merchants and organisations lost their entire stocks and a vast number of ordinary people were left completely destitute. The first company was Phoenix (or Phenix), established in 1680, followed by the Sheaf of Arrows (1683), Friendly Society (1683) and Amicable Contributionship (Hand-in-Hand) in 1696. Many more followed in the 18th and 19th centuries, all over Britain, although London remained the centre of the industry and supplied insurance to properties even further afield.

The Great Fire of London. 'In sixteen hundred and sixty-six, London burned like a pile of sticks.'

A crucial aspect of fire insurance was prevention. When the Great Fire broke out, Charles II and his courtiers had to turn out to organise efforts to fight it. It clearly benefited the insurance companies not to leave matters to similar regal intervention, so they established their own liveried brigades with horse-drawn carriages carrying water and hoses – fire engines – to go galloping out to quench conflagrations. The earliest engines were those of the Hand-in-Hand Company (1707), followed rapidly by the Sun Fire Office (1716) and Westminster Fire Office (1720). In 1791, the Phoenix, Sun Fire Office and Royal Exchange Assurance Co. joined forces to create a single service, to which was added London Assurance in 1826. Similar brigades were also established elsewhere in the country, from the early 18th century onwards. The early companies who had fire brigades, together with their dates of foundation, are given by Richardson (see page 127).

The state's first involvement was in 1865, when it created the Metropolitan Fire Brigade, paid for jointly by national and local government and the insurance companies: it was retitled the London Fire Brigade in 1904 and was again followed by other state-funded services throughout the realm.

When fire brigades were run by private companies, their services were for members only. To enable people to prove they had an insurance policy in an emergency, the companies invented those well-known features of many old houses – and a massive boon for tracing the history of your home – fire plaques. Best known are the Sun plaques, depicting a stylised sun with a human face. The earliest fire plaques were made of lead, later ones of copper and iron, all with the insurance policy number engraved on them.

Beware of mistaken identity, though. Old fire plaques are very attractive and modern home-owners have been known to buy them in junk shops and attach them to their homes, simply for effect.

ABOVE

An 18th-century fire plaque attached to a beautifully decorated timbered building in Palace Street, Canterbury.

Fire insurance records

Fire insurance company records can be very detailed and are definitely worth seeking. You may know the householder had a policy because of a surviving plaque on the outside wall of your home. If not, and the property is a reasonably sized one, or was formerly used for business purposes, it can be worth undertaking a speculative search. The records tend to be well indexed, but by policy holder, not address. Surviving records of the companies are scattered among county record offices and can be found using the notes on tracking down business archives given on pages 166–9.

|| Notable companies are the Royal Exchange, Hand-in-Hand and Sun, whose records are at Guildhall Library, London; Phoenix at Cambridge University Library (West Road, Cambridge CB3 9DR; tel: 01223 333000; **www.lib.cam.ac.uk/** (but covering London and the provinces)) and Westminster Fire Office at the City of Westminster Archives

Stoke Newington's original fire engine house (1821), with added watch house and lock-up (1824), now a very distinctive-shaped private home.

Centre (10 St Ann's Street, London SW1P 2DE; tel: 020 7641 5180; **www.westminster.gov.uk/archives/**).

|| The Sun Fire Office, also called the Company of London Insurers, operated from 1716 to 1863. Its records are at the Guildhall Library, and include many properties both within and far beyond the boundaries of London. Besides insuring many domestic dwellings, the Sun Fire Office acquired a virtual monopoly of industrial property all over Britain. Thirty of its registers, covering the period 1816 to 1824, have been indexed online by the Place in the Sun Project. You can search these to see if the owner or occupier of your home had a policy at **www.a2a.org.uk**: click on 'search the database', enter a name and choose 'Guildhall Library' from the 'location of archives' dropdown menu. For further guidance on using the index, see **www.history.ac.uk/gh/sun.htm**.

LEFT
The Sun Fire Office logo.

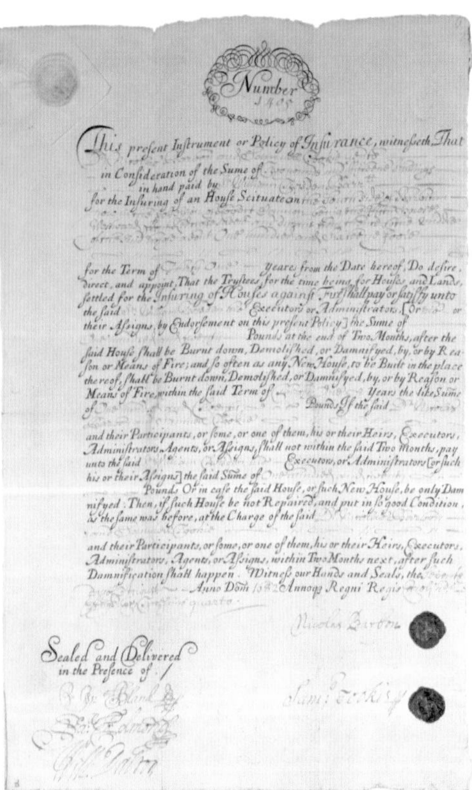

Number
1405

This preſent Inſtrument or Policy of Inſurance, witneſſeth That in Conſideration of the Sume of in hand paid by for the Inſuring of an Houſe Scituate

for the Term of Years from the Date hereof, Do deſire, direct, and appoint, That the Truſtees for the time being for Houſes and Lands, ſettled for the Inſuring of Houſes againſt Fire ſhall pay or ſatiſfy unto the ſaid Executors or Adminiſtrators [Or or their Aſſigns, by Endorſement on this preſent Policy] the Sume of Pounds at the end of Two Months, after the ſaid Houſe ſhall be Burnt down, Demoliſhed, or Damnifyed, by, or by Reaſon or Means of Fire; and ſo often as any New Houſe, to be Built in the place thereof, ſhall be Burnt down, Demoliſhed, or Damnifyed, by, or by Reaſon or Means of Fire, within the ſaid Term of Years the like Sume of Pounds If the ſaid

and their Participants, or ſome, or one of them, his or their Heirs, Executors, Adminiſtrators, Agents, or Aſſigns, ſhall not within the ſaid Two Months, pay unto the ſaid Executors, or Adminiſtrators [or ſuch his or their Aſſigns] the ſaid Sume of Pounds Or in caſe the ſaid Houſe, or ſuch New Houſe, be only Damnifyed: Then, if ſuch Houſe be not Repaired, and put in ſo good Condition, as the ſame was before, at the Charge of the ſaid

and their Participants, or ſome, or one of them, his or their Heirs, Executors, Adminiſtrators, Agents, or Aſſigns, within Two Months next, after ſuch Damnification ſhall happen. Witneſs our Hands and Seals, the Anno Dom 1682 Annoq Regni Regis

Sealed and Delivered in the Preſence of

BELOW LEFT
Nicholas Barbon's insurance policy, 1682. Barbon was one of the great post Great Fire building speculators and an early advocate of fire insurance.

The records include names and statuses of owners and occupiers; the address, and sometimes other details, such as how the place was built and laid out, what it was used for, what it was worth; surveyor's reports; and details of claims. The records may also detail specific fire risks.

The great fun of the records is in the details they provide. All manner of specific items were insured, so you can discover that your home once contained anything from books and musical instruments to ostrich feathers; fine linen to old umbrellas. The records also reveal a lot about people's lives: men claiming to be living on their own incomes are revealed to have had wives working as schoolmistresses or laundresses. In her exploration of the records, local historian Isobel Watson (see page 127) identified a coal dealer who sold oysters, a barrel maker who also made hats, and an iron-plate worker who had a sideline dealing in pigeons.

Insurance plans

Insurance plans of properties and of general urban areas were produced from the late 18th century onwards. Most, however, date from 1885 to 1968 and were made by the firm of Charles E. Goad. The plans were updated every five years or so. They were extremely detailed, showing the dimensions of buildings and adjoining streets. They improved on Ordnance

A Christmas tradgedy

A newspaper report, from the *Birmingham Daily Post* (26 December 1863), describes a dreadful fire that took place on Christmas morning 1863 in the Hill Street Tavern, Birmingham. The report first helpfully states where this was – 'on the left hand side of Little Hill Street from the Horse Fair, and opposite the end of Bow Street'. It then states the exact layout of the property:

The house itself has a double front, and is three stories high. On the ground floor to the front is – on one side of the door, a tap room, and on the other, a bar, from which the various drinks are served. On the ground floor in the rear are the private sitting room of Mr [George] Gameson [the landlord], in which the fire originated, a pantry, and the door of the stairs leading to the upper storeys. A large room used for the meetings of clubs and other large gatherings of a similar nature, runs the whole width of the first floor, and behind it are the stairs communicating with the second floor and the bedroom occupied by Mr and Mrs Gameson. On the third and highest floor to the front are two garrets, used as the sleeping apartments of the junior members of the family and the servants. In the rear of the premises is a large yard and outhouses.

After the last customers had gone carousing away ruddy cheeked at midnight, Mrs Gameson had put the plum pudding 'near a fire, which had been kindled for the purpose in the sitting room, to boil until morning'. Unfortunately, the safety-conscious Mr Gameson overlooked a cloth hanging by the fire.

During the night, two young men passing saw flames and shouted up to Mr Gameson who, going downstairs, found the sitting room, 'with its entire contents, was one glowing mass of fire. As though glad of a means of exit the eager flames rushed out with a volume of smoke, upsetting Mr Gameson, stifling him with vapour, rushed across the passage and up the stairs'. Recovering, and being unable to return upstairs, Mr Gameson ran into the street, where he, 'wept and cried for his children's safety, and had he not been prevented by sheer force would have rushed again into the burning house, and as he put it "and saved his darling children or shared their fate"'.

Mrs Gameson escaped by a ladder – but the others were trapped:

... the crowd, unable to render any assistance, stood with white upturned faces, looking intently at the window of the rooms in which it was known that the six children, the servants and the old lady were – cut off from all apparent hope of avoiding the terrible death which threatened them. After a few minutes ... one of the garret windows was thrown up and the girl [Elizabeth] Hancocks, with a fearful cry, threw herself into the street, where she fell with a dull sound upon the hard pavement.

Elizabeth survived with only bruises. The older boy, John, then threw his younger brother out onto the pavement and jumped himself – both were seriously injured but had at least survived the flames.

By this time, 'the engines from the various offices, with their superintendents, and fully manned, arrived on the spot', but it took an hour before the flames were subdued. When the firemen entered the upper chamber, the old lady, the nurse and the four younger children were found dead, suffocated by smoke, and some of their bodies subsequently charred black. The firemen, it was reported, 'dashed the tears from their eyes with their hard and grimy hands as they carried the charred and disfigured remains of the recently happy children from the scene of their violent and untimely death'.

The paper also tells us the financial implications of the tragedy:

The loss to Mr Gameson will be serious, for although the property in the tap room, club room and bar is not injured to any serious extent, the remainder of the house has been gutted. His loss will probably amount to some £150. The damage to the property is considerable, walls, ceilings, and doors being destroyed completely. His loss will, in all probability, amount to some £200 or more, which is covered by a policy in the District fire office ... in addition to this, the young serving woman, Hancocks, who saved her life by jumping from the window, has lost everything she possessed in the world – her box, clothing, and little savings all being swallowed up in the general ruin.

A politic policy

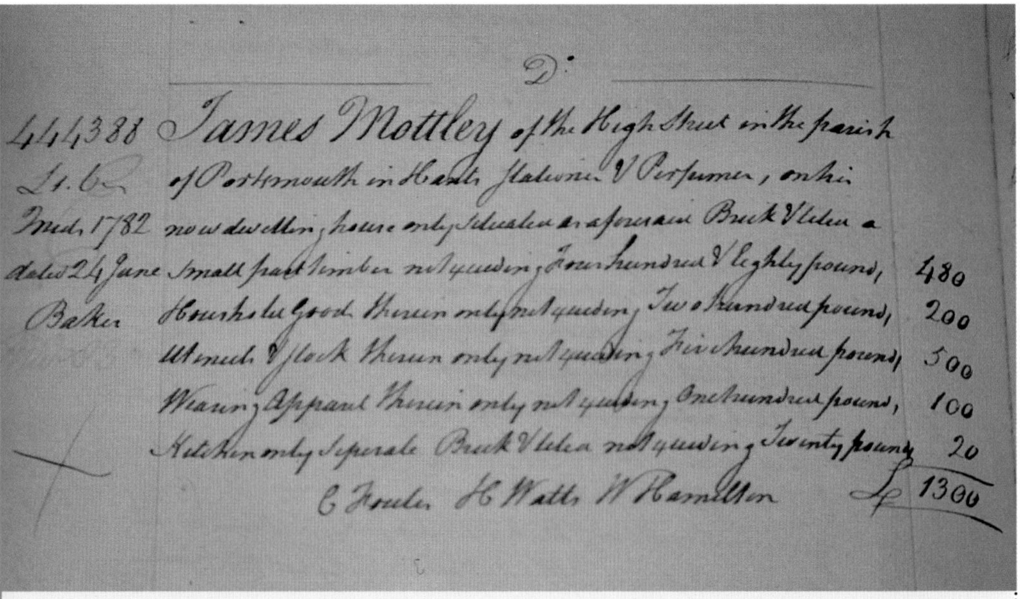
D:
444388 James Mottley of the High Street in the parish
£1.6 of Portsmouth in Hants Stationer & Perfumer, on his
Mid. 1782 now dwelling house only situated as aforesaid Brick & tiles a
dated 24 June small part timber not exceeding Four hundred & Eighty pounds, 480
Baker Household Goods therein only not exceeding Two hundred pounds, 200
Utensils & stock therein only not exceeding Five hundred pounds, 500
Wearing Apparel therein only not exceeding One hundred pounds, 100
Kitchen only separate Brick & tiles not exceeding Twenty pounds 20
C Fowles H Watts W Hamilton £ 1300

James Mottley has the unusual distinction of having been the grandfather of Mary Mottley, wife of the French political thinker Alexis de Tocqueville (1805–59), who wrote the first analysis of the American Constitution. James lived in Portsmouth, and had a fire insurance policy with the Sun Fire Office. The record is at Guildhall Library in SFO/MS11936/292, policy no. 444388:

444388m 24 June 1782, Baker.

James Mottley of the High Street in the parish of Portsmouth in Hants, stationer & perfumer, on his now dwelling house only situated as aforesaid Brick & tiles, small part timber not exceeding Four hundred & Eighty pounds 480

Household Goods therein only not exceeding Two hundred pounds 200

Utensils & stock therein not exceeding Five hundred pounds 500

Wearing apparel therein only not exceeding One hundred pounds 100

Kitchen only separate Brick & tiles not exceeding Twenty pounds. 20

£1,300

[signed] C Foules H Watts W Hamilton

Therefore, we know exactly what James owned, and how much it was valued at. It does not say what premium he paid, though. 'Baker' was simply an internal reference: the three names at the end were the appraisers.

James also paid for redemption of Land Tax – a lump sum in lieu of ever having to pay the annual tax again. The returns for Portsmouth dated 24 November 1798 (Hampshire Record Office, ref: 50M63/C49/113) state that redemption of £1-15-0 was paid for the year starting 25 March 1798. 'Mr James Motley' (sic) of Portsmouth paid taxes on 'a free hold messuage or tenement with appurtenances situate in the High Street in the borough of Portsmouth in his own occupation'.

It will be noted this does not say where in the High Street James lived. That would require more searching through rate and poll books, deeds and so on.

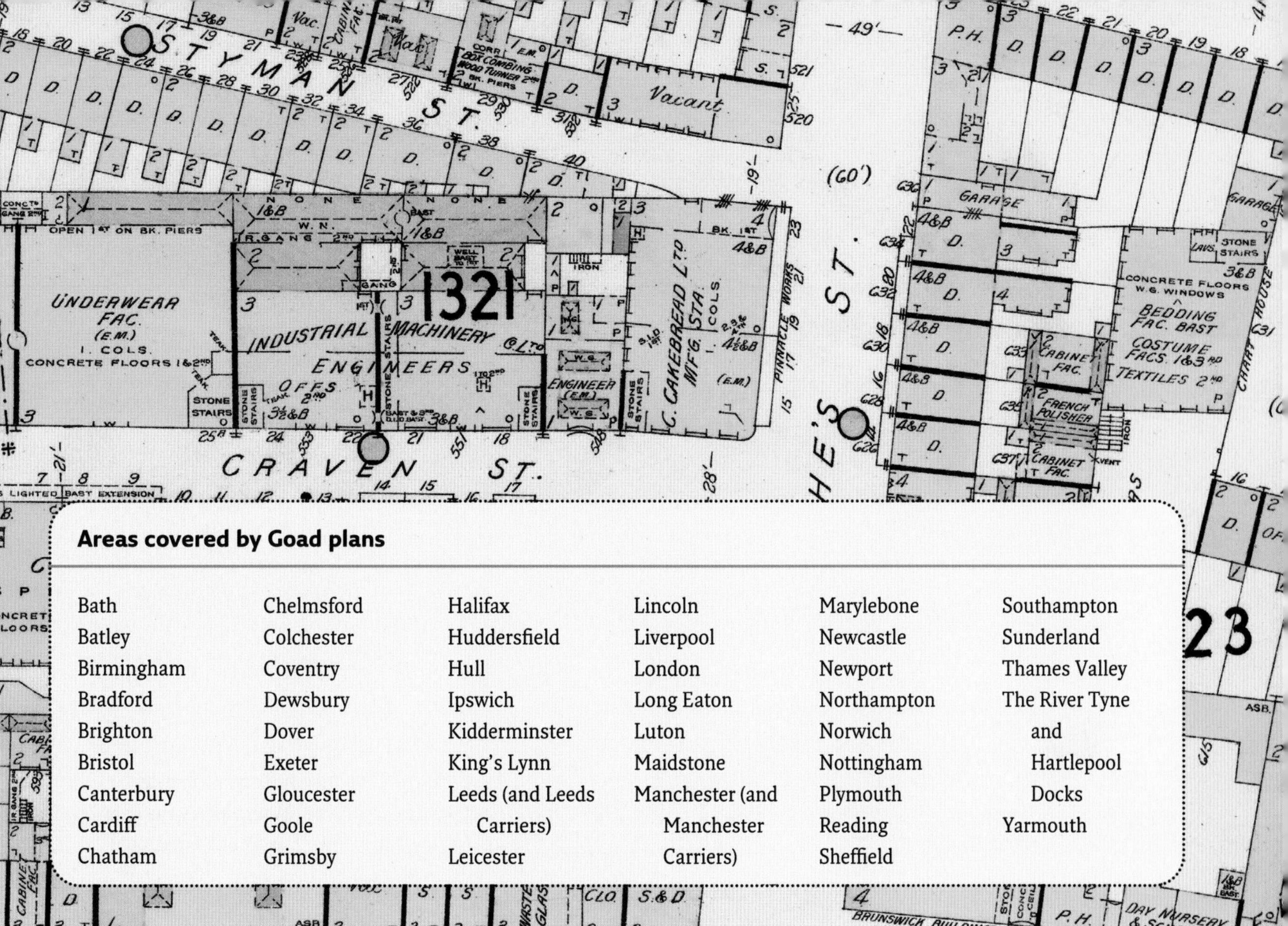

Areas covered by Goad plans

Bath
Batley
Birmingham
Bradford
Brighton
Bristol
Canterbury
Cardiff
Chatham
Chelmsford
Colchester
Coventry
Dewsbury
Dover
Exeter
Gloucester
Goole
Grimsby
Halifax
Huddersfield
Hull
Ipswich
Kidderminster
King's Lynn
Leeds (and Leeds Carriers)
Leicester
Lincoln
Liverpool
London
Long Eaton
Luton
Maidstone
Manchester (and Manchester Carriers)
Marylebone
Newcastle
Newport
Northampton
Norwich
Nottingham
Plymouth
Reading
Sheffield
Southampton
Sunderland
Thames Valley
The River Tyne and Hartlepool Docks
Yarmouth

A sample Goad plan, this one including an underwear factory!

Survey maps by including house numbers; details of how properties were built and used – sometimes the buildings were actually illustrated; and recorded matters relating to fire risk, such as boilers and engines, and the location of fire hydrants or other water supplies. Mostly the properties concerned were used commercially, not domestically, but, of course, many old factories and warehouses have since been converted into homes. The main areas covered by Goad's plans are listed in the box above.

- The maps were leased, not sold, to insurance companies, but some still end up in the archives of such organisations.
- Copies are also scattered around many archives, especially since the sale of the now defunct Goad company's archives – many local archives and libraries brought the sections of the archive relevant to their own area.
- Others can be sought by contacting 01707 663090 or goad-sales@experian.com.
- There are also collections of Goad plans at the British Library and Guildhall Library in London.

BOOKS

- **H. A. L.Cockerell and E. Green, *The British Insurance Business, 1547–1970* (Sheffield Academic Press, 1994)**
- **D. T. Hawkings, *Fire Insurance Records for Family and Local Historians: 1696–1920* (Francis Boutle, 2004)**
- **J. Richardson, *Local Historian's Encyclopaedia* (Historical Publications, 1993)**
- **G. Rowley, *British Fire Insurance Plans* (Hatfield, 1984)**
- **I. Watson, 'A Kaleidoscope of Early-19th-century London Life' (*Family History Monthly*, July 2004, issue 106, pp 25)**

CHAPTER 21

Mid-late 17th century: Hearth Tax and other matters

Hearth Tax returns (1662–89) are tax lists that tell you not only who lived where, but also how many fireplaces they had.

In May 1660, the Cromwellian Commonwealth collapsed and Charles II came home from exile to a multitude of cheering crowds, a joyful nation – and an empty Exchequer. Besides the crippling debts he and his father Charles I had incurred during the Civil War and Interregnum, his palaces were in ruins and the Crown lands – the monarchy's traditional first port of call for income – were unmanaged. To rectify the problem, Charles II's ministers came up with a number of ingenious taxes, of which the foremost was a tax on all householders assessed on the number of fireplaces in their homes.

The idea for this probably came from the spread of chimneys in the 16th century. In 1577, William Harrison wrote of 'a multitude of chimneys lately erected'. Indeed, it was an exceptionally cold period, and besides simply lighting more fires, people were starting to use coal rather than wood. Both required more than simply a hole in the ceiling, and thus chimneys started to be added to houses.

Parish constables or tithing-men compiled assessments and delivered them to the local Justice of the Peace, whose clerk enrolled them in the Quarter Sessions records and sent a copy to the Exchequer. The tax was massively unpopular because inspectors were allowed to enter homes to count the fireplaces – a frightful intrusion. Sometimes, the collectors even left marks on fireplaces to show they had been taxed – a fascinating thing for the home historian to identify.

The idea was that the bigger the house you occupied, the more money you were likely to have and therefore the more you could pay towards national government. Those occupying property worth less than 20 shillings in yearly rent, had less than £10 worth of movable goods, or were receiving poor relief or alms, were let off. Also exempt were charitable institutions, alehouses, kilns, furnaces and blowing houses. The rest had to pay 1 shilling per half-year for every fireplace or stove. After May 1664, anyone who had two hearths had to pay regardless of other circumstances.

Initially, money was collected by the parish constables, but so much resistance and corruption was encountered that the Treasury

Certificates of residence

The National Archives also holds related certificates of residence in E 115. These were issued to people who owned several properties, but only lived in one – thus proving that they were not liable to pay Hearth Tax on houses they owned but did not inhabit.

appointed Receivers-General in 1664 and 1669. They farmed out collection to self-employed agents in 1666 and 1674, and appointed a Special Commission to do so in 1684. In 1689, along with many other hangovers from Medieval taxation systems, Hearth Tax was ditched, as 'a badge of slavery upon the whole people exposeing every mans house to be entred into and searched at pleasure by person unknown to him'. It was replaced by Land and Window Taxes (see pages 112–13 and 118–21).

With few exceptions – such as the inclusion of 'senior', 'junior', 'widow' and so on after names – Hearth Tax returns simply provide a list of each householder's name and the number of hearths in their home, for each parish. Sometimes, assessments include subsidiary lists of those exempt due to poverty, and of unoccupied and therefore non-taxable houses.

Where to search for Hearth Tax returns

- Gibson's guide (see page 132) provides a full list of surviving material.
- You may find returns at county record offices. Much has been published, especially by county record societies, and by a joint project of the British Records Society and the University of Surrey at Roehampton – all such material published by 1996 is listed in Gibson.
- Because of the different collection methods used, most of the Hearth Tax records that are now at the National Archives are for 1662–6 and 1669–74. Finding out which Hearth Tax records have survived there for the parish you want is now very easy. The records are arranged by hundreds (units of land comprising several parishes), which date back to Anglo-Saxon times, as areas from which 100 soldiers could be raised in times of emergency.
- To find out in which hundred your parish was, you can look it up in a 19th-century directory or old gazetteer, or type the parish into **www.nationalarchives.gov.uk/e179/**. This will tell you both the name of the relevant hundred and what Hearth Tax records have survived for the parish.
- Scottish Hearth Taxes survive from 1661 to 1695 and are at the National Archives of Scotland.
- Ireland's records are called Hearth Money Rolls. These have survived in places, as listed in Ryan's book (see also page 132).

Using Hearth Tax returns

The slight drawback to Hearth Tax records is that they list occupiers, not houses *per se*.

The famous 17th-century chimney-piece at 'Albyns', Stapleford Abbots, Essex. Chimneys and fireplaces could be lavishly decorated as status symbols, though few as finely as this.

The General Council of the Parliamentarian Army meet to declare the remonstrances of Charles I in 1647.

Indeed it is most unusual to find a precise address stated. It is best to approach these records already knowing – or having an idea of – who occupied your home at the time.

If you do not know, you can sometimes work out which was the right property by the number of hearths. Generally, if any given room had a chimneystack running down a wall, you would expect it to have a hearth. If two chimneystacks ran down its walls, you would expect two hearths, and so on. Armed with some architectural knowledge of your home from that period, you can work out roughly how many hearths there were likely to have been.

Like rates, censuses and many other tax lists, the returns were usually listed in order of the homes the collectors encountered when walking around the village or town. You can thus sometimes work out which your home was by its place in the sequence. Once you have identified your home, you can examine earlier or later returns and see if any changes occurred in occupancy, and indeed in the number of hearths. If someone extended their home during the period the tax was being levied, this should be reflected in an increase in the number of hearths being taxed. The returns may reveal that your home at the time had fewer hearths than it did later on, thus enabling you to put an 'earliest possible' date on their construction. Indeed, it's quite possible that many hearths were constructed after 1689 *because* the Hearth Tax had been abolished.

Most homes with only one hearth were probably little cottages, but there were still some ancient, rambling manor houses that had not been modernised and contained only one or two fireplaces. Sometimes, the grander the property, the sparser its amenities. When Winston Churchill was born at Blenheim Palace in 1874, for example, the massive and magnificent mansion had only one bathroom.

The Civil War

In 1642, Civil War erupted between Charles I and his Parliament. It raged until 1646 and flared up again between 1647 and 1649. After this came the Commonwealth period, presided over by Oliver Cromwell. When 'that great hellcat', as the prominent London developer Henry Jermyn once called him, died in 1658, the Commonwealth began to unravel, resulting in the Restoration of Charles I's son, Charles II, in May 1660.

|| The run-up to war generated a number of lists, compiled parish by parish, including the Solemn League and Covenant and the Protestation Oaths, which name the adult men who occupied your home – though, sadly, properties themselves are not identi-

Hearth and Hall

I wanted to find the Hearth Tax returns for the tiny Norfolk parish of Thelveton (or Thelton) at the National Archives. In order to do so, I opened the search facility on **www.nationalarchives.gov.uk/e179/**, selected 'place' and typed in 'Thelveton'. I was told that Thelveton is a parish in the hundred of Diss (if you click on 'notes' it even gives you a map reference). I then clicked on the word 'Thelveton' and selected 'Tax' from the menu, and then clicked on 'date and/or tax type' and selected 'Hearth Tax' from the menu. I clicked 'search', and was told that the surviving returns for Thelveton are:

- E179/154/697 1673 March x Sept 19
- E179/154/709 c.1664 Sept 29
- E179/253/42 c.1666 March 25
- E179/253/45 1664 Sept 29

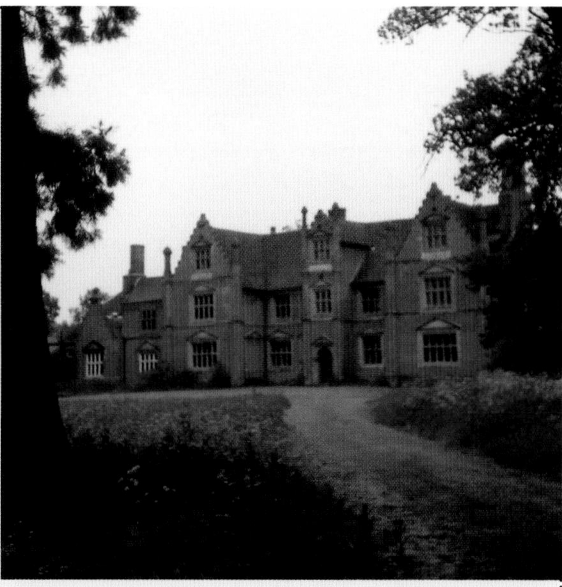

Gibson's guide (see page 152) also indicated that the Diss assessments for 1664 and 1666 have been published in *Norfolk Genealogy* volumes 15 and 20 respectively. Gibson also detailed what was in the National Archives and showed that the Norfolk Record Office's only assessments for Norfolk are some for Erpingham hundred.

The 1666 printed version for Thelveton tells us the following (see below). Here, as in many other cases, the assessments (what people were supposed to pay) and returns (what they actually paid) are one and the same, because the former lists were annotated to become the latter:

of Wm Havers Esqr	*12s*
John Smith	*7s*
Stephen Hamblinge	*4s*
Robert Harman	*2s*
Thomas Bitton	*2s*
Robert Kempe	*4s*
James Barnes	*1s*
John Hasell	*2s*
John Le Grice gent	*4s*
Eliz Gostlinge widd	*1s*
Thomas Chandler	*6s*
Robert Bird	*3s*
John Harrold	*2s*

We can see immediately that William Havers had by far the biggest house, paying 12 shillings per half-year on his 12 hearths. In fact, he owned the manor house, Thelveton Hall. Messrs Smith and Chandler were the next most substantial inhabitants, while the only other 'gent', John le Grice, does not seem to have been quite so prosperous. Mrs Gostlinge was a poor relation of the Havers family, and a beneficiary of William's will, which he wrote the same year and was found proved in the Prerogative Court of Canterbury (see page 158).

Thelveton

Sr Wm Havers Esqr 12
John Smith 7
Stephen Hamblinge 4
Robert Harman 2
Thomas Bitton 2
Robert Kempe 4
James Barnes 1
John Hasell 2
John Le Grice gent 4
Eliz Gostlinge widd 1
Thomas Chandler 6
Robert Bird 3
John Harrold 2

02 – 10 – 00

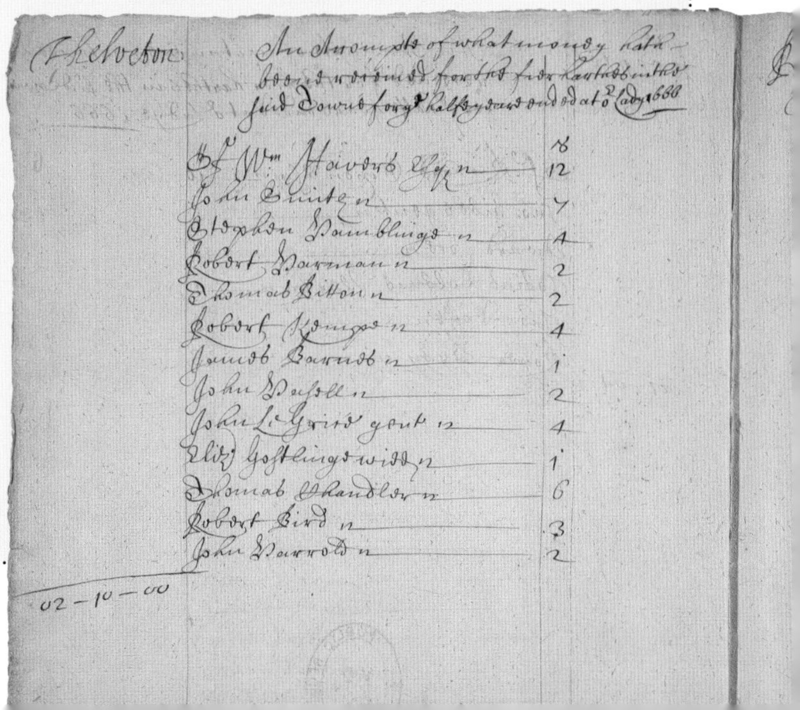

'And when did you last see your father?': W. F. Yeames' famous 19th century painting of Roundheads questioning the children of an escaped Royalist commander vividly evokes the mood of the Civil War, and shows what the interior of a mansion of the time would have looked like.

fied. These records are in county record offices.

The Civil War caused considerable damage to buildings, such as stones pitted by musket fire, some traces of which still remain. More usefully, it generated some interesting records when Royalist land came under Parliamentarian scrutiny.

Under the Commonwealth, the huge amount of land belonging to the Crown was largely sold off to raise money for the new régime.

|| Records are mainly at the National Archives in the Exchequer Records, especially E 317 (searchable in **www.catalogue.nationalarchives.gov.uk**), and can include room-by-room description of properties.

|| Material relating to Charles II's repossession of his family's lands in 1660 appear particularly in the State Papers, which have been abstracted and published, and are easily searchable in good libraries. More will be found in the records of the Crown Estates

BOOKS

- **J. Gibson, *The Hearth Tax, and other Later Stuart Tax Lists and the Association Rolls* (FFHS, 1996)**
- **M. A. E. Green (ed.), *Calendar of the Proceedings of the Committee for the Advance of Money, 1642–1656, Preserved in the State Paper Office of Her Majesty's Public Record Office* (HMSO, 1888)**
- **M. A. E. Green (ed.), *Calendar of the Proceedings of the Committee for Compounding, etc., 1643–1660, Preserved in the State Paper Office of Her Majesty's Public Record Office* (HMSO, 1889–92)**
- **D. Hey, 'No Smoke Without Fire' (*Ancestors*, February 2005, pp 74)**
- **J. G. Ryan, *Irish Records: Sources for Family and Local History* (Ancestry, 1997)**

Commissioners in E 134 and E 178 in the National Archives. Claims made by dispossessed Parliamentarians are in CRES 6/1–8 (1660–8).

Parliamentarian committees

From 1642 onwards, a Parliamentarian committee forced people, Royalist and Parliamentarian alike, to loan money to the Commonwealth. From 1646, only defeated Royalists had to make these loans although, to be fair to Parliament, efforts were made to pay the money back with interest.

From 1643 onwards, a Parliamentarian committee called the Committee for the Sequestration of Delinquents' Estates sat in judgement on landowners who had supported the King, and seized their land. The Committee for Compounding, which was not wound up until the Restoration, then gave the land back in return for an oath of loyalty to the Commonwealth and a hefty fine.

- The records of the committee's highly intrusive activities have been indexed and calendared in Green's edited volumes on the Committee for the Advance of Money (see box opposite).
- The original records, called Royalist composition papers, are in National Archives class SP 23 and have been calendared and indexed in Green's edited volumes. Both can provide some fascinating information on Royalists and their homes.

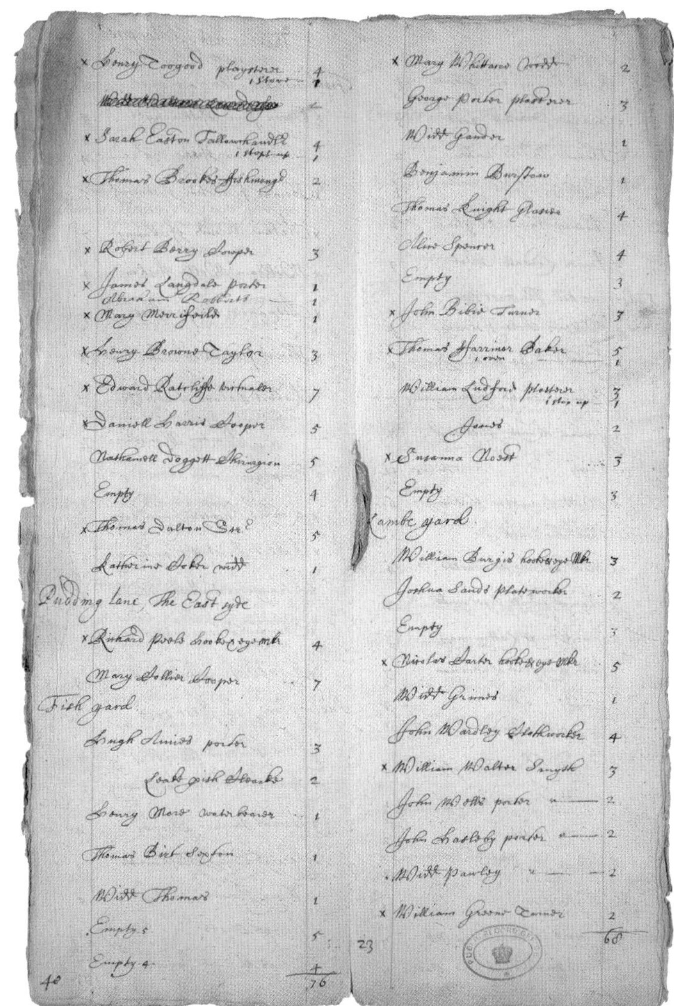

x Henry Toogood playsterer 4
x Sarah Easton Tallowchandler 4
x Thomas Brookes fishmonger 2
x Robert Berry Cooper 3
x James Langdale porter 1
Abraham Roberts 1
x Mary Merrifield 1
x Henry Browne Taylor 3
x Edward Ratcliffe Vintner 7
x Daniell Harris Cooper 5
Nathaniell Doggett Skinner 5
Empty 4
x Thomas Dalton Esq 5
Katherine [illegible] widd 1
Pudding lane the East syde
x Richard Poole [illegible] 4
Mary [illegible] Cooper 7
Fish yard
Hugh [illegible] porter 3
[illegible] 2
Henry More waterbearer 1
Thomas Bird Sexton 1
Widd Thomas 1
Empty 5
Empty 4
48 76

x Mary Whittaker widd 2
George Porter plaisterer 3
Widd Gander 1
Benjamin Burstow 1
Thomas Knight Glasier 4
Olive Spencer 4
Empty 3
x John Bibie Turner 3
x Thomas Farriner Baker 5
William Ludford plaisterer 3
[illegible] 2
x Susanna [illegible] 3
Empty 3
Lambe yard
William Burgis [illegible] 3
Joshua Sands plateworker 2
Empty 3
x Nicolas [illegible] 5
Widd Grimes 1
John [illegible] Silkweaver 4
x William Walton Smyth 3
John [illegible] porter 2
John [illegible] porter 2
Widd Pawley 2
x William Greene Turner 2
23 68

Hearth Tax return for 1666, featuring Thomas Farrinor, owner of the bakery in Pudding Lane where the Great Fire of London started.

CHAPTER 22

Old maps

Middle Ages–early 19th century

Unless you live in a country pile, early maps are highly unlikely to depict your home. But they can tell you, with varying degrees of accuracy, what your area was like in the past.

Britain was first described by Pytheas, a member of the Greek colony at Marseilles, France, who made an extraordinary journey to these shores, in *On the Ocean*, published in 320 BC. It was not until AD 150, however, that another Greek, Ptolemy of Alexandria, produced an accurate survey of these islands in a work called *Geographia*. This single work formed the basis of most maps of Britain right through the Dark Ages into Medieval times. Remarkably, Ptolemy's measurements were still being used as an important source of reference into the 18th century.

Aside from these, a handful of local maps and plans survive from the Middle Ages. They are detailed in Skelton and Harvey (see page 138), who found that they were all created for specific purposes, such as showing the effects of flooding in Cliffe, Kent; the location of concealed water pipes in such places as Islington and Clerkenwell (Middlesex), Canterbury (Kent) and Wormley (Hertfordshire); and other strangely contemporary-sounding matters.

It was in the Tudor period, and particularly thanks to the influence of William Cecil, Lord Burghley (1520–98) that the English really started producing maps for widespread use. As Secretary of State to Elizabeth I between 1558 and 1572, Cecil recognised the importance of information and organised a ruthlessly efficient spy network. Cecil did much to encourage the production of maps, for purposes ranging from accurate taxation to keeping tabs on where prominent Catholics lived. Cecil's enthusiasm for cartography coincided with great advances in mapmaking on the continent. The theodolite, and other instruments of mapmaking, including the circumferentor and plane-table, started to be used. The principles of compass surveying and triangulation were first published in English in 1559. Thanks to these factors, maps started to be used – and made – far more widely than before.

County maps

Christopher Saxton, a former employee of one of Lord Cecil's mapmakers – if not actually an amanuensis of the great Secretary of State himself – went on to survey and print a series of 34 decorative maps of English counties. Produced between 1574 and 1579, they depicted each county with its main rivers, settlements, hills, parks and mansions. While some buildings were drawn as they appeared, most were stylised, as were the 'sugar-loaf' hills. Saxton's maps sold very well, as they still do to this day.

Saxton was followed in the 1590s by John Norden, who worked mainly in southern England (and the Channel Islands), and whose

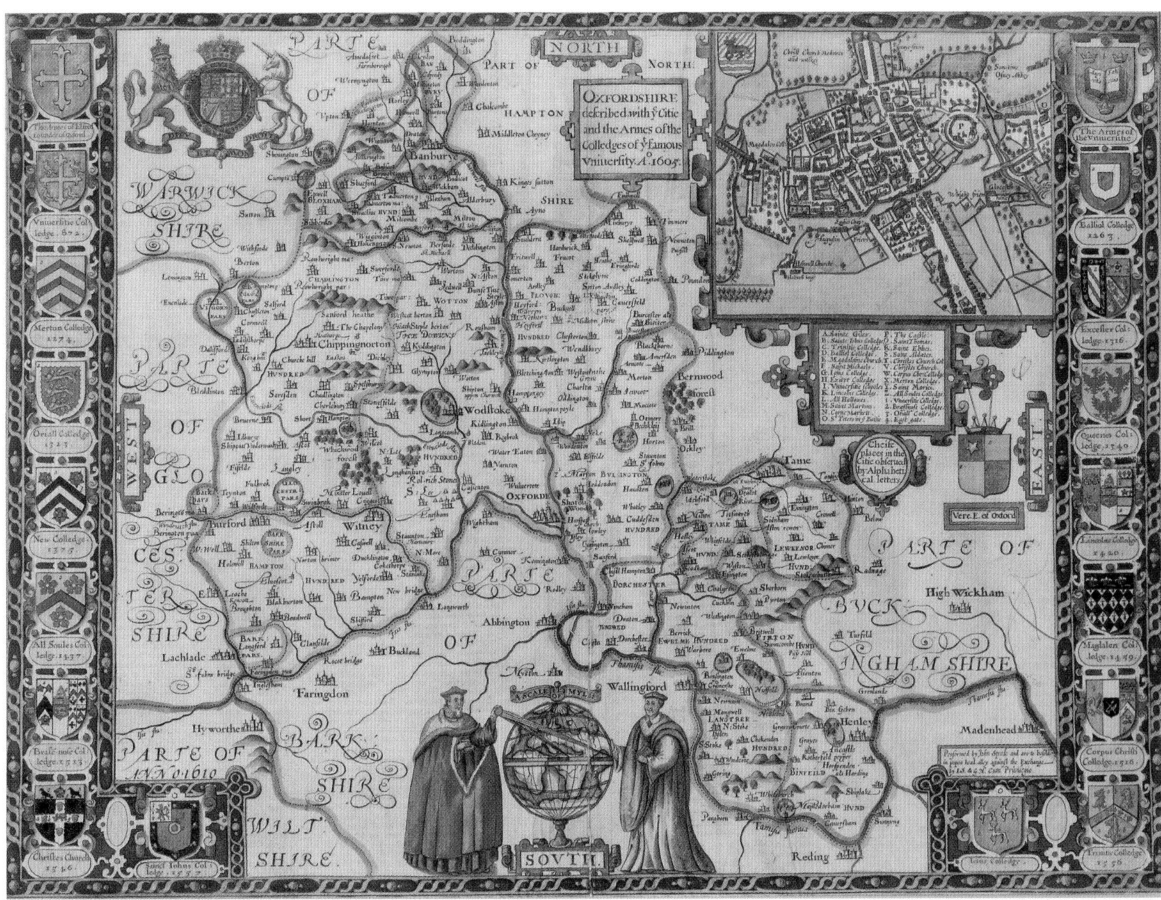

maps, unlike Saxton's, included roads. From 1610, John Speed also started producing county maps, adding plans of the main towns to the otherwise blank corners of the sheets. To a certain extent, both Norden and Speed copied Saxton's work: to a very large degree, subsequent county mapmakers – and there were many – copied all three. Most 17th- and early-18th-century county maps are more or less altered reproductions of the original Tudor and Stuart ones.

The old county maps of Saxton and his colleagues are, of course, highly stylised. As accurate representations of the counties at the time, they are a very far cry from the later Ordnance Survey maps. For our purposes, this doesn't really matter. I like the idea of my ancestors looking out to sea where monstrous narwhals and dolphins rear out of the depths, or travelling up to the north of their shire past red-spired churches to view the gigantic royal coat of arms suspended in the sky over the blank reaches of the neighbouring county. Such maps are immensely evocative of their eras, and that's why they are still immensely popular.

John Speed's beautifully coloured map of Oxfordshire.

Map developments

With the appearance of Ogilby and Morgan's map of London in 1683, a new genre of map was born – environ maps. Rather than showing counties, they depicted cities and their

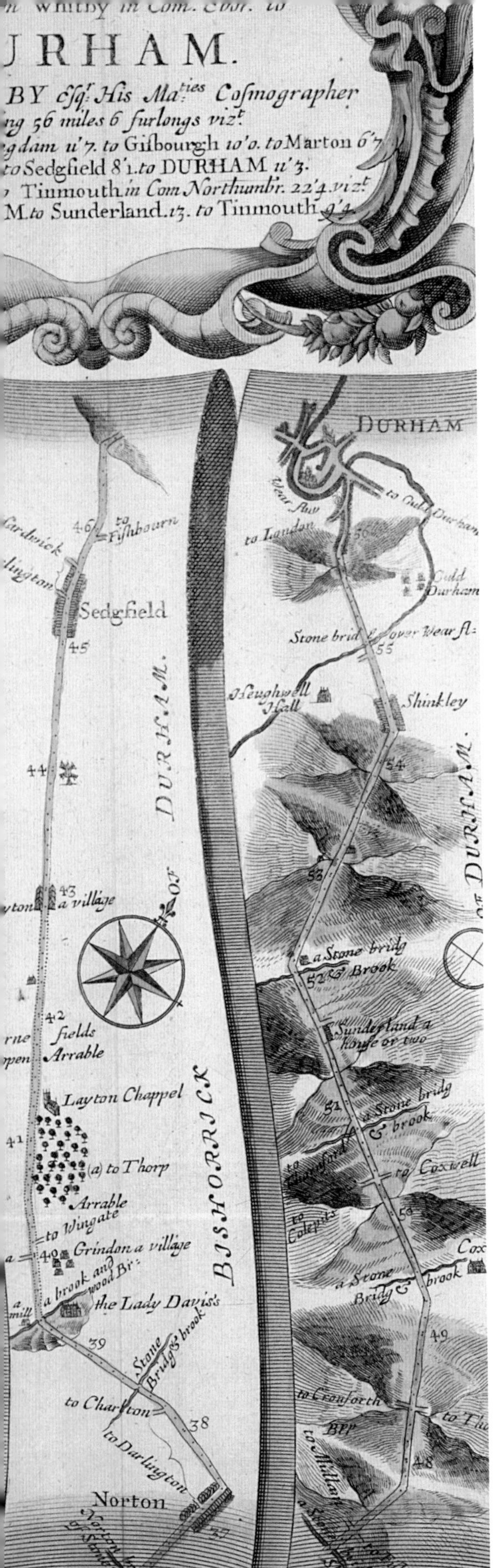

Detail of a John Ogilby road map of Durham, 1675.

surroundings, in this case showing roads extending as far out as Sevenoaks and Colnbrook. These were developed in the 19th century to show such excitements as cycling routes and even cab fares around towns and cities.

A style of map of minimal use to home historians are route maps – not modern ones, showing all roads in an area, but long, thin maps just depicting specific routes between major towns. Of these, the best known are in Ogilby's *Britannia* (1675), now available from Archive CD Books, 5 Commercial Street, Cinderford, Gloucestershire GL14 2RP; tel: 01594 829870; **www.archivecdbooks.org**. Ogilby drew what the traveller would encounter on the journey – the towns; turnings; hills; castles and mansions; and, once in a while, inns and other smaller buildings. If your home is next to a major old route, however, these maps are worth a look.

Most counties were re-surveyed from the mid-18th century onwards. The results were highly detailed and are worth studying for your home area. Standards of accuracy vary and can be misleading. John Rocque's 1761 map of Berkshire, for example, purports to show field boundaries, but if so, the Berkshire countryside would have resembled the prairie-farm landscape of today, for most of the smaller hedges were ignored. Equally, Burdett's Cheshire map (c.1770) shows the location of salt mines, but it turns out that he simply peppered the salt-mining area with pictures of salt mines to show their general presence, without bothering to pinpoint each one accurately.

Other maps, such as Yeakell and Gardner's 1783 one of Sussex, produced at a scale of two inches to the mile, are probably more accurate and show many individual buildings. For Selsey Bill, for example, on an otherwise apparently deserted stretch of coast, we can see 'Bill Barn' and a 'Fish Shop', while in nearby Selsey village there are various square dots representing houses, and one marked 'High House'.

In the period 1817–39, Christopher Greenwood, his competitor Andrew Bryant and others re-surveyed the whole country, producing some 46 new maps that included canals, railways and turnpikes.

County maps were largely superseded in the 19th century by the one- and six-inch to the mile Ordnance Survey maps (see pages 59–63).

|| Finding county maps is usually a matter of visiting a local library or museum (or local museum's bookshop). Most counties have county map bibliographies, listed on page 13 of Paul Hindle's book (see page 138).

Town plans

Besides a map of Bristol drawn in 1479, town plans started being produced in the late 16th century. The first printed plan was Cunningham's map of Norwich (1559); the earliest of London, probably drawn by Wyngaerde in the 1550s, was copied in the 1560s in the map usually attributed to Ralph Agas. The first five volumes of Braun and Hogenberg's *Civitates Orbis Terrarum* included plans of Bath, Bristol, Cambridge, Canterbury, Chester, London, Norwich, and Oxford. The year 1612 saw the publication of John Speed's *Theatre of the Empire of Great Britaine*, containing many town plans. Copies of these can be seen in good libraries, such as the British Library, but you'll come across most of these maps in relevant local histories. Town maps remained a popular genre throughout the ensuing three centuries, generating much valuable material for historians of homes situated in the older parts of towns.

|| Many have been reprinted. The early ones for London, for example, have been republished by H. Margary (of Lympne Castle, Kent), and are on sale in the bookshop of Guildhall Library.

|| Copies of originals can be found in local libraries and archives.

Most early town plans were commercial ventures: the surveyor would pace the streets, quickly sketching what he needed, conscious of the cost of accommodation in the local inn and anxious to press on to the next conurbation on his itinerary before his funds ran out. For all that, they are immensely evocative of their subjects. Many are perspective views – as seen from a (usually imagined) high hill nearby. Others are 'bird's eye plans' – drawn from the imagined perspective of bird flapping past, looking down from an angle of between 30 and 60 degrees. The main buildings, such as the cathedral, churches, town hall and principal residences, were sketched in profile, along with prominent features such as gates and walls. Streets were filled with standardly drawn houses, or even left blank (prompting a comment made of Cunningham's 1559 map of Norwich: 'one is left ... to wonder where the poor lived'!) But as long as you don't take the representation of houses in your street as being accurate, you can have great fun studying these old town plans and imagining life in the area at the time.

In some cases, where one family, guild or church body owned a large part of a town, early town plans were, in fact, estate maps. There is a 1690s plan of parts of London by J. Ward, for example, showing estates owned by Goldsmith's Company.

During the 18th century, some areas were surveyed in much more detail. Rocque's 1746 map of London is a true map, depicting the metropolis from above, and is quite accurate. Richard Horwood's 26-inch to the mile London maps, produced between 1792 and 1796 (there were later, updated editions), were accurate down to each house and alleyway.

In and just after 1832, some 294 English and Welsh town plans were issued by Reform Bill Commissioners, showing new electoral boundaries. Many were based on the new Ordnance Survey plans, but there were towns that had not yet been surveyed by the Ordnance department, so in some of these cases the maps created were original. They were published by Hansard, and later many appeared in Samuel Lewis's history of England (see box below).

Town plans were largely superseded in the late 19th century by the Ordnance Survey five- and ten-feet to the mile town maps (see page 63). A partial bibliography to old town plans is provided by West (see box below).

- The National Archives has a substantial collection of maps of all sorts and ages. Most are now indexed in their online catalogue, **www.catalogue.nationalarchives.gov.uk**.
- Many old maps can now be viewed online – see box right.

BOOKS

- **P. Christian, 'Exploring Historical Maps Online' (*Ancestors*, December 2004, pp 36–8)**
- **P. Christian, 'London Calling' (*Ancestors*, September 2004, pp 28–31)**
- **P. Hindle, *Maps for Historians* (Phillimore, 2002)**
- **S. Lewis, *A Topographical Dictionary of England ... and the Islands of Guernsey, Jersey and Man ... with Maps ... and a Plan of London, etc.*, 5 vols (with a supplementary volume comprising a representative history of England, with plans, etc.) (S. Lewis & Co., 1835)**
- **R. A. Skelton and P. D. A. Harvey, *Local Maps and Plans from Medieval England* (Clarendon Press, 1986)**
- **L. Smart, *Maps that Made History: The Influential, the Eccentric and the Sublime* (National Archives, 2004)**
- **J. West, *Town Records* (Phillimore, 1983)**

Websites for viewing old maps

Also included here are some useful associated gazetteers and place-name finders.

http://contueor.com.beadeker/great_britain Maps from Baedeker's 1910 *Great Britain Handbook for Travellers*.

http://dewey.library.upenn.edu/sceti/printedbooksNew/index.cfm?textID=stow&PagePosition=1 John Stow's *Survey of London*, 1618.

http://faculty.oxy.edu/horowitz/home/johnspeed John Speed's early-17th-century maps of around 30 English towns and cities, and also Edinburgh.

http://freepages.genealogy.rootsweb.com/~genmaps Old maps for England, Wales and Scotland, including many links to other map sites.

http://hermes.reading-college.ac.uk/LearningResources/Sources/maplinks.doc A substantial listing of links to organisations connected with all forms of mapping.

http://homepage.ntlworld.com/tomals/index2.htm Samuel Lewis's county maps of the British Isles.

www.chartingthenation.lib.ed.ac.uk/project.html Scottish maps dating from 1550 to 1820.

www.clarelibrary.ie/eolas/coclare/history/parliamentary_gazeteerJl845.htm Clare County Library's transcription of Clare places in the *Parliamentary Gazetteer of Ireland* of 1845.

www.Collage.cityoflondon.gov.uk Contains many plans and maps, mostly from Guildhall Library's own Print Room, with a good place-search facility.

www.cyndislist/com/maps.htm Entitled 'Maps, Gazetteers and Geographical Information', this section of the popular genealogy site contains many links to sources for maps.

www.devon.gov.uk/library/locstudy/gazet.html Devon Library Services' Historic Devon Gazetteer.

www.dur.ac.uk/picturesinprint Old maps of Durham.

www.freepages.genealogy.rootsweb.com/~genmaps/genfiles/COU_Pages/ENG_pages/lon.htm 'Genmaps' scans of some 70 million historical maps, plans and panoramas of London from the 1560s to 1920, including John Roque's map of 1746.

www.gazetteer.co.uk Gazetteer of some 50,000 British place names and details on their present-day administrative divisions.

www.gendocs.demon.co.uk/lon-str.html Gendoc's Victorian London Street Index – an excellent site including details of churches; cemeteries; lodging houses; Irish areas; institutions; inns, and taverns; and census indexes.

www.genuki.org.uk This genealogy site has index pages for each county and thus each parish, from which there are links to relevant maps, including some individual parish maps. The gazetteer is at **www.genuki.org.uk/big/Gazetteer/**.

www.geo.ed.ac.uk/scotgaz/Anyword.html A useful Scottish gazetteer. It's best to use the 'any words' rather than the 'place' field to search for the location you want.

www.geog.port.ac.uk/webmap/hantsmap/hantsmap/hantsmap.htm and **www.envf.port.ac.uk/geo/research/historical/webmap/sussex.html** Old maps of Hampshire and Sussex from the 16th century onwards.

www.manchester2002-uk.com/towns/gazetteer.html Gazetteer of Greater Manchester.

www.nls.uk/digitallibrary/map The National Library of Scotland's extensive map collection, which includes maps of Scotland from 1560 to 1920, including Pont's maps of Scotland dating from about 1583–96 and military maps of Scotland from the 18th century.

www.nwkfhs.org.uk/PARINDEX.HTM The North West Kent Family History Society's West Kent Parish Gazetteer.

www.perseus.tufts.edu/cgi-bin/city-view.pl The Bolles Collection of old and new maps of London. The site allows you to overlay maps from different eras for comparison.

www.proni.nics.gov.uk/geogindx/geogindx.htm PRONI's Geographical Index of Northern Ireland, listing counties; baronies; poor law unions; dioceses; parishes and townlands.

www.seanruad.com The IreAtlas database of all Irish townlands, with details of the county and civil parish to which each belonged.

www.visionofbritain.org.uk This is a project in progress at the time of writing, part of the Great Britain Historical Geographical Information System (GIS). The aim is to collect data on places for the period 1801–2001, including historical maps and descriptions. For each place, the site will tell you the historic county and poor law union, the hundred it was in, and other useful data. Its 'descriptive gazetteer' will contain the entire text of three 19th-century gazetteers: John Goring's *Imperial Gazetteer of England and Wales* (1870–2) (still in progress); Frances Groome's *The Ordnance Gazetteer of Scotland* (Edinburgh: Thomas C. Jack, Grange Publishing Works, 1882–5); and the first edition of John Bartholomew's *Gazetteer of the British Isles* (1887), including all of Ireland.

www.tomorrows-history.com Maps of north-eastern England from the 19th century.

www.yourmapsonline.org.uk An ever-growing collection of out-of-copyright maps submitted by users.

CHAPTER 23

Before the mid-17th century

They might be approaching 400 and more years old, but Britain's earlier records can still tell you a lot about your home. Even if it was not built by then, you can still find out who owned the land and how it was used. If a Medieval knight once hunted wild boar across my front garden, I'd like to know about it!

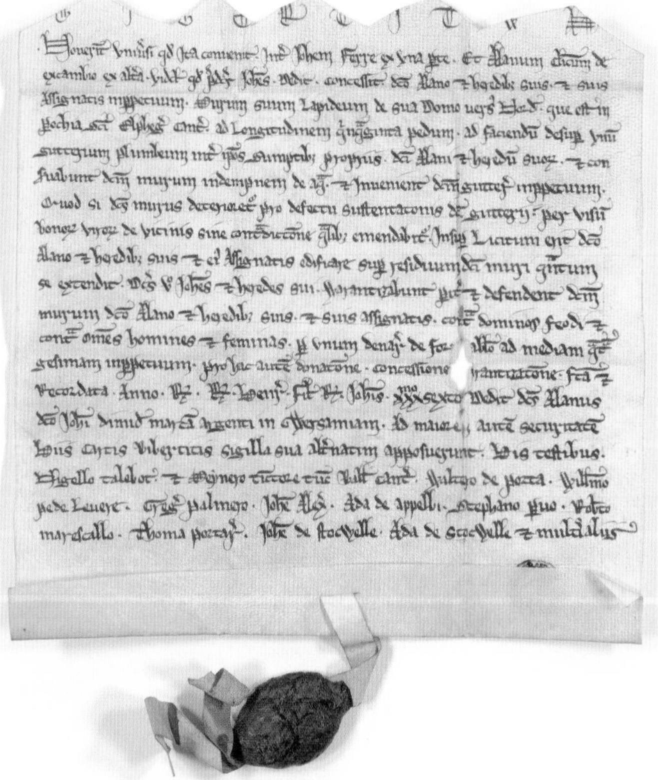

Grant relating to a wall in St Alphege parish, Canterbury, dateable to around 1251.

Inquisitions post mortem

(1235–1649)

'IPM', as they are usually called, were taken from 1235 to 1649. They record the deaths of those who held land direct from the Crown, stating what the land was; under what terms it was held; and who the heir was. Although unlikely to mention even great mansions, they are helpful for tracing the descent of the estate in which your home now stands.

- The records are at the National Archives, mainly in classes C 132–49 and E 149–50.
- Abstracts of many have been published by county record societies and similar works and can be identified through Mullins (see page 145).
- Those for Ireland are at the Genealogical Office, Dublin, **www.nli.ie**, (and on microfilm via Mormon Family History Centres).

The dissolution of the monasteries

(1524–mid-1500s)

Some homes dating back to the 16th century, especially those called '— Priory' or '— Abbey', may be former monastic buildings. Many more that were built in the 16th century may incorporate stones taken from dissolved religious houses.

The Protestant Reformation in England and Wales (1534) was caused by Henry VIII's desire to divorce Catherine of Aragon and marry Anne Boleyn, against the Pope's wishes. His gripes with Rome's authority in this country, however, went back much earlier. The Church was a major

Battle Abbey, Sussex

Battle Abbey was dissolved in the Reformation and became the family home of the Browne Viscounts Montague. Legend has it that the last monk to leave turned round and cursed the Montagues to extinction by fire and water. All seemed to go well until 1793, when the 8th Viscount was drowned in a stupid attempt to cross the Schauffenhausen Falls in Switzerland in a flat-bottomed boat. Unbeknown to him, the monk's time bomb had gone off back in England, too, for another of his homes, Cowdray Park, burned to the ground. In 1815, his two nephews were drowned while bathing in the sea at Bognor. His remaining heir, Mark Anthony Browne, last Viscount Montague, died childless – the monk's curse was thereby fulfilled. (The story isn't all bad, though: as a result of the foregoing, Mark Anthony's young widow, Frances Manby, was able to remarry – and thus became my 4 x great-grandmother.)

landowner and, because of the claimed supremacy of the Pope, it behaved semi-independently from the Crown. This was too much for Henry, who, in 1524, inveigled the Pope into allowing 30 small monastic houses to be closed down, the proceeds being used to found new colleges in Oxford and Ipswich.

Once the final breach with Rome was made, Henry, via his Vicar-General, Thomas Cromwell, appointed church commissioners to survey all Church property and income. In 1536, the smaller monastic houses were closed down. Four years later, all the remaining ones were dissolved. The buildings were either demolished or merely de-roofed, in both instances to discourage monks and nuns from returning to live in them. Most of the land was then sold off by the specially created Court of Augmentations (called the Augmentations Office from 1554).

|| The court's records are mainly in the Exchequer Records at the National Archives, partially indexed in the online catalogue **www.catalogue.nationalarchives.gov.uk**. Here you may find a rich supply of deeds and other information on your home – some monasteries were surveyed down to the contents of each room – or at least the land on which your home stands.

|| The best place to start a search, however, is in local antiquarian histories (see page 73) and the Victoria County History series (see also page 73).

Medieval Canterbury

The Priory of Christ Church, Canterbury, compiled a series of long rentals detailing their extensive property in the city, from which they received income. Their records, supplemented by some 500 charters, enable us to trace the history of properties inside (and just outside) the city walls back to within a monk's whisper of the Norman Conquest. Some of these rentals, such as Rental D, thought to date from about 1200, are so detailed as to provide names of tenants; annual rents paid; on which religious feast the rent was due and a description of the holding, often including measurements.

In the 1960s, the late Bill Urry produced a series of detailed maps showing Canterbury in the 12th century, based on surviving rentals and charters in the city's archives. Furthermore, by studying the whole series of rentals in chronological order, it is even possible to observe changes in ownership between different unrelated individuals, or more often from father to son or daughter, man to widow and so on – thus 'Norman the plumber' was succeeded by 'Ingenulph the plumber son of Norman the plumber' and 'Alan the Alderman' by 'Heirs of Alan the Alderman'.

This section of Bill Urry's map for 'about 1200' shows that the land now occupied by St Edmund's

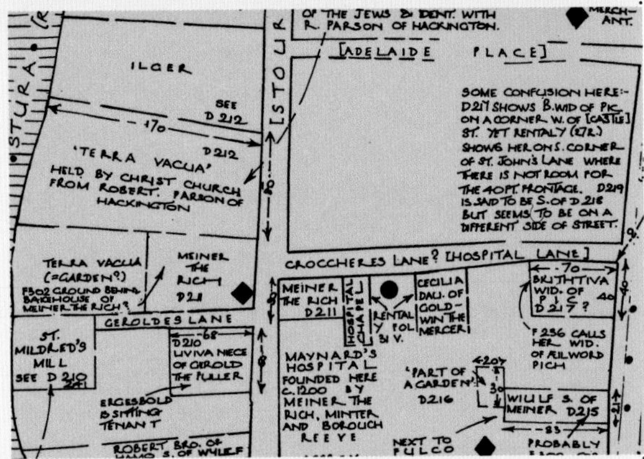

Street (pictured above) was then the bakehouse of Meiner the Rich, and the garden was behind it. The backs of the houses on the left of the photograph stand on what was then open ground ('terra vaccia') held by Christ Church Abbey from Robert, parson of nearby Hackington. The street opposite St Edmund's Street is called Hospital Lane because of Maynard's Hospital, founded there in about 1200 by the self-same Meiner. Meiner made his money by being the local minter and also borough reeve, jobs that enabled him to have a great deal of ready cash at his disposal at any given time.

Domesday Book

(1086)

After William the Conqueror invaded England in 1066, he parcelled out the land he had conquered among his nobles. Twenty years later, he wanted an accurate means of taxing his subjects. He therefore sent monks out to every corner of England with instructions to assess the value of the land in 1066, and its current values. Because the penalty for non-compliance with William's monastic inquisitors was having your entire village razed to the ground, it is generally reckoned that the survey's results were highly accurate – perhaps, indeed, it was the most accurate of its sort ever undertaken.

The details recorded are mainly concerned with people – who had held the land in 1066; who had it now; the numbers (but not names) of freemen, slaves, villeins, cottars and sokemen toiling in the fields. Some buildings were mentioned, though. If your home is a very ancient manor house, church or mill, there's a chance you may find it mentioned in *Domesday Book* – even though it's quite likely it will have been substantially rebuilt since then.

The real fun of *Domesday Book* is in having a peek at your home parish almost a thousand years ago. In practical terms, it's one of the earliest sources of documentary evidence you can use to underpin the history of your home.

Sadly, some areas of England had been so badly devastated by the Conquest that there

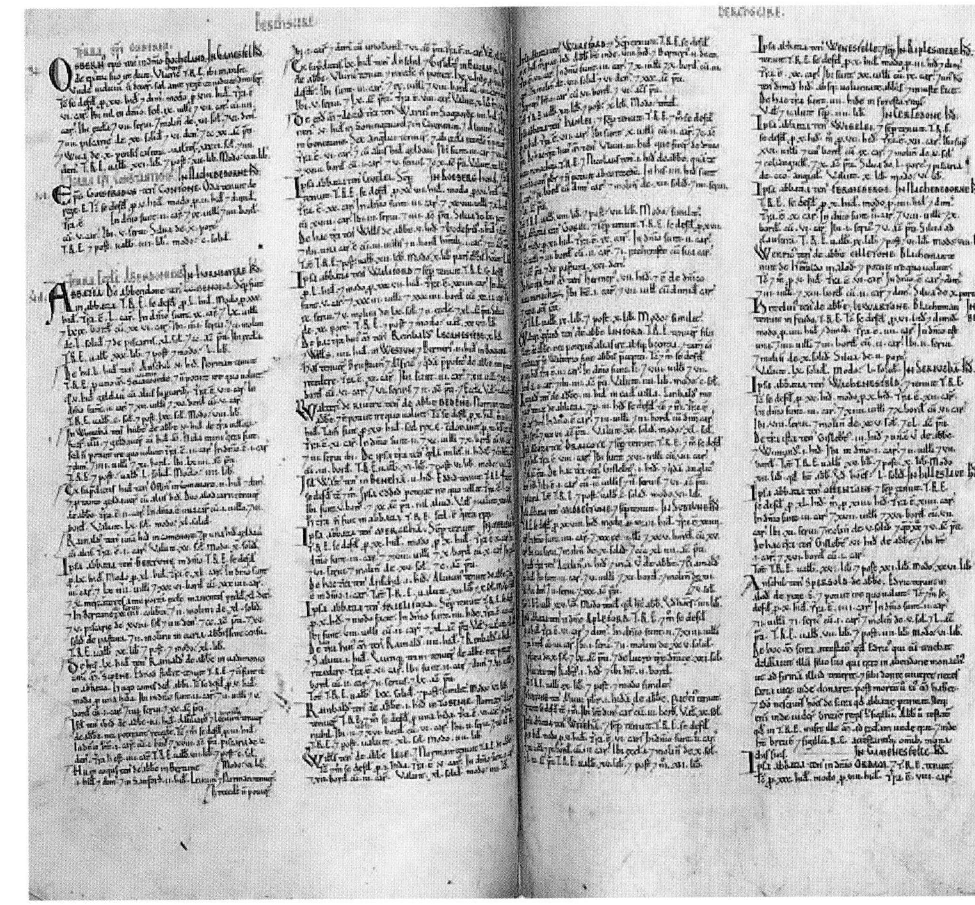

Extract from *Domesday Book*.

Medieval descriptions, rentals and charters

Some areas have exceptionally long runs of records stretching right back into the Middle Ages.

Battle, Sussex *The Chronicle of Battle Abbey, Sussex* (*Chronicon Monasterii de Bello*, ed. J. S. Brewer, London, 1846, pp 12–16) lists the inhabitants of the town of Battle c.1111.

Bristol William of Worcester's description of Bristol in his *Itinerary*, has been edited by Nasmith (see box opposite). This work is so splendidly detailed as to include measurements and dimensions of the port's streets and buildings.

Cambridge See Oxford and Cambridge, right.

Chester A similar description exists of Chester, written by the monk Lucian, recently edited and published by Taylor (see also box opposite).

City of London William FitzStephen's biography of Thomas Becket, *Vita Sancti Thomae*, is prefixed by a 'Description of the City' in the late 12th century, reproduced in *English Historical Documents* II (no. 281, Norman London) and by Barraclough (see also box opposite).

Fordwich, Kent A charter of 1111 (British Library MS Cotton, Claudius D X, 175r) made by Hamo Dapifer names 25 of the town's inhabitants.

Gloucester From the 15th century there is a detailed 1455 rental of Gloucester, edited by Stevenson in 1890 (see also box opposite).

Gloucester and Winchcombe 11th-century descriptions exist (see Ellis's *General Introduction to Domesday Book*, 11, pp 446–7).

Hull 13th-century surveys have been analysed by Bilson (see also box opposite).

Newark on Trent A late 12th-century rent roll containing some 500 entries, published and edited by Barley, Stevenson and Cameron (see also box opposite).

Oxford and Cambridge Both of these cities are very well charted through their Hundred Rolls and the vast archives of deeds held by the colleges, as studied by Salter for Oxford, and Willis and Clark for Cambridge (see also box opposite).

Sandwich and Dover Early-13th-century inhabitants appear in records in Canterbury Cathedral Archives.

Winchester Two short descriptions were made c.1110 and in 1148, and used in the Victoria County History volume covering that city (Hampshire, 1, pp 527 ff).

was no point surveying them. These were Durham, London, Winchester, Northumberland and northern Westmoreland.

- The Victoria County History series (see page 73) contain detailed analyses of *Domesday Book* entries.
- Copies of *Domesday Book* are available in a variety of forms from Phillimore & Co. Ltd. You can choose between volumes for each county, with translations printed next to facsimiles of the original Latin text.
- Phillimore also sells county maps either on paper sheets or CD-Rom. These are based on Ordnance Survey sheets, showing county and hundred boundaries; *Domesday Book* place-names; vills; manors; and special features such as castles, salt mines and so on.

A surprising number of Medieval buildings are still inhabited. This section of Canterbury, looking down Mercery Lane to the cathedral's Christ Church Gate, is still little changed from the Middle Ages.

BOOKS

- M. W. Barley, W. H. Stevenson and K. Cameron (eds), 'Documents Relating to the Manor and Soke of Newark on Trent' (*Thoroton Society Record Series*, xvi, 1955)
- G. Barraclough, *Social Life in Early England* (Routledge and Kegan Paul, 1960)
- J. Bilson, 'Wyke upon Hull in 1239' (*Transactions of the East Riding Antiquarian Society*, xxvi, pp 37–105)
- H. Ellis, *A General Introduction to Domesday Book* (Muller, 1971)
- E. L. C. Mullins' *Texts and Calendars: An Analytical Guide to Serial Publications* (RHS, 1958) and vol. II 1957–82 (RHS, 1983)
- J. Nasmith (ed.), *Itineraria Symonis Simeonis et Willelmi de Worcestre* (Cambridge, 1778)
- H. E. Salter, *Map of Medieval Oxford* (1934) (edited and republished by W. A. Pantin in vol. 1 of the *Oxford Historical Society, New Series*, xiv, 1960)
- W. H. Stevenson (ed.) and Robert Cole (compiler), *Rental of All the Houses in Gloucester, A.D. 1455* (J. Bellows, 1890)
- M. V. Taylor (ed.), 'Liber Luciani de Laude Cestrie' (*Lancashire and Cheshire Record Society Publications*, vol. 69, 1912)
- W. Urry, *Canterbury under the Angevin Kings* (Athlone Press, 1967)
- J. Willis and J. W. Clark, *Architectural History of the University of Cambridge, etc.* (CUP, 1886)

PART 3

Digging deeper

By now, you should have formed a fairly detailed knowledge of your home and its history. If your case is a reasonably normal one, then you will probably have made some great finds, while being left with a few niggling mysteries – was it Mr X or Mr Y who lived in your house in the 1770s? Was the coal shed that appears on old maps located in your back garden or next door's? Were the chimneys built in 1600 or 1568? Whatever you have found, one thing is certain – there is still much more you can do!

This section should fulfil two purposes, by providing details of other sources that may give you more information about your home and its past inhabitants, and helping you overcome problems that may have arisen. Using the sources described here you can go into greater depth in areas that particularly interest you and find out more about your home's history than maybe you ever thought possible.

CHAPTER 24

General Registration and parish registers

1538–present

Thanks to information discovered by the family history movement, we now know that families in the past tended to be quite mobile, moving from place to place regularly to seek work. However, it's worth bearing in mind that most family trees relate to children, unless it was an only child – usually the eldest son – who inherited the family home. Most daughters and younger sons ended up moving away from home, thus making family trees so geographically diverse. But when you look at the history of an old home, you will generally encounter the line of the family as it descended through the eldest son – the one who did not have to move away.

You may find that the surnames of inhabitants changed from one generation to another. This can be due to complete change of tenancy or ownership. Often, however, especially once you have traced back to the early to mid-19th century, this will be because of inheritance through the female line, i.e. sons-in-law or maternal grandchildren succeeding their fathers-in-law and maternal grandparents respectively.

Even if the occupancy of a home changed outside such immediate family circles, you may find that the new occupants had moved in because they had some more remote family link with the previous ones.

General Registration

You can use many of the records discussed in this book – censuses, wills and so on – to help reconstruct the relevant family trees. Of most use, however, are parish registers (see page 151) and, for the past 150 years, General Registration.

General Registration records of births, marriages and deaths provide some evidence for the history of homes in their own right, and are extremely useful for unravelling the stories of the people who once lived under your roof. They all include spaces for addresses. As we have seen with census returns (pages 46–55), precise addresses were rarely recorded in the 19th century: most homes were, in fact, identified by who lived in them and how they stood in relation to other buildings. Therefore, while a great number of precise addresses do appear on General Registration certificates, many just state the name of the village or the name of a street but without a number. When combined with other evidence from directories, electoral lists and so on, however, the precise addresses can often be inferred.

These records can add a lot of detail to the history of your home. For example, the 1851 census may show a young man living with his parents, and that of 1861 might then reveal him residing in the same home with his widowed mother, his wife and young child. It is interesting then to search for records of the death of the father, the marriage of the young man and the birth of his child. This will add precise dates and other details to your home's story. The death and birth may actually have taken place in your home. If they took place nearby, perhaps in a local hospital, and if the marriage took place at a local church or chapel, then these records show how your home and its inhabitants stood in relation to the community around them.

Equally, obtaining a General Registration certificate for someone who you thought lived in your home may reveal that they actually lived somewhere else – frustrating for you, but at least alerting you to your having made a mistake.

How to search

General Registration records started being kept on 1 July 1837. They are indexed by the four quarters of the year in which they were registered: January–March (called the 'March quarter'); April–June (the 'June quarter'); and so on. Marriages were registered on the spot, but death registration could be delayed by inquests, and births by simple tardiness. Up to 1875, births were registered voluntarily; thereafter, they had to be registered within six weeks of the event. For this reason, you should always look in the likely quarter and the one after, though as ages are often given inaccurately, it is usually worth looking for an event a few years either side of when you expected it to happen. If you have no idea when an event took place, you can simply search through each quarterly index, year by year, looking for it.

- Copies of the indexes are at the Family Records Centre, Mormon Family History Centres and good libraries, but increasingly the easiest way to search is on the internet.
- A complete set of indexes is at **www.1837online.com**.
- At the time of writing, sections of the indexes are fully indexed at a pay-to-view site, **www.familyrelatives.org** (by the time this book goes on sale this will probably be complete).
- A free, random but increasingly large index of references up to 1901 is at **www.freebmd.rootsweb.com**.
- Several counties now have websites containing composite computerised indexes to local registrars' indexes: details of these appear at **www.ukbmd.org.uk**.
- Certificates can be ordered via the Registration Online Ordering Service at **www.gro.gov.uk**, at the Family Records Centre or from the relevant local registrar. Certificates cost £7 each. If you find a couple of possible entries but do not know which is right, you can have a check made based on a confirmed piece of information and £4 will be refunded for entries that do not match up. The checking point may, for example, be the father's name on a birth certificate, when you already know this from a census return.

What the indexes tell you

Birth indexes: The General Registration birth indexes give the name (surname, forename and with initials for middle names); the registration district in which the birth was registered; a reference number and, from September 1911, the mother's maiden name. Be aware, though, that some birth and death certificates may give a hospital's address but not state that the building was actually a hospital.

Marriage indexes: These give the names of the parties marrying, the registration district where the event took place and a reference number. You can search under the more unusual of the two surnames and then seek a corresponding entry for the other party's name – you can find the other spouse's name from the birth certificate of one of their children. If the reference number and registration district match up, then it's probably the right entry. From March 1912, the name of the other spouse appears as part of the index entry. It's best to start from the date when the first child was born – the idea that couples dutifully waited until their wedding night is fanciful and seldom borne out by the facts. On marriage certificates, the groom's address will often not be his permanent one but a temporary residence adopted solely to give him the right to marry in his bride's parish.

Death indexes: These give the deceased's name, the district in which they died and a reference number. Between March 1866 and March 1969, they include the deceased's age, and thereafter the date of birth. The place of death will not always be the person's permanent home, but in many such cases a home address is given in the 'occupation' column. There is also a column for the informant and their home address, which may be the same as the deceased's.

Deaths were often also recorded by newspaper obituaries and wills. If the death was followed by an inquest, this will be stated on the certificate. Coroners' reports can be traced through Gibson and Rogers' book (see box opposite), though invariably a more accessible and colourful account will be found in the local paper (see pages 66–7). Alcock makes the point in his book (see box opposite) that:

... perhaps half of the deaths by misadventure took place in the home and details in the inquests can be very revealing of, for example, the strength of walls and doors, shared sleeping arrangements, the location of ovens in house yards, the stones around the open hearth supporting pots of boiling water.

If a death requiring an inquest took place in your home, take a deep breath before you read it – you never know what macabre details you may discover!

General Registration in Scotland

- Scottish General Registration dates from 1 January 1855. The records are with the Registrar General of Scotland at New Register House, Charlotte Square, Edinburgh EH1 3YT; tel: 0131 334 0380; **www.gro-scotland.gov.uk**.
- The website **www.scotlandspeople.gov.uk** has indexes and downloadable copies of the certificates. These will probably provide complete coverage by the time this book is published: at present they cover births, 1855–1902, marriages 1855–1928 and deaths 1855–1953.

Scottish records are slightly more detailed than English and Welsh ones: the date and place of marriage appears on birth certificates. Most marriages took place not in church but at home, and this is usually recorded.

General Registration in Ireland

Civil registration for Protestant marriages started on 1 April 1845 and on 1 January 1864 for all births, marriages and deaths. The records and registration districts were organised as in England.

- The records are kept by the Registrar General of Eire at Joyce House, 8–11 Lombard Street, Dublin 2; tel: 00 353 1635 4000; **www.groireland.ie**.
- Civil records for Northern Ireland from 1922 are kept by the Registrar General of Northern Ireland at Oxford House, 49–55 Chichester Street, Belfast BT1 4HL; tel: 0232 235221, and certificates can be ordered online at **www.groni.gov.uk**.

Parish registers

The odd boundary change aside, your home has probably always been in the same parish, so you are likely to find helpful details of past inhabitants in the parish registers. These started in 1538, though very few survive for before 1600. Indeed, many do not survive from before the disruption of the Civil War and Interregnum (1642–60), or, if they do, they contain a gap for those years. From 1598, copies, called Bishops' Transcripts, started being made.

The details given in parish registers are usually fairly minimal, but they are often enough to piece together a family tree. Until 1754 for marriages and 1812 for baptisms and burials, clergymen could record whatever extra details they wanted, so you may be lucky and find your home named as the place of residence for people being baptised, married or buried. Between 1754 and 1837, precise addresses should not be expected in marriage registers. From 1812, the place of residence is recorded for baptisms and burials, but this could vary from a precise address to merely the name of the village. If you're lucky, therefore, the registers will confirm who lived in your home. In most cases, though, parish registers will help you most by revealing how people who you have already identified as occupants of your home were related to each other.

- You will usually find both parish registers and Bishops' Transcripts in the county record office: if they are not there, ask the staff or consult the *Phillimore Atlas* and Gibson's guide (see box right). The record office may also have printed, and sometimes indexed, transcripts of registers.
- Marriages often took place in the bride's parish. There are many marriage indexes, often accessible in the record office. Many also appear on **www.familysearch.org**.
- Non-Anglicans avoided having their children baptised in parish churches – in such cases, you should seek records of their particular denominations. However, as many Catholic families eventually gave in and became Anglicans, and many Protestant non-conformist families could also lapse back into Anglicanism, you may still find useful information in the parish registers.
- From 1754 onwards, marriages of all except Quakers and Jews had to be performed in parish churches to be legally valid. Further, regardless of denomination, Anglican parish churches were often the only available place for burying bodies, so burial registers tend to provide reasonably complete coverage of all those who died in the parish.
- Scottish parish registers – those of the Presbyterian Church – are kept at New Register House, and are indexed on **www.scotlandspeople.gov.uk**. Some non-Presbyterian registers are indexed on **www.FamilySearch.org**.
- Irish parish registers are not normally as useful for most families as those of the Catholic Church, which are still generally held by parish priests or in county heritage centres. Sadly, they rarely go back much further than the 1830s.
- For further specialist help on tracing ancestry, see the accompanying Collins guide *Tracing Your Family History* (see box below).

BOOKS

- **A. Adolph, *Tracing Your Family History* (Collins, 2004)**
- **N. W. Alcock, *Documenting the History of Houses* (British Records Association, 2003)**
- **J. Gibson, *Bishops' Transcripts and Marriage License Bonds and Allegations: A Guide to their Location and Indexes* (FFHS, 1997)**
- **J. Gibson and C. Rogers, *Coroners' Records in England and Wales* (FFHS, 1997)**
- ***The Phillimore Atlas and Index of Parish Registers* (Phillimore, 2003)**

James Paterson and family

At the point when census returns and directories enable you to write 'between about 1868 and 1879 Whithorn House, Stoke Newington, was occupied by James Paterson and his family ...', you could do one of two things: move back to the house's history in the 1860s, or pause and find out more about the Patersons' time there.

The 1871 census, for example, shows the Patersons at Whithorn House as follows:

James Paterson, head, married, 40, carrier railway agent, born Scotland

Isabella, 38, born Marylebone

Mary A.C., daughter, 17, born Northumberland

John J., son, 16, born Northumberland

Harry L., 5, born Islington

Thomas, 3, born Deptford, Kent

Edith J., 2, born Deptford

Janet L., 2 months, born Stoke Newington

William Arnott, visitor, 22, brass finisher, born Clerkenwell

Hannah Thomas, servant, domestic cook, born Chester

Emily Suare, 17, nurse, born Brandon, Suffolk

Ann Mason, 15, housemaid, born Little Downham, Cambridge

Janet was clearly a new arrival in the home, but where exactly did she come screaming into the world? Was it in Whithorn House? Her birth certificate, found in the March quarter of the 1871 General Registration indexes, confirms that this was indeed the case. She was born Janet Louise Paterson on 26 January 1871 at Whithorn House, Stoke Newington, daughter of James Paterson, a carrier, and his wife, 'Isabella Lorraine Paterson', formerly Wilkins. 'Carrier' was a bit of an understatement,

RIGHT
James Paterson and his daughter Mary Ann, pictured before he moved to London. The interior shown was not his own house, however: like most pictures of the time, it was taken on a set in the photographer's studio.

ABOVE
'Whithorn House and the churchyard': watercolour by T. H. Shepherd.

BELOW
An 1871 census return for Whithorn House, showing the Paterson family in residence.

		John J	do	Son	do	16		do
		Harry L	do	do	do	5		Islington do
		Thomas	do	do	do	3		Deptford Kent
		Edith J	do	daughter	do		2	do do
		Janet L	do	do	do		2 Mo	Stoke Newington Middx
		William Arnott	Visitor	do	22		Brass Finisher	Clerkenwell do
		Hannah Thomas	Serv	do		[illegible]	Cook Domestic	Chester
		Emily Suare	do	do		17	Nurse do	Brandon Suffolk
		Ann Mason	do	do		15	Housemaid do	Little Downham Camb
Church St	1	Richard Bird	Head	Marr	32		Coachman	[illegible] Shropshire
The Lodge to "Clissold"		Eliza Bird	Wife	do		33		[illegible]
		Mary C Bird	daughter	do		4		Stoke Newington Middx
Total of Houses	[illegible]			Total of Males and Females	6	19		

as James was in fact the senior proprietor of the enormous luggage carrying firm of Carter, Paterson & Co.

Further exploration of General Register Office certificates for the family reveals other family events involving Whithorn House. On 29 April 1879, James's eldest daughter, 25-year old Mary Ann Collingwood Paterson, married the Rev. Patrick Henry Kilduff of nearby Tottenham, at 'the parish church of Stoke Newington'. The certificate is one of those annoying ones that does not give a precise place of residence for either party, but just states Mary Ann's residence as 'Stoke Newington'. Luckily, directories provide evidence that the family were still living at Whithorn House at the time.

This broadens the story of Whithorn House outwards a little. Originally 2 Church Row, Whithorn House became the first house in Church Row when number 1 was demolished in the mid-19th century so that the graveyard of Old St Mary's parish church could be extended. Whithorn House therefore adjoined the graveyard and was next door to the old parish church. However, it's unlikely this was where Mary Ann was married, for local histories show that the old church, which dates from 1563, was superseded by a much larger one over the road, commissioned in 1853 from the highly fashionable Gothic architect George Gilbert Scott (1811–78), who also built Glasgow University, St Pancras Station and the Albert Memorial in London – he founded the Society for the Protection of Ancient Buildings as well.

It's likely, then, that the Patersons left Whithorn House on the morning of 29 April 1879 and crossed the road in order to enter the grand new parish church to celebrate the wedding. As a final twist in the tale, however, it seems that the church was not quite as it is today: the towering spire wasn't added until 11 years later.

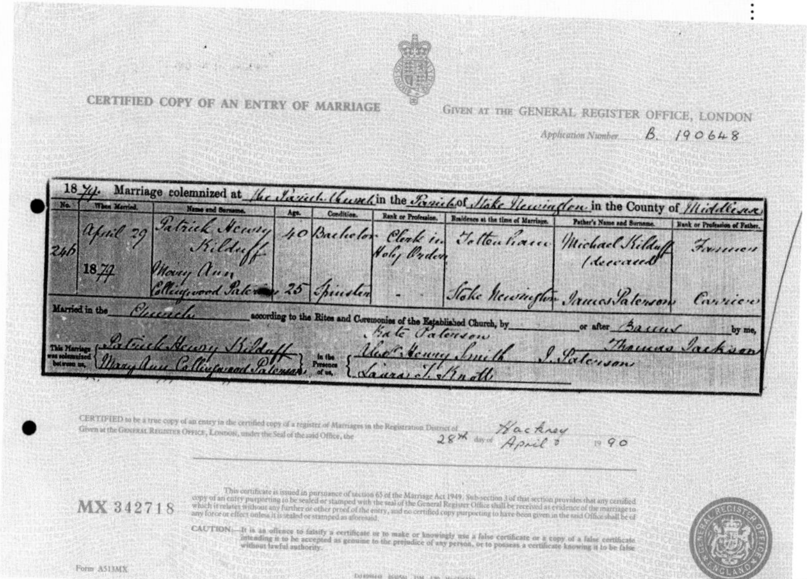

CERTIFIED COPY OF AN ENTRY OF MARRIAGE — GIVEN AT THE GENERAL REGISTER OFFICE, LONDON

Application Number B. 190648

1879. Marriage solemnized at the Parish Church in the Parish of Stoke Newington in the County of Middlesex

No.	When Married	Name and Surname	Age	Condition	Rank or Profession	Residence at the time of Marriage	Father's Name and Surname	Rank or Profession of Father
246	April 29 1879	Patrick Henry Kilduff	40	Bachelor	Clerk in Holy Orders	Tottenham	Michael Kilduff (deceased)	Farmer
		Mary Ann Collingwood Paterson	25	Spinster	-	Stoke Newington	James Paterson	Carrier

Married in the Church according to the Rites and Ceremonies of the Established Church, by or after Banns by me, Thomas Jackson

This Marriage was solemnized between us, Patrick Henry Kilduff, Mary Ann Collingwood Paterson. In the Presence of us, Kate Paterson, Alex. Henry Smith, J. Paterson, Laura J. Knott

CERTIFIED to be a true copy of an entry in the certified copy of a register of Marriages in the Registration District of Hackney. Given at the GENERAL REGISTER OFFICE, LONDON, under the Seal of the said Office, the 28th day of April 1990

MX 342718

CAUTION:—It is an offence to falsify a certificate or to make or knowingly use a false certificate or a copy of a false certificate intending it to be accepted as genuine to the prejudice of any person, or to possess a certificate knowing it to be false without lawful authority.

Form A513MX

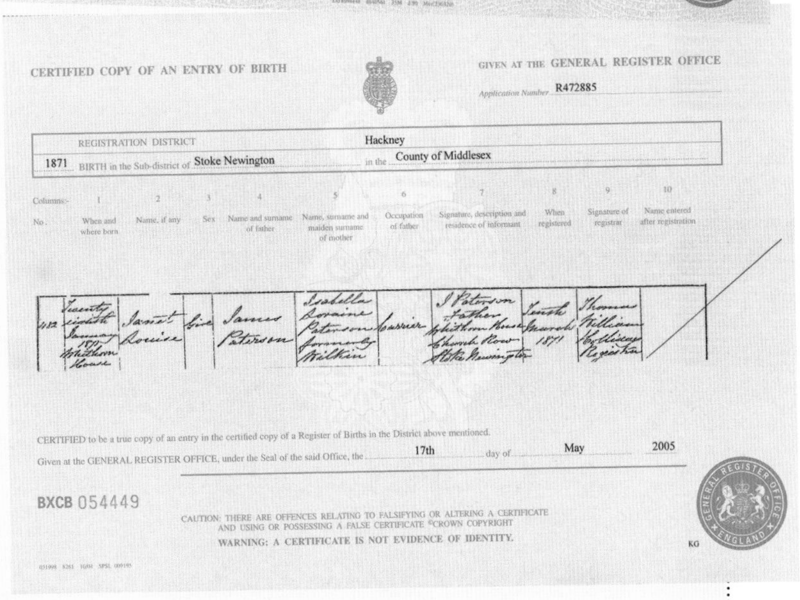

CERTIFIED COPY OF AN ENTRY OF BIRTH — GIVEN AT THE GENERAL REGISTER OFFICE

Application Number R472885

REGISTRATION DISTRICT Hackney

1871 BIRTH in the Sub-district of Stoke Newington in the County of Middlesex

No.	When and where born	Name, if any	Sex	Name and surname of father	Name, surname and maiden surname of mother	Occupation of father	Signature, description and residence of informant	When registered	Signature of registrar	Name entered after registration
482	Twenty sixth January 1871 Whithorn House	Janet Louise	Girl	James Paterson	Isabella Lorraine Paterson formerly Wilkin	Carrier	J Paterson Father Whithorn House Church Row Stoke Newington	Fourth March 1871	Thomas William Kilburn Registrar	

CERTIFIED to be a true copy of an entry in the certified copy of a Register of Births in the District above mentioned.

Given at the GENERAL REGISTER OFFICE, under the Seal of the said Office, the 17th day of May 2005

BXCB 054449

CAUTION: THERE ARE OFFENCES RELATING TO FALSIFYING OR ALTERING A CERTIFICATE AND USING OR POSSESSING A FALSE CERTIFICATE ©CROWN COPYRIGHT

WARNING: A CERTIFICATE IS NOT EVIDENCE OF IDENTITY.

ABOVE
Janet Louise's birth certificate.

TOP
Mary Ann Collingwood Paterson's 1879 marriage certificate. She only stated 'Stoke Newington' as her address.

CHAPTER 25

Wills and inventories

Middle Ages–present

Wills may well turn up in your research, in a bundle of title deeds, or in other family papers. It is always worth searching out wills for people who lived in or owned your home. Besides providing some extra information about the people in their own right, they will often mention properties, furniture, leases and so on.

Generally, the better off someone was, the more likely they were to write a will. Often, the poor did not make wills, but there are plenty of examples of labourers and factory workers who bucked the trend. Don't automatically assume that, just because your home was not inhabited by the well-to-do, that they have not left any wills.

Thomas Braithwaite of Ambleside (d. 1607), looking in poor shape, makes his will.

Wills were written by people (called 'testators') during their lifetimes and taken to a probate court after their deaths to be registered ('proved'). Often, when there was no will, letters of administration would be taken out – quite interesting for someone's potted biography, but much less useful for us unless accompanied, as were many wills, by an inventory. Inventories could list all the deceased's possessions, sometimes room by room, providing fascinating detail about the contents of their homes. Inventories are also useful as a means of comparing your home with what was normal at the time. Barley and Wetheril's books (see page 161) both offer yardsticks with which to compare inventories for your home against general trends. Besides name and date of death, the main things you will learn from a will are how much the deceased's estate was worth, where they lived and where they died.

Be aware that some terms have changed considerably in meaning over the centuries. A 'loom' for example, was not always a weaving machine but could mean a bucket, and a 'map' was invariably not a chart but a tablecloth or napkin. Milward's book is a useful guide on this subject (see also page 161).

From 1540, men aged 14 or more and women aged 12 or more were allowed to write wills.

From 1837, the age for both sexes was raised to 21 years. Those who were excommunicated, mad or imprisoned could not write wills. While spinsters and widows often wrote wills, married women seldom did so until 1882, because until the Married Women's Property Act of 1882 they could not legally own anything.

Wills could be proved just after someone died, but the process could take years, so don't make your search too restricted. As with all records, take into account possible variant spellings too.

Where to search

- From 1858, probate matters have been handled by the Principal Probate Registry, now called the Principal Registry of the Family Division (First Avenue House, 42–49 High Holborn, London WC1V 6NP; tel: 020 7936 7000; **www.courtservice.gov.uk**), where copies of the wills cost £5, either to view or be posted to you.
- The annual indexes to wills and administrations can be searched there, or, up to 1943 only, on microfiche in major libraries. Alternatively, postal searches cost £5 for a four-year search plus a copy of the will, with £3 for each extra four-year period you want searched. Postal applications should be sent to the Principal Registry of the Family Division's Postal Searches and Copies Department, The Probate Registry, Castle Chambers, Clifford Street, York YO1 9RG.
- Wills before 1858 were proved by a variety of church authorities. Most were proved by the most local ecclesiastical authority – usually the archdeacon or bishop. You can find out where to search by looking up your

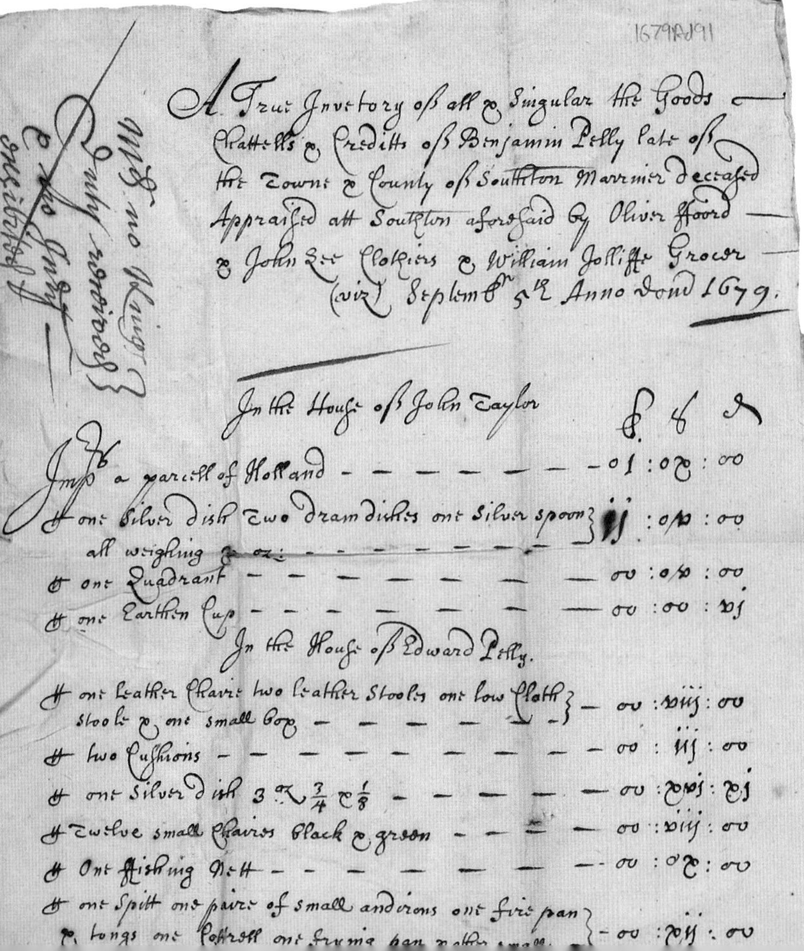

1679A/91

A True Inventory of all & Singular the Goods Chattells & Credits of Benjamin Pelly late of the Towne & County of Southton Marriner deceased Appraised att Southton aforesaid by Oliver ffoord & John [illegible] Clothiers & William Jolliffe Grocer (viz) Septemb 5th Anno Dom 1679.

In the House of John Taylor — £ s d

Imps a parcell of Holland — 01 : 02 : 00
It one Silver dish two dram dishes one Silver spoone all weighing [illegible] oz — ij : 0[illegible] : 00
It one Quadrant — 00 : 0[illegible] : 00
It one Earthen Cup — 00 : 00 : 0j

In the House of Edward Pelly.

It one leather Chaire two leather Stooles one low Cloth stoole & one small Box — 00 : viij : 00
It two Cushions — 00 : iij : 00
It one Silver dish 3 oz 3/4 & 1/8 — 00 : xvj : 0j
It Twelve small Chaires black & green — 00 : viij : 00
It One fishing Nett — 00 : 02 : 00
It one Spitt one paire of small andirons one fire pan & tongs one [illegible] — 00 : xij : 00

Pelly's possessions

The inventory of Benjamin Pelly from Southampton, a mariner, dated 5 April 1679, lists the property he owned in three different people's houses, the main being that of Edward Pelly, who happened to be his father. This starts with 'one leather Chaire two leather stooles one low Cloths stoole & one small box', together worth 8 shillings, and includes such other items as 'one Bible three sea books & other books' (value 15 shillings).

In 1864, the old estate of Thelveton Hall, bought by Thomas Havers in 1592, was sold. The sale papers provide much detail concerning the estate itself, down to individual cottages (see pages 174–5). They also tell us a lot about the house itself. The ground floor, for example, consisted of an 'Entrance Hall with Stone Porch, Drawing Room 21 ft. 6in. by 19ft., Dining Room 20ft. by 19ft. 6in., Library or Morning Room, Water Closet, Lobby and door to Garden'. There was, one reads, only one 'water closet' or loo in the whole mansion.

It is interesting to note the mention on the first floor of 'a large room with arched roof being the chapel and a sacristy adjoining approached by a separate staircase', for the family were Catholics. What is not described here is the priest hole, used for hiding priests (16th and 17th centuries), that was said to be in a space between the ceiling of the entrance porch and the small chamber above it. Hodgetts provides a full list of known priest holes (see page 161).

The estate papers are interesting in their own right, but they also bear fascinating comparison with earlier Havers wills that make specific reference to the rooms of Thelveton Hall. Writing his will in 1666, William Havers (grandson of the first Thomas and 5 x great grandfather of the man who sold the Hall in 1864) described the ground-floor rooms as 'the Great Parlour'; 'my Great Hall'; 'Inner Chamber'; and 'Hall Chamber and the inner chamber in it'. The 'Hall Chamber' was presumably the 1864 'Entrance Hall'; this leaves three rooms in 1864 (drawing room, dining room and library or morning room), to correspond with the three rooms of 1666 – great parlour, great hall and inner chamber. The loo, if it existed back then, was not, of course, mentioned in the 1666 will.

Picture of Thelveton Hall from the original sale papers, in the family papers of a descendant of the Havers family.

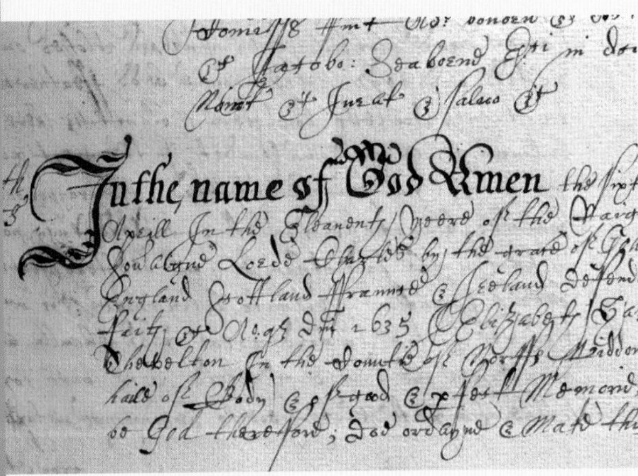

In the name of God Amen

The beginning of Elizabeth Havers' very detailed will.

Going even further back, rooms appear again in the 1635 will of Elizabeth Havers, widow of the original Thomas. She actually tells us what was in the rooms. The great parlour contained, among other things, 'a wainscot chayer, two trunks, danske chests, two chayers, wicker chayer, two chestes of purndell and hangeings'; the hall had 'two tables' and a 'greate cubberd; while in the 'Inner Great Parlour Chamber' were a 'postedd bedstead, downe bedd, fether bedd, curtains, trundle bedstead, redd rugg'. Three main rooms again: the fact that a bedroom was on the ground floor was entirely in keeping with the social norms of the time.

(3)

OF PRODUCTIVE

ARABLE, PASTURE, MEADOW AND WOOD LAND,

Lying exceedingly well together and affording first-rate shooting.

The sub-division of the Estate is as follows:—

THE MANSION, GARDENS, WOODS, PLANTATIONS, &c.

THE ACCOMMODATION OF THE MANSION CONSISTS OF

ON THE UPPER FLOOR–

Two Attic Bed Rooms or Nurseries, Two Store Closets, Men's Room, Lumber and Box Rooms.

ON THE FIRST FLOOR–

A Large Room with arched roof being the Chapel and a Sacristy adjoining, approached by a separate Staircase; Five Large Bed Rooms, Four Dressing Rooms, and Book Room or Store Closet.

ON THE GROUND FLOOR–

Entrance Hall with Stone Porch, Drawing Room 21ft. 6in. by 19ft., Dining Room 20ft. by 19ft. 6in., Library or Morning Room, Water Closet, Lobby, and door to Garden.

DOMESTIC OFFICES–

Consisting of Large Kitchen, Butler's Pantry, Cook's Pantry, China Closet and Store Room, and Capital Wine and Beer Cellars, and Larder on the Basement.

Paved Court Yard, Servants' Hall, Coal-house, Bake-house, and Wash-house.

CAPITAL STABLING,

Consisting of 3 loose Boxes and 8 Stalls, Harness Room, Coach House, Hay and Straw Lofts, Large Fruit Room, Brew-house, with Carpenter's Shop over.

AT A CONVENIENT DISTANCE ARE

THE FARM BUILDINGS,

Comprising Three Farm Yards, Wagon and Implement Sheds, Large Barn, Cattle Sheds, Stabling, Piggeries, Granary on Stone Piers, &c.

EXTENSIVE GARDENS,

PARTLY LAID OUT IN

Lawn ornamented with Flower Beds and planted with luxuriant Shrubs and Evergreens,

AND

THE REMAINDER IN PRODUCTIVE KITCHEN GARDEN,

The whole surrounded by lofty Brick Walls, clothed with Choice Fruit Trees in full bearing,

PLANTATION AND SHRUBBERY WALKS, SUMMER HOUSE,

OUTER FRUIT AND VEGETABLE GARDENS,

ABOVE

Page 3 of the sale papers of Thelveton Hall, showing the level of detail provided.

RIGHT

The entrance porch and chamber above: between the two, it is said, was a priest hole.

...of 1851 Religious Census Return

A RETURN

OF THE SEVERAL PARTICULARS TO BE INQUIRED INTO RESPECTING THE UNDERMENTIONED

PLACE OF PUBLIC RELIGIOUS WORSHIP.

[N.B.—A similar Return will be obtained from the Clergy of the Church of England, and also from the Ministers of every other Religious Denomination throughout Great Britain.]

I. Title ...orship	II. Where Situate; specifying the Parish or Place (1)	District (2)	County (3)	III. Religious Denomination	IV. When Erected	V. Whether a Separate and Entire Building	VI. Whether used exclusively as a Place of Worship (Except for a Sunday School)	VII. Space available for Public Worship: Number of Sittings already Provided: Free Sittings (4)	Other Sittings (5)	VIII. Estimated Number of Persons attending Divine Service on Sunday, March 30, 1851	Morning	Afternoon	Evening	IX. REMARKS
[illegible]	Thelton	Depwade Union	Norfolk	Roman Catholic	before 1800	attached to the mansion and offices under it but never been used but as a place of worship –	used exclusively as a place of worship but private	50	10	General Congregation	15	15		This Chapel is supplied from Bungay. The catholic priest of that place attends at Thelton about 8 times in the year being sometimes Sunday but always on a week day – Prayers are therefore read morning and Evening by the Proprietor – To this chapel (tho' private) no person is refused admittance at any time –
										Sunday Scholars	none			
										TOTAL ..				
								Free Space or Standing Room for		Average Number of Attendants during months (See Instruction VIII.)				
								none		General Congregation				
										Sunday Scholars				
										TOTAL ..				

...certify the foregoing to be a true and correct Return to the best of my belief. Witness my hand this 26 day of March 1851.

x (Signature) ..... Thos. Havers. – Justice of Peace for Norfolk & Suffolk

(Official Character) Proprietor of the above-named Place of Worship.

(Address by Post) Thelton Hall. Scole. Norfolk

LEFT

The entry in the 1851 religious census showing the Catholic chapel at Thelveton Hall. It was 'attached to the mansion and offices under it but never been used since built but as a place of worship'. It could sit 60 people, after which there was – perhaps not surprisingly – no standing room!

parish in the *Phillimore Atlas*, or consulting Gibson and Churchill's guide (see page 161). Sometimes, if someone had property in more than one jurisdiction – or had pretensions to being the sort of person who might – their will may have been proved by a higher authority. These too are indicated by Gibson and Churchill. The highest authorities were the Prerogative Courts of York and, above that, Canterbury. During the Cromwellian Interregnum (1653–60), *all* wills were proved at the secularised version of the Prerogative Court of Canterbury. You may therefore have to look in a number of courts for a will, but the search is invariably worth it.

|| Most pre-1858 wills are in county record offices, and many are accompanied by indexes – Gibson and Churchill will tell you this. Pre-1858 wills for Wales are at the National Library of Wales. Some are searchable on their record offices' websites (Cheshire's, for example, are at **www.cheshire.gov.uk/recoff/eshop/wills/search.html**).

|| Some categories of wills have been transcribed or summarised. Those for the period 1558–1603 in Essex, for example, are abstracted in Emmison's book (see also page 161).

|| The Prerogative wills for York are at the Borthwick Institute for Archives (University of York, Heslington, York YO10 5DD; tel: 01904 321166; **www.york.ac.uk/inst/bihr/**), and those for Canterbury (including wills from anywhere in the British Isles) are at the National Archives and are searchable at **www.documentsonline.nationalarchives.gov.uk**, from which you can download copies at £3 each.

|| Sometimes, if one was made, a probate inventory will be attached to the will or administration, but often they are stored separately in the same archive – Spufford's book provides a useful backup if a search does not prove straightforward (see also page 161). Inventories will generally be found for the period 1660–1750, but if you are lucky you may find some going back to 1539, the year they were generally introduced – though some actually go back even earlier. As they are not so useful for family history (this is the main reason why wills *are* so extensively indexed), inventories tend to be rather neglected, but for the histories of homes they can be amazingly useful.

|| Sadly, most pre-1858 wills proved in Somerset, Devon and Cornwall were destroyed in the bombing of Exeter in 1942. The county record offices keep what survives, and they also hold abstracts of other wills, extracted from secondary sources, such as solicitors' records.

|| For 1796–1903, many wills were abstracted in Estate Duty (also called Death Duty) registers. These are at the National Archives in class IR 26, indexed in IR 27, with copies available in the Family Records Centre and fully if rather poorly indexed on a pay-to-view site, **www.nationalarchivist.com**. These provide a useful partial substitute for the lost West Country wills, and have the advantage of saying what actually happened after someone died, rather than (as in wills) simply what was intended to have taken place.

|| Similar abstracts for estates including government stocks, covering 1717–1845, are held in the Bank of England Archive Section, Threadneedle Street, London EC2R 8AH; tel: 020 7601 5096; **www.bankofengland.co.uk/archive.htm** and indexed in **www.Englishorigins.net**.

Harvards in London

John Harvard founded Harvard University using money inherited from his family in Southwark, London. His brother Thomas's will was written on 15 July 1636 and proved on 5 May 1637 in the Prerogative Court of Canterbury and mentions various premises owned by the family in London, including (with numbers added by me):

1 messuages and Tenementes with thappurtennces And the rentes issues and proffites of them scituate lyinge and beinge att or neere Towerhill in the parishe of All Saintes Barkinge in London which I hould ioyntly togeather with my brother John Harvard by vertue of a lease to us thereof made by the brothers and sisters of the Hospitall of Saint Katherines neere the Tower of London.

2 All that messuage or Tenement with thappurtennces and the rente and revercon thereof scituate and beinge in or neere Shippyard in the pishe of Saint Saviours in Southwark now or late in the tenure or occupacon of Owen Jones or his assignes.

3 my moitie or halfe parte of the lease of the said Tenem'e with thappurtennces att or neere Tower hill in the said pishe of All Saintes Barkinge holden of and from the Hospitall of Saint Katherines and the moitie of any rentes and revercons thereof, and all my estate tearmes of yeares and demaund therein.

Rewritten in modern spelling, this means:

1 messuages and tenements with the appurtenances and the rents issues and profits of them situate lying and being at or near Tower Hill in the parish of All Saints Barking in London which I hold jointly together with my brother John Harvard by virtue of a lease to us thereof made by the brothers and sisters of the Hospital of Saint Katherine near the Tower of London.

2 All that messuage or tenement with the appurtenances and the rent and reversion thereof situate and being in or near Shipyard in the parish of Saint Saviours in Southwark now or late in the tenure or occupation of Owen Jones or his assigns.

3 My moiety or half part of the lease of the said tenement with the appurtenances at or near Tower Hill in the said parish of All Saints Barking held of and from the Hospital of Saint Katherine and the moiety of any rents and reversions thereof, and all my estate terms of years and demand therein.

Wills

James Paterson, whose residence, 'Melrose', in Stamford Hill, Stoke Newington, is described on page 54, died on 19 November 1887. The General Registration death certificate reveals that he died at Melrose. His will, obtained from the Principal Registry of the Family Division at First Avenue House, was written at Melrose on 30 September 1887. He wrote that the *lease* of Melrose was to be maintained for his wife Mary – the ex-governess Mary Sutton – and his children and sister Janet. His estate (in other words, his possessions and money), which amounted to a very impressive £67,302-5-5, was to be used to pay for 'other outgoings and domestic servants, gardener's wages and other outdoor charges', giving us, again, a hint at what life was like there at the time. A further clue is found in the bequest to his son Harry Lorraine Paterson of 'all my portraits pictures and books' – which, of course, would have been in Melrose. By 1891, when the next census was taken of Stamford Hill, James's family (despite his intention to have the lease of Melrose maintained after his death) had left.

James Paterson, shortly before he died. The photographer's address, 77 De Beauvoir Road, Kingsland. De Beauvoir Road, oddly enough, is where Hackney Archives are now: Kingsland Road is the same road that becomes Stamford Hill as it rises up north from Stoke Newington.

Wills in Scotland

Until 1868, the inheritance of land was fixed rigidly, going automatically to the eldest surviving son (or his heir), or, if there were no sons, to the eldest surviving daughter. Technically, therefore, there were no wills. There were testaments, however, in which people could bequeath their movable goods to whomever they liked. These can tell you something about people and their possessions. The equivalents of letters of administration, in which was appointed an administrator to distribute the goods of someone who had died intestate, these were called 'testaments dative'. Probate matters were dealt with in church courts until 1560 when, unlike England and Wales, probate was handed over to secular commissary courts or commissariots under the overall jurisdiction of the Principal Commissariot of Edinburgh. This court also dealt with Scots who had goods in Scotland but who had died elsewhere.

- The *Phillimore Atlas* and Gibson and Churchill's book (see box opposite) indicate where to look. All records have been indexed and are at the National Archives of Scotland.
- Testaments from 1824 were proved in the county sheriffs' courts. Most of their records up to 1875 are at the National Archives of Scotland, with annual national indexes up to 1959 – called calendars of confirmations and inventories.
- An index to 350,000 Scottish wills, 1500–1875, is on **www.scottishdocuments.com**.
- The Scottish Archive Network's online catalogue, SCAN (**www.scan.org.uk**), contains catalogues for 52 of Scotland's main

archives, including an index to some 500,000 Scottish wills and testaments.

Wills in Ireland

|| Wills proved from 1922 are at the National Archives, Dublin, and PRONI. Most proved before then were destroyed by IRA bombing, though copies of the majority from 1858 survive and are at the National Archives, Dublin, and PRONI, which also hold abstracts of some otherwise lost wills from before that date.

|| There are also English Inland Revenue copies of Irish wills 1828–39 (indexed at the National Archives, Dublin) and abstracts of wills from the deeds registry (1708–1832), indexed in Eustace's book (see box below).

|| Another large collection of will abstracts up to 1858 is in the Land Commission records at the National Archives, Dublin.

BOOKS

- **M. W. Barley, *The English Farmhouse and Cottage* (Sutton, 1987)**
- **F. G. Emmison, *Essex Wills (England): The Archdeaconry Courts 1597–1603* (Essex Record Office, 3 vols, 1558–1577; National Genealogical Society, Washington, 1982, 1983, 1986), supplemented by a further series of 3 vols, 1578–1603, and eight more covering the Commissary Court, 1558–1603 (Essex Record Office)**
- **P. B. Eustace, *Registry of Deeds, Dublin: Abstracts of Wills*, 3 vols (Irish Manuscripts Commission, 1954–84)**
- **J. Gibson and E. Churchill, *Probate Jurisdictions: Where to Look for Wills* (FFHS, 2002)**
- **M. Hodgetts, 'A Topographical Index of Hiding Places' (*Recusant History*, vol. 23, no. 4, and vol. 24, no. 1, 1998)**
- **R. Milward, *A Glossary of Household, Farming and Trade Terms from Probate Inventories* (Derbyshire Record Society Occasional Paper no. 1, 1986)**
- **P. Spufford (ed.), *Index to the Probate Accounts of England and Wales* (British Record Society, vols 12 and 13, 1999)**
- **L. Wetherill, *Consumer Behaviour and Material Culture in Britain 1660–1760* (Economic and Social Research Council, 1988)**
- ***The Phillimore Atlas and Index of Parish Registers* (Phillimore, 2003)**

CHAPTER 26

Parish rates

16th–20th centuries, mainly surviving from the 18th century onwards

Rate books can provide annual lists of parish ratepayers. Using them you can often work back through many successive generations of occupants of your home.

During the 16th and 17th centuries, parishes took over many of the functions previously exercised by manorial courts, and were granted the right to raise rates for such matters as looking after bridges (1531); building prisons (1532); caring for the poor (1598); and maintaining roads (1654). These and other specific rates were gradually consolidated during the 18th century, so some parishes had several rates, and some only a single, multi-purpose one. Some new rates were then added and assessed separately, such as the sewer rates, raised to build and repair sewers in the 18th and 19th centuries, especially in towns and cities.

In 1834, the Poor Law Amendment Act transferred rate collection to local councils. Rates were combined into one single rate in 1930, and continued until Margaret Thatcher famously abolished them in favour of the Poll Tax in the 1980s.

Rate books record the levying and payment of rates in each parish. The list was usually compiled by the collector walking around, listing each head of household as he went. Careful study of the lists in conjunction with maps should enable you to retrace the route the original compiler took. In towns and cities – as with records of sewer rates – rate books tend to be arranged by named streets. Sometimes you may find house numbers, though these may not, of course, be identical to modern numbering systems.

After 1834, besides names of occupiers, you will sometimes find the owner's name listed as well, together with the value of the property, the amount of rates paid and perhaps the house name or other description of its location.

Each subsequent rate book was copied from the last, with appropriate alterations made to account for changes in occupancy due to death; inheritance; sale and purchase; replacement of tenants due to leases ending; and, of course, a new house occupying the old site. Rate books after 1834 are often annotated to show changes in occupation. Those before may be annotated. More likely, though, you will simply see one name being replaced by another. You can then investigate why – you could, for example, seek reference to the death of the previous occupant.

- Rate books are best sought at local archives and county record offices.
- Where rate books do not survive, you may find the valuations on which they were based, in local archives or county record offices. In some cases these may tell you what rents were being collected and details of tenancies.

Using the records

Working out which entry in a rate book relates to your home can be something of an intellectual challenge. In the absence of addresses, it is often

Rugby Street, Holborn. In this case, the St Andrew's Holborn rate books were used to discover exactly where someone known only to have resided in the parish lived. William Havers (d. 1770) was a Catholic barrister at Gray's Inn, Holborn. The sewer rates for 1767 reveal him to have been rated in Church Street, Holborn. No such street exists now, but local histories of Holborn show that its name was changed to Rugby Street. This survives as a street of fine Georgian houses – just the sort of place, in fact, where you'd expect a successful lawyer to have lived.

a question of establishing which way round the village the initial list went, and pinpointing your home's occupier in the context of how many doors he was away from other people. For example, if your home was occupied in 1790 by Nicholas Crowe, you may find a rate book listing:

Michael Kan
Roland Back
Nicholas Crowe
Malcolm Clark

That for 1789 may then list:

Michael Kan
Roland Back
Simon Crowe
Malcolm Clark

This probably indicates that Simon Crowe died about 1789 and was replaced by his son – or maybe another relative – Nicholas. The parish burial register could well confirm this. On the other hand, 1789 might read:

Michael Kan
Roland Back
Dominic Stinton
Malcolm Clark

That would suggest that Nicholas Crowe may have acquired the lease of the house in 1789/90 from Dominic Stinton, something you could check (for example) through manorial records (see pages 178-83). Or, Crowe may have been Stinton's son-in law, or maternal grandson, or other sort of relation, and could have been bequeathed the property – further study of the parish registers, wills and manorial records could also indicate whether any of these options were the case.

Clearly, the best option is to work back

SCHEDULE A.—FORM 4.

RATE BOOK.

Parish of *Boulton*

"*A Rate Book.* In this Book shall be inserted the Particulars of the Assessment and Collection of the Poor Rate of the Parish, as set forth in the Form Numbered 1; and in addition to the Declaration required by the Act passed in the seventh year of the reign of King William the Fourth, intituled 'An Act to regulate Parochial Assessments,' such Overseers shall, before any Rate is presented to the Justices for their allowance, sign a Declaration in words at length, of the Total Amount of Rate so presented for allowance, according to the form or to the effect set forth in the said Form numbered 1."

Derby: Chadfield & Sons,

PRINTERS AND PUBLISHERS OF ALL BOOKS AND FORMS REQUIRED BY THE POOR LAW BOARD.

The cover and a page from the 1856 rate book of Boulton, Derby.

2

SCHEDULE A. FORM 1. PARISH OF *Boulton*

No. (1)	Arrears: Due or If excused (2) £ s. d.	Arrears: If Excused write the word 'Excused.' (3)	Name of Occupier (4)	Name of Owner (5)	Description of Property Rated (6)	Rate: Name or Situat[ion] (7)
11			Cantrell late Revd Wm Trust.	Messrs Cantrell	Land	Brough[…] Boulto[n]
12			Derby Canal Compy	Themselves	Towing Path & Tools	do
13			Dolman Elizth	Herself	House & Land	do
			Do	Jno Curzon Esqr	Land	do
14			Etches Edwd & Co	Earl of Harrington	Fishery	do
15			Fearson John	Chas Holbrooke	House & Garden	do
16			Fearson James	do	do	do
17			Foster Robert	Sir I H Crewe Bt	do	do
18			Garratt Thos	do	House & Land	do
19			Garner Joseph	do	House & Garden	do
20			Garner Thos	do	do	do

through these records very methodically, noting changes not just in what you think is your home, but also the neighbouring ones. It is also worth bearing in mind that the amount charged seldom adjusted, so the sums being paid are a good indication of which building was being referred to.

It should be noted that paupers were exempt from paying rates, so neither they nor, by inference, their homes, will be listed. As paupers' homes are less likely to have survived than others', this omission is not as serious a drawback for the home historian as it may at first sound.

For towns, the building of a street can be pinpointed fairly accurately through rate books, because the local authority was obviously anxious to start charging rates as soon as it could.

Parochial assessments

(1836–1840s)

The Act to Regulate Parochial Assessments was passed in 1836. The aim was to reorganise the chaotic parish rates, many of which – more so in the country than the towns – by then bore no relation to the original values of the buildings. The local Poor Law Commissioners were instructed to survey each parish and compile assessment reference books. Creating a map was optional. Some did so, while others copied existing tithe maps instead. By 1843, some 4,000 parishes (about a quarter of the total) had been assessed, 1,267 of which had accompanying maps. The maps' quality varied but their advantage over tithe maps is that they covered the whole parish, not just the parts liable for tithe payment, and also included many town parishes not covered by the tithe survey.

- The records for London are in the Guildhall Library.
- Those for the shires – insofar as they survive – are in county record offices.

Marriage assessments

Between 1695 and 1704, the City of London charged a 'rate' on married couples. The assessments are indexed and arranged by street, providing a form of mini-census. Surviving records (those of only 17 parishes do not survive) are at the Corporation of London Record Office, c/o London Metropolitan Archives, 40 Northampton Road, London EC1R 0HB; tel: 020 7332 3820; **www.cityoflondon.gov.uk**.

Oliver escapes being bound apprentice to the sweep – from *The Adventures of Oliver Twist* by Charles Dickens, 1838.

House row

House row was a system of choosing parish officers and deciding which families should take in parish apprentices, by rotation based on the order in which the house came in the village. Records of house row can provide a useful addition to any study of the location of houses based on the order in which they appear in rate books.

CHAPTER 27

Estate records and sale papers

Middle Ages–present, but mainly 1550–1900

You do not have to trace very far back into the past before finding that most land in Britain belonged to a landed estate of one sort or another. About half the present population of Wales, for example, live within the former boundaries of only two landed estates, those of Bute and Tredegar in Monmouthshire and Glamorganshire. And the purpose of *Domesday Book* (1086) was precisely to identify who held the estates into which England had been parcelled after the Norman Conquest 20 years earlier (see pages 143–5). Records of estates are therefore likely to be useful at some point in your research.

Finding records

|| First, find your estate owner. If your home is part of a development of houses, you may be able to learn the name of the family who used to own the land (or that still does) in a novel way – by walking around and noting the names of the roads. Not infrequently, when selecting road names, developers or councils chose ones associated with the area's past.

|| Estates usually passed down the male lines of families, but remember that they could pass by inheritance to daughters, or be sold: the records are likely to be archived under the latest owner.

Whitehaven, Cumbria, showing Flatt Hall, c.1730–35; painting by Matthias Read. Originally a village, Whitehaven was developed as a port and its streets laid out in a grid by the Lowthers of Flatt Hall in the late 17th century.

- You can find past owners' names from many sources, particularly books covering your local history, such as the Victoria County History series (see page 73); the Manorial Documents Register (see page 169); and 19th-century directories. A list of known manorial lords in 1925 is in HMC 5 at the National Archives.
- Estate records are found in many different places. Many, especially those of the great estates owned by the Crown, are in the National Archives. You can search for what you want in the online catalogue, **www.catalogue.nationalarchives.gov.uk**. The main records of Crown estates in the National Archives are in CRES, particularly CRES 2/1613 (Crown manors in 1827) and CRES 60 (annual reports of administration of the estates 1797–1924).
- Records for the royal Duchy of Cornwall, currently held by HRH the Prince of Wales, include large tracts of Cornwall and also parts of south London. The duchy provides revenue for Princes of Wales before they become kings. It was therefore usually more intensely managed, and thus better recorded, in periods, such as now, when there was a Prince of Wales. In periods when there was not one, they are less useful. The records are at the Duchy of Cornwall Office, 10 Buckingham Gate, London SW1E 6LA. They are on closed access, but the archivist will pass your enquiry to one of the small group of record searchers who are allowed in.
- The National Archives, plus those of Scotland and Ireland, PRONI, and the National Library of Wales also have extensive holdings of private estates, searchable online. The latter, for example, has records of 54 estates of over 3,000 acres, totalling some 750,000 acres, along with those of 600 smaller ones.

The National Register of Archives indexes

The National Register of Archives incorporates two indexes. First is the Family and Estate Index, relating mainly to landowning families. In many cases, you will find that records listed here will be searchable in the form of copies or abstracts in the National Archives. Some are too brief to mention homes, but others go into considerable detail.

The second index is the Business Index. Many homes are built on old industrial sites, or indeed are converted warehouses or factories. To find what you want, you'll need to know the name of the firm that once owned your home or its site. The Business Index also includes about 600 entries for builders and some 300 for architects.

The mushrooming of Masborough

Business archives often provide a great deal of information on individual homes. The journal of Samuel Walker, founder of the great iron and steel firm of Samuel (later Joshua) Walker & Sons at Masborough, near Rotherham, Yorkshire, includes the following examples:

From Nov. 1747 to Nov. 1748 we made 110 tons supposed value £1300. Built bay of warehouse at Grenn[oside], fenced Hind Farm round, repair'd house &c. Mr Booth and me built Steel Furnace.

From Nov. 1751 to Nov. 1752 we made 256 tons, stock valued £3600. Built Cart House, and one bay of Warehouse at Grenn, Smith's Shop, and my upper Barn, and Aa[ron's] parlour at Rotherham and mill at Dunn Close.

From Nov. 1752 to Nov. 1753 we made 283 tons supposed value £4200. Built the Keel Providence, Built Mrs Buck's Land & House at Masper, built John Booth Barn and Warehouse by it, &c.

From Nov. 1753 to Nov. 1754 we made 318 tons, supposed value with £800 S.W. & J.C. added stock, £5600. Built Forge and Warehouse, Warehouse at Bridge, 2 houses and Smithy in Yellands, and one New House, and repaired and divided the Old House at Masbrough, &c.

Heraldic highways

Cann Hall, Leytonstone, Essex used to be a lovely country estate. Now, it is an intensely built-up area, apparently far removed from its historical past. Yet when the modern roads were laid out, many of the names were chosen with an awareness of the estate's history.

Cann Hall Road is obvious, of course. Colegrave Road is named after William Colegrave, a London property speculator who bought the estate in 1670, using the money he had received as the dowry for his marriage to Frances Bourne (hence Bourne Road). Colegrave already owned the Norfolk Manor of Little Ellingham (Ellingham Road). His grandson, also called William Colegrave, married Mary Manby from Downsells Hall, Essex (Downsell Road), whose family also owned the manors of Wragby and Elsham, Lincolnshire (Wragby and Elsham Roads), and were descended from the families of Thorpe (Thorpe Road), Cary (Cary Road) and Selby (Selby Road). The descendants of the marriage, the Manby-Colegraves, later married into the families of Stewart, Chichester and Cayley-Worsley, hence Stewart, Chichester and Worsley Roads.

The street names of this part of east London, therefore, correspond to the pedigree of the rather grand family who had once farmed the land here.

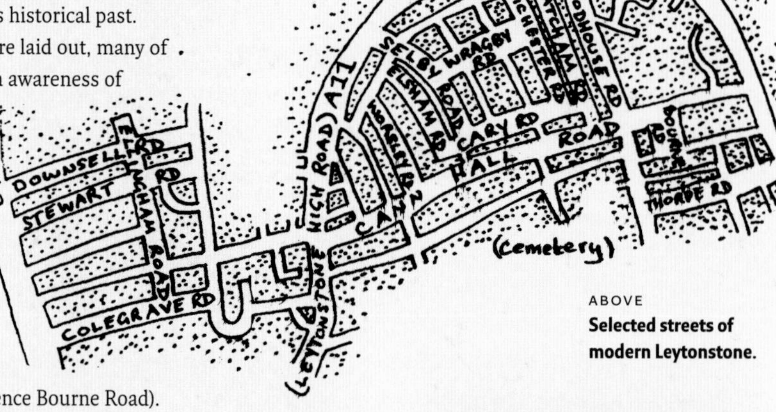

ABOVE
Selected streets of modern Leytonstone.

RIGHT
The arms of many of the families now commemorated in Leytonstone's street names appear as quarterings in the Manby-Colegrave's coat of arms. Those of Selby, for example, *Barry of ten, Or and Sable*, are third down in the left column.

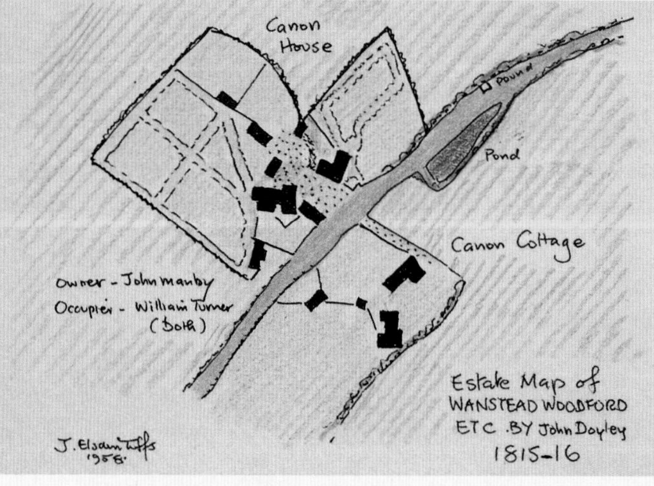

Drawing made by J. Elsdon Tufts in 1958 of Canon House and Canon Cottage, Leytonstone, East London, Wanstead, from an estate plan drawn by John Doyley in 1815. It shows the owner as John Manby and the occupier as William Turner. The houses' names hark back to the pre-Reformation ownership of the land by the canons of Wanstead Priory.

- Many more private estate records are deposited in county record offices. As estates often stretched across county boundaries, and great landowners frequently inherited several estates in widely different parts of the realm, you should not automatically expect estate records for your home parish to be in your nearest county record office. The best way to establish what is where is to examine the Access to Archives website **www.a2a.org.uk**.
- You can also search under the place, estate owner's name or other key words likely to produce the right result in the National Register of Archives database on **www.nra.nationalarchives.gov.uk/nra/**. See also the box right.
- Further records of businesses may be traced through the Registrar of Companies (main office), Companies House, Crown Way, Maindy, Cardiff CF14 3UZ; **http://ws6.companieshouse.gov.uk**, with public search rooms at Companies House, 21 Bloomsbury Square, London WC1B 3XD, and regional offices in Leeds, Manchester and Birmingham. The Registrar of Companies (Scottish office) is at 37 Castle Terrace, Edinburgh EH1 2EB. All share the same number, 0870 333 3636. Irish company records can be traced through the Irish National Archives in Dublin and PRONI in Belfast or the Companies Registry, Customer Counter, 1st Floor, Waterfront Plaza, 8 Laganbank Road, Belfast BT1 3BS; tel: 0845 604 8888; **www.detini.gov.uk/cgibin/get_builder_page?page=1966&site=7**.
- Further business archives may be traced through the local record offices, the National Archives and the Business Archives Council, **www.businessarchivescouncil.org.uk**.
- Many estate and manorial records are still in private hands. Some manorial lords belong to the Manorial Society of Great Britain, 104 Kennington Road, London SE11 6RE; tel: 020 7735 6633; **www.msgb.co.uk**.
- Notable in terms of church-held estate records are those of the Welsh Church Commission at the National Library of Wales, whose surveys, conducted in the 1940s, contain much detail on buildings, including parsonages and churches. They also include many other church-owned buildings – many now homes – with details going back, in some cases, to the 16th century.

The Manorial Documents Register

A great deal more information about estates may be found through the Manorial Documents Register of the Historic Manuscripts Commission, now at the National Archives. This comprises two paper indexes:

The first lists which manor or manors covered your home parish – manorial and parish boundaries were by no means always the same. The index is not complete, so it is also wise to check whether your parish has yet been covered by the Victoria County History series (see page 73), which goes into much detail on manors.

The second index tells you what records have survived for each manor and who the last lord of the manor known to the Commission was.

- The register is being computerised – Wales, Yorkshire, Hampshire, the Isle of Wight and Norfolk are now online (at the time of writing Surrey and Middlesex will be next), in a subsection of the National Archives website, **www.mdr.nationalarchives.gov.uk/mdr**.
- In addition, for Welsh manors, you can consult Helen Watt's book (see page 177) and the National Library of Wales's own database.

If none of the foregoing give a current owner's name and address, you may have to use genealogical techniques – using particularly the Burke's publications (see page 74), wills (see pages 154–61), and General Registration records of births, marriages and deaths (see

Bacons & Dagness Farm in

No	William Havers Esqr	Tithe Free	Meadow	Arable	Quantity A	R	P	June 23 1810	June 24 1811	June 1812
	House Yard Orchard &c				3	0	12	Mead	Mead	Mead
	Oxyard or Sawpit Hoppet		Mead	"	1	0	30	do	do	do
	Little Mead adjoining the Moat		Mead	"	5	0	14	do	do	do
	Great Bushy Lease		"	Arable	16	2	14	Barley	Wheat	Fallow
	Little do		"	Arable	10	3	12	Wheat	Fallow	Wheat
	Long Meadow } laid together A R P 10.0.7 / 3.0.36 / 6.3.11 Laid to Wm Francis		Mead		"	"	"	"	-	"
	Further do		Mead		6	3	11			
	Further Bushy Lease Laid 9.2.22 to Wm Francis			Arable	"	-	-	"	"	"
	Great Bartholomews Laid 22.1.4 to Staines		"	Arable	"	"	-	"	"	"
	Little do Laid 14.2.26 to Francis			Arable	"	"	"	"	"	"
	Lodge Field		"	Arable	23	3	2	Leave for Wheat	Fallow	Wheat
	Kitchen or Cross Path Field		"	Arable	11	2	26	Wheat	Fallow	Oats
	Stable Mead		Mead		11	1	16	Mead	Mead	Mead
	Great Cross Field or Claypitt Field		"	Arable	13	0	30	Clover	Wheat	Fallow
	Little do going to Buttsbury Green			Arable	12	1	24	Fallow	Wheat	Clover
	[illegible]		"	Arable	8	2	24	Fallow	Wheat	Clover
	[illegible]			Arable	10	2	11	Tares for Fallow	Barley	Clover

William Havers, tenant gentleman farmer of Bacons.

ABOVE

Pages from Lord Petre's account books for Mountnessing, Essex, showing Bacons Farm, leased by William Havers, detailing that the house, yard and orchard comprised 3 acres and 12 perches, and also its location among its (named) fields. The field names are wonderful – 'Little Bushy Lease', 'Gores Lay' and 'Farther Flood Field' are my favourites.

pages 148–50) – to trace forward down the family line and then seek living descendants in telephone directories. Some people will let you see their records for free; others will charge a fee; others simply won't reply – there's nothing much you can do about that. However, the more polite and courteous your initial written approach is, the more likely you are to have a happy outcome.

Your research may indicate that the estate owner was a corporation, such as an Oxford or Cambridge college, or church body. Their records will be found using the foregoing methods. You may also find estate records among the solicitors of landowners. Over 1,000 solicitors' practices appear in the business index of the National Register of Archives (see above).

ABOVE LEFT
Bacons Farm, showing part of its distinctive moat (photographed by the late Philip Coverdale).

LEFT
Part of Chapman and André's map of Essex 1773 showing Bacons, Mountnessing. It is detailed enough to include the moat around the farmhouse.

Many more solicitors' records will turn up through searches in record office catalogues. The Law Society, 113 Chancery Lane, London WC2A 1PL; tel: 0870 606 2511; **www.library.lawsociety.org.uk** will tell you, for a fee, the current incarnation of old solicitors' partnerships and where surviving old records may be.

As a last resort, though, you can make enquiries of solicitors in your area, or the area where the last known owner of the estate lived, and see what they have in their private archives.

It must be admitted that, since the abolition of the manorial system in 1922, many manorial records were thrown away, or embarked on new careers (like old deeds) as pub lampshades. However, it is certainly worth working from the assumption that the records you want still exist somewhere – they are invariably worth the effort of seeking.

What you might find

Estate records can include all manner of papers concerning the management and improvement of the estate and its buildings.

You may find correspondence between the owner and his employees, particularly builders and architects, concerning the design of new buildings. Where they survive, minutes of the estate's management may enable you to watch projects – such as the building of your home – as they progressed. Beware, though – estate records can include modified or failed projects too!

A particular type of property you may find in estate records are dower houses. These are often rather elegant buildings, situated for no other obvious reason on the edges of estates. They were built for widows of former heads of the family. Provision for dower houses is often found in marriage contracts and mentioned in wills. Details of their construction and maintenance may also appear in the records of the estate itself.

Estate surveys (also called 'rentals') list each parcel of land, detailing how it was farmed, who tenanted it and how much rent was paid. These surveys are very often accompanied by maps (see page 173). For smaller estates, surveys may, in fact, be written in the otherwise blank spaces around the edges of an estate map.

'Scant fit for a farmer'

Ingatestone Hall today.

The sort of material you may find in estate records is beautifully illustrated by an early, detailed survey of Ingatestone, Essex, compiled by Thomas Larke in 1566. 'When Sir William Petre first bought the manor,' wrote Larke, he found an old house

... scant fit for a farmer to dwell upon ... he caused all the old houses to be pulled down and instead of them has at his own great costs and charges elected and builded other new houses very fair large and stately made of brick and embattled ... the situation of the inner houses is dewly proportioned four square with a fair large hall, one parlour, and a great chamber over it, with other fair chambers both above and beneath the north part of the house, besides the armory which is over the hall ...

The estate papers also include a 'trew and perfect platt' or plan of the house in 1605, drawn by the John Walkers, father and son – all in all, a remarkable record of a building over 400 years ago.

Ingatestone Hall, Essex, from an old postcard produced about 1920: its chapel can be seen, contrasting with the Elizabethan architecture of the rest of the building.

Estate maps and plans

Maps and plans were commissioned by estate owners for all sorts of reasons, ranging from a desire to manage their land better, or to sell it off, or simply to remind them how rich they were.

When maps exist, they can vary greatly in quality, from rough sketches to magnificently surveyed works of art. A tip for working out if you are examining an accurate map is to compare it to a modern Ordnance Survey one. In many cases, accuracy and detail will vary within the map, depending on what the surveyor thought was important. If he was concerned with boundaries, not buildings, he may not have given much, if any, attention to buildings, and those that appear away from boundaries may not be depicted at all accurately.

When estates were surveyed in the Middle Ages, the results were usually presented as a narrative. With few exceptions, estate maps really started during Elizabeth I's reign, as an offshoot of the great enthusiasm for cartography shown by her Secretary of State, Lord Cecil (see page 134). Twenty-five estate maps were produced by the great cartographer Christopher Saxton, along with plans of two towns, Manchester and Dewsbury. Some early town plans were, in fact, estate maps: John Walker's map of Chelmsford and Moulsham of 1591, for instance, was compiled because the town was part of a substantial local estate.

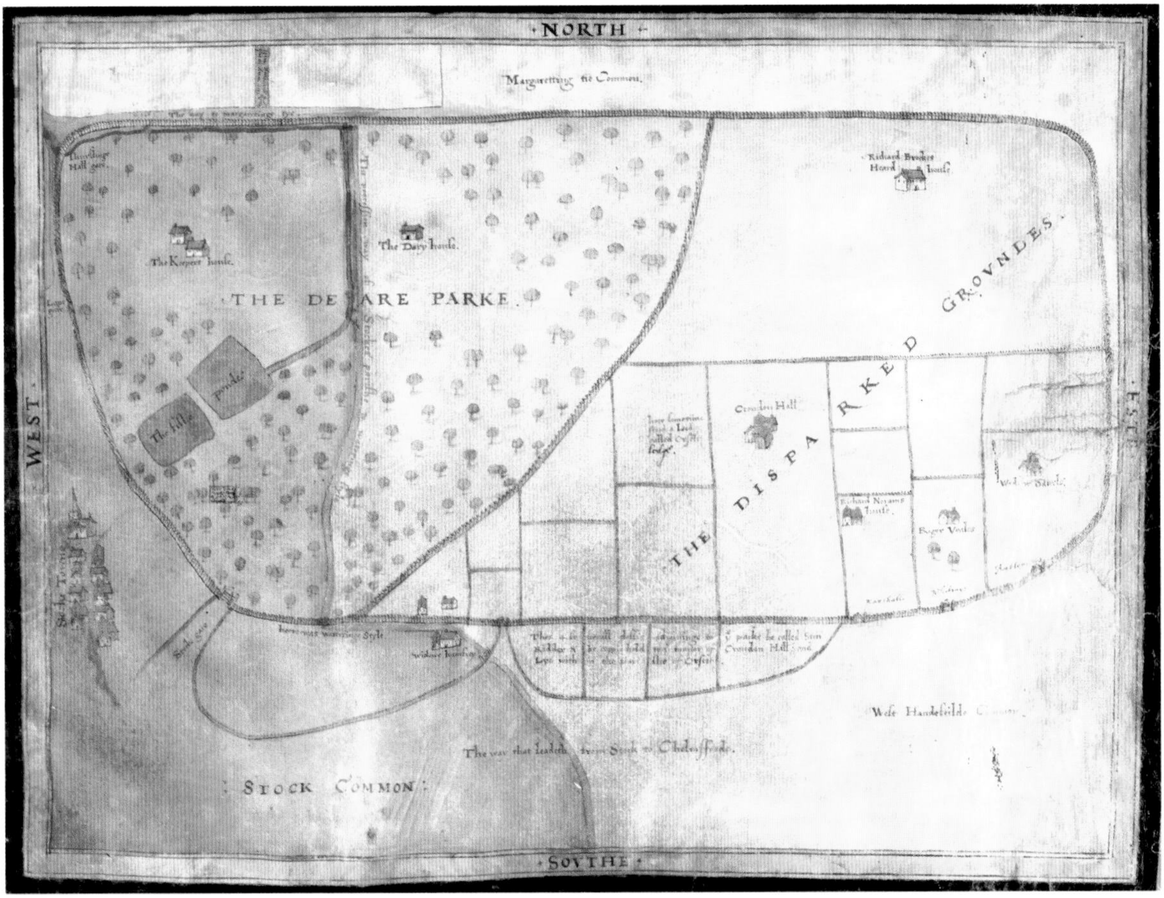

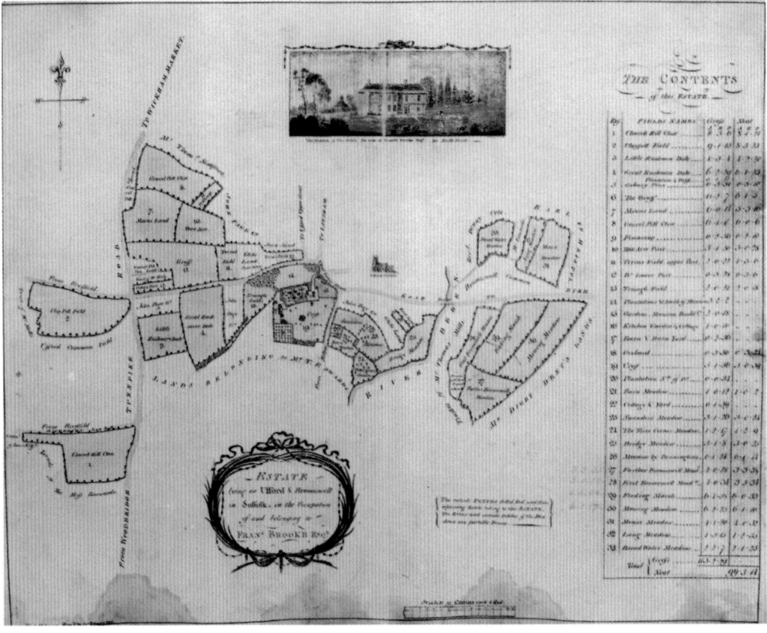

LEFT

Estate map and illustrations drawn by Isaac Johnson of Woodbridge, Suffolk (1754–1835) in 1788.

ABOVE

An old estate map of Crondon Park, Stock, Essex, from an unknown date in the 17th century. Crondon Park became the leased home of the Mason family, who maintained a Catholic chapel there (see page 240). The map shows the houses of Widow Sawel and Roger Veale, side by side: a contemporary witch trial described how Widow Sawel allegedly bewitched poor Mr Veale, but for doing so, paid with her life.

The Thelveton Estate

Thelveton Hall, later called Thelton Hall, was bought by Thomas Havers, steward to the Dukes of Norfolk, in 1592, and rebuilt by him as an 'E'-shaped Tudor mansion. His family occupied it for the next 272 years. In 1864, the heir, also called Thomas Havers (1810–70), was desperately in need of money. He had served a rather unsuccessful spell as Colonial Manager of the Falkland Islands, and had also seen the profits from his rents slump due to the general agricultural depression that struck East Anglia thanks to the import of much cheaper American grain. Consequently, the estate was sold. It was the end of an era, but it generated a wonderfully detailed set of sale papers.

The papers include a plan of the estate (see opposite). The fields and cottages are all numbered, and the areas occupied by individual estate farms were designated in the original by a coloured wash, with the names of the farmers, 'Calver', Moore', etc., written over them in ink. The corresponding sale papers then state the names, extents and values of the plots (see below). The building marked 139, for example, was not a single dwelling, but 'three cottages and gardens' covering one rod and 29 perches, rented for a total of £9 a year – presumably £3 per cottage. This was probably an old farmhouse dating back to Medieval days, but which had been divided into workers' cottages after the estate had been consolidated by the Havers family.

NORFOLK.

PARTICULARS OF

"THE THELTON HALL ESTATE,"

A VALUABLE AND EXCEEDINGLY COMPACT

FREEHOLD PROPERTY,

SITUATE IN THE PARISHES OF

Thelton (otherwise Thelveton), Scole, Shimpling, Billingford, & Dickleburg,

About Three miles from Diss, Seven from Harleston, Six from Eye, and Eighteen from the City of Norwich, in a fine Agricultural part of the

COUNTY OF NORFOLK.

IT CONSISTS OF A

SUBSTANTIAL OLD ELIZABETHAN MANSION

MANTLED WITH IVY,

Approached by a Lodge Entrance and Carriage Drive, very Productive Gardens, and Shrubberies, Stabling, Carriage Houses, and Offices of every description; several convenient

Farms with Farm Houses, and Agricultural Buildings,

ACCOMMODATION LAND & COTTAGES FOR LABOURERS,

THE WHOLE EXTENDING OVER ABOUT

ELEVEN HUNDRED AND NINETY-THREE ACRES;

WHICH WILL BE SOLD BY AUCTION, BY MESSRS.

NORTON, HOGGART & TRIST,

At the Guildhall Coffee House, near Guildhall, in the City of London,

On FRIDAY, 5th AUGUST, 1864, at 1 o'clock precisely.

May be Viewed and Particulars had at "The King's Head" Hotel, Diss; "The Swan," Harlestone; "The Royal Hotel," Norwich; of H. Dixon, Esq., Solicitor, Sunderland; of Messrs. Harrisons, Solicitors, 5, Walbrook, City; of Messrs. Muskett & Garrod, Solicitors, Diss; of Messrs. W. W. Elliott & Sons, Auctioneers, Thelton; at the Guildhall Coffee House; and of Messrs. Norton, Hoggart, & Trist, 62, Old Broad Street, Royal Exchange, E.C.

Printed by T W. Nicholson, 3 & 4, Bell Yard, Gracechurch Street.

ABOVE
The front page of the sale papers of Thelveton Hall, Norfolk.

COTTAGES AND GARDENS.

No. on Plan.		A.	R.	P.	RENTALS. £	s.	d.
139	Three Cottages and Gardens	0	1	29	9	0	0
143	Two Cottages and Gardens	0	1	16	6	0	0
144	Two Cottages and Gardens	0	1	10	6	0	0
146	Two Cottages and Gardens	0	0	32	5	10	0
163	A Cottage and Garden	0	2	18	6	0	0
167	Two Cottages and Gardens	0	1	30	8	15	0
182 pt.	Cottage and Garden				2	10	0
183 pt.	Cottage and Garden				3	0	0
193	Two Cottages	0	0	37	6	5	0
197	A Cottage and Garden	0	1	10	5	0	0
77*a*	Two Cottages and Gardens				8	0	0
	A.	2	3	22	£66	0	0

The quantities of Nos. 182 and 183 are included in the occupations of Atkins and Foreman, and that of No. 77*a* in Mr. Elliott's Farm.

PLAN OF THE

THELTON HALL ES

NORFOLK

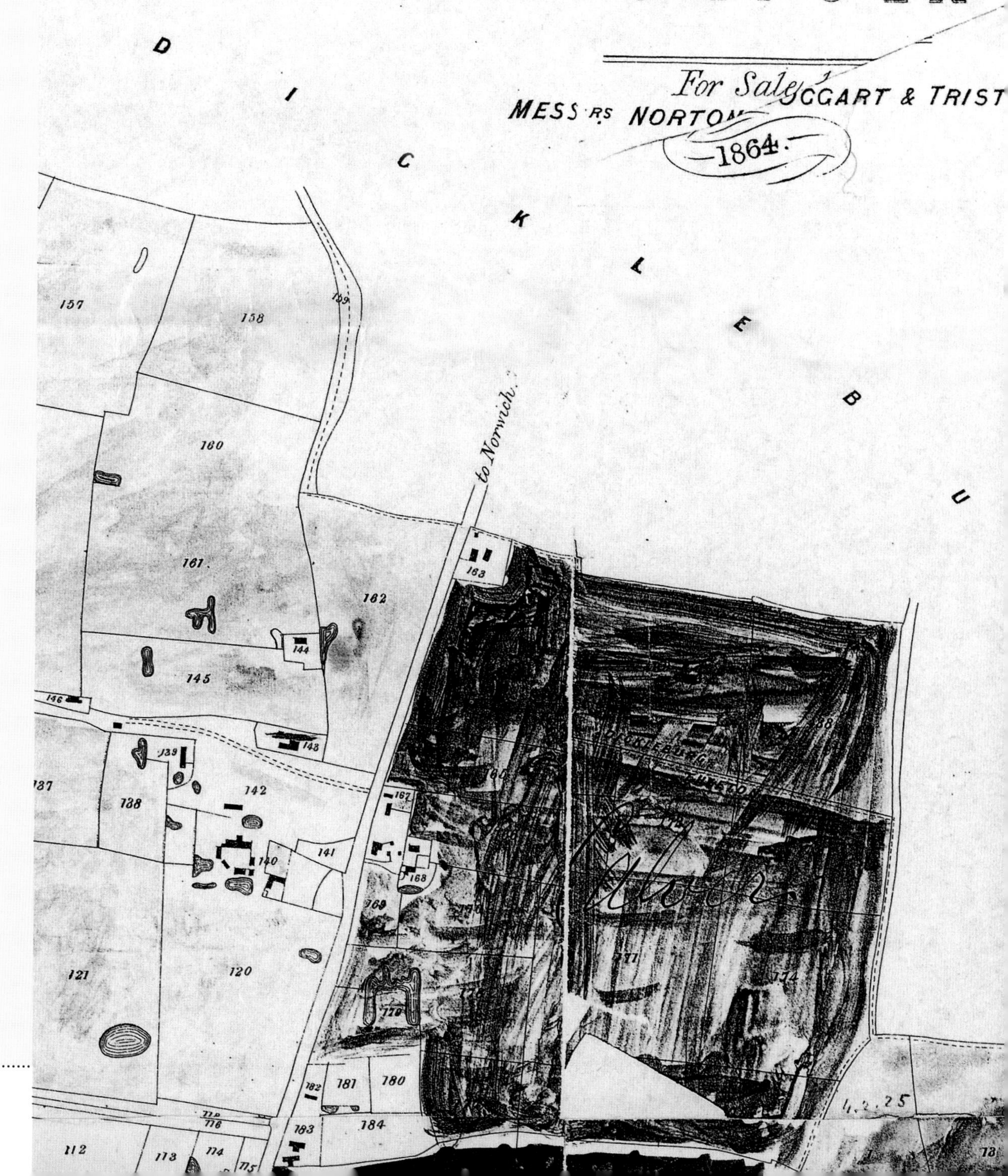

"Florence Villa," 212, Park Road, Milton Regis.

CATALOGUE of HOUSEHOLD FURNITURE, &c., to be SOLD BY AUCTION by Mr. HEDLEY PETERS, at the above address, on THURSDAY, DECEMBER 5th, 1912, at One o'clock precisely, the property of Mrs. Smart, who is leaving for Canada.

SCULLERY.

LOT
1 Four iron saucepans and 3 fry pans
2 Pembroke table
3 22in. patent mangle
4 Two chairs, galvanized pail, 2 hand bowls, and sundries
5 Three galvanized baths
6 Kitchen fender, 3 cocoa mats, and sundries
7
8

KITCHEN.

9 Stained-frame dining table
10 Wicker cradle, hearth rug, and fender
11 Bassinette perambulator on C springs and ball bearing wheels
12 Child's high chair
13 Mantel glass and sundries
14 Set of jugs and sundry earthenware
15 2 Windsor Chairs
16

BACK BEDROOM.

17 4ft. 6in. brass-mounted iron French bedstead
18 4ft. 6in. woven-wire mattress
19 Deal dressing table and mahogany dressing glass
20 Iron fender, 2 cane-seat chairs, and child's chair
21 Painted washstand and chamber ware
22
23

MIDDLE BEDROOM.

24 4ft. 6in. brass-mounted iron French bedstead
25 4ft. 6in. woven-wire mattress
26 4ft. 6in. wool mattress
27 Deal dressing table and dressing glass
28 Painted washstand and chamber ware
29 Iron fender, cane-seat chair, clock and sundries
30 Box & Sundries
31

FRONT BEDROOM.

32 4ft. 6in. brass-rail iron French bedstead
33 4ft. 6in. woven-wire mattress with cable edge
34 4ft. 6in. wool mattress
35 Mahogany duchesse dressing-table with bevelled swing glass
36 Mahogany marble-top washstand
37 Set of chamber ware
38 3ft. 10in. antique mahogany chest of 5 drawers with brass handles
39 Child's cot with spring mattress attached

LOT — 12 | 14
40 Three cane-seat chairs, towel airer, and fender — 6
41 Mahogany chest of 4 drawers — 11
42 Cornice pole, bamboo table, and trinket set — 1
43 4 Pictures & Mantle Ornaments — 2
44 Cheese Dish & Ware — 2
45

LIVING ROOM.

46 Linoleum, cloth hearth rug, and set of fire irons — 5
47 Teak-framed dining table — 5
48 Upholstered wicker chair — 3
49 "Simplex" hand sewing machine and cover — 18
50 Antique inlaid mahogany table — 7
51 Striking clock in walnut case — 11
52 Cornice pole and 3 pictures — 1
53 Four coloured prints (framed) — 1
54 Tapestry carpet — 5
55 Walnut Folding Chair — 5
56 Tea Ware — 3

FRONT SITTING ROOM.

57 Brass-rod fender — 3
58 Set of brasses — 5
59 Mahogany Pembroke table — 3
60

Walnut-framed Dining Room Suite in American Leather :—

61 Spring-seat couch
62 Gentleman's easy chair
63 Lady's ditto
64 Six occasional chairs — 4 | 4
65 Two bamboo tables — 2
66 GOOD-TONED 7-OCTAVE PIANOFORTE in walnut case, iron frame, full trichord and check action, by Squire — -
67 Set of stained bookshelves — 2
68 Lloyd's Encyclopædic Dictionary, in cloth, 7 vols. — 8
69 John Bull gramophone and 56 records — 2 | 10
70 Mandoline and case — 4
71 Pair of 14in. floral vases — 4
72 Pair of vases and sundry ornaments — 1
73 Bamboo music Canterbury and shaped mantel board — 2
74 Oil painting in gilt frame — 2
75 Ditto — 3
76 Large coloured print in fancy frame — 3
77 Ditto — 3
78 Oil heating lamp — 7
79
80
81 — £ 26 | 12

W. J. PARRETT, LTD., PRINTERS, SITTINGBOURNE.

Saxton's maps indicate that he spent some time sketching the main buildings as they really were, but other houses and cottages were treated pretty summarily, or ignored. Walker's Chelmsford map, on the other hand, shows each house and cottage in its own plot. The buildings look different to each other and this suggests he was drawing what was actually there.

The period 1700–1850 has been described by the cartographic historian J. B. Harley as the 'golden age of the land surveyor'. From 1850 onwards, estate maps tended to be based on tithe, enclosure or, mainly, Ordnance Survey maps. The information the estate surveyors added to the already very detailed maps can still, of course, be invaluable to home historians.

Estate maps vary in the amount of names of tenants they provide. When a property appears on a map but does not belong to the estate, though, the owner's name will often be given. Similarly, the names of adjoining landowners may appear around the edges.

- In addition to following the above recommendations, you can also seek estate maps in the British Library's map collection.
- Some record offices, such as those of Essex and Cambridge, have produced specific catalogues of the estate maps they hold.

Sale papers

Whether your home was part of a great estate or a private estate of just one building, each time it was sold it may well have been described in sale papers. Sales of properties and their contents have often generated printed material in the form of posters, newspaper advertisements, sale papers and auction catalogues.

Especially from about 1850, sale papers are usually accompanied by an estate map. Sale papers may also give the 'roots of title', outlining the owner's right to sell the property – in other words, its history!

You may find details of your home – or a piece of land destined to become your home – being sold. You may also find the sale of people's effects accompanied by their emigration, bankruptcy, or death – often, in wills, you will find the testator leaving instructions for the sale of their belongings after their death. In such cases, you may be lucky enough to find a room-by-room description of the contents of your home at some point in the past.

- Most local archives have collections of sale papers and associated documentation. These are especially useful for the most recent decades – a period not so well covered by many of the other sources suggested in this book.
- Sale catalogues, such as that for Thelveton Hall (see pages 174–75 and also referred to on pages 76 and 156–7), were produced by estate agents and land agents. Many are therefore found in the archives of solicitors and of estates themselves, or in family papers. Others were generated by the forced sales of estates after the 1911 Finance Act introduced death duties.

FACING PAGE

Sale papers for a modest town bungalow. This offers a marvellous mixture of furniture – beds and tables – with artefacts very much of their time, such as the '"Simplex" hand sewing machine' and the 'John Bull gramophone and 56 records'.

BOOKS

- **E. A. Baskerville, 'Estate and Related Records at the National Library of Wales' (*The Local and Family History Handbook*, 8th edn, pp 203–6, see page 75)**
- **J. Gurney, 'The Manorial Documents Register' (*Ancestors*, July 2004, pp 28–35)**
- **H. Watt, *Welsh Manors and their Owners* (National Library of Wales, n.d.)**

CHAPTER 28

Manorial records

13th century–1920s

Manorial records are records of land tenure dating back far into the Middle Ages. They were primarily concerned with land, not buildings. For all that, they can provide copious information on homes, and also structures such as barns that later became houses.

Most of the records you will need will be in court rolls, where the inheritance of copyhold tenants is recorded (see page 180). There is much, too, to be found about both freehold and leasehold properties from manorial surveys and rentals. Welsh land expert Eirionedd Baskerville wrote of Bute and Tredegar estate records (see page 183), 'by studying the rentals of these two estates you can see before your very eyes the green fields being turned into streets'.

|| How to find manorial records is discussed under estate records (see pages 166–69).

Dealing with the records

Manorial rolls (or, later, books) can survive from the 13th century. Up to 1732, including the Cromwellian Interregnum period (c.1653–60), they were usually written in Latin. Scary? Yes, somewhat, but the clerks who wrote the records were in reality barely more adept in Latin than

Cheney Court, Herefordshire, photographed by the late Philip Coverdale, whose ancestors (and mine) lived there. Buildings named '__ Court' usually started off as Medieval manorial courthouses. Age oozes from this picture, and indeed the building has a very long history.

1960s schoolchildren. The vocabulary was usually simple, the word order often the same as English, and many stock phrases and formulae were used.

Guides to these are Palgrave-Moore (which outlines the formulae) and Stuart's books (see page 183). At the worst, if you see a reference to your home but cannot decipher it, you can always refer it to a Latin translator (some advertise in local family and history magazines): they usually charge very modest rates.

Manorial origins

Manors are derived from the estates of the Saxon thegns and comprised the lord's hall with its outbuildings, the village and its surrounding farm, common and woodland. The re-allocation of manors to his followers was the basis of William the Conqueror's feudal system. The Saxon villagers retained their land and livelihood solely by virtue of the services they performed for their new Norman masters. The Norman lords in turn held their manorial lordships in return for the military service they owed the monarch. In time, services on all levels became broadly converted into money payments.

Frequently, manorial boundaries, some probably dating back to those of Roman estates, came to form the borders of parishes. Equally, the manorial lord's chapel was often the seed from which the parish church grew. After the Reformation, many of the administrative functions of the manors were transferred to the parish and their law-and-order functions to the Quarter Sessions. Yet the manorial system remained the basis under which most property was held until its abolition in 1922 – the final pieces of copyhold land being turned into freehold in 1926.

Manors have inescapable Medieval associations, and conjure up images of snivelling peasants cowering under the oppression of greedy and lusty lords. Such stereotypes were sometimes true but, while most of us would no doubt have found life in a Medieval village excruciatingly unpleasant, manorial tenants were generally well fed and unmolested. The laws and customs of manors were designed to ensure continuity of tenure in their ancestral homes to a degree that might be envied by many struggling to find or keep flats or houses in today's aggressive property market.

Originally, parish and manorial boundaries were pretty much the same, but centuries of buying and selling little bits of land, amalgamations and subdivisions put paid to that. Some manors ended up as little more than a house and garden. The largest, the manor of Wakefield, Yorkshire, conversely covered over 150 square miles.

Nobody knows how many manors there were – estimates vary between 25,000 and 65,000. They were administered by the lord's steward, who managed the manor, with a bailiff to collect rents, a reeve to collect fines, a hayward to maintain the infrastructure of fences, barns and so forth, and a constable to keep law and order and see off vermin.

Manorial courts

When the officials and tenants of a manor met together, their meetings were called 'courts' (and homes whose names incorporate the word 'court', such as 'Cheyney Court', especially in rural areas, are often former locations of such

Understanding manorial records

In manorial records, buildings are referred to as follows:

Capital messuage The manor house.

Tenements Usually houses.

Messuages Usually cottages. These were often built of non-durable materials so are less likely than tenements to have survived.

meetings). Manorial courts came in several varieties, the main being as follows:

Court leets: Derived from the earlier Views of Frankpledge, they were mainly concerned with regulating behaviour. They can be interesting, should you chance across your home as the site of a brawl, for example, or lapsing into dilapidation.

Courts customary market, swain and portmote: These concerned themselves with markets, forests and ports, which could be useful if your home was in one of these. Courts customary were often absorbed within a court baron, though may sometimes be found being held in their own right.

Court barons, also called halmotes: The main courts concerned with landholding – and hence homes – within the manor. Manorial tenants had obligations to fulfil, either by labour or surrender of produce or money, but the right to inhabit their ancestral homes was inviolable.

Court rolls

These were where obligations and rights were recorded. When someone became a tenant, whether by inheritance or purchase, they would be given a *copy* of these obligations and rights, and were thus known as copyholders.

When a tenant died, their heir would appear at the next court baron, state their right to inherit the tenancy, and, of course, say what it was they were tenanting. When their right was acknowledged, they were 'admitted' to the tenancy, paying a forfeit to do so. The forfeit was traditionally a 'heriot', the tenant's best beast (payment of which was sometimes recorded separately in estreat rolls), but after the Restoration (1660) a money payment was made instead.

Copyhold tenancies were hereditary and could not technically be sold, but of course they were, all the time, both to neighbours and incomers. This involved a little pantomime, by which the vendor would attend the court baron and surrender their holdings to the lord, who would then admit the purchaser, while cash changed hands behind the scenes.

Copyhold land fell into two categories, heritable copyhold and copyhold 'for lives'. Heritable copyhold passed to the holder's heir on their death according to the custom of the manor. The heir was usually the eldest son, but manors in some areas practised 'gavelkind'. This was the dividing up of land between all sons, with the family home going to the youngest. Another system, Borough English, allowed the youngest son to inherit.

Copyholders sometimes managed to overcome these strict inheritance rules by attending the manorial court to surrender the holding – as they termed it – 'to the use of another's will', and then bequeathing the land to whomever they wanted. Copyhold for lives allowed the holding to remain in the family during the lives of a set number of people, usually three – holder, wife and son. When all three had died, the land reverted to the lord, though the custom of 'free bench' allowed the widow of the last 'life' to keep her deceased husband's holding for life. Copyhold for lives often altered over time to become straightforward leasehold land.

The records of court barons are thus full of specific pieces of land and buildings within the manor. These will usually be described or named, or at the very least identified in terms of who held it. Therefore, when a long run of court rolls survive, you should be able to reconstruct a detailed history of your home and, of course, learn a great deal about the people who inhabited it.

A typical court baron will provide information on your home in the 'proceedings before the jury'. This recorded which people were brought to book for breaking rules; not paying

The Roebuck revisited

This is an example I used in my book *Collins Tracing your Family History*. There, I showed how a sequence of manorial records could help trace a family tree. Here, however, the same records also show how they can be used to trace the history of a family home - 'the Roebuck' - and, of course, remind us that the history of buildings and homes often coincided.

The manorial records of Petworth, Sussex, cover the nearby village of Tillington. At a court held on 3 September 1822, the following was recorded:

Death of Thomas Elliott a freeholder

Also the homage present that Thomas Elliott late of Tillington, Sussex, yeoman ... who held a freehold tenement barn stable orchard and croft and several new built tenements thereon near the church in Tillington and formerly called the Roebuck (late copyhold and enfranchised to the Lord to the said Thomas Elliott deceased) ... died ... (no heriot, as no living beast) now at this Court comes Thomas Elliott only son and heir ... and acknowledges to hold ... by the said yearly rent of two shillings and six pence heriot relief ffealty suit of court and other services And thereupon pays to the lord for a relief two shillings and six pence and doth to the lord his ffealty.

This is marvellous, for the record tells us not only what the buildings were - a small house with a barn, stable and so on - but also that some were 'new built' and, what's more, roughly where they were in the village.

Earlier in the manorial records, on 8 September 1789, there appears an earlier step in the story, under the heading 'death of Sarah Day':

Also the homage presents that Sarah Day widow who held of the Lord all that copyhold or customary messuage or tenement barn garden orchard land and premises with their appurtenances formerly called the Roebuck lying in Tillington the yearly rent of two shillings and sixpence since the last court [26 August 1788] *died thereof seized (no heriot as no living beast) NOW ... comes Hannah wife of Thomas Elliott of Tillington shopkeeper ... and produces the will of Sarah Day bearing date 29 December 1788 - wherein she devises said premises to her niece Hannah Elliott wife of Thomas Elliott and her Heirs for ever. She is admitted. Fine £10-00-00.*

It is amusing that, although the holding was 'formerly called the Roebuck', the name was still being used as the only practical means of identifying it - not least when the surname of the holder had changed from Day to Elliott.

rent on their holdings; disputing a boundary with a neighbour; or a host of other interesting things that will add colour to your home's history. Most importantly, you should find the inheritance or transfer of the copyhold of your home. If you are really lucky, you'll discover a jolly good argument breaking out over which of several members of the family was to inherit a house.

Manorial surveys

Manors generated other sorts of records too, including surveys (also called extents) of the lord's holdings, which can include maps; the tenants' names; rents due; and details of boundaries that can mention specific buildings. 'Custumals' set out the manor's customs, including how copyhold land and buildings were to be inherited. 'Relief' rolls recorded free-holders paying what was usually the equivalent of a year's rent to inherit freehold land within the manor. Most relevant for house histories are the rent rolls, in which homes and outbuildings are usually noted and named. Stewards' accounts, also called ministers' and receivers' accounts, may contain details of properties on which rent was owed, or expenses paid out for the repair of properties owned by the manorial lord.

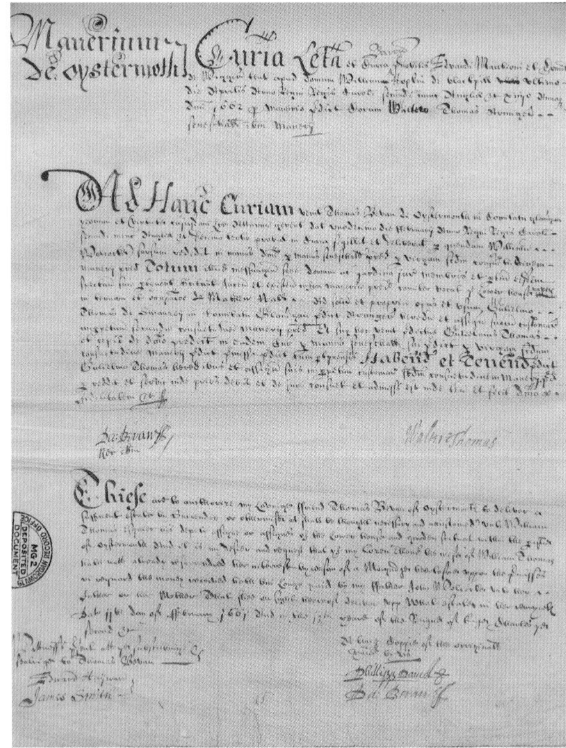

Part of a manorial court roll from Oystermouth, Glamorgan, Wales, known to most people as 'The Mumbles'.

Enfranchisement

In manorial records you may find a copyhold property being converted into freehold by a deed of enfranchisement, including a money payment to extinguish future copyhold rent and entry fines. This is how all remaining copyholds were converted into freeholds in the 1920s. Before then, however, you may find freehold properties still being mentioned in manorial records if the heir was still obliged to pay a 'relief' to the lord on inheriting them.

Lordships of manors

The manorial system was abolished in 1922, but the system had started to unravel long before.

|| Records of the conversion of copyhold to freehold, naming countless homes, are at the National Archives. Records run from 1841 to 1924, and are in MAF 9, arranged by county and then by manor. Subsidiary papers are in MAF 13, 27, 48 and 76.

Although the system ended in 1922, the Lordships of Manors survived. For a long time they were considered to be entirely worthless, but then it was realised that they still carried certain rights and were perceived by many to hold great social kudos. Tied to manorial lordships may be fishing and hunting rights, the right to fine the local council for digging gravel, or to charge British Telecom rent for the parts of their telephone poles embedded in the soil

Letters patent of a charter granted by Henry VIII to Stephen Beckingham for the Manor of Tolleshunt, Essex.

of the manor. Others carry feudal rights which are still extant, such as the privilege of the Lord of the Manor of Worksop to attend the coronation in person and provide a glove for the monarch (at Elizabeth II's coronation, the manor was owned by a firm, and the claim was consequently disallowed. A few years ago I was at a manorial auction in London where the lordship was bought by a private individual, no doubt eager to obtain an invitation to the next coronation).

Many people simply like the idea of being lord or lady of the manor, either because they live in an area that was a manor, or just because Fred Smith, Lord of the Manor of Twatcham, sounds much more impressive than plain Fred Smith. By the 19th century, though, a lord of the manor was basically a glorified landlord. Fred could just as well title himself Fred Smith, Proprietor of the Launderette. Fred might think he can call himself Lord Frederick Smith, or that his 'title' has anything at all to do with the peerage titles bestowed by the monarch to denote nobility, but he would be wrong. Manorial titles have no more in common with titles of nobility than they have with the titles of books.

Having said that, I know of a number of people who have bought manor houses, and then gone to great pains to acquire the lordship of the manor, and the associated records. They have done so to reunite their historic home with an equally historic title and records. Good for them.

BOOKS

- **E. A. Baskerville, *Estate and Related Records at the National Library of Wales (The Local and Family History Handbook*, 8th edn, pp. 203-206,** **see page 75****)**
- **P. Palgrave-Moore, *How to Locate and Use Manorial Records* (Elvery Dowers, 1985)**
- **D. Stuart, *Manorial Records: An Introduction to their Transcription and Translation* (Phillimore, 2004)**
- **J. West, *Village Records* (Phillimore, 1997)**
- **See also the National Archives' leaflet on manorial research** www.catalogue.nationalarchives.gov.uk/researchguidesindex.asp

CHAPTER 29

Property deeds

Early on in this book we looked at title deeds, and how you can try to obtain those for your home from its present owner, or the person (or building society) from which you bought it.

In some cases, the results may be disappointing. However, there is a good chance that other deeds relating to your home are out there, somewhere. If you do track down original deeds, remember to treat them carefully. Your local archives will provide free advice on conserving them. Better still, you can deposit your deeds with your local archives on long- or short-term loan, and they'll conserve them for you.

A deed from the Cromwellian period, dated 1653.

Seeking deeds

- You can start looking for renegade deeds by asking the solicitor who handled the most recent sale. Failing that, ask other solicitors in the area who may have handed transactions during the 20th century. Remember that in 1925 the Law of Property Act allowed deeds relating to property transactions before 1895 to be disposed of, and many solicitors sadly took advantage of this to free up space in their cellars. However, if you can find out who owned your home in 1925, it's worth tracing their descendants to see if they kept their older deeds.
- Fortunately, many deeds were disposed of by depositing them in record offices. Try your local ones, but remember that they may be deposited in the archive most local to the previous owner, who may have resided somewhere completely different.
- Many archives have catalogued their deeds, and many of the catalogues are now accessible through the Access to Archives website, **www.a2a.org.uk**.
- Many homes – or the land they stand on – once belonged to larger estates. You can try seeking the deeds of the estate owners (see pages 166–9), as these may shed light on the early history of the ground below your home.
- Deeds may also be in solicitors' offices and in archives. A large number were enrolled in the Quarter Sessions and so will be in county record offices.

- Many deeds are also catalogued in the Historic Manuscripts Commission's National Register of Archives database, **www.nra.nationalarchives.gov.uk/nra/**.
- A substantial number of deeds are at the National Archives. Pre-17th-century deeds there are described as 'ancient'. They are mainly among the records of the Palatine Courts and Courts of Chancery (C 146–9) and Exchequer (E 40–4, E 132, E 210–14, 326–30 and 354–5). Some of those in C 149, E 40 and E 210 have been transcribed and indexed in *A Descriptive Catalogue of Ancient Deeds in the Public Record Office*, 6 vols (HMSO, 1890–1906), available in the Reading Room at the National Archives.
- Many more, ancient and modern, are in the following groups of records at the National Archives: Courts of Chancery (especially Close Rolls and Patent and Charter Rolls); Exchequer; King's Bench; Common Pleas; Chanceries of the Duchies of Lancaster, Chester and Durham; Treasury Papers; and Charters Rolls. Most were enrolled voluntarily, by people wishing to create an official record of their private transactions, for use in the event of disputes. During the 18th century, however, between the Jacobite uprising of 1715 and the Catholic Relief Act of 1791, well-off Catholics (and, theoretically, other non-conformists unwilling to pledge loyalty to the Crown and Church of England) were compelled to enrol their deeds. These are in NA E 174 and FEC 1 – a line well worth pursuing especially if you know your home was owned by a well-to-do Catholic family.
- There are many indexes and calendars to enrolled deeds at the National Archives. Many are now accessible through the National Archives' catalogue, **www.catalogue.nationalarchives.gov.uk**, and the *Guide to the Contents of the Public*

Types of landholding

Deeds recorded land holding, either by outright possession or tenancy. Traditionally, there were four common types:

Fee simple land The land could be transferred freely.

Fee tail or 'entail' A lease to one person and their descendants, so long as there were any, after which the estate reverted to their heir of the grantor. The holders of fee tail could sub-lease the land but such sub-leases became void when the holder died. There were many cases when holders wished to end the entail and dispose of the land. This might have been to free property of charges, such as providing widows' dowries or, of course, to be able to sell it. From 1285, fee tail could be converted into fee simple by what was known as the 'levy of a fine' and, in the 15th century, by a 'common recovery'. From 1833, tenants in tail could break the entail by enrolling a deed at the Court of Chancery.

For life or lives This was a lease that expired on the death of one or several people. While the lease was running, the holder of the fee simple owned what was termed the 'reversion', which meant the estate would pass to them or their heirs once the life or lives had expired. The lives were usually a close family unit, such as a man, his wife and son. Often, the third person in the lease might pay the landlord to extend the lease for further lives, thus ensuring continued tenure for the family. Needless to say, such leases provide highly reliable material linking different generations of the family tree. Leases for lives were particularly common in the West Country.

Term of years This was a lease for a set term of years.

Other types of tenancy you may encounter are **tenancies at will**, which were created by the landlord and often used by the Crown as a means of rewarding loyal servants. At the other end of the scale, **tenancies by sufferance** were tenancies that had expired, but the tenant refused to leave!

Local deeds registries

Middlesex (c.1709-1938)
London Metropolitan Archives, 40 Northampton Road, London EC1R 0HB; tel: 020 7332 3820; **www.cityoflondon.gov.uk**

Bedford Level (1600 onwards)
Cambridge Record Office, Shire Hall, Castle Hill, Cambridge CB3 0AP; tel: 01480 375842; **www.cambridgeshire.gov.uk**

West Riding of Yorkshire (1704-1972)
West Yorkshire Archive Service, Newstead Road, Wakefield, Yorkshire WF1 2DE; tel: 01924 305980; **www.archives.wyjs.org.uk**

East Riding and Hull (1708-1976)
East Riding of Yorkshire Archives and Records, County Hall, Beverley, Yorkshire HU17 9BA; tel: 01482 392790; **www.eastriding.gov.uk/learning**

North Riding of Yorkshire (not York itself) (1736-1972)
North Yorkshire County Record Office, County Hall, Northalerton, Yorkshire DL7 8AF; tel: 01609 777585; **www.northyorks.gov.uk**

Record Office, vols. 1-3 (HMSO, 1963-8). An extremely detailed guide to deeds relating to house histories is given in Barratt (see page 191).

- If your home stands on land that was once owned by the Crown, or the Duchies of Lancaster, Durham and Chester, then it's probably worth investigating these records further: otherwise, it's very much a lucky dip, and not for the faint-hearted.
- Some deeds at the National Archives and elsewhere have been published, especially in the volumes of county record and archaeological societies. What is available for your area may be identified through Mullins (see also page 191).

Ireland

- Irish deeds are best sought through the Irish Registry of Deeds (from 1708), at the National Archives in Dublin.
- PRONI has microfilm copies. The registry holds abstracts, called 'memorials', of the original deeds (which were kept by the landowners).

Scotland

Scottish land records are covered on pages 196-9.

Deeds registries

Before the establishment of the Land Registry in 1862, Middlesex, Yorkshire (but excluding York itself) and part of Bedfordshire had deeds registries, whose dates and locations are given in the box left.

These records include memorials of deeds relating to property transfer, especially those of freehold sales; mortgages; leases of 21 years or more; and wills concerning property transfer. The East Riding registry has a good place-name index. Although the others are not desperately easy to search - it is best to look under the names of any people who could conceivably have had an interest in the property - the results can be well worth it, providing details of ownership, and even of when buildings were first put up, dating back into the 18th century.

Dealing with deeds

Deeds will hopefully tell you who owned your home at different times, and when it changed hands. They will probably also shed considerable light on people who leased or rented the property. Occupiers (as opposed to owners) were usually mentioned in deeds only in passing when the property was changing hands.

Deeds can be daunting, but bear in mind that many local history societies will decipher the documents for you in return for being allowed use of the information they contain. However, the fact that you are reading this book means you have an investigative mind, so you'll probably want to have a stab at them yourself.

James I recovery dated 22 November 1624.

Start by sorting them out by age. If you see any obvious abstracts on paper, begin by deciphering them, as they should provide a framework for the whole collection. As later deeds often recite earlier ones, look at the most recent first. The details of previous transactions usually come after the word 'WHEREAS'.

Most deeds were indented. This means that the text was written out twice on the same sheet, and the two copies were then cut apart along a wavy line, to deter subsequent forgery. They usually recorded, in this order:

- Date
- Names of the vendor/leasor and purchaser/leasee
- Type of transaction and earlier relevant ones
- Name of the vendor/leasor again
- Value of purchase/lease (prefixed 'in consideration of the sum of ...')
- Type of transaction again (in terms of the vendor/leasor 'demising' to the purchaser/leasee)
- Details of the property
- If a lease, the length or type, how the rent would be paid and any obligations incumbent on either party
- Signatures of parties and witnesses.

Types of deed

The aim of a deed was to transfer land holding from one person to another. There were a number of ways of doing this.

Feet of fines: In *Domesday Book* (1086), William the Conqueror's clerks recorded who held the land. Transfer of land, however, continued to be performed verbally and, by the 12th century, disputes over who owned what became widespread.

To try to guarantee future legal recognition of sales, therefore, lawyers devised a legal pantomime acted out in the Court of Common Pleas, whereby the purchaser ('plaintiff' or 'queriant') would claim he had always owned the land and that the seller ('deforciant') was squatting in it. The two parties would agree to settle the affair by the purchaser paying the vendor to go away and renounce any future

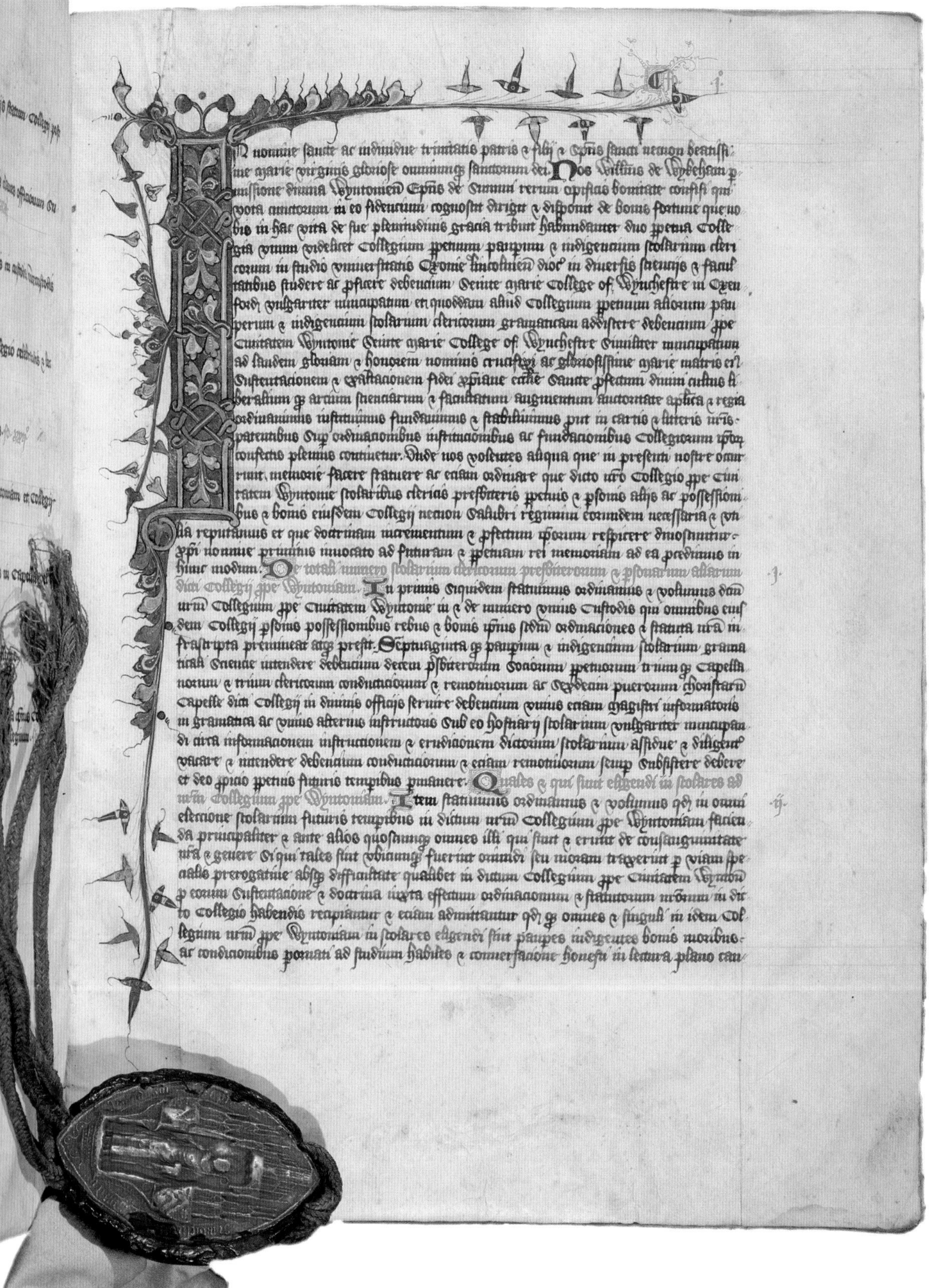

claim to the land. Their 'final agreement' of the case, also termed 'finalis concordia' or just a 'fine', was written out three times on the same sheet and then cut with a jagged line, the top two being given to the two parties and the bottom part being kept by the court. The latter were called 'feet of fines'.

Fines also started being used to break old encumbrances on property, such as entails, to enable women to sell land and to create family settlements. Besides the names of the purchaser and vendor, they will mention, where relevant, wives, heirs or people to whom they were heirs. The system lasted until 1833.

|| Many feet of fines have also been published by county record societies and HMSO. The originals are at the National Archives, enrolled in the records of many courts, such as those of the Court of Common Pleas. There are no overall indexes, but there are many indexes to parts of the collection, published by HMSO and county record societies, and these indexes can be viewed at the National Archives.

Common recoveries: This type of property transfer developed in the 15th century. The purchaser ('demandant') would pay the vendor for the land, but in order to gain legal recognition for the sale, the purchaser then took the vendor to court. The vendor would not appear but would deputise the task of proving his right to the property to a vouchee, who would leave and not turn up again, thus allowing the court to rule in favour of the purchaser. If the intention was to break an entail, the purchaser would claim he had owned the property but had been thrown out by a non-existent person called Hugh Hunt. The tenant who occupied the entailed property would not contradict the purchaser's claim, enabling the court to grant possession of the property to the purchaser. Sometimes, the tenant in tail then purchased the land back off the purchaser, the whole rigmarole having been solely for the tenant in tail to keep the land but under different conditions than the entail.

|| These records, which provide similar property details to feet of fines, are at the National Archives in Plea Rolls (CP 40, indexed in CP 60); Recovery Rolls (CP 43), indexed 1538–1835 in IND 1/17183–216); and records of the Palatine Courts (CHES 29–32 1259–1830; DURH 13 1344–1845; and PL 15 1401–1848).

Trusts: Otherwise known as 'uses', trusts were devices enabling people to settle land on whomsoever they wished. They would transfer the land to trustees, who were to hold it but allow a third party to 'use', profit from and bequeath it. The third party was often the original owner himself, who was now able to write a will allowing fre use of the land. The system was sometimes also used to avoid having to perform feudal service for the land, because neither the original holder nor the trustees were in full possession of it.

The state tried to prevent this practice with

FACING PAGE

The archives and muniments of old institutions can contain much that is of great interest not least because of the land with which they were endowed. This is from the records of Winchester College, founded in 1832 by William of Wykeham , Bishop of Winchester, and bears his episcopal seal.

A super settlement

An example of a settlement comes from the records of the Mason family of Crondon Park (see page 173), now at Essex Record Office. In a settlement of 3 June 1833 (D/D.Ge 182) relating to the marriage of Isabella Margaret Mason of Butsbury and George Porter of Writtle, various family properties were described, including Wood Farm in the parishes of Great Badow and Moulsham, containing 95 acres and a copyhold messuage (divided into three dwellings) called Goodman's Garden, held of the Manor of Great Baddow. If you were interested in Goodman's Garden, you could go on to see what the manorial records of Great Baddow had to say about it.

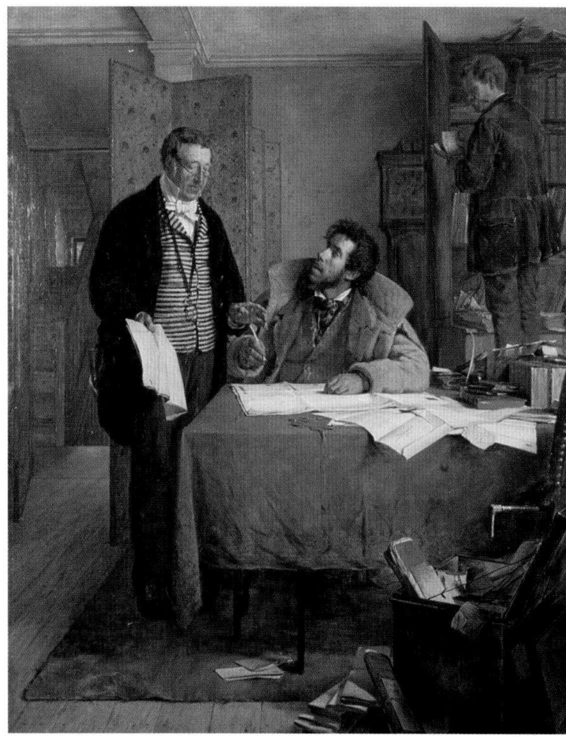

Erskine Nicol's painting 'Signing the New Lease' (1868) shows a typical scene played out in solicitors' offices up and down the land.

the Statute of Uses in 1535. This proved so unpopular, however, that the state subsequently gave people the right to bequeath land to whomsoever they wished by the Statute of Wills in 1540. Uses remained, however, as trusts whereby a landowner could ensure continuity of land ownership within the family – preventing profligate heirs from mortgaging or selling the land, for example – by creating a settlement by will or deed specifying the descent of the land, usually to the landowner's wife, then their eldest son and his heirs, or failing any, the second son and his heirs, and so on. Such records of settlements can obviously provide a great deal of useful information on the history of your home.

Bargain and sale: Deeds of bargain and sale started to be made after the Statute of Uses in 1535, as secret transfers of land, or interest in land, from one person to another, in consideration for a sum of money. The sale created a 'use', meaning that the purchaser had the use of the land. Because no actual change of ownership – no 'enfeoffment', as it was called – had taken place, however, the vendor still technically owned the land. The state responded in 1536 with the Statute of Enrolments, forcing bargains and sales to be enrolled at a court, so they were no longer secret.

|| Most bargains and sales were enrolled in Quarter Sessions, now at county record offices, though many are at the National Archives in the Chancery Close Rolls, C 54.

Lease and release: This was devised by lawyers to get around the Statute of Enrolments. It operated up to 1845. The vendor bargained and sold a six- or 12-month lease of a piece of land to the purchaser for a nominal rent. The purchaser thus acquired the 'use' of the land, but as it was only by a lease, not a conveyance of freehold, it did not have to be enrolled. The following day the vendor and anyone else with an interest in the property released their right to the reversion of the property once the lease had expired. As this was effectively the transfer of a right, not actually of a piece of land, it did not have to be enrolled either.

Leases and releases are often tucked one within the other. In practical terms it is only necessary to examine the release, as this will include details of the lease as well.

Mortgages: A landowner in need of money might mortgage his land, still occupying it but granting a long lease of it to the lender of the money, who would gain possession of the land if the owner failed to pay back the money in full.

Strict settlements: By the mid-19th century, about half the country was covered by strict settlements, designed to ensure the descent of land and estates from father to son. These usually took the form of a deed starting with the date and names and occupations of the parties involved, followed by a clause beginning 'WHEREAS', followed by an account of the property's descent. After this came a clause starting 'WITNESSETH', in which the purpose of the deed was stated, and then one beginning 'ALL THAT', in which the property was described. Then came 'TO HAVE AND TO HOLD', followed by any trusts and annuities to be paid out of the estate. The property was then conveyed to trustees for a set period, and the way in which the property was to be inherited by descendants alive or as yet unborn was specified. The trustees were then given powers to administer the estate, after which the deed was witnessed and signed. From the 1925 Settled Land Act onwards, strict settlements were created by two deeds, one vesting the land in its owner and detailing the trustees' names and powers, and the second being the trust settlement itself.

The reality of leasing

You can tell quite a lot about your home and its inhabitants from leases. Those who rented on a weekly or monthly basis were invariably very poor. A lease for a year or more indicates tenants who were somewhat better off.

Sometimes, several layers of tenancy could exist on the same property. Often, the builder would pay the landowner an agreed yearly ground rent and hold long lease of the property himself. He would either grant this to someone else as a short lease at a 'rack rent', which was usually fairly high, or keep the lease itself and sublet the property, usually with the obligation to pay the ground rent included. Alternatively, the builder might mortgage the long lease to acquire more funds for the next building project.

The right to receive lucrative ground rents might be sold by the original landowner to raise money, and bought by someone else as an investment. Equally, rack-renters often sublet their properties, often at very short (sometimes weekly) rents.

By the early 20th century, most people leased under various different terms, the occupants often being the bottom of substantial pyramids of people with different interests in the property.

BOOKS

- **N. W. Alcock, *Old Title Deeds: A Guide for Local and Family Historians* (Phillimore, 1986)**
- **N. Barratt, *Tracing the History of Your House* (Public Record Office, 2002)**
- **M. Brown, *Understanding Three Life Leases and Other Post-Medieval Deeds: A Practical Guide for Family Historians* (Dartmoor Press, 1998)**
- **M. Deacon, 'House Specials' (includes the history of Howard House, Cardington, Bedfordshire, being traced through deeds in the archives of Whitbread Brewers, now at Bedfordshire and Luton Archives) (*Ancestors*, July 2004, pp 60–2)**
- **A. A. Dibben, *Title Deeds* (Historical Association, 1971)**
- **J. Groves, 'Leases and Rental Surveys: Their Relevance to Family Historians' (*The Local and Family History Handbook*, 8th edn, pp 133–8, see page 75)**
- **E. L. C. Mullins, *Texts and Calendars: An Analytical Guide to Serial Publications* (RHS, 1958) and vol. II, 1957–1982 (RHS, 1983)**

CHAPTER 30

Court cases

Middle Ages–present

The records of civil courts, in which people enacted their personal quarrels, are rich sources of information about homes. Indeed, apart from hard cash itself, there has seldom been anything more sought after or worth fighting over than buildings and land.

Civil cases involving property may appear in one of several courts. There were the Courts of Chancery (1199) and Exchequer (most records from 1558), specifically concerned with financial matters; the Court of Requests, which heard (among other things) disputes over property and contracts, such as assignments of dower lands to brides; the Court of Wards and Liveries, in which matters of inheritance by young heirs could be heard; and the Star Chamber, which concerned itself with such matters as arguments over boundaries.

When cases involved property, delightfully detailed plans and maps could be produced as evidence ('exhibits') and left behind in the

The Court of Chancery, Lincoln's Inn Fields, 1808.

records. From these and the cases themselves, you may learn much about the buildings, their occupants and owners.

- With the exception of Quarter Sessions and ecclesiastical courts, these records are all at the National Archives.
- In some cases, you may find a specific reference – in a newspaper report or solicitors' records, for example – either to your home, or to the people who owned it, having been involved in a court case. If not, the records are very much a lucky dip: deciding simply to start ploughing through them on the remote offchance that your home might be mentioned would be a highly impractical approach. However, there are some easily accessible indexes to some sections of the records.
- The main one is the National Archives' online catalogue, **www.catalogue.nationalarchives.gov.uk**. This includes, for example, Chancery cases between 1386 and 1714 and Exchequer Exhibits E 140 between 1319 and 1842. As time passes, more cases are being indexed on this catalogue: at some point in the future, all court records will probably be indexed – but certainly not yet!
- Barratt's book (see page 195) provides a detailed breakdown of what other search aids are available at the National Archives – many of these are already on the National Archives catalogue.
- The National Archives of Scotland factsheet provides similar detail for Scottish holdings.
- Some court records have been published and indexed. Your local archives should have copies of relevant publications, or can advise you on where such books could be found. For example, some of the Kent assize records have been edited by Cockburn (see page 195). Here we read of homes being used as unlicensed alehouses and 'tippling-houses', or

Carry On Caulking!

Some of the Portsmouth Borough Quarter Session papers have been published and they contain wonderful examples of what can be found out about people's homes. Most buildings are identified simply in terms of their occupants, but once you know who these were, you may find that all sorts of goings-on had been taking place under your roof. Actually, it's extraordinary how many of the cases did indeed involve events in people's homes.

[83/12/3], 8 December 1684, Ann Spashot of Portsmouth, spinster, said that last Thursday afternoon she was in the house of her mistress, Ann Crowcher, in the wash-house washing clothes. Henry Cumings came and asked her why she abused his wife. She said she did not and asked him to go. He would not but came and struck her three blows; she threw a stick at him and then he tried to put her into the tub of water but could not and then dragged her about the house by the hair of her head till she was almost dead.

[83/12/4] 24 November 1684, John Tailer of Gosport, caulker [caulking was part of the process of shipbuilding] said that last Saturday night he found in the chest of his apprentice, Hub. Bessent, in his house stage ropes he thought worth 4s a set bolt and a few nails to the value of 6d, which were the King's goods and which Bessent had stolen. Hub. Bessent, apprentice of the above John Tailer, said that the ropes his master found were not in his chest but under his bed. He found them in his master's wood-house but who brought them there he did not know. About a month ago he brought them into the house thinking that some time he might have occasion for them. The bolt he found astern of the new ship amongst the chips and sea ore, the nails he found in his master's house on the shelves ...

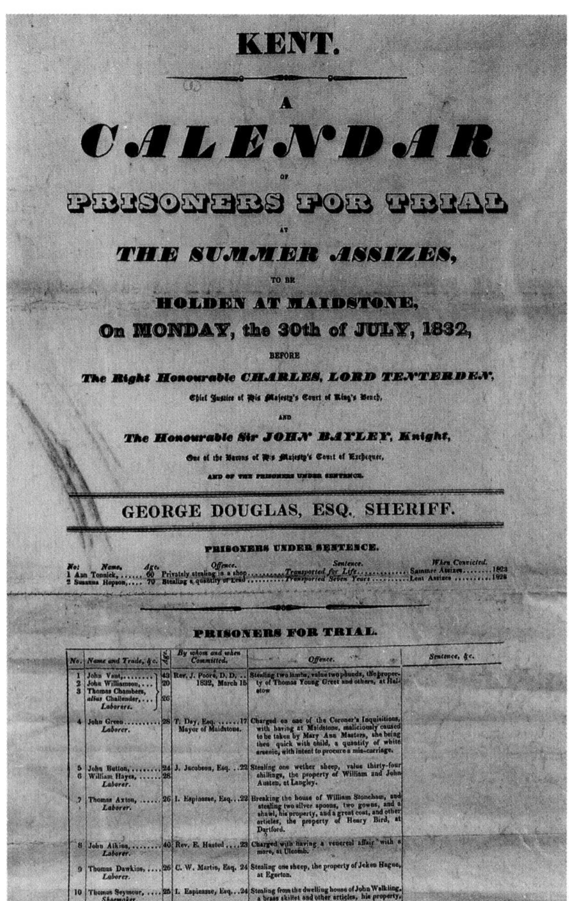

KENT.

A

CALENDAR

OF

PRISONERS FOR TRIAL

AT

THE SUMMER ASSIZES,

TO BE

HOLDEN AT MAIDSTONE,

On MONDAY, the 30th of JULY, 1832,

BEFORE

The Right Honourable CHARLES, LORD TENTERDEN,

Chief Justice of His Majesty's Court of King's Bench,

AND

The Honourable Sir JOHN BAYLEY, Knight,

One of the Barons of His Majesty's Court of Exchequer,

AND OF THE PRISONERS UNDER SENTENCE.

GEORGE DOUGLAS, ESQ. SHERIFF.

PRISONERS UNDER SENTENCE.

No.	Name.	Age.	Offence.	Sentence.	When Convicted.
1	Ann Tonnick, ...	60	Privately stealing in a shop	Transported for Life..............	Summer Assizes........1823
2	Susanna Hopson,....	70	Stealing a quantity of Lead	Transported Seven Years	Lent Assizes 1828

PRISONERS FOR TRIAL.

No.	Name and Trade, &c.	Age.	By whom and when Committed.	Offence.	Sentence, &c.
1 2 3	John Vant,........ John Williamson,... Thomas Chambers, alias Challender,... *Laborers.*	43 20 26	Rev. J. Poore, D.D. .. 1832, March 15	Stealing two lambs, value two pounds, the property of Thomas Young Greet and others, at Halstow	
4	John Green.......... *Laborer.*	28	T. Day, Esq. ......17 Mayor of Maidstone.	Charged on one of the Coroner's Inquisitions, with having at Maidstone, maliciously caused to be taken by Mary Ann Masters, she being then quick with child, a quantity of white arsenic, with intent to procure a mis-carriage.	
5 6	John Button,........ William Hayes, ... *Laborer.*	24 28	J. Jacobson, Esq. ..22	Stealing one wether sheep, value thirty-four shillings, the property of William and John Austen, at Langley.	
7	Thomas Axton, ... *Laborer.*	26	I. Espinasse, Esq...22	Breaking the house of William Stoneham, and stealing two silver spoons, two gowns, and a shawl, his property, and a great coat, and other articles, the property of Henry Bird, at Dartford.	
8	John Aikins, ... *Laborer.*	40	Rev. E. Hasted 23	Charged with having a venereal affair with a mare, at Ulcomb.	
9	Thomas Dawkins, ... *Laborer.*	26	C. W. Martin, Esq. 24	Stealing one sheep, the property of Jeken Hague, at Egerton.	
10	Thomas Seymour, ... *Shoemaker.*	25	I. Espinasse, Esq...24	Stealing from the dwelling house of John Walkling, a brass skillet and other articles, his property, at Eynsford.	

intended to be made throughout the borough immediately.

The following prisoners are already committed for trial at our Assizes, which commence on Monday week:— *Richard Woodward*, aged 28, *John Archer*, 22, & *John Stansor*, 28, charged, on the oaths of Wm. Reed and others, and on the voluntary confession of the said John Stansor, with feloniously murdering Elizabeth Longfoot, at Easton, on the 6th of March last.

James Cooper, 38, charged with maliciously cutting and wounding Wm. Wallace, at Towcester, with intent to murder him, and also with stealing a half-crown, pair of trowsers, a shirt, and other articles, his property.

Henry Hammond, 22, charged with having, in company with other persons, on the Daventry turnpike-road, in the parish of Towcester, feloniously robbed Thomas Butcher of 15s. in silver.

Joseph King, 29, charged with feloniously killing and

LEFT

A poster showing forthcoming court cases in Maidstone, Kent, 1832.

RIGHT

Newspaper extracts from a Northamptonshire paper showing news of forthcoming trials, and commitments to gaol, February 1839.

LEFT BELOW

Wandsworth Gaol records, 1873.

Commitments to the County Gaol.—Richard Woodward & John Archer, charged, upon the oaths of Wm. Reed and others, on strong suspicion of having, with others, on or about the 6th of March last, at the parish of Easton, feloniously killed and murdered Elizabeth Longfoot.—William Basketfield, charged with being found, with a felonious intent of stealing wheat, in a barn, the property of Joseph Johnson, of Handley.—Thomas Harper, charged with stealing, at Weedon Beck, a jacket, value 5s. the property of Thomas Harper.—James Ploughwright & Henry Ford, charged with stealing several tame fowls, at Easton, the property of Charles Whitehead.—William Woodward, charged with stealing nine tame fowls, at Easton, the property of John Trasler.—Charles Newey, charged with stealing, at Easton, five tame fowls, the property of Gregory Bateman.—Jacob Earl, charged with stealing, at Easton, two sheep, the property of Thomas Thompson.

To the House of Correction.—Peter Hall, for one month, for allowing several flat baskets to remain in the High-street, Daventry, for a longer time than was necessary, and not paying the adjudged penalty of 5s. and 8s. 6d. costs for such offence.

Borough Commitment.—Lucy Jeffery, charged with stealing upwards of £2 in money, and a muslin collar, value 2s. the property of her master, Samuel Betts, leather-seller.

Name, No. Henry Miller - 6456 — 16 Aug 73
and Aliases

Description.
Age (on discharge) 15
Height 4 ft 11 in
Hair Brown
Eyes Blue
Complexion Fresh
Where born Boro.
Married or Single Single
Trade or occupation Labourer
Distinguishing marks Scar on back

Address at time of apprehension 9 Kaal Street Boro Road.
Place and date of conviction Southwark 5 Aug 73.
Offence for which convicted Simple Larceny. S.A. Stealing a loaf of Bread.
Sentence 10 Days Hard Labour & whipped
Date to be liberated 14 August 1873
Intended residence after liberation 9 Kaal Street Boro Road.

Previous Convictions
Summary
By Jury

Remarks, antecedents &c.

as illegal meeting places for religious services, such as the indictment of:

George Weldishe jr, baker of Goudhurst, and others including clothiers, who assembled illegally at Cranbrook and attended the conventicle in the house of William Hervey, 23 July 1642.

Quarter Sessions

Quarter Sessions dealt with a vast amount of business, criminal and civil, including much that dealt with homes and their occupants. They are kept in county record offices and can be a fabulous resource for the history of homes, though few are indexed.

Quarter Sessions were courts held from 1361 to 1971 in each county four times a year, i.e. quarterly; those held at other times, 'petty sessions' or 'divisions'. They were presided over by Justices of the Peace (JPs), also called Magistrates, whose modern equivalents still deal with cases in Magistrates' Courts. Quarter Sessions tended to deal with less serious crimes than the Assize Courts. Their concerns were with such matters as theft and poaching; licensing innkeepers; prosecuting Catholics; maintaining the highway; enforcing the poor law; taking oaths; local militias; maintenance of roads and bridges; presiding over tax collection; and overseeing matters relating to apprenticeship and qualification of craftsmen.

Different sorts of cases in Quarter Session records relevant to the history of homes are referred to at appropriate places in this book.

Ecclesiastical courts

These were law courts maintained by the Catholic Church before the Reformation and thereafter by the Church of England. They dealt with moral matters, but records often provide passing mentions of homes. Everything from priest holes used by Catholics to harbour priests, to illegal fornication, is mentioned.

- These records are usually to be found in the county record office of the archdeaconry (and hence the bishopric) covering your area: directories and the *Phillimore Atlas* (see box above will all tell you which this was). Tarver's book (see box above) is an excellent guide to this subject.
- A useful short cut to some of the otherwise unindexed records are the appeals made against sentences. These were heard at the Archbishop of Canterbury's Court of Arches (records at Lambeth Palace Library, Lambeth Palace Road, London SE1 7JU; tel: 020 7898 1400; **www.lambethpalacelibrary.org**), indexed in Houston's book (see box above).

BOOKS

- **N. Barratt, *Tracing the History of Your House* (Public Record Office, 2002)**
- **J. S. Cockburn (ed.), *Calendar of Assize Records: Kent Indictments*, 6 vols (HMSO, 1975–97)**
- **J. Houston, *Cases in the Court of Arches, 1660–1913* (BRS, vol. 85, 1972)**
- **A. Tarver, *Church Court Records: An Introduction for Family and Local Historians* (Phillimore, 1995)**
- **A. J. Willis (M. J. Hoad, ed.), *Portsmouth Record Series Borough Sessions Papers 1653–1688* (Phillimore, for the City of Portsmouth, 1971)**
- ***The Phillimore Atlas and Index of Parish Registers* (Phillimore, 2003)**
- **See also the National Archives of Scotland's fact sheet on the history of buildings (including much useful information about Scottish court records) at www.nas.gov.uk/miniframe/fact_sheet/buildings.pdf**

A country attorney and his clients, 1800.

CHAPTER 31

Scottish land records

Middle Ages–present

If your home is in Scotland, you may find much valuable information on the building itself, or else on the land on which it stands, from Scottish land records. Sinclair (see page 199) provides a detailed guide to these, written from the point of view of tracing family history, though the principle of using them for researching the history of land and buildings is broadly similar.

In Scotland, owners of land were generally described as 'of' a place, whereas tenants were 'in' somewhere. Brian Crowley of Kirkintilloch would have owned Kirkintilloch, whereas Alexander McLeod 'in' Lenzie would merely have been a tenant.

In the Middle Ages, all Scottish land was held from the Scottish Crown by grants known, north of the border, as 'feus'. Land was granted to people or burghs, who were thus vassals or 'feuars', paying for the privilege with military service or, later, with cash. These feuars could, in turn, sublet land on similar terms.

Besides being inherited or sold, land could be used as security for a loan, called a 'wadset', whereby the lender became the holder of the land until the loan was paid off.

Charters

The granting of Crown land, either by the Crown itself, or by those to whom Crown land had been granted, was accomplished by charter. These record the name of land holder (called the 'superior'); a description of the land concerned; to whom the grant was made; and sometimes – especially good for home historians – details of earlier ownership. Most charters were written in Latin.

|| Charters granted by the Crown are in the Register of the Great Seal (*Registrum Magni Sigilli Scotorum*) at the National Archives of Scotland, but have been abstracted, printed and indexed by place and person for the period 1314–1668.

|| From 1668, there is a typed index to lands and grantees, but no abstracts. However, there is a series of 'signatures for Crown charters' covering the period 1607–1847, and for this there is a typed index to grantees and lands.

Progresses of writs

Family muniments sometimes contain 'progress of writs', listing all the family's charters, precepts and subsequent sasines.

|| There is a large collection of these at the National Archives of Scotland, indexed by the National Register of Archives at **www.nra.nationalarchives.gov.uk/nra/** (see also page 167).

Sasines

Changes of land ownership, be they sales, unusual inheritance or loans (wadsets), were conducted before witnesses in a public ceremony called a 'sasine' (from the French *sasir*, 'to seize', i.e. to be in legal possesion of). Originally, the giving of a sasine was accomplished symbolically, the previous holder handing over a wad of turf from the land concerned to the new owner. This was later translated into a written transaction, also called a sasine.

|| Sasines were recorded in notaries' protocol books, which can be found at the regional record offices and the National Archives of Scotland. Up to 1599, sasines were recorded by notaries on an ad hoc basis. They can be very hard to search, but luckily many have been published by record societies such as the Scottish Record Society, and are listed in D. and W. B. Stevenson (see page 199).

In 1599, an official register of sasines was established, which proved unpopular and was shortlived. In 1617, however, a new and lasting system, the Register of Sasines, was established.

There are, in fact, several registers, in which the sasine you want may appear. The General Register of Sasines covers all of Scotland. It was often used when the property being conveyed spread over more than one district. It is indexed 1617–1720. The Particular Registers of Sasines covered certain areas, such as a county, like Perthshire, or several counties, such as Roxburgh, Selkirk and Peebles. Some are indexed for the period 1617–1780, others for part of that period, and some not at all. This makes searching difficult, though in the cases of unindexed registers, a short cut can sometimes be made by searching the minute books instead. There were also separate registers of sasines for royal burghs.

|| These are all at the National Archives of Scotland. For buildings in burghs, you can also search the records of the Dean of Guild Courts, in local archives.

|| From 1781, searching becomes much easier, for the sasines in the General and Particular Registers for the counties – but not the royal burghs – have been abridged in English, printed and indexed. These abridgements of sasines are indexed by person and, with the exception of the period 1830–72, by place. These too are at the National Archives of Scotland. Copies up to 1868 are also available on microfilm at other libraries and Mormon Family History Centres (see page 47).

TOP
Crofts in Stornoway c.1900 with roped roofs, peat stacks and chimneys.

BOTTOM
Early-20th-century interior, Orkney.

Sasines are usually rather repetitious documents. Most of the salient detail will be given in the first section, and then repeated. They state the terms of the transfer: the person buying the land is indicated by the phrases 'gets disposition' and 'registers disposition'. If the sasine was

THE EVICTIONS AT BARRA, &c.

COL. GORDON of Cluny has written an answer to an application made to him by Mr Ross, for relief for the destitute Barra men now in Edinburgh, in which he very curtly says:—"*Of the appearance in* Glasgow of a number of my tenants and cottars from the parish of Barra I had no intimation previous to the receipt of your communication; and, in answer to your inquiry—'What I propose doing with them?'—I say—*Nothing.*" The Colonel's letter is from Cluny Castle, and is dated the 18th inst.

COLONEL GORDON'S DEFENCE.—Mr Baird, the Secretary of the Highland Relief Committee, having written Colonel Gordon regarding the parties who, it was stated, had been ejected from Barra, has received an answer, which he has sent to the newspapers. This letter was written prior to the one above quoted; and in it Col. Gordon writes as follows:—"The only notice I think it worth my while to take of what is said of me in the newspapers is to disabuse the public from the false assumption that the Barra people now in Glasgow were mercilessly turned out of their dwellings by me, or by my orders, at this inclement season of the year. So far from that being the case, I had no intimation of man, woman, or child having left Barra at this time. Nor do the letters which I had from Uist, dated 6th inst., make any allusion to such an occurrence. They must have left Barra of their own free will, and I am not sorry they did so; for it may be expected that they will tell their story as favourably as they can for themselves, which must lead to investigation, and then, I hope, the truth will appear. It should be borne in mind that the majority of the present inhabitants were not originally natives of

In 1850 *The Scotsman* protested so vociferously against Col. Gordon's forcible 'clearance' of Barra, that he was forced to pay for 1700 of them to emigrate.

concerned with inheritance, the phrases 'registers special or general service' and 'under precept of clare constat' will be used. Sometimes, you will encounter a husband transferring land to his wife as part of a marriage contract. If the sasine was to secure a loan (or wadset), the terms of the loan will be outlined – here the person lending money and thus being seized of the property was deemed to be 'getting' a bond and disposition for a sum of money 'over' property: when the loan was paid off, another sasine was registered, whereby the lender renounced his rights over the land.

Deeds

Deeds, for everything from land transfer to marriage contracts, could be enrolled at any Scottish court, so unfortunately the variety of different courts sometimes makes searching complicated. From 1804, thankfully, the power to enrol deeds was limited to the Royal Burgh, sheriff and Sessions courts.

Major tenants held leases that were often called 'tacks'. These can be recorded in registers of deeds at Books of Council and Session, Sheriff Court deeds, Regular Burgh Court registers of deeds, deeds of franchise courts, or family papers and many state conditions and improvements to be carried out under the terms of the lease.

|| The National Archives of Scotland has registers of deeds enrolled in various courts, such as the register of deeds in the Court of Sessions (called Books of Council and Session: NAS series RD, from 1554 onwards); Sheriff Courts (NAS series SC, mainly from the 19th century onwards); Royal Burgh Courts (NAS series B, covering various dates); and Commissary Courts (NAS series RH 11, dating from before 1748).

Service of heirs

Scottish land could not generally be bequeathed by will. Instead, it passed down strictly to the next living heir who, in the case of those holding land from the Crown, had to prove their right to inherit at a sheriff's inquest. The resulting decisions to allow inheritance were recorded in the Court of Chancery and are termed 'retours' or 'services of heirs'. The same procedure was followed when inheritance of land was unusual (i.e. not from parent to child).

|| Services of heirs from 1544 onwards have been printed and indexed and are now also available on CD-Rom by the Scottish Genealogy Society, 15 Victoria Terrace, Edinburgh EH1 2JL; tel: 0131 220 3677; **www.scotsgenealogy.com/**. The records are excellent, though they are incomplete and do not record every single unusual inheritance that has ever taken place. The published abstracts usually give all the relevant

information in the original retour, including details of the land concerned, but this is not always the case.

|| Sometimes an inspection of the original Chancery record may reveal more. Also, in the case of a complicated inheritance, extra papers may have been presented to a Sheriff's Court and may survive in their records. Challenges made to services of heirs are in National Archives of Scotland C 22 and C 28.

Tailzies

From 1685, landowners could decide who was to inherit certain heritable property in future generations by creating a legal document called a 'tailzie'.

|| The National Archives of Scotland has a Register of Tailzies from 1688, indexed up to 1938.

Scottish land valuation

From 1854 up to 1988, land was valued annually and names of owners, tenants and occupiers paying £4 or more per annum were recorded in valuation rolls. They were compiled by local authorities, and detail owners and occupiers of properties; details of the properties; and occupations. The lists are arranged by street.

|| Timperley's book (see box right) is a special resource for land ownership, listing the proprietors of land in each parish in 1770, though sadly her descriptions of the lands held are not complete.

|| The records are at the National Archives of Scotland, arranged annually by counties and burghs.

|| Copies of relevant sections are in local archives and libraries, although in neither case are records complete. Note that side streets, called wynds, vennels and closes, may be listed with the street they lead off, or separately.

Now a resident of London, Glaswegian Scott Crowley revisits the tenement, built about 1895, where his late grandfather Walter Hooks lived – 12 Lawrence Street, Partick, Glasgow.

BOOKS

- **R. Bigwood, 'A Foothold on the Land: Exploring the Records of Scottish Landlord and Tenant' (*The Local and Family History Handbook*, 8th edition, pp 227–32, see page 75)**
- **E. Reid, 'Close to Home' (on Scottish local archives) (*Ancestors*, September 2004, pp 44–8)**
- **C. Sinclair, *Tracing Your Scottish Ancestors: A Guide to Ancestry Research in the Scottish Record Office* (HMSO, 1997)**
- **D. and W. B. Stevenson (eds), *Scottish Texts & Calendars: An Analytical Guide to Serial Publications* (RHS (London) and Scottish RHS (Edinburgh), 1987)**
- **L. Timperley, *Landownership in Scotland c.1770* (Scottish Record Society, 1976)**
- **See also the National Archives of Scotland's fact sheet on the history of buildings at** www.nas.gov.uk/miniframe/fact_sheet/buildings.pdf

PART 4

Broadening the picture

The last two sections have been concerned with written records. Using these you can build up a detailed picture of your home's history. However, it is important not to be blinded by the scale of the archival research that can be undertaken and forget that there are other ways of looking at the histories of homes.

You can use this section once you have completed your archival research, or you can study it in parallel with your other investigations. If possible, I'd recommend the latter. The following chapter on architectural history will help you get a lot more out of individual record sources that touch on architecture. The chapter on what's below your foundations is one you can use at any stage in your research. And, if you have a resident ghost, some of the sources suggested in Chapter 35 can help you find out who he or she may originally have been!

CHAPTER 32

Your home in its historical context

Your home does not exist in isolation. Every building in which people eat, play and sleep is part of Britain's long architectural history. Whenever your home was built, and whatever has happened to it since, you'll get more out of your study of its own history by understanding how it fits into the wider context.

Greyfriars, Canterbury, Kent, in the 1940s, from a watercolour by Jack Merriott.

Nomad origins

For most of human existence we have been nomadic – some people, such as gypsies, still are. For the rest, the transition from nomad to farmer started in the Middle East some 10,000 years ago, spreading slowly to Britain about 4,000–5,000 years later.

Before then, though, we weren't homeless. Most people were nomadic within a specific territory, using temporary shelters of branches, brushwood and hides in campsites that were visited regularly. If they were lucky, our forebears' patches included **caves**. Some of these were in periodic use over tens of thousands of years. Besides offering safety and shelter, they also represented connections with the underworld – the realm of the ancestral spirits. Our earliest fixed homes thus had deep-seated connotations of permanence, security and contact with the dead.

This link between homes, continuity of occupation and the spiritual world is fascinating. It probably has much to do with the reasons underlying why we are so interested in the histories of our own homes. In most cases, indeed, we know that the space we occupy was not inhabited by direct forebears of ours, yet this does not seem to lessen our wish to know more. Maybe the concept of living in the same space as our ancestors is so deeply buried in our psyches that we can't help but treat the former inhabitants of our home as surrogate or honorary ancestors. The connections we make with those who have lived in our homes before us may, therefore, not only be very interesting, but also quite psychologically important as well.

Once agriculture was firmly established, different types of home developed around Britain, from the stone-built, beehive-shaped **brochs** of northern Scotland, such as those at Skara Brae in the Orkneys, to the **round houses** of southern England. These were thatched with turf, reeds or corn, and had walls of wattle and daub – interwoven brush and twigs coated with mud and dung that dried to give a hard and relatively strong surface. These homes, like caves, combined practical and sacred functions, and rituals would have informed many aspects of daily life.

The Romans marched into England in the first century with an impressive array of new home-building techniques. Their architecture fused Greek columns with Etruscan domes and arches. Homes tended to be rectangular **villas**, with brick walls and tiled roofs. Some even had underfloor heating. Under the Romans, British towns, which had been ad hoc, rambling affairs, became well-planned conurbations with clearly defined centres.

The Romanesque and Gothic periods

After the Roman legions left in the 5th century, their successors, the Romanised Britons and the Anglo-Saxon invaders, reverted to a less sophisticated style of architecture. They favoured **aisled halls**, built with timber frames, constructed as a series of bays set up side by side and then linked together by long beams. The angular roof timbers were usually supported by internal rows of posts, thus creating aisles. Roofs were thatched or covered with wooden shingles and walls were of rubble or, more often, wattle and daub. These halls housed whole communities, eating and sleeping

RIGHT
Detail of Greyfriars, showing its Medieval flint walls and the obviously later addition of a brick chimney. Originally it would have been thatched, not tiled. This charming building of flint and brick stands astride the Stour in a quiet garden in the very heart of Canterbury. Alderman John Digge gave the site to the Grey Friars – disciples of St Francis of Assisi – in 1267, and here they built Britain's first Franciscan monastery. It was dissolved at the Reformation and only this building, the monks' dormitory, survived. In the 17th century it was the home of Colonel Richard Lovelace, the Royalist poet who later, when captured by Parliamentarians, wrote the famous lines in 'To Althea', 'Stone walls do not a prison make / Nor iron bars a cage'.

BELOW RIGHT
This picture shows Greyfriars' unusual situation, straddling the River Stour.

The magnificent Romanesque external staircase at King's School, Canterbury.

around a large central fireplace. At the upper end, the lord's family would eat on a raised dais and sleep behind curtains or, later, partition walls. At the lower end were chambers for storing bread and booze, later called the pantry and buttery ('butts' were barrels) respectively. The kitchen was usually an outhouse, to reduce the risk of fire.

While the Saxons used stone to build some of their churches, its use in houses really only dates from after the Norman Conquest of 1066. The typical '**King John**'-style home comprised two storeys, the lower being an undercroft for storage or livestock and the upper being a living area or 'solar', so called because it was lit by the sun. Access was via an external staircase leading to the solar. Sometimes, for security when it was used solely for storage, the undercroft would not have an external door. As the 12th century progressed, such houses started incorporating features of the new Gothic architecture found more usually in churches, such as high pointed arches and buttresses.

From the 13th century in the war-torn north, especially on the Borders and in lowland Scotland, defensive rectangular towerhouses or **pele houses** rose to two or three storeys in height, the ground floor being for animals and the upper solars providing living space. Stone was also used in the north and in the extreme southwest for **longhouses** – long, rectangular homes in which the family occupied one end, and their animals munched hay in the other. Both regions boast some fine homes built of square-cut blocks of stone called ashlars. Sometimes, though, ashlar stone might be used to provide a handsome front or impressive window- and doorframes, while the side and back walls were of cheaper materials.

Stone houses, however, were unusual until the 16th century. Even in areas, such as the Cotswolds, which we now associate with stone

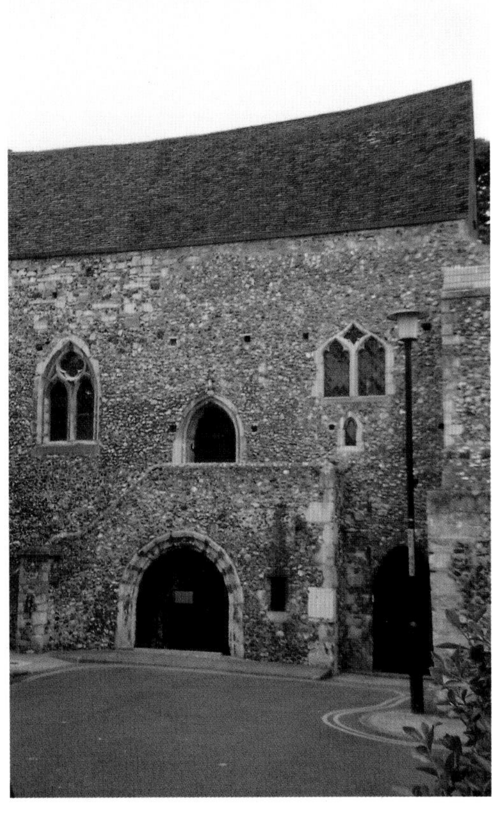

dwellings, readily available, easily workable wood was the norm. Admittedly, Richard I (1157–99), wanting to prevent the spread of fires, ordered that all London houses should have three-foot-thick party walls of stone, but this requirement was generally ignored.

The two main Medieval methods of constructing wooden homes did away with the inconvenient internal posts of aisled halls to create the earliest **hall houses**. These were called cruck and boxframe homes. **Crucks** were curved timbers – oak was best, followed by chestnut or elm – split down the centre to form pairs of arches, erected in a series of bays, linked together by horizontal timbers. The roof was formed by the inward curve of the crucks. **Boxframes** were literally that – boxes of timber that could be erected to form a series of bays,

The Sudbury Tower, one of the towers in the ancient city walls of Canterbury, is a rare example of a 14th-century building still used as a home, albeit much restored in 1870. Its walls are of local flint, with stone door and window frames and quoins – the name for the blocks of stone forming the building's corners. It is crenelated – the top has battlements.

A King John-style building in Canterbury, with outside steps leading to the solar, and round-arched doors leading into the undercroft below. As this was in the centre of a walled city, security was not as pressing a matter as it was in parts of the countryside.

A mid-15th-century cruck-framed cottage, Didbrook, Gloucestershire.

and covered with a pitched roof, whose timbers would be held together by tiebeams to stop them pushing the frames apart. In both cases, cottages usually had only one or two bays, while larger homes could have many more.

However tall they were, most early timber-framed homes had only a ground floor. A central fireplace produced smoke that curled up to the roof and escaped through the thatch, or through slatted flaps in the gables called louvres. Larger houses followed the Anglo-Saxon model of having the hall partitioned at each end to form chambers – the lower end for pantries and the upper for the lord's family to sleep in. As the Middle Ages progressed, it became normal for these end chambers to be divided horizontally to create a first floor, usually used as a solar for sleeping or socialising, hence their name, parlour, from the French *parler*, 'to talk'.

Usually, homes were rectangular, with one of the long sides facing the street. Their shape was dictated by the difficulties of creating roofs. Therefore, when greater depth was required, instead of building wider houses, people would simply build another rectangular house behind the existing one, with its own roof, thus creating an 'M' shape, the gulley between the two roofs being 'sproketed' with tiles or, later, filled by a lead gutter. A simpler method of creating more space was to allow the rear roof to run down diagonally to the ground, thus forming a lean-to. In towns, the front chamber was often used as a shop, with living rooms behind and a yard at the back. Fifteenth-century examples of such buildings survive, particularly in Canterbury, Shrewsbury and York.

Regional styles developed from this. In Kent and Sussex, **Wealden** or **Yeomen's houses** incorporated the two-storey end-chambers (containing the parlour, solar and so on) under a single roof. **Crosswing houses**, however, found especially in East Anglia, allowed these end-chambers to extend outwards under their own roofs to form wings running at right angles to the central hall, forming an overall 'H' shape. In grander homes, these wings sometimes grew enormous, including chapels and all manner of other domestic rooms. Sometimes they formed a courtyard. In all cases, however, the central hall, extending from the floor to the high-pitched roof, remained the building's focus.

Timbers were either fashioned on the building site, or in carpenter's yards. In the latter case, they were marked with Roman numerals, or by special carpenter's marks that can sometimes, under expert eyes, be dated or even identified to a specific craftsman. The timber wall frames were usually filled in with wattle and daub. In areas where they were readily available, though, turf, flints or cobbles might be used. In the southwest, mud and straw were mixed together to create 'cob', a style made

RIGHT
A classic 'M'-shaped roof on a flint-walled home next to Norwich Cathedral. This one has been adorned with magnificent brick crowstep gables.

BELOW RIGHT
A Canterbury hall house, built facing the street lengthwise. The end sections are of two floors, but the central section is still as it was in the Middle Ages, a single space stretching from the ground to the roof. All other similar buildings in Canterbury have had a first floor inserted.

ABOVE
A drawing of an 18th-century lead rain waterhead, from Chester.

Roof shapes

There are two main roof shapes, hipped and gabled. Hipped roofs slant in at the ends, whereas in a gabled design the end walls rise up to meet the peak of the roof. These can be hybridised. The 'gambrel', for example, combines the gable and hip, the very tops of the gables leaning inwards to provide a hipped peak: in pre-chimney days this created a slanted space at the top of the gables through which smoke could escape.

Although hipped roofs are found in the Medieval and Tudor periods, they are especially associated with the influx of Dutch style after the Restoration of 1660.

In the 17th century, the French architect François Mansard invented a way of creating more living space in the roof. Mansard roofs have two pitches, the lower steep and the upper shallow. They can be either hipped or gabled.

ABOVE
A Mansard roof.

RIGHT
A gabled roof. This is a hall house in Mill Lane, Canterbury, whose gabled ends display its original timbers in-filled with brick, and an enormous chimney.

BELOW
A hipped roof on a boxframed house in North Lane, Canterbury.

distinctive by its thick walls, rounded corners and deep-sunk door- and windowframes.

Medieval doors were thick vertical planks held together by internal cross-members. Doorways were usually quite low – not because everyone was very short, but to minimise heat-loss – and wide, for they might be used by both people and animals. Iron strips ran round the door and formed loops used to hang them on pegs in the wall. Doorframes and hinges were generally Tudor innovations. Under the Tudors, doors started being made of frames in-filled with thin wooden panels, usually six or eight in number.

Sometimes exterior and interior walls might be plastered and painted white, vermilion or cobalt blue. Bull's blood mixed with plaster produced a pink tone particularly associated with Suffolk. East Anglian plasterers also specialised in decorative exterior plaster mouldings and carvings called pargeting. Towards the end of the Middle Ages, exterior walls might also be decorated by extra timberwork that was not structurally necessary, producing elaborate patterns that were highlighted by painting the timbers black against the white plaster in-filling. This 'magpie' style was a particular speciality in Cheshire.

Although cruck frames continued to be built into the 18th century, it was box frames that really took off, not least because, by putting one on top of another, you could create multiple-floored **jettied houses**. These were especially popular in crowded towns, where each floor's box frame would be made larger than the one below, thus creating more space. The characteristic jetties that stuck out over the road might be decorated with elaborate decorations, while the protruding corners might be carved as dragons, hence their name – dragon posts. Such houses

Weatherboarding was a popular way of waterproofing the exposed sides of homes, as this jettied timber-framed house in Canterbury demonstrates.

Herringbone brick in-filling to the jettied stage of a half-timbered house in Canterbury, built in 1503, later to become the Sun Hotel and a favourite haunt of Charles Dickens.

RIGHT

The House of Agnes, St Dunstan's, Canterbury. Charles Dickens is believed to have had this 16th-century house in mind when he described Mr Wickfield's home in *David Copperfield* (1849-50) as a 'very old house bulging out over the road, a house with low lattice windows bulging out still further, so that I fancied the whole house was leaning forward, trying to see who was passing on the narrow pavement below'.

A carved bracket helping to support the jetty of a wood-framed building built in 1620.

might reach up to five or six storeys, with the protruding jetties projecting out so far that it is said people living on opposite sides of the street could reach across and shake hands.

The Tudor period

Towards the end of the Middle Ages, Britain faced a crisis. Timber, the main material for building homes, carts, ships, bows and arrows – as well as being the principal fuel – was becoming ever scarcer. By the Tudor period, timber in buildings was being cut ever thinner (in general, the thicker the timber, the older the building), but this was not a permanent solution. Timber's scarcity led to two extraordinary developments in British architecture – the widespread use of bricks and tiles, and the erection of chimneys.

All these had been used to a limited degree in the Middle Ages. Clay tiles imported from the Low Countries had been used for London houses from the 13th century in a further attempt to reduce the metropolis's regular and devastating conflagrations. Equally, Roman bricks were frequently re-used in the Middle Ages and new bricks had been made here from the 13th century. Little Wenham Hall, Suffolk, built in the mid-14th century, is one of the earliest significant brick-built homes to have survived.

Brick production did not take off, however, until the Tudor period, when brickyards started making bricks and tiles in large numbers. The trend started in East Anglia and Kent – the parts of Britain nearest the Low Countries – where brick was already widely used, and quickly spread across the realm. In 1605, the use of brick (or stone) instead of timber was required for all London homes – a law that Londoners generally ignored, to their great peril.

The innovations of brick and stone led to many older homes being torn down and rebuilt in what is known as the 'great rebuilding' of the

Highly decorative magpie timbering on the Palace of the Stanleys in Chester, c.1600.

Earthen floors

In the Middle Ages, floors were sometimes flagged with stone, but were more usually made of carefully beaten earth and strewn with reeds. This distinctive feature of old buildings took a long time to disappear. Boulge Cottage, near Woodbridge, Suffolk, was described by Edward Fitzgerald (1809–83) – translator of *The Rubáiyát of Omar Khayyám* – in 1844, as follows:

a hut with walls as thin as sixpence: windows that don't shut: a clay soil safe beneath my feet: a thatch perforated by lascivious sparrows over my head ... at evening [I can] *sit with open windows, up to which China roses climb, with my pipe, while the blackbirds and thrushes begin to rustle bedwards in the garden, and the nightingale to have the neighbourhood to herself... And such verdure! White clouds moving over the newly-fledged tops of oak trees, and acres of grass striving with buttercups.*

Though built in an old style, however, Boulge Cottage had been built to a traditional style not many decades before Fitzgerald started his periodic occupancy.

Before mass-production, bricks were usually slightly irregular in size.

In the 14th and 15th centuries, they tended to be 2 inches high and 12 x 6 inches across. The 1571 Statute of Bricks attempted to regulate brick size to 2½ x 9 x 4½ inches. Between 1784 and 1850, bricks were taxed, however, so it made sense to make them larger – up to 3 inches high – fewer bricks meaning less tax (in some cases people hung tiles resembling bricks to the fronts of their wood-framed homes to avoid paying any tax at all). Since then, bricks are usually 2½ inches high.

In the 16th, 17th and 18th centuries, bricks were made locally, and thus gave the resulting buildings distinctive regional colours. Many ponds, lakes and patches of rough ground remain to this day as relics of old brickfields.

In the 19th century, however, the railways meant that bricks could be mass-produced and transported anywhere – the age of regional variety in bricks was waning.

Fashion also dictated choice of brick colour. Red was the most popular between the 16th and 18th centuries, changing towards the end of this period to a fondness for grey and brown for walls, and red for corners and openings. London's familiar local yellow and grey bricks, called 'stock', fell out of fashion in the late 19th century and a demand for red bricks increased.

ABOVE
Early-19th-century print showing one of the small brickfields which sprang up whenever there was a demand for building materials.

RIGHT
A beautiful mosaic of handmade Tudor bricks from the mid-16th century on Roper Gate in Canterbury.

RIGHT
The Roper Gate, St Dunstan's, Canterbury, surrounded by much newer brick buildings. It is part of the home of Margaret Roper (1505–44), daughter of Sir Thomas More. When her father's head was chopped off by Henry VIII, Margaret bought it from the executioner. It was found when her coffin in nearby St Dunstan's church was opened in 1824. The gate dates from about the time of Margaret's death, and includes a fine Dutch crow-step gable, which at the time was a very avant garde cross-Channel innovation from Holland. Dutch gables caught on in the southeast and East Anglia, but later spread throughout Britain: their similarity to battlements led to them becoming a key feature of Scots Baronial style in the Victorian era.

Buildings with upper storeys hung with tiles are a common feature of Kent and Sussex.

Tudor period. Relatively few homes built before the 16th century have survived. Those that have are generally ones built to high standards by the middle and upper classes, but many of them have been altered extensively, often disguising their true antiquity. Thatched roofs were often replaced by tiles, and wattle and daub walls were superseded by bricks or hung with tiles. With walls, more effort was usually made on the front than the sides and back, where you may find traces of the original, pre-brick in-filling.

Thatch is an inefficient means of creating a roof, as the outside parts are prone to rot. It thus needs changing every generation or so. The most protected areas of thatch, however, could remain dry and be re-used many times over. Some old roofs contain thatch so old that it is blackened by soot from the days before chimneys. The replacement of thatch by tiles was largely due to their being much less of a fire hazard. Also, threshing machines, invented in the 18th century, broke the long straws used for thatching, which traditional methods had left intact.

One clue to altered roofing is the pitch. Tiled roofs need a much shallower pitch than thatch to allow the rain to run off them. Purpose-built tiled roofs, therefore, tend to be angled at no more than 30 degrees, while those originally intended to bear thatch were built to a much steeper 45-degree angle to stop rainwater soaking in. The pitch, therefore, can be the key to recognising a building that's much older than its initial appearance suggests.

Another ruse practised in the 18th and 19th centuries was to raise the height of the walls and thus lower the pitch of the roof. Such alterations are usually given away by the presence of slightly newer building material at the tops of the gable ends and signs of alteration around chimneystacks.

Many people are surprised to learn that **chimneys** have only been in general use since the Tudor period. Before then, smoke made its way up from the central hearth into the outside world by snaking through the thatch, or via specially made holes in the roof. In the 15th century, some larger homes had their fireplaces moved to be against walls and were covered by wooden hoods that funnelled the smoke up and out. The spread of brick, combined with the increased use of slow-burning coal – both symptoms of the wood shortage – led to the development of chimneys proper. Fireplaces surmounted by chimneystacks were sometimes built in the centre of the home. More usually, though, deeply recessed fireplaces were built into the walls. In new houses, the chimneystack was often the most durable structure – the only thing, ironically, likely to survive a fire!

Chimneys rapidly became status symbols and could be topped by many more decorative flues than there were fireplaces beneath. Fireplaces, equally, became highly decorated with linenfold panelling and relief plasterwork.

Because two hearths, back to back, could be fed by one chimney, more rooms could be heated and regularly inhabited. This suited the growing Tudor taste for privacy. Large manor and farmhouses ceased to be communal spaces for families and their servants and became more like the homes with which we are familiar today. When the chimney was installed at the lower end of the house, the pantry and buttery became nice and warm and developed into parlours, while the old parlour at the upper end of the house, unless it too received a chimney, might now be used as a summer parlour, or for storage. The upper parts of old halls, which used to stretch floor to ceiling, were usually divided vertically to create a first floor. The chamber

TOP
A Tudor townhouse in Norwich, showing a striking combination of Dutch crow-step gables, elaborate Tudor chimneys and some wonderful Norfolk thatch: the relentless advance of tiled roofs passed this building by.

BELOW
Oakhurst Cottage, Hambledon, Surrey, preserved by the National Trust as a beautiful, timber-framed cottage with lead-light casement windows. Its steeply pitched roof shows that the tiles have been used to replace the original thatch. (Photographed by Mrs H. Weaver.)

The fine Tudor chimneys and classically influenced gateway of Woodbridge Abbey, Suffolk, are both clearly visible in this pen and ink sketch by Perry Nursey (1771–1840).

below, formerly the focal point of the house, became merely another room, or even just an entrance hall. It was in the Tudor period that the upper rather than the lower floor became widely used for sleeping.

The undersides of the wooden floorboards of the first floor could be left bare, or plastered over to create elaborately carved and moulded ceilings. The gap between the plaster and the boards might be stuffed with straw. Besides many mouse droppings, these spaces may include some interesting Tudor rubbish for the home historian to sift through.

With the upper half of the home now fully usable, attention turned to the roof space. **Dormer windows** – from the Latin *dormire*, 'to sleep' – stuck out from the roof to allow light into the upper part of the home for the first time. From the mid-17th century, these started being built as a standard part of new homes. It was not until the 20th century that the unpleasant box-dormer – dormer windows extending across almost the entire length of the roof – spoiled this otherwise very attractive architectural feature.

The existence of upper floors necessitated proper **staircases**. Especially in the 17th century, these, like fireplaces, could be prominent, decorative features, sometimes dominating the entrance hall, or else snaking up around the chimneystack, or rising in dog-leg form in the space created between a central chimneystack and an external wall.

Rooms might now be panelled in oak or hung with tapestries. While homes remained generally rectangular, grander ones started adopting an **'E' shape**, comprising two wings and a central protruding porch, leading into the grand entrance hall. This era also saw the decline of ground-floor living quarters in favour of first-floor galleries – precursors of the *piano nobile*, the grand first-floor reception rooms favoured by Renaissance Europe.

The **Renaissance** was the revival of Classical learning, arts and architecture which had started in the Italian city-states in the Middle Ages. In architecture, it led to a rejection of Gothic style and a revival of earlier, Roman styles, making much use of Classical pillars, arches and pediments. Instead of being driven by ease of construction and dominated by functionality, Renaissance architects strove to achieve precise proportions and impressive overall visual effects.

In Tudor and early Jacobean England, Renaissance ideas were slow to catch on, not least because of Henry VIII's breach with Catholic Europe. Ideas trickled in, however, mainly via France and the Low Countries. They caused a modification of traditional building style and the adoption of various Classical decorative techniques, such as the incorporation of pillars or pilasters (flat pillars attached to the fronts of buildings), pediments and balustrades, in otherwise Gothic edifices. The first known Classical ornamentation in Britain was on the tomb of the first Tudor monarch, Henry VII (d.1509). Longleat, Wiltshire, is an example of a Tudor mansion built symmetrically, in reasonably Classical proportion, and was begun in 1541. It was not until the 17th century, however, that true Classical architecture would take root on these shores.

The 17th century

True **Classical architecture** was introduced to Britain by Inigo Jones (1573–1652). The son of a London clothworker, Jones developed an early enthusiasm for architecture and was fortunate in finding a patron who paid for him to visit Italy. Here Jones studied ancient ruins, the writings of Vitruvius, a first-century Roman architectural theorist, and Renaissance revivals of older building practices, particularly the works of the Padua-born Andrea Palladio (1508–80), who had studied and revived many ancient

The same building, now the Abbey School, Woodbridge, showing how little has changed since Perry Nursey's time. (Photographed by Mrs D. Kneebone.)

Classical principles in Italy, especially in Vincenza and Venice. Returning to England and working under aristocratic and royal patronage, Jones produced many British 'firsts', including the first piece of town planning – the piazza of Covent Garden (1630) – and the first fully Classically styled villa, the Queen's House at Greenwich (see picture on page 220).

Commissioned by James I's wife Anne of Denmark and finished by Charles I's wife Henrietta Maria, the Queen's House was constructed of brick and stone and covered with white plaster. Its exact proportions and crisp straight lines made it shine out among the mass of haphazard wood and red brick structures of London. Most people thought it avant garde, foreign and unpleasant, but, along with the rest of Jones's work, such as old Somerset House and the Banqueting House at Whitehall, it would revolutionise the appearance of British buildings. Especially after the Restoration (1660) and ensuing Great Fire of 1666, Classical style became extremely fashionable.

Townhouses built by Jones and his successors were of brick, dressed with stone. They had tall, elegant façades and symmetrical windows, the tallest being on the first – and now the principal – floor, the *piano nobile*. Features included parapets or balustrades concealing the roof, pilasters, pediments and porticos, and especially sash windows.

These developments took place in grander homes. Cottages tended to retain older casement-style windows. In fact, thanks to taxes on glass and the Window Tax that was first levied in 1696 (see pages 118–21), many poorer houses remained unglazed until the 19th century.

Until the 17th century, most houses were built to commission. Especially after the 1660 Restoration, however, speculators started building single homes or whole streets of houses that

A word on windows

ABOVE
Hexagonal leaded windows and some beautiful carved timbers adorn this timber-framed home and shop in Palace Street, Canterbury.

OPPOSITE TOP
A row of timber-framed homes facing the River Stour in Canterbury, of various dates: the one on the left is from 1680. With its large, vertical rectangular sash windows and dormer windows, it anticipates the later Georgian style. The two to the right of it are in older 'Tudor' style, with casement windows and prominent timbers (the front doors are much more recent), while to the right of the picture is a much older hall house, whose dormer windows and chimney are almost certainly later additions.

OPPOSITE MIDDLE
These steep-pitched, flint-walled houses by Norwich Cathedral would originally have been thatched with Norfolk reeds. We can see clearly on the middle house how the original small casement windows were bricked up and larger, more elegant sash windows added instead, probably some time in the 18th or 19th century.

As indicated by the word's Saxon origin *windi-durs* – 'wind doors' – windows were originally gaps in the walls to let in air, covered by wooden shutters. Interestingly, our Medieval ancestors had a widespread belief that the south wind was bad for them: they were convinced that certain sorts of air were bad for their health. South was considered the most dangerous as epidemics such as the plague tended to spread north from the Mediteranean. Consequently, houses often had blank south-facing walls. Although glass was used extensively in Roman times, glass windows were very unusual in the period between their departure and the 17th century. When they existed, Medieval glazed windows were lead frames holding small pieces of glass – lead lights – that were usually detachable: if you moved house, you took your windows with you, until this practice was forbidden by a law of 1579.

From the 15th century, windows had generally opened on hinges attached to the window frame on one side – what are termed **casement windows**. Improvements in glass technology in the 17th century allowed for larger panes held together by ever-thinner lead glazing bars. More significant was the development of the **sash window**, whose tall, rectangular shape perfectly suited the proportions of Classically styled homes. The system of weights and counter weights to enable the lower panel of a sash window to slide up and remain open was perfected in the 1670s by Charles II's Office of Works.

Sash windows became popular throughout Britain and her colonies – hence their presence from America to India – though strangely hardly anywhere else. One of the few places you're likely to see sash windows in Europe is Gibraltar. To surround these windows – which were often set back at least 10cm (4 inches) from the front of the house to decrease the risk of fire – later generations developed elaborate Classical architraves.

RIGHT
A Canterbury hall house with a solid front door of timber planks and wooden barred windows, only later filled in with glass.

The Queen's House, Greenwich, in the 18th century. It doesn't look that extraordinary to us, but when it was first erected there was nothing like it on this side of the Channel.

were then sold or leased. This often led to reduction in building quality and an increase in standardised styles. Following the Great Fire the 1667 Rebuilding Act demanded – and this time enforced, through inspectors – measures to reduce fire risk and also to make the city a cleaner, safer place. The use of brick and slates instead of wood and thatch was now compulsory, but there were also rules governing everything from the width and paving of streets to the thickness of walls and the heights of ceilings. Such rules were copied in many other cities and this again helped create a standardisation of architectural practices across the realm.

The effects of the enclosures

In the countryside, the enclosures (see pages 114–15) brought about enormous social changes that rebounded on buildings. Until land was enclosed, most farmers held strips of land in the large communal fields which dated back to the Middle Ages. As a result, they usually lived in large farmhouses in villages, built in the old style of a hall with pantry and buttery at one end and parlour at the other. The enclosures resulted in some farmers receiving consolidated blocks of farmland within which they built large, sturdy farmhouses. From the Stuart era, these tended to be square rather than rectangular, with rooms at the front and back. Sometimes, if there was already a hall house on the site, this might be retained as a kitchen and storehouse at the rear of the new building. The old village farmhouses that these farmers had abandoned would be divided into cottages for labourers. In the 20th century, as the demand for agricultural labour dropped, the reverse tended to happen, and rows of cottages were knocked through to make single homes once again.

Other farmers were ruined by enclosures. They remained in their village homes, but turned them into shops or pubs. Pubs next to churches, however, are usually of earlier origin. In the Middle Ages, the village guild often brewed its own ale in a guild house next to the church. At the Reformation, guilds were dissolved and the guild house often became an inn.

The 18th century

The growth of the British Empire and influx of goods from all over the globe stimulated the enormous spread of housing in ports, especially Liverpool, Bristol, Southampton and London. The Georgian era also saw the inception and growth of the resort towns, such as Bath and Brighton, with their many elegant squares and crescents. It is an astonishing fact that over a million Georgian homes are still in occupation today.

The late 17th and very early 18th century saw the emergence of two different Classical styles in Britain, Palladianism and the over-blown, elaborate grandeur of **Baroque** with its giant Corinthian pilasters and massive pediments. Blenheim Palace (1705), built by John Vanburgh (1664–1726) is a fine example of this short-lived style. Its Catholic, European connotations made it generally far less popular than the elegant restraint of **Palladianism**, which was championed by the Earl of Burlington and architects such as William Kent (1684–1748) as being far better suited to English Protestantism. It must be said, however, that English architects sometimes interpreted Palladianism in a fairly heavy way, with substantial triangular and half-circle pediments over the first-floor windows, and ground floors clad with extremely rusticated – that is, artificially pitted to look rough – stone.

A typical house of the period is the '**Queen Anne Villa**', built in reality from the 1660s onwards right through the 18th century. Such houses tended to be rectangular or, increasingly, square, with steeply pitched hipped or Mansard roofs; a pedimented centre; and sash windows arranged in Classical proportions – the tallest being those of the *piano nobile*.

As new dyes were developed, outside walls

Dr Johnson's House, Gough Square, London. 'If you wish to have a just notion of the magnitude of this city,' Johnson wrote, 'you must not be satisfied with seeing its great streets and squares, but must survey the innumerable little lanes and courts.' Samuel Johnson (1709–84) lived in this splendid house, built of sturdy red brick in 1700, between 1748 and 1759. It was here that he compiled the first comprehensive English dictionary. The house is fully restored and open to the public. It is a wonderful example of what homes were like in the mid-18th century.

RIGHT
The front door shows how few hostages Dr Johnson left to fortune when it came to protecting his belongings from London's burglars.

Henry Jermyn and the growth of the West End

One of the most influential 17th-century British developers was Henry Jermyn, Earl of St Albans (1605–84). Jermyn rose to prominence as the favourite courtier of Charles I's wife, Henrietta Maria of France. Indeed, some said Jermyn became her lover, and even that he was Charles II's real father. During the Civil War and the rule of Cromwell, Jermyn lived with the exiled royal family in France, and raised loans equivalent to some £25m in modern money, to help restore the monarchy. In 1660, Charles II was indeed restored but, unable to repay Jermyn in cash, he offered him the lease of the Bailiwick of St James's, Westminster instead.

St James's, the area to the north of St James's Palace, was then largely undeveloped rough ground used for hunting and recreation. Stuart bureaucracy being what it was, the 'lease' was, in fact, a series of leases granted by the Crown, each lasting for different periods of time, with subsequent ones granted to extend them up to, variously, 1711, 1720 and 1748. They were so complex that sometimes land under two halves of a single plot might be covered by leases of differing terms and lengths.

Jermyn began laying out the area as a series of streets in 1662. He sublet areas to speculative builders who were in some cases master masons, and in other cases gentlemen who in turn sublet their plots to masons. By 1666, Jermyn Street was finished, followed by Pall Mall, whose houses backed onto St James's Square (1670), St Albans Street (1671) and Bury Street (1672) – so called because Jermyn's family came from near Bury St Edmunds, Suffolk. Wanting to create a fully developed area, Jermyn built a provisions market, the Haymarket, and commissioned his protégé Sir Christopher Wren to design a church, which became St James's, Piccadilly.

Jermyn had grown up in Charles I's court and had known Inigo Jones. In exile in Paris he had seen the influence of the Renaissance first hand. These two factors had a massive influence on Jermyn's designs. The streets were wide and paved; a sewerage system was installed (no provision was made for street lighting, though); and the buildings were of brick, not wood. Most importantly, they were built to Classical proportions, with tall rectangular sash windows in evenly spaced bays.

Nowhere was Jermyn's Classical vision more apparent than in the centrepiece of the development,

Jermyn's masterpiece and his greatest legacy to posterity, St James's Square, pictured here in the 18th century, viewed looking towards St James's Church in Jermyn Street, both of which he also built.

St James's Square. This was to have had a fully unified façade, behind which were to stand 'thirteene or fourteene greate and goode houses, fit for the dwelling of persons of quality and needed for the beauty of the town and convenience of the Court'. He set an example by building one house himself, but others were reluctant to fund such great mansions on land that was only leasehold. Jermyn resolved his problem by persuading Charles II to grant him the freehold of the square, and allowed builders to buy smaller plots. In the end, 20 houses looked out onto the square from behind the unified façade of the west, north and east sides.

Due to several mix-ups, the south side was developed separately with houses facing away from the square, and looking south onto Pall Mall instead. For this and other reasons, St James's Square did not end up quite as impressive as Jermyn had intended. It was, nonetheless, the first of London's (almost) fully unified squares that, unlike its predecessors – such as Jones's Piazza at Covent Garden (see page 218) – was solely for the upper classes, with no shops on the ground floor. It had, admittedly, a rival in Lord Southampton's almost exactly contemporary Bloomsbury Square. While St James's Square ended up not being fully symmetrical, however, this was due to accident, not design. Lord Southampton's was only ever intended to present three unified sides to his own grand mansion's rather dull garden wall.

St James's Square was also a political statement. Jermyn was a passionate Royalist. Unified squares symbolised order imposed by the state on its people, and to ensure the unity of his square's façade Jermyn placed supervision of its development in the hands of the King's Office of Works. Its enclosed nature gave it the feeling of a palace courtyard, and, of course, it was only a few hundred yards away from St James's Palace. Classical and orderly, St James's Square was a microcosm of what Jermyn hoped Stuart Britain would eventually become.

It didn't, but not for his want of trying. Jermyn's development of St James's, however, had a massive influence on the growth of the West End. His insistence on wide, well-drained and paved streets of well-proportioned brick houses anticipated and had a great influence on the Building Acts that were framed after the Great Fire of 1666 and which, in turn, had a massive influence on urban architecture throughout Britain. Jermyn's work also inspired subsequent building developments such as the streets created by George Downing and Sir Thomas Bond and the square designed by his cousin John Berkeley, followed by King's Square, Soho. Such developments spread west, engulfing Chelsea and Fulham, at a seemingly unstoppable rate. Writing a century later, a character in Tobias Smollett's novel *Humphry Clinker* (1771) says:

I am credibly informed that in the space of seven years eleven thousand new houses have been built in one quarter of Westminster ... if this infatuation continues for half a century, I suppose the whole county of Middlesex will be covered by brick.

He was not wrong. It was not for nothing that the *Survey of London* volume covering St James's acknowledges Jermyn as 'the founder of the West End'.

LEFT
A restrained Doric porch c.1792–3, in Stoke Newington Church Street.

ABOVE
Fine five-bay Georgian house, also in Stoke Newington, built in 1769, with a Doric porch.

could now be painted in an increasing variety of colours, especially new shades of blue, green and yellow. Inside, walls were panelled in painted wood, plastered or, especially from the mid-18th century onwards, hung with wallpaper. Basements became popular, especially in towns, for use as kitchens. Ground floors, which might have been laid with brick or clay tiles from the 17th century, could now be covered with glazed tiles or timber. Roofs might be covered with curved tiles or sometimes with 'S'-shaped interlocking pantiles. A more traditional roofing material, the oak shingle, was also sometimes used. Generally measuring about 2 feet x 7 inches, shingles weather to a distinctive pale grey colour that sometimes leads to them being confused with slate. From the mid-18th century, however, thanks to their easy distribution by the canals, blue-grey Welsh slates became very popular, and were near universal in the 19th century, not least because their relative lightness allowed roofs to become lower-pitched and wider than before. The 18th century also saw the development of cast-iron and especially zinc gutters.

Speculative development continued from the 17th century. This, coupled with London's 17th- and 18th-century Building Acts and the popularity of standard pattern books, such as those of Batty Langley (1696–1751), led to ever greater uniformity of style across the nation. Town-houses were often two bays wide, with a single room running along the front, the rear room being narrower to allow space for the staircase.

In the later 18th century, Palladianism was challenged by a new style – **Neoclassicism**. Although Britain was no stranger to Classical architecture, this was generally Classical style as interpreted by the Italian Renaissance. Now, architects such as the Adam brothers, particularly Robert Adam (1728–92), were inspired by the discovery of Pompeii in 1748 and other Classical finds in Italy, and started looking back to ancient Roman remains for fresh inspiration. Grander and more detailed pediments and pilasters surmounted by decorated capitals appeared, as did recesses in walls, with or without statues and urns. Venetian windows became popular, based on ancient triumphal arches comprising three sections, the centre one being higher and arched.

Robert Adam is particularly associated with **Neoclassical fireplaces**, grand white marble affairs – often imitated in white-painted wood in humbler homes – with architraves incorporating caryatids or atlantes (female and male Classical figures) supporting a massive mantelshelf. Behind these grand fireplaces rose ever thinner chimneys, requiring ever smaller chimney sweeps and eventually mere children to clean them.

Neoclassicism also took inspiration from ancient Greece, whose architecture now became much better known in Britain than before. It was only in 1755, with the publication of Winkelmann's *Reflections on the Painting and Sculpture of the Greeks*, that British architects realised how much Roman architecture had borrowed from Greece. Some started appreciating and studying the latter's much purer, more austere crispness, its noble simplicity and calm grandeur. Greek style was pioneered particularly through the temple-like buildings and Doric porticos of James 'Athenian' Stuart (1713–88) and Sir John Soane (1753–1837). The style flourished in the early-mid-19th century: the British Museum (1823) by Robert Smirke, with its grand Ionic columns, is a fine example, but its effect can be seen on countless surviving Neoclassical porches and elsewhere in homes of the period.

15 St James's Square, rebuilt in 1763–5 by James 'Athenian' Stuart.

Elaborate ironwork adorns this home near Bloomsbury Square, London, in which lived the architect James Wyatt (1808–88).

The late Georgian era and the Regency period of the early 19th century saw the development of iron foundries. These produced much ornamental **ironwork**, used especially on first-floor balconies and balustrades. Most of what has survived can be dated from the catalogues of ironworkers, especially the Carron company of Falkirk, Scotland, whose 'hearts and honeysuckle' pattern was popular everywhere.

The 19th century

Parallel to Neoclassicism in the late 18th century there developed several new trends. Imported Chinese and Indian styles led to the Prince Regent's Brighton Pavilion (1815–20) and to many a small pavilion in domestic gardens, not to mention the addition of inward-curving, pagoda-style roofs to porches and verandas.

These reflected a fascination with the Orient. The Picturesque and Gothic movements, however, resulted from a hankering after our pre-Industrial past. The **Picturesque** movement celebrated the random beauty of nature, reacting against rigid symmetry and straight lines, and opting instead for a deliberately random, haphazard look in both buildings and gardens. But while the Picturesque could still incorporate many Classical features, **Gothic Revival** (initially called Gothick) was a deliberate return to the Middle Ages both in terms of style and spirit. The Classical revival, Gothicists argued, had stifled the native spirit in which lay our love of liberty and individualism. An early enthusiast was Horace Walpole (1717–97), who incorporated into his home, Strawberry Hill, Twickenham, Gothic features such as battlements, towers, decorated gable ends and delicate interior fan vaulting.

Early Gothicism involved decorating existing, usually Georgian, houses. In the 19th century, however, pioneered by the likes of Augustus Pugin (1812–52) and Sir Charles Barry (1795–1860), new buildings started being constructed in an entirely Gothic style. Two prominent buildings that influenced countless new homes were Pugin and Barry's new Houses of Parliament (1836) and the Midland Hotel at St Pancras (c.1868), by the former's pupil George Gilbert Scott (1811–78).

Theberton Hall, Suffolk (drawn by J. Marchant, engraved by D. Buckle), described by Richard Fawcett in the house's guidebook as 'a fascinating building ... an example of the curiously eclectic Picturesque phase of neoclassicism that came to the fore at the turn of the 18th and 19th centuries, and which was also expressed in the more severe, but still essentially Picturesque Greek forms of such as the younger [George] Dance, and the extravagant Gothick of James Wyatt and others. Theberton staunchly refuses to be categorised too closely.' It was probably designed in the 1820s or '30s by Perry Nursey, a local painter and amateur architect and passionate advocate of the Picturesque in all its manifestations.

Throughout the 19th century, Gothicism and Neoclassicism battled it out to become the dominant style. In the end, a general consensus was reached – Classicism was mostly used for public buildings, except for churches and schools, which were usually Gothic. In domestic architecture, while Gothic architecture dominated the Victorian period, it had no monopoly. Developers and private builders could choose from a broad range of styles, from Medieval, Tudor and Jacobean to Renaissance, Classical and Neoclassical, or any mix-and-match combination of these, often therefore causing confusion for those wishing to date a home simply by its outward appearance.

Regardless of style, this was a great period of home building. In the towns and cities, unified developments continued, notably in the great terraces built around Regent's Park by John Nash (1752–1835). In the outer suburbs, **villas** for the upper and upper-middle classes proliferated. Set in their own grounds, they were generally of two storeys, the living rooms on the ground floor and bedrooms above, with a service wing attached. Typical features included shallow-pitched slate roofs and French windows.

Speculative builders created other, sprawling suburbs of brick-walled, slate-roofed **terraces** for the middle classes. Terraces were usually uniform in design, broken occasionally by pubs and corner shops. Homes were generally 'two up, two down', the front ground-floor room being the 'best room', the rear one for daily living, reached by a narrow passage from the front door, and a narrow landing above. The better sort had bathrooms. Most have now been modernised with an extension sticking out from two-thirds of the back wall, with a bathroom above a kitchen. They usually had small front and rear gardens. The front ground-floor bay window, which was curved in the 18th century, became three-sided, usually surmounted by its

RIGHT
A Chinese pagoda-style veranda roof snakes round Abney Park House, Stoke Newington, built c.1792.

LEFT
The Grove, Little Bealings, Suffolk, from a mid-19th-century lithograph. Perry Nursey acquired this property on his marriage to Anne Simpson in 1795. The original Elizabethan farmhouse, to the left of the picture, became the service wing of Perry's new, Neoclassical, Picturesque mansion. Note the Picturesque style of the garden, with its 'natural' curve-edged lake and drifts of plants – quite the opposite to the sterile, regimented landscaping of Capability Brown that had been fashionable in the 18th century.

BELOW LEFT
The Grove today, including a fine Regency-style iron balcony.

ABOVE
Odd bedfellows: a Classically styled home stands in peculiar harmony next to an individualistic example of 19th-century Gothic in Northchurch Road, north London.

RIGHT
A real mixture of pointed Gothic roofs and arched windows and Neoclassical door and window frames adorn these houses near Brook Green, London.

own sloping roof. Front doors started to contain panes of stained or acid-etched glass, while garden paths, hallways and fireplaces were decorated with brightly coloured, or black and white chequerboard tiles.

As the quality of glass improved, the size of panes in all windows, and of windows themselves, increased. Within, ironically, contemporary taste favoured dark-coloured walls either of wood panelling or sombre wallpaper and heavy, elaborately carved plasterwork cornices and roses on the ceilings.

Terraced housing was also built in vast quantities for the poor. It was usually very cheaply constructed, the rear wall of one house doubling as the back wall of the one behind, with homes often grouped around courts. Addresses (as found in censuses, for example) took the form of 'Court 5, off Bubyer Street' – the courts didn't even have the dignity of being accorded their own names. These **back-to-backs** were generally only two or three storeys of one room each, and often had more than one family with numerous children crammed into them. The whole court shared a communal outside washhouse and loo: everything was badly ventilated, badly sanitised – and rife with illness and death. It was not until the mid-20th century that the working class generally started to be able to enjoy indoor baths and loos.

Much of the urban working class did not live in purpose-built back-to-backs: they simply squashed into whatever poor-quality accommodation was available. Some even lived in cellars, with no windows or ventilation at all.

In the countryside, impoverished agricultural labourers – many of whom were descended from the small farmers dispossessed by the enclosures – lived in mud hovels, most of which have long since collapsed, or shared with numerous other families the ramshackle village homes that had once been farmhouses.

TOP
Tudor-style houses with prominent gables and original lozenged windows in de Beauvoir Square, Hackney, built c.1839 by the ground landlord Benyon de Beauvoir.

ABOVE
This row of clean-cut brick houses in Albion Road, Stoke Newington, was built in 1825 by the speculative builder Thomas Cubitt (1788–1855), ship's carpenter turned architect, who also built the east front of Buckingham Palace.

Well-preserved Victorian terraced houses in north London incorporating Classical pillars in the porches and window architraves, and elegant sash windows.

Typical Gothic-style terraced houses in north London, with steeply pitched roofs reminiscent of the towers of an old castle.

Modern 'stone' cladding and paintwork forces this Victorian terraced house to present an entirely new face to the world.

Both in town and country, thanks to philanthropy, middle-class guilt and a growing realisation of the link between poor housing and disease, efforts started being made to provide the poor with better accomodation in the form of **social housing**. Some villages, such as Ovington, Hampshire, contain specially built labourers' cottages while other villages, such as Chatsworth in Derbyshire, were almost entirely replanned and rebuilt – usually some form of commemorative inscription survives. Some industrialists, such as the Walkers of Masborough, Yorkshire, and their relations the Strutts of Belper, Derbyshire, in the 18th century and the Dennys of Dumbarton in the 19th century, built decent terraced housing for their workers.

Concern with urban planning goes back far earlier. A law of 1589, designed to prevent slums, required any homes built on the edges of towns to have four acres of land around them. Such homes could not be divided into two tenements, nor could the householders take in lodgers. Builders failing to comply with this rule could be fined by the Quarter Sessions, while those who maintained such illegally built houses had to pay £10 and 40 shillings a month thereafter. The law was repealed in 1775, having, of course, been generally ignored.

Victorian **town planning** affected wealthy areas and municipal works as well. Over three-quarters of the City of London was rebuilt between 1850 and 1900, and this was a pattern repeated elsewhere. Local authorities redeveloped town centres; erected public buildings; created parks and gardens; and built new harbours, bridges and roads, of which the most famous was Regent Street, which cut straight through the West End.

Most importantly, the Public Health Acts passed between 1848 and 1890 made local authorities responsible for drainage, sanitation and social housing. In London, the Metropolitan Association for Improving the Dwellings of the Industrious Classes started its work of urban regeneration with a block of flats to replace a slum area in Stepney in 1849. The Peabody Trust, founded by American George Peabody (1795–1869), built many blocks of flats around the capital for the poor. **Slum clearance** took place all over Britain: many of the resulting homes were later demolished – condemned themselves as slums – in the post-war era.

Before the Penny Post was introduced in 1840, deliverymen would knock on the front door to receive payment for letters delivered. Thereafter, postmen could slip letters through post boxes. Early letter boxes were small – as were letters in those days – and, as they were unfamiliar items of door-furniture, early ones were marked 'letters'.

In the late 19th century, several new styles of architecture appeared. The artist and social reformer John Ruskin (1819–1900) introduced – rather by accident than design – a **Venetian** style characterised by oval-topped Byzantine windows, used in homes and also offices and

FAR LEFT
An outside loo at the National Trust's restored back-to-backs in Birmingham. NB: this picture is not quite authentic – there is no queue!

LEFT
The kitchen of a restored back-to-back, showing the walls of plaster decorated by hand in blue paint.

warehouses. Pure **Romanesque** style was revived, especially by Alfred Waterhouse (1830–1905), architect of the Natural History Museum (1871–81). **Renaissance** styles re-emerged and various French-style châteaux appeared, such as the Royal Holloway and Bedford College (1879–87) near Egham, Surrey. **Egyptian** style, with its thick, flask-topped pillars, was used, though more for public buildings, such as the Canterbury synagogue and the gates to Abney Park Cemetery, Stoke Newington, than in homes.

Ruskin, along with the Pre-Raphaelite artist and social reformer William Morris (1834–96), was also a leading light in the **Arts and Crafts** movement and the **Vernacular** revival. The idea was to avoid mass-production and return to genuine craftsmanship and 'good design'. Its advocates wanted to turn the clock back to rediscover 'true' Medieval architecture, as opposed to Victorian Gothic, which was merely an interpretation of what had gone before. The results were steep-pitched Medieval-looking buildings, often recalling castles or cottages, made of local materials. The works of Sir Edwin Lutyens (1869–1944) are probably the best known: working closely with the garden designer Gertrude Jekyll (1843–1932), Lutyens tried to make the homes that blended into their surroundings, as if they had always been there. The Arts and Crafts movement also embraced many elements of **Art Nouveau**, of which the Scottish designer and architect Charles Rennie Mackintosh (1868–1928) is perhaps the best-known British practitioner.

The 20th century

In the early-mid-20th century, homes were built in a wide variety of styles, called disparagingly 'By-Pass Variegated': of these, '**mock**

Gibson Gardens, Stoke Newington, was a model mixture of flats and cottages built in 1892 by the Metropolitan Association for Improving the Dwellings of the Industrious Classes. Ironically, with the massive rise in house prices in the area, the flats are now much sought after by young members of the professional middle class. So as not to put off people with social sensibilities, the original entablature proclaiming the buildings' purpose, shown here in 1966 (far right), has been removed.

Terraced workers' houses facing straight onto the cotton mill where the original inhabitants would have worked in Schofield Street, Chadderton, Manchester.

Sun House, Hampstead, designed by International Modern architect E. Maxwell Fry in 1938.

Tudor' was especially popular. Many homes (and cinemas) were built in the **Art Deco** style, which had been inspired by the curved lines of ocean liners and the bright colours of ancient Egyptian tombs.

The **International Modern** movement appeared next, fostered by Modernist architects such as Walter Gropius (1883–1969) and Erich Mendelsohn (1887–1953), who both fled to Britain from Nazi Germany. International Modernism shunned historic references, seeking simplicity and often drawing attention to the materials used. Flat roofs, plain white walls, steel window frames and right angles were especial features. These can be seen vividly at Mendelsohn's De La Warre Pavilion in Bexhill and Gropius's Irpingham Village College, Cambridgeshire, on which he collaborated with E. Maxwell Fry (1889–1987) – the model for much that came after the Second World War.

Whichever style was chosen, however, exteriors became less and less decorative. What ornamentation remained generally retreated indoors, but even here open-plan schemes tended towards simplicity and minimalism. Homes were generally semi-detached, with living room, dining room, hallway and kitchen downstairs and two or three bedrooms and a bathroom and loo above.

The period saw the continuous improvement of metalled roads and railways, leading to many villages being encircled by new leafy housing estates, all of which were within walking distance of a parade of shops and a commuter railway station. Electric railways, such as the Metropolitan Line in London and the Mersey Electric Railway in Liverpool, led to the dramatic growth of Harrow and Southport respectively.

Most estates were created on an ad hoc basis by opportunistic developers. Others were more carefully planned. In the Victorian era, philanthropic industrialists had started creating purpose-built new towns. Port Sunlight near Liverpool was one, where Lord Lever created a new utopia of traditional half-timbered homes for his workers; a similar example is George Cadbury's Bourneville, Birmingham. The planned **garden cities** of the 20th century, however, did not rely on the presence of a single industry. They started with Bedford Park in Chiswick, designed by Norman Shaw (1831–1912), where whole streets were laid out with integral avenues of trees and green spaces. Bedford Park was followed by the first of the garden cities – Letchworth (1903) and Welwyn Garden City (1920). After the Second World War, the British New Towns Act led to the building of more, including Stevenage and Harlow.

Early 20th-century **social housing** got off to a good start with reasonably pleasant, neo-Georgian developments with grass verges and

TOP
Slick, rounded edges and metal-framed casement windows characterise these 1930s flats in north London.

ABOVE
A mock Tudor house in Canterbury with its very distinctive white walls and black 'beams', which are there entirely for effect.

TOP
Modern housing in Alderoot, Chadderton, Manchester.

ABOVE
Post-war social housing in Stoke Newington, comprising two layers of two-storey, self-contained 'houses', the upper ones reached by a communal stairwell. Their austere design is somewhat tempered by the gardens.

tree-lined roads. Soon, however, town planners started turning to International Modernism, whose simplicity made it seem like a cheap option for cash-strapped local authorities. Low-rise developments of plain but inoffensive brick-built semi-detached homes quickly became a feature of many towns and villages.

Tower blocks first became practical places to live when Elisha G. Otis of New York invented the elevator in the 1850s. The French architect Charles-Édouard Jeanneret Le Corbusier (1887–1965) advocated a futuristic world of well-spaced, self-contained and well-maintained tower blocks of steel and concrete. The first Le Corbusier flats in Britain were High Point 1 in Highgate (1930), and are relatively innocuous. Ideas well suited to sunny southern Europe, however, soon took a nasty turn in rain-soaked Britain. Especially from the Second World War onwards, and in areas of slum clearance or bomb damage, 'Festival of Britain'-style tower blocks reared up all over Britain. Rather dreary and soulless, they created a sense of social alienation leading to vandalism and violence. The collapse of the Ronan Point tower block in East London in 1968 signalled the end of the movement. Since then, local authorities have generally tried to return their tenants to low-rise terraced or semi-detached homes, with the hope – often unfulfilled – that communities would reappear.

Under Margaret Thatcher in the 1980s, many council houses and flats started being sold off to their owners. Since then, social housing has largely been handled by **housing associations**, with varying degrees of attention given to quality and individuality.

The older the home, and the more attractive, the worthier it seems as a candidate for having its history traced. Modern high-rise flats, however, belong to the history of British building just as much as palatial Palladian villas. They

LEFT
Council houses in Canterbury. Their original minimalist style with casement rather than sash windows is often now enhanced by the addition of decorative front doors – not to mention satellite dishes.

BELOW
These private flats in Orchard Mews, Hackney, built in 1984, hark back to the Arts and Crafts style of almost a century earlier.

too have a history that can be traced: the stories of their occupants can be investigated – not least their translation from ground-hugging slums to apartments in the clouds. And before any modern homes were built, the ground on which they would stand itself has a fascinating history going back millions of years. Whatever form your home takes and whatever its age, its history is always worth investigating.

The 1960s heralded a concerted movement towards the **conservation** and appreciation of old buildings. While some architects like Norman Foster (1935–) continue to produce ultra-modern designs, many architects have again turned back to the past for inspiration. Instead of trying to make homes look modern, occupiers and owners of older homes are now keen on restoring them to their former glory. An interesting spate of redesigning has also been sparked by the recent plethora of home improvement television programmes. And, for the first time, there has been a huge growth of interest in the history of homes: hence this book.

BOOKS

- **A. Adolph, *Full of Soup and Gold: The Life of Henry Jermyn* (A. Adolph, 2006)**
- **A. I. Dasent, *The History of St James's Square, and the Foundation of the West End of London, With a Glimpse of Whitehall in the Reign of Charles the Second* (Macmillan & Co., 1895)**
- **J. Harris, S. Orgel and R. Strong, *The King's Arcadia: Inigo Jones and the Stuart Court* (Lund Humphries, 1973)**

- **See also architectural bibliography (see page 31)**

CHAPTER 33

Unusual buildings

A sign of Britain's increasing love affair with heritage is the number of old buildings being converted into homes. 'Has Britain become conversion crazy?' the *Telegraph* asked in 2001. Judging by the number of unusual properties you can now find advertised for sale, the answer is certainly, 'Yes.'

Sources for the history of unusual homes, such as railway stations (see pages 96–8), are mentioned elsewhere in this book. Here are some other examples of peculiar places in which people now want to live.

|| Many unusual types of building, such as almshouses, lighthouses and dovecotes, are covered by the Shire Books series (see page 25).

Churches and Church property

With the general decline in religion in Britain, many churches and associated buildings have been sold off to become private homes. Most church histories are very well recorded in local history books of all kinds (see pages 72–3). Many, while still in use, had guides or leaflets, copies of which should not be too hard to track down locally.

The Church was, and indeed remains, a substantial landowner in Britain. Within almost every parish, some land – known as glebe land –

The archpriests's glebe

A glebe terrier for Haccombe, Devon, was made in 1671. It reads as follows:

A Later Terrier of 1671.
A Terrier of the Parsonage House and Glebe Lands of Haccombe.

The dwelling House, one Patter [parlour], *one Hall, one Citchinge* [kitchen] *and a butterie, a patter chamber* [i.e. on the first floor], *a citchinge chamber and an entry chamber.*

These have all mud walls and the roof is covered with shingle [oak tiles], *an outhouse and one barn having mud walls and covered with reeds.*

One orchard, one herb garden adjoining the backside of the said outhouse containing by estimation 3 quarters and one acre, a little meadow before the dwelling house containing about half an acre, one field called the Lane End one acre and a half, one field called the Dewdnie one acre, one field called the Holt Pie 3 quarters of an acre, and the hedges of the outbounds belong to the same. There is also annexed to the Parsonage of Haccombe part of the Sheaf of the parish of Quethiock, in the County of Cornwall, and one field of ground there called Parson's Park 9 acres, etc.

Teste me, Matthew Carew, Archypresbiter.

(from the scrap book of A. W. Searley)

The Archpresbtery was founded in Haccombe – the smallest parish in England – in 1341 by the local landowner Sir John Lecedekene. Valuable background on this comes from Rev. G. Oliver's *Ecclesiastical Antiquities in Devon* (W. C. Featherstone, 1842), in which he states that 'Archbishop Grandison required that the Archpriest and his associates should lodge and board under the same roof ...'. This was probably the ancient parsonage house itself.

had belonged to it. Sometimes, deeds concerning Church land and the homes that stood on it will be found in county record offices. Church property was carefully recorded in glebe terriers. These were not small, ecclesiastical dogs, but they were surveys of parish land made between 1600 and 1850 (Latin for land = *terra*). They are most detailed for the parsonage house itself, often including information on how it was built and how many rooms it had. Terriers can also include other Church property such as glebe farms and cottages.

|| Glebe terriers are best sought in the local diocesan record office, usually the same as the county record office.

|| Non-conformist chapels – those used by denominations other than the Church of England – are also well recorded in local histories, and are listed in directories (see pages 64–6).

|| In addition, they were licensed and registered through Quarter Sessions and diocesan records.

|| Non-conformist chapels' registrations can also be found in the records of the Registrar General in the National Archives, in RG 31, and deeds for property held in trust for such purposes are in C 54 up to 1903, and thereafter in J 18.

|| The 1851 census (see pages 47–9) included a religious census of all places of worship, some of which have become homes, and others of which were then *in* homes.

|| The same applies to the registration of Catholic chapels made under the Catholic Relief Act of 1791, results of which were enrolled in the Quarter Sessions (see pages 94–5).

TOP
St Mary's House, Great Oakley, Essex, a Grade II listed 12th-century church turned home: 'chancel drawing room has dramatic barrel-vaulted ceiling and full height, east-facing stained glass window'.

ABOVE
Glebe Cottage, St Stephen's Green, Canterbury. The name of this box-framed cottage with brick additions tells us that it once stood on Church-owned land, and indeed it is just opposite St Stephen's church.

Factories

|| Material on factories will be found in directories, local histories and the archives, if they

A peek at a Papist

Crondon Park, Stock, Essex (no longer standing, sadly), was registered in the local Quarter Sessions on 4 October 1791 as having a 'Chapel or Room in the Capital Messuage or Mansion House called Crondon Park'.

Family papers I have inherited contain a remarkable biography of a nun, Margaretta, whose father Matthew Mason leased the property from Lord Petre. A paragraph about Margaretta's early life in the 1840s brings the Crondon Park chapel vividly to life:

...[Margaretta] *used on Sundays after Mass to go up to the rails of the Sanctuary and say her Catechism with the other children of the Parish, the Congregation remaining till the instructions were over. One day the priest asked the children if they knew who the famous Father Mathew was who was doing so much good in England. The elder girls could give no answer and catching Margaretta's knowing little face, he turned to her 'Now Margaretta, can you tell me who Father Mathew is?'*

'Oh yes' she answered in an animated tone, 'It's Papa'.

Of course, the Congregation went into fits of laughter to the discomfiture of poor 'Papa' who was sitting just behind her.

One day the priest asked the c
who the famous Father Mathew
so much good in England. – The el
no answer and catching Marg
little face, he turned to her: "No
you tell me who Father Mathew
in an animated tone "Its Papa
gregation went into fits of laugh
of poor "Papa" who was sitting j

Calver Mill.

survive, of the business for which they operated (see pages 64–6 and 72–5). Calver Mill, Calver, north Derbyshire, is now divided into homes, with a beautiful view of the River Derwent – one of the original watercourses that provided waterpower to the early mills of the Industrial Revolution. The advert adds: 'Waterwheel house converted to contain Gymnasium'.

Institutions and public buildings

- An excellent starting point for the history and records of any institution is Ross Brent's institutions website (**www.institutions.org.uk**). It provides coverage for prisons, orphanages, hospitals and much more.
- For almshouses, see also Thompson's article (page 243) and **www.almshouses.org**, though the latter is chiefly concerned with those that are still functioning.
- Many plans and descriptions of public buildings are at the National Archives' WORK series. Buildings on Crown Estates may be found in the series CRES. Local authority records (in HLG, and also in local archives) can also be very helpful.
- Buildings formerly used by the military are generally well recorded and surveyed. Records are especially to be found at the

National Archives in WO 78 and WORK 43–4.

Oast houses

Old Kiln Farm, an old oast house near Farnham, Surrey, was converted in 1933. 'Each of the roundels' – the round towers in which kilns dried the hops used for brewing beer – 'provides three floors of accommodation, with a sitting room and dining room on the ground floor and four bedrooms above'. Sources for the history of farms and farm buildings – such as the National Farm Survey (see pages 89–90) should provide plenty of detail on these unusual constructions.

Lighthouses

Up to 1986, lighthouses were manned by keepers and their families. After that date, a system of automation was introduced. By 1998, most lighthouses had been deserted by resident keepers. However, intrepid families have moved in to many, and converted them into homes. Some, such as the one at West Usk, St Bride's, Newport, South Wales, even offer B&B.

|| Such buildings, many dating back to the early 19th century, are well recorded in the

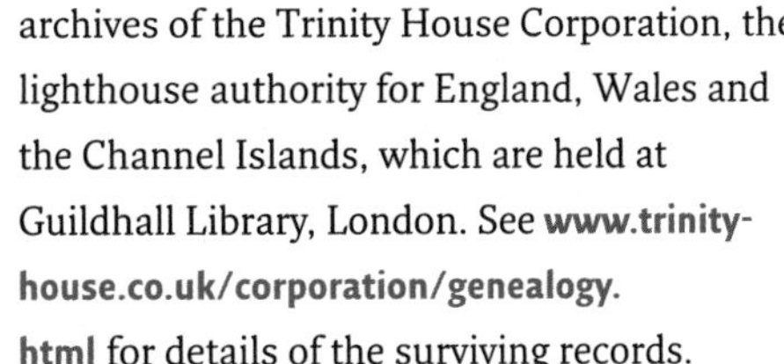

archives of the Trinity House Corporation, the lighthouse authority for England, Wales and the Channel Islands, which are held at Guildhall Library, London. See **www.trinity-house.co.uk/corporation/genealogy.html** for details of the surviving records.

|| Also helpful is **www.history.ac.uk/gh/thouse2htm**.

|| Lighthouses are also extensively covered by local histories and the records of coastguards at the National Archives (mainly in the series ADM).

Post offices

Letters started being carried by mail coaches in 1784, and by train in 1830, the Penny Post commencing ten years later. Purpose-built post offices date from the 1830s, the oldest being Sanquhar sub-post office in Dumfries, dating from about 1834. Recent cuts in sub-post offices are resulting in many becoming private homes.

|| Directories (see pages 64–6) are an excellent source of information on them, while archival sources are at the Royal Mail Archive Service at Freeling House, Phoenix Place, London WC1X 0DL; tel: 020 7239 2570; heritage@royalmail.com.

LEFT
Old Kiln Farm.

RIGHT
West Usk lighthouse.

This home in Castle Street, Cambridge, with its steeply gabled dormer windows, bears a plaque to commemorate its former life as the White Horse Inn. It was the last (or first, depending on your point of view) on the Cambridge to Godmanchester turnpike road (see also page 115 where there is a picture of the turnpike plaque).

|| The Scottish Post Office records from 1803 to 1910 are at the National Archives of Scotland.

Pubs and inns

We are used to modern pubs being rather elaborate affairs. In the 19th century, however, most were literally the public parts of normal, small houses: you'd go in the front door, sit on benches with everyone else, and be served a glass of nice frothy ale out of a big jug by the landlord's wife – and not a salted peanut to be seen. Tragically, these and even some purpose-built pubs have now become private homes.

|| If you live in one, you can seek more information on better times via the Pub History Society, Steve Williams, 15 Hawthorn Road, Peterborough PE1 4PA; **www.pubhistory.freeserve.co.uk/phs/index.htm**, and read Simon Fowler's essay on tracing pub ancestors at **www.pubhistory.freeserve.co.uk/phs/ancestors.htm**.

|| Booze-holes of all sorts can be traced back using directories (see pages 64–6).

|| Before directories, you can turn to Victuallers' Licences in Quarter Session records (in county record offices). Licences were granted each year, but you will usually have to search under the licensee, the name of the establishment itself not generally being recorded.

|| An unusual source for information is **www.alanroulstone.com/** from which you can get access to the collection of some 8,000 images of interiors and exteriors of pubs from the 1950s and '60s, drawn by Alan Roulstone.

Shops

Shops converted into homes often retain their distinctively large front windows. Some shops changed use frequently, but others that required particular fixtures and fittings generally stayed the same, even if owners changed. Butchers' shops, for example, would be fitted with fairly immovable stone slabs for carving the meat. Bakers' ovens, equally, did not lend

Not what you'd expect in an Inn

Newspapers (see pages 64–6) provide much information on pubs, not least in terms of all the public meetings that used to be held in them. Incidents, too, were reported. One of the most bizarre I have ever seen was sent to me while I was writing this, by David Courtier-Dutton. It is from a Berkshire newspaper, dated 21 August 1879:

... the horse commenced kicking and got free of the carriage though the shafts were attached; after running about a quarter of a mile it turned into the Horse and Jockey Public House, the door being open, it ran in, and was going down the cellar stairs when the landlord (Mr Hawkins) met it as he was coming out with some beer ...

Extraordinarily, everyone/–thing concerned got off with nothing worse than slight bruises.

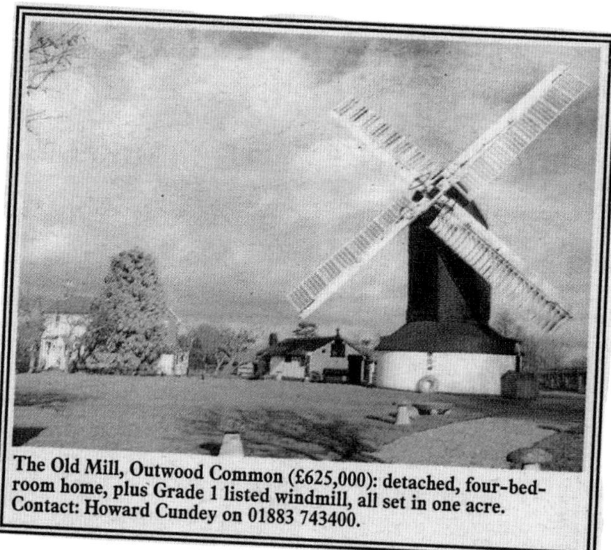
The Old Mill, Outwood Common (£625,000): detached, four-bedroom home, plus Grade 1 listed windmill, all set in one acre. Contact: Howard Cundey on 01883 743400.

themselves to easy transportation, so the buildings tended to remain as bakeries.

- Directories (see pages 64–6) are a particularly good source for shops, as most were listed and some also advertised.
- Morrison's book (see box right) provides interesting background.

Windmills

Outwood Mill, Outwood Common, near Kenley, Surrey (see above newspaper cutting), is one example of many converted windmills now used as houses. Windmills were special buildings of much concern to local communities, and therefore appear extensively in many of the records described in this book. As objects of fascination, many have also been the focus of special booklets. The windmills and watermills of some counties, such as Essex, have also been the subject of books. One 'converted' windmill, in Wraysbury, Berkshire, however, is nothing of the sort: it was purpose-built as a home by its present owner and proud occupant, Glyn Larcombe, for the cost of only £45,000.

BOOKS

- **K. A. Morrison, *English Shops and Shopping* (Yale University Press, 2003)**
- **A. Thompson, 'A Call to Alms' (*Family History Monthly*, no. 109, October 2004, pp 52–4)**

CHAPTER 34

Heraldry

The builders or alterers of your home may have left behind a visual clue as to who they were in the form of a coat of arms. Coats of arms appear painted on or carved into the fabric of homes, from outside walls and doorframes to internal fixtures and fittings, such as the fireplace. It is important to determine whether the coat of arms was part of the original building or a later addition, and take this into account when you assess its contribution to your home's history.

A coat of arms is a shield depicting various heraldic symbols to make it distinctive. Associated with the coat of arms – the shield – are various other elements of the whole 'achievement' of arms. These include the helm, sitting over the shield, and above it the crest, often repeating an element from the arms. Originally, the actual crest was tied to the helm by a twisted torse of cloth: in illustrated heraldry, this is often stiffened out to resemble a stick of candy. Equally, the mantling, the cloth that stopped the helm overheating in warm

In the 1950s, a house in Mayfield Lane, Wadhurst, Sussex, was owned by two cousins of mine, Thomas Gerald and Tizzie Havers. Their family coat of arms was *Or, on a fess Sable, three chess rooks of the field*, so they called their house 'Chess Rooks'. They are now dead, but the house has retained its attractive name.

weather, can be depicted very ornately. Below the arms (or above them in Scotland) you may find a motto, usually written in Latin, on a scroll. The helm, crest, mantling and motto are sometimes left out of depictions of achievements of arms, and sometimes you may find just the crest being shown. Grander families, usually just those of noble rank, also had supporters, taking the form of two creatures standing on either side of the shield, holding it up.

The system dates back to the 12th century. The original purpose was to tell one knight from another on the field of battle. Heraldry rapidly became a means of identification on written documents, the largely illiterate nobility using wax seals depicting their arms as a substitute for signatures. Most original deeds, wills and other legal documents you encounter in your researches will include such seals, though many older ones will have fallen off. As the centuries passed, most families of noble and knightly rank acquired coats of arms, and the use of them permeated down to the middle classes, the merchants and professionals, especially those in the process of acquiring enough wealth to buy up landed estates from the impoverished gentry. By the Victorian era, virtually any respectable middle class family sported a coat of arms, invariably without proper authority to do so.

The right to use coats of arms is regulated by the Crown, delegating its powers to the heralds – the College of Arms in London covering England, Wales and Ireland, and Lord Lyon presiding over Scottish heraldry in Edinburgh. Since independence, Southern Irish heraldry has been dealt with by the Genealogical Office in Dublin.

|| Useful contacts are: College of Arms, Queen Victoria Street, London EC4V 4BT; tel: 0207 248 2762; **www.college-of-arms.gov.uk**; Lord Lyon King of Arms at New Register House, Charlotte Square, Edinburgh EH1 3YT; tel: 0131 334 0380; **www.gro-scotland.gov.uk**; the Genealogical Office, National Library of Ireland, 2–3 Kildare Street, Dublin 2; tel: 00 353 1603 0200; **www.nli.ie**.

The Havers' coat of arms, showing the heraldic representations of chess rooks on the fess (horizontal stripe).

These bodies keep excellent records of families to whom arms were granted, and their pedigrees. Many people, however, have simply adopted arms and used them without any authority. This can lead to confusion, but can still be helpful: if your home is marked with a coat of arms that was legitimately granted to one Howard family, for example, but then was misappropriated by another Howard family, you may be temporarily misled into supposing which Howard family built your home, but at least you know that the builders of the place were called Howard.

|| Many British coats of arms – correct and bogus alike – are listed, by surname, in Burke's *General Armory* (see page 247). If you know whose arms are attached to your home, you can look the family up in many printed works on armigerous families (see page 247).

More often than not, though, you will want to

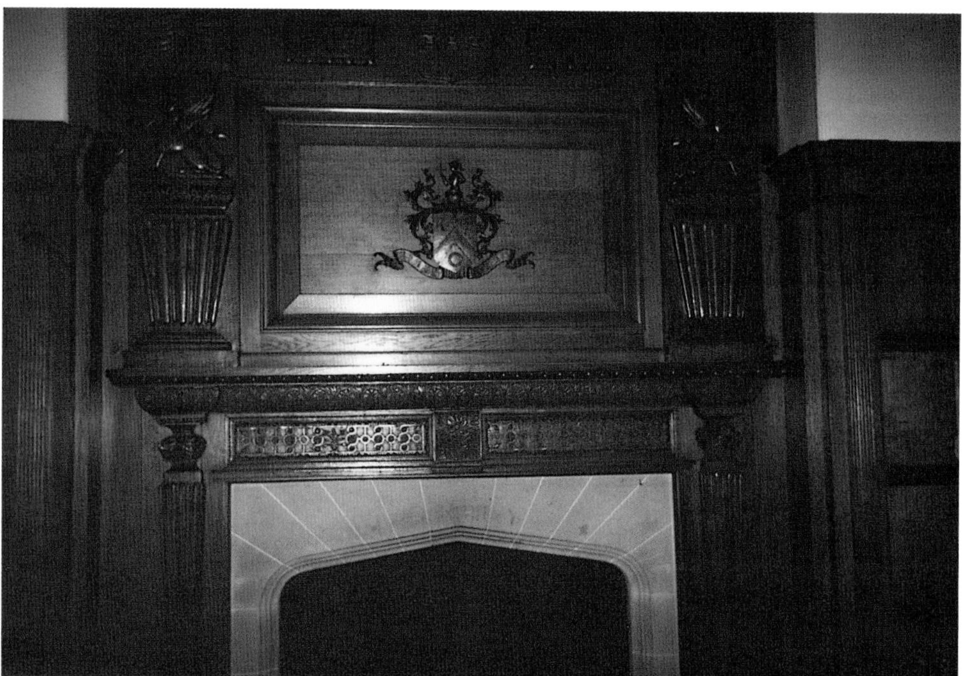

The dining room fireplace at Thelveton Hall, Norfolk. The fireplace was carved by Thomas Havers and his son George in 1849, and shows the family's griffin crest on either side of the main panel. After the house was sold in 1864, however, the coat of arms in the centre was replaced with that of the new owners, the Mann family. An unwitting home historian, going on the main coat of arms and ignoring the griffins, could therefore erroneously date the fireplace to after the Manns' arrival in 1864.

identify a coat of arms from scratch. This is done by breaking it down into its component parts, looking them up in Papworth and Morant or, for Scotland, in Balfour Paul (see box opposite). To identify the symbols and assign them their correct heraldic names you will need a guide to heraldry, such as Fox-Davies or Friar and Ferguson (see also box opposite) – in reality, though, you are likely to find several useful guides on the same library shelves as the copy of Papworth and Morant you are using.

You can check that your identification is right by looking up the results in Burke's *General Armory* (see box opposite), or seeking pedigrees of the relevant family as outlined above. All being well, the pedigrees will confirm the family's link to your home, and open up many new avenues of research for you.

Dating buildings

Arms can also be used to help date buildings (and objects on which they are found, such as old pieces of furniture). Finding out when the arms were granted can give an 'earliest possible' date. Impalements and quarterings can provide very accurate dates, though. If two coats of arms are 'impaled' together on the same shield (displayed on either side), this means a marriage has taken place. The arms on the left are those of the husband, and those on the right are those of the wife (confusingly, heraldic language describes the arms from the viewpoint of the bearer of the shield, i.e. from behind, so the husband's side is 'dexter' (right) and the wife's is 'sinister' (left)). Such impaled arms can only date from the period during which the couple were married. If the dexter arms are those of a bishopric, however, those on the right-hand side will be those of the bishop himself, who was symbolically 'married' to his see – equally useful for dating.

Sometimes, a wife had no brothers to continue her family line, so was termed an heraldic heiress. Once her father died, the husband placed her arms on a small shield in the centre of his, called an escutcheon of pretence. When the wife died, her arms vanished from her husband's shield altogether, and appeared as hereditary 'quarterings' on the arms of her children. A quartering can be a quarter of the shield, but in fact a shield can bear many sub-divisions, all reflecting the intermarriages of many generations with heiresses (for an example, see the Manby-Colegrave coat of arms on page 168). Once you know which arms are which, you can establish the dates of the marriages and deaths of the relevant parties, and thus date your shield - and therefore, hopefully, the home on which it appears sometimes to a specific year.

BOOKS

- **Sir J. Balfour Paul, *An Ordinary of Arms Contained in the Public Register of all Arms and Bearings in Scotland* (William Green and Sons, 1903) and *An Ordinary of Arms*, vol. 2 (1977)**
- **Sir B. Burke, *The General Armory of England, Scotland, Ireland and Wales, Comprising a Registry of Armorial Bearings from the Earliest to the Present Time* (1842, repr. by Harrison & Sons, 1884, and this, in turn, by Burke's Peerage, 1961)**
- **A. Fox-Davies, *A Complete Guide to Heraldry* (T. Nelson & Sons, rev. edition by J. P. Brooke-Little, 1969)**
- **S. Friar and J. Ferguson, *Basic Heraldry* (Bramley Books, 1993)**
- **J. W. Papworth and A. W. Morant, *An Alphabetical Dictionary of Arms Belonging to Families of Great Britain and Ireland Forming an Extensive Ordinary of British Armorials*, T. Richards (1874), repr. as *Papworth's Ordinary of British Armorials* introduced by *G. D. Squibb and A. R. Wagner* (Tabard Publications, 1961)**

This chimney iron was found during the renovation of the Logis de la Badinière near Tours, France. Extensive searching through works on French heraldry eventually revealed it to be the arms of the Milon de Mesne family, of whom several members were clergymen. One, Alexandre, almoner to the King of France, was also provost of Oë, attached to the church of Saint-Martin de Tours, in the 18th century. Carpenter's marks in the attic indicate that the house was built in the mid-18th century. This makes it most likely, therefore, that Alexandre, or his nephew, who was also a clergyman in Tours, built the house.

MILON DE MESNE (Alexandre), seigneur de Varenne et autres lieux, docteur de Sorbonne, prieur de Villers-Saint-Sépulcre, prévôt d'Oë, en l'église de St-Martin de Tours, aumônier du Roi.

Il avait été nommé évêque et comte de Valence, puis député de sa province à l'assemblée du clergé, tenue aux Grands-Augustins en 1735. Ce prélat mourut vers 1772.

De gueules, à la fasce d'or chargée d'une merlette de sable, accompagnée de 3 croissants d'or, 2 en chef, 1 en pointe.

CHAPTER 35

Ghosts

Much of the story of your house is bound up with the people who lived in it – and died there. For those who don't believe in ghosts, this chapter won't be of much interest, so I suggest turning straight to the next. For those who do – or aren't entirely sure – this could be an opportunity to add an extra layer to your home's history.

I know from experience that many people start tracing the history of their homes because they have encountered, or suspect the existence of, a ghost.

Ghostly images may appear in photographs taken in your home. Pets or small children may react strangely in parts of it, at certain times. You may experience a feeling of coldness in a particular room. I worked for a long time in a part-Medieval, part-Tudor building in Canterbury. There was a small, narrow stairway, near a radiator, leading up from a heated room into a heated library. Yet although I used the stairway several times a day, it never failed to make me shiver. If I was there on my own in the evenings, I would always avoid it and take the long way to the library. There was indeed, I discovered a few years later, an established story of a ghost on the stairs.

You may actually have heard or seen a ghost. My father, who is one of the most rational people on the planet, tells the story of staying as a small boy in the house where his great-grandmother had died not long before, and waking one morning to see her standing at the foot of his bed. The case-study (on pages 250–1), which comes from an account written by that same great-grandmother's own mother, records an experience similar to that experienced by many.

Ghosts can take many forms. They may be invisible, manifesting themselves as a feeling (like coldness), or by making sounds (footsteps, heavy breathing, rattling chains), or actions (turning door handles, pushing or throwing things). People with psychic abilities claim to be able to communicate with them, and in some cases say they can obtain information from them about who they are, why they are there and what they want. If you yourself are not psychic, you may want to consider inviting or hiring someone who is.

One of the most well-known and successful psychic mediums is Derek Acorah (**www.derekacorah.org**). Derek's Living TV programme, *Most Haunted*, was one of the first satellite shows to rival the ratings of the terrestrial channels, and has a dedicated audience of some two million worldwide. In each episode Derek visits a different haunted building, and attempts to communicate with or identify the ghosts present there. Elsewhere, he also uses psychometry, which involves picking up the 'residual energies' left behind in objects by past owners. For Derek, these energies can enable him to gain a picture of who the person was, and provide some useful details about them. He demonstrated this skill admirably in *Antiques Ghostshow*, another Living TV programme that he made with myself and antiques expert Chris Gower.

Working with Derek gave me a good idea of what you can expect to learn from a psychic. Ideally, you'd like them to say something like, 'Your ghost is Mark Ellison. He was bludgeoned to death by his Spanish lover when he was 36, in 1854.' Unfortunately, even the best psychics are unlikely to achieve that level of detail. This is not, I understand, through lack of ability, but because, however good you are, communicating with the dead is not particularly easy. Also, the sort of information conveyed by ghosts seldom provides the sort of pithy data you could use to help identify them. In other words, the psychics will pick up on all sorts of other information – the dead person smoked, had a northern accent, he hated paella – and of the essential data you need you may only get one or two things – his name was Mark and he died violently in his mid-30s, for example.

Your job will then be to research the history of your home and see if you can find a record of someone called Mark who lived and died in his mid-30s. If you do find a Mark living there, say, in the census of 1851, but not in the next census in 1861, you could seek a death certificate, and follow this up by looking for reports of an inquest or murder trial in local papers.

Psychic ability varies a lot across the board: there are many excellent, dedicated psychics who seem extremely good at their work. There are many charlatans too, or at least people who think they are psychic, but aren't really anything special at all. You can find psychics available for hire in most local newspapers, or in *Psychic News* (The Coach House, Stansted Hall, Stansted, Essex CM24 8UD; tel: 01279 817050; **www.snu.org.uk**). You may feel safer choosing a psychic who has been trained by the Spiritualist National Union (Redwoods, Stansted Hall, Stansted Mountfitchett, Essex CM24 8UD; tel: 0845 4580 768; **www.snu.org.uk**) or the Institute of Spiritualist Mediums (121 Church End Lane, Runwell, Essex SS11 7DN; **www.ism.org.uk**). As with any other profession, though, there are some trained psychics who aren't very good, and some untrained ones who are.

A ghostly presence on the stairs can add real frisson to your home's history.

As information from ghosts and psychics can sometime be rather ambiguous, it is open to misinterpretation. When tracing the history of your home through written records, I'd advise you to make sure any information obtained via the paranormal is clearly identified as such. If some of it fits with documentary evidence, then do say so: but if you find a contradiction between record-based and psychically obtained data, my advice would be to base your history on the former.

I also think, however, that ignoring the ghostly element of home histories would be a terrible shame. After all, if you're investigating people who lived in your house in the past, what could be better than meeting one of them?

A Greenwich ghost story

On the evening of 8 September 1866, a boy appeared on the doorstep of St Mary's Lodge, Croom's Hill, Greenwich. It was an unexceptional event, and would have gone unrecorded, save for one extraordinary fact: the boy had died two days earlier, in Jamaica.

Since 1858, St Mary's Lodge had been occupied by Arthur Oldfield Hammond (1822–81), a non-underwriting member of Lloyds of London who travelled to work each day via the tunnel that still runs under the Thames from Greenwich to the London docks. He and his family were staunch Catholics, and had been attracted to the house because it was three doors away from the local Catholic church of St Mary, Star of the Sea, and next door to a Catholic boys' orphanage, run by Dr William G. Todd (1820–77).

According to a memorandum written by Mrs Hammond, the family soon became closely involved with the orphanage:. *'I was there daily,'*

and took great interest in the boys, so that many of them looked upon me as a mother and confided their troubles and sorrows to me. Thomas Potter was an orphan boy [there. He] ... was a good boy but troublesome and often getting into scrapes. He took to the sea when he left the Orphanage which I suppose was when he was fourteen or fifteen.

The 1861 census shows the Hammond family in residence in Croom's Hill (the house is not named). Thomas, aged 11, was listed as one of the 80 boys in residence at Dr Todd's orphanage next door. Naval records at the National Archives show him joining up on 12 December 1863, his widowed mother Ann signing her consent. Tom was described as 4 feet 11½ inches tall, with a fresh complexion, brown hair and blue eyes.

While Tom started his career in the navy, Mrs Hammond wrote that 'his mother who had married again and bore the name of Cooper was with me as [an] extra maid to the children who were home for Christmas holidays 1865'. When Tom left on a voyage to Jamaica, to help quell riots there, he 'parted with his mother at my house'.

Mrs Hammond's account of Tom Potter's life continues:

On the 8th of Sept. 1866 on a Saturday at 11 o'clock at night there was a ring at the street door bell. We had all gone up to bed except Mr Hammond who was reading in the library (which is close to the street door). The servant who came down to answer the bell had only been with me a short time. Her name was Eliza Mann. I heard her speaking to someone whose voice I at once recognised as Tom Potter's. When Eliza came up I called her into my bedroom and asked her who had come. She replied 'only a sailor boy who wanted Mrs Cooper and I told him she did not live here'. I said what kind of boy was he? She described him as fair with blue eyes and handsome but pale and without shoes then I said that cannot be Tom for he always had a good colour.

However on Sunday morning the 9th I saw Dr Todd and said

ABOVE
Arthur Oldfield Hammond.

RIGHT
Part of Mrs Hammond's memorandum.

RIGHT
St Mary's Church and Croom's Hill today.

to him 'So Tom has run away again and came to my house (which was next door) last night'. He replied 'nonesense that is impossible for I had a letter from him two or three days ago and he was then in Jamaica'. I said 'I <u>cannot</u> help that he was here last night' and I told him that he had asked for his mother and that when Eliza told him she did not live here, he put his hand to his forehead and seemed in great distress and said with a sigh 'What shall I do and <u>you</u> also are strange'. He then disappeared or as Eliza thought went away.

On Monday morning the 10th Dr Todd brought in his album and asked Eliza if she could say which boy out of the number (over 510) was the one she saw. She went through the book and pointed to two: one was Tom before he became a sailor the other was in the sailor's dress (she had never seen the boy before as he left the orphanage for the <u>last</u> time during the Christmas holidays of 1865 and Eliza came about midsummer of 1866). Dr Todd to try her called her attention to another boy and said 'you must be mistaken this is a more likely boy to run away', but she persisted that the photographs of Tom Potter were the same as the boy she had seen.

We were puzzled and Dr Todd sent to Mrs Cooper to know if she had seen her boy. No one could tell us anything about him nor could we trace him. In the next month which was October Dr Todd received a letter from the Admiralty stating that Tom Potter had fallen from the masthead on the 24th of July and died on the 6th of September and that during his illness he called for his mother.

What Dr Todd told Mrs Hammond was true. Tom's naval discharge papers show that he died at Port Royal Hospital on Jamaica on 6 September 1866.

Mrs Hammond was, naturally, somewhat incredulous at what had happened, which is why she wrote down Tom's story. It survived for well over a century among her family's papers, before coming to light recently. She added, apparently as a postscript, that 'Mr H[ammond] who was in the library never heard the ring nor the voice', but, besides this, she was confident that Tom's ghost really appeared at her front door.

Besides enjoying this story in its own right, I like it because it brings the 19th-century St Mary's Lodge very much to 'life' – albeit due to Tom's tragically early death.

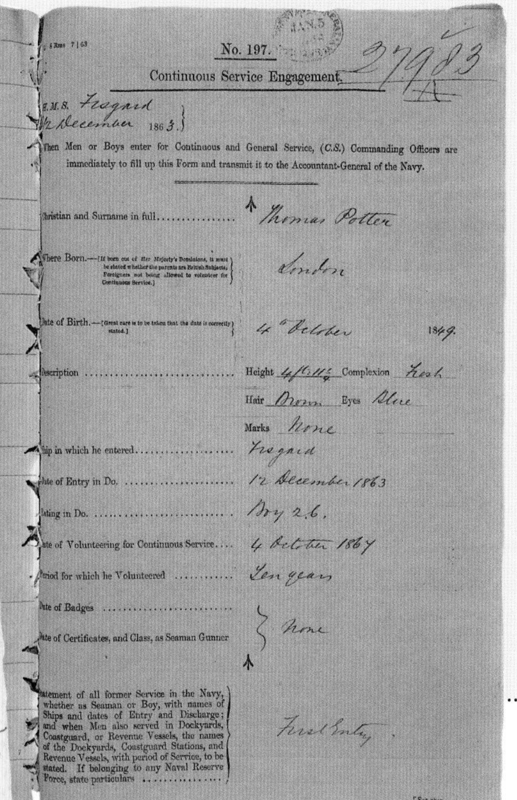

No. 197. 27983

Continuous Service Engagement.

H.M.S. Fisgard
12 December 1863.

When Men or Boys enter for Continuous and General Service, (C.S.) Commanding Officers are immediately to fill up this Form and transmit it to the Accountant-General of the Navy.

Christian and Surname in full .... Thomas Potter

Where Born.—[If born out of Her Majesty's Dominions, it must be stated whether the parents are British Subjects, Foreigners not being allowed to volunteer for Continuous Service.] London

Date of Birth.—[Great care is to be taken that the date is correctly stated.] 4 October 1849.

Description .... Height [illegible] Complexion Fresh
Hair Brown Eyes Blue
Marks None

Ship in which he entered .... Fisgard

Date of Entry in Do. .... 12 December 1863

Rating in Do. .... Boy 2 C.

Date of Volunteering for Continuous Service.... 4 October 1867

Period for which he Volunteered .... Ten years

Date of Badges ....
Date of Certificates, and Class, as Seaman Gunner } None

Statement of all former Service in the Navy, whether as Seaman or Boy, with names of Ships and dates of Entry and Discharge; and when Men also served in Dockyards, Coastguard, or Revenue Vessels, the names of the Dockyards, Coastguard Stations, and Revenue Vessels, with period of Service, to be stated. If belonging to any Naval Reserve Force, state particulars .... First Entry.

[See over.

BELOW
Part of Tom's naval service papers.

CHAPTER 36

Chancel repairs

Chancel repair liability is the obligation of the owners of certain property to contribute to repairs to the chancel of the parish church. The chancel is the part of the church occupied by the rector, as opposed to the nave, where the congregation sit. Originally, in pre-Reformation churches, the funds to repair the chancel were raised from land owned by the rector. Over the centuries, however, much of this land has changed hands. But even in cases where the liability to contribute to repairs has not been explicitly recorded or registered in title deeds, land registry entries and so on, liability to help repair the chancel remained.

Examining a Record of Ascertainment

On the first page of the record will be a series of numbered paragraphs. Existence of Chancel Repair liability affecting certain properties in the parish is usually indicated by any entries against either or both paragraphs 2(c) or 2(d). You will then need to examine the written records of ascertainments and maps to determine which particular pieces of land in the parish carry liability. Chancel repair costs are divided proportionately among such lands according to their size. The procedure for this is explained in National Archives Leaflet 33.

It should be noted that the 'local' parish church was that of the parish in which the property was situated in 1836, not necessarily the civil parish in which it lies now. Old directories and original one-inch to the mile Ordnance Survey maps will tell you which this was.

Due to recent publicity, the Church of England has become more aware than before of its right to demand such funds from unsuspecting householders, some of whom have received very substantial bills for repairs to their local parish church's chancel, completely out of the blue. Now many people are reluctant to buy property in villages without having first established that the building concerned does not carry chancel repair liability.

Fortunately, this iniquitous system applies only to some 5,200 parishes in England and Wales and the unfairness inherent in it provoked a partial change in the law. Until 13 October 2013, under the Land Registration Act 2002, property owners may still unexpectedly find themselves liable to chancel repair liability. After that date, however, only those whose liability is recorded by an entry in the Land Registry will be liable.

Where to search

Naturally, many people will want to know whether their property, or one they want to buy, is liable.

- As a first step, you can ask your local diocesan authority – the relevant address can be found via **www.cofe.anglican.org/location/** or in copies of Crockford's *Clerical Directory*, available in good libraries. For Monmouth and Wales ask the Representative Body of the Church in Wales, 39 Cathedral Road, Cardiff CF11 9XF; tel: 029 2034 8200; **www.churchinwales.org.uk/reference/padmin/patronage_e.html**.

- The National Archives holds records that can give a good idea of whether any liability exists, but the law is complex and no single document can give a legally definitive answer. Indeed, this section of the book is intended only to give broad advice. For further information you should consult the National Archives' Legal Records Information Leaflet 33 (**www.catalogue.nationalarchives.gov.uk/RdLeaflet.asp?sLeafletID=223**).
- The best place to start looking is in the Record of Ascertainments (IR 104), indexed in IR 104/107 and 108. If your parish is not listed, your property is probably safe, though sadly even this cannot be stated definitively. Next, if your parish is listed but is annotated with letters other than R/A, R/A (L) or R/A (SA), then you are likely to be non-liable. If one of the foregoing letters appear, there will be a Record of Ascertainment that you can examine (see box opposite).

Beautiful churches they may be, but how much are you prepared to fork out for their upkeep? Top: St Michael's, Cockington, Devon (painting, 1889); and above: St Kenelm's Church, Clent, Worcestershire (19th-century painting).

It should be noted that such searches only determine the existence or not of rentcharge liability. There are several other sources of liability too, such as allotments of land or corn rents in lieu of tithes made by enclosure awards, or private acts and merger of tithes with the land by the 1839 Tithe Act. These too are explained in Leaflet 33. In all cases, seek the advice of a solicitor.

CHAPTER 37

What lies beneath?

You may well be content with knowing when your house was first built or who owned the land before then. However, in some cases, it's possible to go even further back, into prehistory. This is, after all, relevant to your studies – and you may turn up some extraordinary results. Did Romans once march across what is now your dining room? Did Neolithic farmers tend their swine under your kitchen? Did a tyrannosaurus dismember a hapless cynodont in your back garden? Quite possibly, yes – and in some cases you can find out more precise details.

You can discover lots of information on local prehistory in your local museum; the Victoria County History series (see page 73); and local histories (see pages 72–5). Some old directories (see pages 64–6) go into quite a lot of detail on ancient history and archaeology as well.

Down the garden path

If your home has a garden, it may yield some interesting secrets.

First, you can turn amateur archaeologist. Unusual mounds and bumps may indicate the presence of old outside loos; air raid shelters; sheds; patios; water features; workshops; and so on. By digging beneath the soil you may unearth any amount of old rubbish, from broken clay pipes and coins to pottery and rusting metalwork, which could yield any number of clues as to who lived there before you, and what their lives were like.

Then it's time for your botanist's hat. Old fruit trees are a sure sign that the ground has been cultivated in some way for at least as long as the tree has been growing there. Old woodland trees could be survivors of the area's transition from countryside to built-up area.

I grew up in Hatch End, Middlesex, in a house with an average-size but actually quite extraordinary garden. In the front garden grew a gigantic monkeypuzzle tree, with sharp scales that passed for leaves that would fall onto the lawn as a constant hazard for small bare feet. In the back garden was a yucca in a circular flowerbed, beyond which a path ran down across a rockery into a small grove of fruit trees. Not really what you'd expect in the garden of a semi-detached house. When my parents asked the neighbours why they had such an unusual garden, they learned that the previous occupants-but-one had been sisters who had worked at Kew Gardens.

Sometimes, gardens can reveal much more astonishing information. One family did some digging in their Staffordshire garden and found the funerary urn of a Roman prefect in the 6th Legion called Gellius. That would have been exciting in its own right, but the family who owned the garden knew their ancestors must have lived there for longer than any records could show – their surname was Gell.

Archaeology

A surprising number of archaeological surveys and reports have been made all over the country. You may find that the ground below your own home has been the subject of investigations. If not, you will almost certainly find that sites nearby have. From the results of the latter you may be able to make at least some educated guesses about the ancient history of your own plot.

Finding out what is known already is surprisingly simple. Archaeology UK's Place Name Finder, **www.digital-documents.co.uk/archi/archi.htm**, contains details of 85,000 archaeological sites, derived from archaeological journals and identified by Ordnance Survey map references and an aerial map. You can undertake free searches for limited results: for full details, however, you have to subscribe (£34.95 at the time of writing). A free search for Stoke Newington, for example, revealed the existence of Roman walls, Medieval channels, a Roman building and a Saxon coin from the reign of King Egbert discovered just up Stamford Hill.

|| The National Monuments Record Centre (NMR) (see page 27) has an archaeological database, and you can consult their Sites and Monuments Record (SMR) by postal enquiry for free. County councils hold County Sites and Monuments Records and many towns

London has been busy for a very long time

I applied to the National Monuments Record Centre for a free search for any records they held for Evering Road, Stoke Newington, where I wrote this book. The NMR had nothing on the road itself, but provided a fascinating report on several finds in the immediate area.

There was very little for the Medieval period, and no evidence of Roman activity, which is disappointing as the nearest main road, variously called Kingsland Road and Stamford Hill, is actually the Roman Ermine Street. For the Stone Age, however, there was a surprising amount on record, suggesting that, if I could turn the clock back a few hundred thousand years, I would find the area around my home was a veritable hive of ancient activity.

A couple of minutes' walk takes me to the corner of Northwold and Osbaldeston Roads. Here in 1981, 30 flint flakes, by-products of Stone Age tool making, and two handaxes were excavated.

A few doors down Northwold Road was a 'scatter' of flint tools. Ancient man must have camped there and spent much time making tools, although the actual 'chipping floor', as it is known, was not discovered. Benthall Road, also just round the corner from my home, is where four Lower Palaeolithic handaxes were discovered. These would have been made between half and a quarter of a million years ago by offshoots of our human family tree, probably either *Homo heidelbergensis*, or their Neanderthal descendants, and long before our own species, *Homo sapiens*, had evolved.

Stoke Newington Common, all of five minutes' walk from my home, was excavated in 1878 and again in 1971. Here a vast hoard of Lower Palaeolithic artefacts were collected, including 230 handaxes and 20 flint cores, from which tools were shaped and then detached. Considering that, during the Lower Palaeolithic, the population of what is now Britain was never more than about 5,000 people, these finds may seem remarkable, yet, in fact, they reveal how very rich the remnants of our prehistoric past really are.

Some local finds can be seen in the Museum of London (London Wall, London EC2Y 5HN; tel: 0870 444 3852; **www.museumoflondon.org.uk/**), little more than half an hour's journey from my home. Here you can also see other remarkable survivals from the past – a lion's skull from Crayford; a macaque monkey's skull from Grey's Thurrock; and an elephant's tusk from Aveley, Essex – not to mention the remains of a woolly rhinoceros that once grazed happily near what is now Fleet Street!

and cities have their own archaeological databases held by local archaeological trusts or similar bodies. These urban archaeological databases are called heritage environment records. In theory, these, and the county and national SMRs, contain identical information: in practice, the levels of data on specific places may vary so it can be beneficial to consult two or even all three.

Geology

Most of this book concerns the works of humankind. However, it is both sensible and fascinating to look at the much more ancient, natural history of the ground below your home's foundations as well.

Using the BGS website

Enter the website at **www.bgs.ac.uk/geoindex/home.html**, then click on 'Enter Geoindex', followed by 'Collections'; then tick 'Fossil Specimens' and 'Fossil Localities'; then 'Redraw Map'. Using the 'I' for information button, you can see more information on the finds. If you click on a red star when you have the 'current query' layer set to 'Fossil Localities', you will see a collection registration number: you can email this to the BGS and they will confirm what data they hold.

If you click on a blue square when you have the 'current query' layer set to 'Fossil Specimens', you should see the collection registration number of the fossils, the fossil groups, formal identifications and ages.

BOOKS

- **J. Duffield, 'Mapping Missing Neighbourhoods' (*Family History Monthly*, no. 116, April 2005, pp 26–7)**
- **I. Jackson (ed.), *Britain Beneath Our Feet* (British Geological Survey occasional publication no. 4, 2004)**

Britain is composed of various layers of rock laid down over millions of years. The oldest were laid down some 3,000 million years ago, at the very dawn of life on Earth. Since then, many successive layers have been deposited and, in different parts of the country, rocks from different ages lie on or near the surface. The surface rock of the Hebrides and the most extreme northwest fringe of Scotland is 3,000 million years old. The surface rock of Northumberland, Durham and West Yorkshire (among other areas) was created in the Carboniferous era (355–290 million years ago), not long after our ancestors had crawled onto land, when millennia of forests were compressed down to create seams of rich, black coal for our more recent forebears to mine. A broad swathe of Britain from the Wash down to Portland Bill dates from the Jurassic era (210 million years ago), and contains many dinosaur fossils to remind us what lived here then.

In some parts of Britain, rock is just below the topsoil, or stands out in exposed outcrops. Elsewhere, particularly in the Midlands and the north, glaciers left layers of 'superficial deposits' of sand, silt or gravel that are, in some cases, up to 70m (76yd) deep.

The nature of the rock and superficial deposits below your home affects a lot of things. The type of building materials used locally were traditionally determined by what could be mined: from Cotswold stone to London clay, geology affected the appearance of homes and settlements. Geology affected local work too, from coal mining to sheep farming on the South Downs. It can also have some very immediate effects: radon produced by the radioactive decay of uranium and radium is second only to smoking for the numbers of people it kills through lung cancer each year and has high concentrations in certain areas, such as Cornwall and parts of the Welsh borders. On a more benign level, geology affects the type of flora and fauna in your area – and even what will grow best in your garden: azaleas, for example, thrive on acid soils, and are averse to chalky areas such as downlands.

|| The geology of your area can be explored more fully though the British Geological Survey (BGS), Kingsley Dunham Centre, Keyworth, Nottingham NG12 5GG; tel: 0115 936 3105 and 0115 936 3241; **www.bgs.ac.uk**, **www.geologyshop.com**. Their maps date back in part to 1835. It is worth pointing out that many surveys were undertaken just prior to and because of building developments so can be helpful in dating when your home was built as well.

|| You can learn some basic details about all the foregoing, and much more, from the BGS's *Britain Beneath Our Feet*, (see box opposite) a series of maps of Britain summarising many of their categories of data.

|| The BGS also provides detailed reports based on grid reference or postcode. These can be ordered via its website, **www.bgs.ac.uk/georeports**. A report on the geology of the area immediately around your house costs £23.75 at the time of writing.

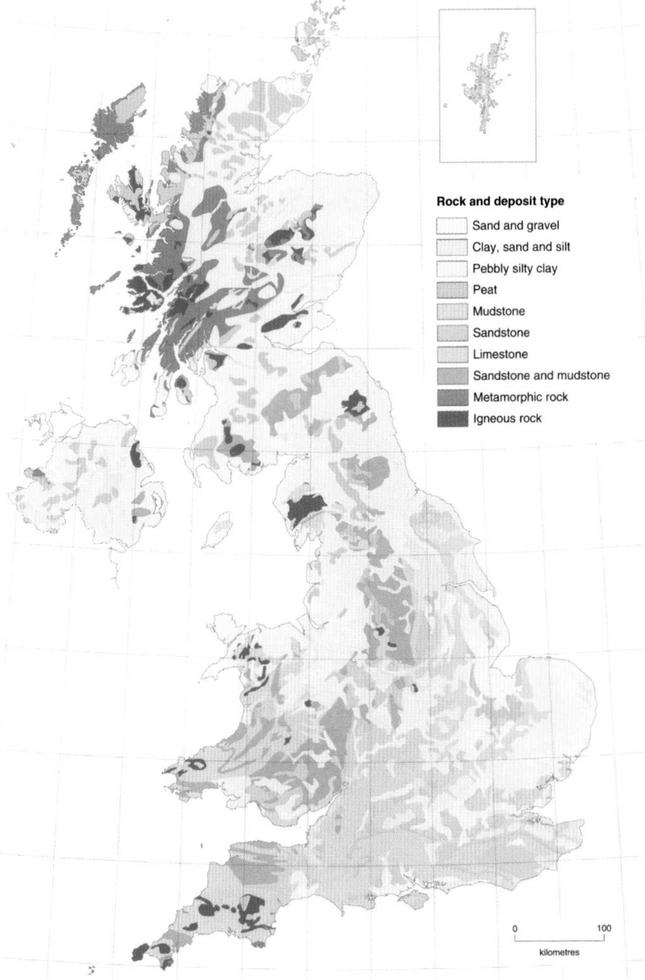

The British Geological Survey's overview map of rock and deposit types. As well as it simply being interesting to know on what type of rock your foundations stand, local geology also plays a substantial part in determining local building materials, both in terms of minerals and the types of plants that grow.

Fossils

The best place to seek information on any fossils found under or near your home is your local museum. Most museums have excellent local collections and their curators are a great store of local knowledge. Within minutes of talking to Ralph Anderson at the museum in Canterbury, for example, I had discovered that mammoths once roamed the area of Wincheap near the gasometer, and that an iguanodon had been found under a house in Maidstone in the 1830s.

|| Besides local collections, you can also enquire at the Natural History Museum in London (Cromwell Road, London SW7 5BD; tel: 020 7942 5000; **www.nhm.ac.uk/**), which holds a formidable collection of fossils from all over the country, although it is catalogued by type, and by location only within types.

|| The Geographical Information System of the BGS also has a substantial database of finds. Its website is somewhat complicated, but can be used to see if finds have been made in given localities. The project is ongoing and they have only, at the time of writing, reached the Carboniferous era. For tips on using the website, see the box opposite.

Postscript

The quest for James Paterson

When I was commissioned to write this book, I was living in Stoke Newington in north London. I had always known of an ancestral connection with the place through my great-great-grandmother Mary Ann Collingwood Paterson, who had married at the parish church in 1879, and her father James Paterson, who lived up the road in Stamford Hill. Being busy with other things, though, I had done no more than wonder exactly which house had been his. It was only when I received the commission to write this book that I decided I must find out more. Besides thinking I could use the results as examples – which I have done – the idea appealed to me that, even though I was a newcomer to this busy part of north London, I would be able to point to a small bit of it and say, 'My family once lived there!'

The rear of Church Row: James Paterson's house was the furthest on the right.

James Paterson was an interesting character. He was born in Scotland on 8 April 1830, scion of a family of tailors from Selkirk. James's own father became a customs officer, and James took a job as master of the then relatively new railway station at Alnwick in Northumberland, where he would no doubt have doffed his hat to the Duke of Northumberland, who lived in Alnwick Castle.

This was the time when railways were taking over from canals as the main means of transporting goods around the country. However, in those days, arranging for private goods and luggage to be delivered to one railway station and collected from another could involve a large amount of effort. Seeing a gap in the market, this Victorian entrepreneur started a firm of 'carriers', in partnership with his brother Robert and a Mancunian, Walter Carter. In time this grew into a nationwide network of horses and carts positioned at railway stations to collect and deliver private goods and luggage, with an accompanying bureaucracy to ensure safe delivery of all items entrusted to their care. The extraordinary success of the firm of Carter, Paterson & Co. made it a household name until it was nationalised in 1948. It also won a curious fame through being mentioned in Bram Stoker's *Dracula* (1897) as the firm employed by the count to transport his coffin.

James's success brought him down to live in London where he could best control his growing empire. The 1881 census told me that James

Paterson lived at 'Melrose', Stamford Hill, the name given to a stretch of the Roman Ermine Street that leads out of London towards East Anglia. The bottom of Stamford Hill is ten minutes' walk from my home: the top takes about half an hour to reach. I slogged up it on a snowy day, looking out in vain for a house labelled 'Melrose', but to no avail. Later research (see pages 54–5) showed that 'Melrose' had been at the furthest end of the thoroughfare – a stretch entirely covered by modern developments. Nowadays, it is a wide, busy street crowded with cars and buses, ploughing on mile after mile. When I examined Ordnance Survey maps from the 1880s, I was struck by the enormous contrast between then and now. When James Paterson lived there, he could walk out of his leafy driveway, and, by turning left and walking north, would soon have found himself surrounded by birdsong and of lush meadows.

The disappointment of not finding James's house spurred me to more research, in the course of which I found that in 1871 he had been living at Whithorn House, Church Row, Church Street, Stoke Newington – the street in which stands St Mary's Church, where his daughter Mary Ann married in 1879 (see pages 152–3). As I spent most weekends enjoying Church Street's pubs and restaurants, I was delighted to find that I had an ancestral connection to one of its buildings. Church Row, however, proved rather hard to find. Imagine my disappointment when I found that, among all the beautifully preserved 17th-, 18th- and 19th-century buildings in Church Street, Church Row had been completely demolished in the 1930s to make way for the library and council offices. My closest tangible connection with Church Street, I discovered, was the council office car park.

Visiting local historian Derek Baker, who lives a few minutes away from where Church Row was, I was shown some wonderful old pictures of James Paterson's home as it was in the late 19th century. This partly made up for the disappointment of the building itself not being there any more. While we were talking, however, Derek, who had lived near Church Street all his life, said he thought the name Carter, Paterson & Co. rang a particular bell. After rummaging among his wonderful collection of files, he produced a directory entry showing that not only had James lived in Church Street, but he had opened an office and warehouse there as well.

I found a court case of 1884 reported in *The Times* (easily found by a name search in Guildhall Library's copy of the *Times Digital Archive*), in which Mr Jordan of 110, Church Street successfully sued Carter, Paterson & Co. for £3-40-0 damages for spoiling his property by erecting a hospital for their sick horses next

Myself standing in the council office car park on the site of what was once Whithorn House. The view behind is broadly what the Patersons would have seen in the 1870s, only the spire of New St Mary's had not been built by then.

house & manufs. of closed uppers, 54, 56, 58, 60 & 62 Kingsland rd E
Carter Joseph & Co. office furnishers & fitters, 12, 13 & 34 Lime street E C & Beehive passage E C
Carter, Paterson & Co. carriers & railway agents, 126 & 128 Goswell rd E C; George yd. Aldermanbury E C; 20 Peel st. Notting hill gate W; 32 Chalk Farm rd NW; 182 High st. Deptford S E; Lamb alley, 151 Bermondsey street S E; Baker street, Brixton rd. SW; Birkbeck st. Cambridge rd E; 8 Milner st. Chelsea SW; 46A, Millbank street, Westminster SW; 35 Church street, Stoke Newington N; & Old distillery, High st. Brentford & Maple rd. Penge; depôt for W. A. Ross & Co. Belfast, Ireland
Carter & Payne, carvers & gilders, 98 Wigmore street W
Carter Richard & Co. wholesale stationers & linen & parchment label makers, 4 Bury court, St. Mary axe E C
Carter Robert & Sons, wholesale cabinet makers, dealers in old

Carter Hy. Alfd. tob
Carter Henry Aylin
Carter Henry Charl
Carter Hy. Christn.
Carter Henry Willia
Carter Hy. Wm. ship
Carter Horace, civil
Carter Howard Bew
Carter Hugh, artist,
Carter Isaac, greeng
Carter Isaac, tobacc
Carter Isabella Mari
Carter James, boot
Carter James, build
Carter James, fancy

TOP
A page from an 1882 directory of London, showing Carter, Paterson & Co.'s different metropolitan outlets, including the office James had opened in Church Street.

BOTTOM
James Paterson's family vault at New Southgate Cemetery, north London.

door at number 108. Mr Jordan's barrister, it was reported, 'drew a most humorous and pathetic picture of his client ... whose peace and repose were utterly ruined by the glandered horses coughing away their weary souls next door'. Just how appalled Mr Jordan would have been at the smells and noise of the traffic zooming up and down the street nowadays defies imagination.

Derek and I pored over old maps to work out where the offending site had been. 'Oh dear,' said Derek at length. The site of the office was now under a row of modern flats.

I now really wanted to find some tangible connection with James Paterson. He died in Stamford Hill in 1887, so I wondered if he was buried in nearby Abney Park Cemetery, on the corner of Church Street and Stamford Hill – but no. He had three wives – my ancestress Isabella Collingwood from Alnwick, then Isabella Lorraine and finally his children's governess Mary Sutton. My family papers stated James's first wife, Isabella, was buried at 'Colney Hatch', which I worked out must have been the Great Northern Cemetery, now called New Southgate Cemetery, about four miles away. The response to my enquiry to the cemetery made me gasp with exasperation – yes, James was buried there, but there was no gravestone.

The census returns I had examined showed that James had lived briefly in Islington, where his son Harry Lorraine Paterson was born. That was not far away, and must have survived, so on 9 June 2005 I decided to visit the cemetery to take a photograph of the patch that *didn't* contain James's gravestone, and then go and see what surely must be a surviving home that he'd actually inhabited.

At Southgate Cemetery I saw James's burial record, showing that the plot had been inherited by Harry Lorraine Paterson. Harry was certainly an unusual character – he died of pneumonia having gone out riding a horse during a thunderstorm on Hallowe'en, wearing only his nightshirt.

As I approached the spot where James was buried, which was just through the main gates of the cemetery and within sight of the cemetery office, there was indeed a blank patch of grass. As I looked at it wistfully, however, my eyes slid to the right to a huge obelisk and then widened with disbelief when I saw what was written at its base: 'THE FAMILY VAULT OF JAMES PATERSON, MELROSE, STAMFORD HILL'. The front of the obelisk commemorated James and his second wife, Isabella Lorraine Paterson, and three of their children who had died young. The rear commemorated James's first wife, my ancestress Isabella, and a daughter of theirs who had died as an infant (Mary Sutton, the family governess and third wife, did not get a look-in).

Delighted that the cemetery records had been wrong I continued my journey to the delightfully preserved old streets of Canonbury to Canonbury Street, where, at 1 Westrop Villas, Harry Lorraine Paterson had been born in 1865. Rounding the corner, I found – modern flats! Surely not? But yes: Westrop Villas, a local told me, had been flattened by Second World War bombs.

My journey was at end. On the way home, I stopped for a drink in the Rose and Crown, looking out through its curved 1930s glass windows at the council office car park where once had stood James Paterson's home, Whithorn House, and consoled myself that at least I'd found his grave. I had learned a lot more about him and his family from the directories; General Registration certificates; his will; census returns; tithe records; and the wonderful old pictures Derek Baker and Hackney Archives had of the area. My researches had given me a much stronger connection with the area where I lived.

And then came one of the extraordinary twists that take place when you get deeply involved in researching the past, be it home, family or local history. The sort of bizarre coincidence that completely wrong-foots you and makes you wonder if it could possibly be a coincidence, and not some sort of carefully laid scheme of fate.

When I traced my Paterson ancestors in the late 1980s, I contacted a number of James's descendants including a portrait artist called Tinka Paterson, a grandson of Harry Lorraine Paterson. Tinka had been extremely kind and helpful, and had even sent me a couple of original photographs of James, which I have used in this book. We had, however, lost touch, and had both moved from our old addresses. I was therefore delighted when I received a postcard from Tinka forwarded successfully from my old address. It seemed extraordinary that, four days before I discovered James's grave, one of his great-grandchildren should have decided to contact me.

The portrait of James Paterson back in Stoke Newington after a space of some 115 years.

Tinka's reason for doing so was that he was nearing 80 and, not having children, wanted some of his family heirlooms to go to new homes within the family. Among his treasures were two original oil paintings, showing James Paterson and his first wife, my ancestress Isabella Collingwood. 'I thought you'd like them, as you're descended from them both, and are so interested in the family,' he explained. Abashed and astonished by such generosity, I gratefully accepted his offer to travel up to Norwich to collect them. And so it was that, on Midsummer's Eve 2005, I returned from a lovely day out in Norwich, bringing the portraits of James and his wife back to Stoke Newington after a gap of some 115 years.

James Paterson had finally come home.

Useful addresses

The addresses are listed here in alphabetical order according to the name of the organisation or person and on page 265 there is a collection of specialist CD-Rom suppliers.

The addresses in the main part of the book only appear the first time they are mentioned; thereafter you should refer to these pages for contact details.

Alan Godfrey Maps
Prospect Business Park
Leadgate
Consett
Durham DH8 7PW
01207 583388
www.alangodfreymaps.co.uk

Bank of England Archive Section
Threadneedle Street
London EC2R 8AH
020 7601 5096
www.bankofengland.co.uk/archive.htm

Blue Plaques Team
English Heritage
23 Saville Row
London W1S 2ET
020 7973 3794
www.english-heritage.org.uk/blueplaques

Borthwick Institute for Archives
University of York
Heslington
York YO10 5DD
01904 321166
www.york.ac.uk/inst/bihr/

British Association for Local History (BALH)
PO Box 6549
Somersal Herbert
Ashbourne
Derbyshire DE6 5WH
01283 585947
www.balh.co.uk mail@balh.co.uk.

British Geological Survey
Kingsley Dunham Centre
Keyworth
Nottingham NG12 5GG
0115 936 3105 and 0115 936 3241
www.bgs.ac.uk and www.geologyshop.com

British Library
96 Euston Road
London NW1 2DB
020 7412 7873
www.bl.uk

British Library Newspaper Library
Colindale Avenue
Colindale
London NW9 5HE
020 7412 7353
www.bl.uk/collections/newspapers.html

British Telecom Archives
3rd Floor
Holborn Telephone Exchange
268–270 High Holborn
London WC1V 7EE
020 7492 8792
www.btplc.com/archives

Business Archives Council
The Clove Building
4 Maguire Street
London SE1 2NQ
020 7407 6110
www.caritasdata.co.uk/charity4/ch007084.htm

Cambridge University Library
West Road
Cambridge CB3 9DR
01223 333000
www.lib.cam.ac.uk/

City of Westminster Archives Centre
10 St Ann's Street
London SW1P 2DE
020 7641 5180
www.westminster.gov.uk/archives/

College of Arms
Queen Victoria Street
London EC4V 4BT
0207 248 2762
www.college-of-arms.gov.uk

Companies House
21 Bloomsbury Square
London WC1B 3X
0870 333 3636

Companies Registry
Customer Counter
1st Floor, Waterfront Plaza
8 Laganbank Road
Belfast BT1 3BS
0845 604 8888
www.detini.gov.uk/cgi-bin/get_builder_page?page=1966&site=7

Corporation of London Record Office
c/o London Metropolitan Archives
40 Northampton Road
London EC1R 0HB
020 7332 3820
www.cityoflondon.gov.uk

David & Charles Ltd
Brunel House
Forde Close
Newton Abbott
Devon TQ12 4PU
01626 323200
www.davidandcharles.co.uk

Duchy of Cornwall Office
10 Buckingham Gate
London SW1E 6LA

Eneclann Ltd
Unit 1b, Trinity College Enterprise Centre
Pearse Street
Dublin 2
03531 671 0338
info@eneclann.ie

Family Records Centre
1 Myddleton Street
London EC1R 1UW
020 8392 5300
www.familyrecords.gov.uk/frc

Francis Frith Collection
Charlton Road
Andover
Hampshire SP10 3LE
01722 716376
www.francisfrith.co.uk

Geffreye Museum
Kingsland Road
London E2 8EA
020 7739 9893
www.geffrye-museum.org.uk/

Genealogical Office
National Library of Ireland
2–3 Kildare Street
Dublin 2
00 353 1603 0200
www.nli.ie

Grimsay Press
57 St Vincent Crescent
Glasgow G3 8NQ
www.thegrimsaypress.co.uk

Guildhall Library
Aldermanbury
London EC2P 2EJ
020 7332 1868
www.cityoflondon.gov.uk

HIPs Direct Ltd
7 Grosvenor Street
Chester
Cheshire CH1 2DD
01244 340159
mail@hipsdirect.com

HM Greffier
General Register Office
Royal Court House
St Peter Port
Guernsey GY1 2PD
01481 725277

HM Land Registry
32 Lincoln's Inn Fields
London WC2A 3PH
020 7917 8888
www.landreg.gov.uk

House of Lords Record Office
Palace of Westminster
London SW1A 0PW
020 7219 3074
www.parliament.uk

Hulton Getty Collection
Unique House
21–31 Woodfield Road
London W9 2BA
0800 376 7977
www.gettyimages.com

Imperial War Museum
Lambeth Road
London SE1 6HZ
020 7416 5320
www.iwm.org.uk

Institute of Historical Research
University of London
Senate House
Malet Street
University of London
London WC1E 7HU
020 7862 8700
www.ihrinfo.ac.uk

Institute of Spiritualist Mediums
121 Church End Lane
Runwell
Essex SS11 7DN
www.ism.org.uk

Jersey Library
Halkett Place
St Helier
Jersey JE2 4WH
01534 759991
www.jsylib.gov.je/

Kent Historic Buildings Committee
Michael H. Peters
Hon. Secretary
CPRE Kent
24 Evegate Park Barn
Station Road
Smeeth
Ashford
Kent TN25 6SX
info@cprekent.org.uk

Lambeth Palace Library
Lambeth Palace Road
London SE1 7JU
020 7898 1400
www.lambethpalacelibrary.org

Land Registers of Northern Ireland
Lincoln Building
27–45 Great Victoria Street
Belfast BT2 7SL
02890 251515
www.lrni.gov.uk

Law Society
113 Chancery Lane
London WC2A IPL
0870 606 2511
www.library.lawsociety.org.uk

London School of Economics
Archives and Rare Books Department
10 Portugal Street
London WC2A 2HD
020 7995 7223
documents@lse.ac.uk

Lord Lyon King of Arms
New Register House
Charlotte Square
Edinburgh EH1 3YT
0131 334 0380
www.gro-scotland.gov.uk

Manorial Society of Great Britain
104 Kennington Road
London SE11 6RE
020 7735 6633
www.msgb.co.uk

Manx Museum
Kingswood Grove
Douglas
Isle of Man
01624 648000
www.gov.im/mnh/heritage/museums/
manxmuseum.xml

Mitchell Library
201 North Street
Glasgow G3 7DN
0141 287 2999
www.glasgow.gov.uk/en/Residents/
Leisure_Culture/Libraries/Librarylocations/
themitchell.htm

Museum of London
London Wall
London EC2Y 5HN
0870 444 3852
www.museumoflondon.org.uk/

National Archives
Ruskin Avenue
Kew
Richmond
Surrey TW9 4DU
020 8876 3555
www.nationalarchives.gov.uk

National Archives of Ireland
Bishop Street
Dublin 8
00 353 1407 2300
www.nationalarchives.ie

National Archives of Scotland
General Register House
2 Princes Street
Edinburgh EH1 3YY
0131 535 1334
www.nas.gov.uk

National Art Library
Victoria and Albert Museum
South Kensington
Cromwell Road
London SW7 2RL
020 7942 2000
www.vam.ac.uk/nal/ with its catalogue at http://ipac.nal.vam.ac.uk

National Library of Scotland
George IV Bridge
Edinburgh EH1 1EW
0131 466 2812
www.nls.uk

National Library of Wales (Llyfrgell Genedlaethol Cymru)
Panglais
Aberystwyth
Dyfed SY23 3BU
01970 623816/7
www.llgc.org.uk

National Monuments Record Centre
Great Western Village
Kemble Drive
Swindon SN2 2GZ
01793 414600
www.swindon.gov.uk.nmrc

New Register House
Charlotte Square
Edinburgh EH1 3YT
0131 334 0380
www.gro-scotland.gov.uk

Office for National Statistics
Segesworth Road
Titchfield, Fareham
Hampshire PO15 5RR
0845 601 3034
www.statistics.gov.uk/

Old House Books
Old Police Station, Pound Street
Moretonhampstead
Devon TQ13 8PA
01647 440707
www.OldHouseBooks.co.uk

Ordnance Survey
Romsey Road
Southampton
Hampshire SO16 4GU
08456 050505
www.ordnancesurvey.co.uk

Phillimore & Co. Ltd
Shopwyke Manor Barn
Chichester
West Sussex PO20 2BG
01243 787636
www.phillimore.co.uk

Principal Registry of the Family Division
First Avenue House
42–49 High Holborn
London WC1V 6NP
020 7936 7000
www.courtservice.gov.uk

Principal Registry of the Family Division's Postal Searches and Copies Department
The Probate Registry
Castle Chambers
Clifford Street
York YO1 9RG

Psychic News
The Coach House
Stansted Hall
Stansted
Essex CM24 8UD
01279 817050
www.snu.org.uk

Pub History Society
Steve Williams
15 Hawthorn Road
Peterborough PE1 4PA
www.pubhistory.freeserve.co.uk/phs/index.htm

Public Record Office of Northern Ireland (PRONI)
66 Balmoral Avenue
Belfast BT9 6NY
028 9025 5905
http://proni.nics.gov.uk

Registers of Scotland Executive Agency
Meadowbank House
153 London Road
Edinburgh EH8 7AU
0845 607 0161
www.ros.gov.uk

Registrar General of Eire
Joyce House
8–11 Lombard Street
Dublin 2
00 353 1635 4000
www.groireland.ie

Registrar General of Northern Ireland
Oxford House
49–55 Chichester Street
Belfast BT1 4HL
0232 235221
www.groni.gov.uk

Registrar General of Scotland
New Register House
Charlotte Square
Edinburgh EH1 3YT
0131 334 0380
www.gro-scotland.gov.uk

Registrar of Companies (main office)
Companies House
Crown Way
Maindy
Cardiff CF14 3UZ
0870 333 3636
http://ws6.companieshouse.gov.uk

Registrar of Companies (Scottish office)
37 Castle Terrace
Edinburgh EH1 2EB
0870 333 3636

Representative Body of the Church in Wales
39 Cathedral Road
Cardiff CF11 9XF
029 2034 8200
www.churchinwales.org.uk/reference/padmin/patronage_e.html

Royal Commission on the Ancient and Historical Monuments of Wales (Comisiwn Brenhinol Henebion Cymru)
Plâs Crug
Aberystwyth
Ceredigion SY23 1NJ
01970 621200
chc.cymru@cbhc.gov.uk

Royal Geographic Society
1 Kensington Gore
London SW7 2AR
020 7591 3000
www.rgs.org

Royal Mail Archive Service
Freeling House, Phoenix Place
London WC1X 0DL
020 7239 2570
heritage@royalmail.com

Scottish Genealogy Society
15 Victoria Terrace
Edinburgh EH1 2JL
0131 220 3677
www.scotsgenealogy.com/

Shire Books
Cromwell House, Church Street
Princes Risborough
Buckinghamshire HP27 9AA
01844 344301
www.shirebooks.co.uk

Society of Genealogists
14 Charterhouse Buildings
Goswell Road
London EC1M 7BA
020 7251 8799
www.sog.org.uk

Spiritualist National Union
Redwoods
Stansted Hall
Stansted Mountfitchett
Essex CM24 8UD
0845 4580 768
www.snu.org.uk

Sutton Publishing
Phoenix Mill
Thrupp
Stroud
Gloucestershire GL5 2BU
01453 731114
www.suttonpublishing.co.uk

Valuation Office
Irish Life Centre
Abbey Street Lower
Dublin 1
00 353 1817 1000
www.valoff.ie

Victoria and Albert Museum
South Kensington
Cromwell Road
London SW7 2RL
020 7942 2000
www.vam.ac.uk/nal/ with its catalogue at http://ipac.nal.vam.ac.uk

Suppliers of directories, maps and other local history material on CD-Rom

Archive CD Books
5 Commercial Street
Cinderford
Gloucestershire GL14 2RP
01594 829870
www.archivecdbooks.org

Back To Roots (UK) Ltd
16 Arrowsmith Drive
Stonehouse
Gloucestershire GL10 2QR
0800 298 5894
www.backtoroots.co.uk

Cyrene Publications
West Surrey Family History Society
Beverly
17 Lane End Drive
Knaphill
Woking
Surrey GU21 2QQ
www.wsfhs.org

Colin Hinson
119 High Street
Blunham
Bedfordshire MK44 3NW
01767 640503
www.blunham.demon.co.uk/cdroms

Direct Resources
33a Ruskin Avenue
Wakefield
Yorkshire WF1 2BG
0797 4672648
www.direct-resources.uk.com

Eneclann Ltd
Unit 1b
Trinity College Enterprise Centre
Pearse Street
Dublin 2 Ireland
00 353 1671 0338
info@eneclann.ie

Fitzmartyn Publications
10 Fitzwilliam Street
Wath-upon-Dearne
Rotherham
South Yorkshire S63 7HF
www.fitzmartyn.co.uk

JiGraH Resources
85 Heythrop Drive
Acklam
Middlesborough TS5 8QX
www.jigrah.co.uk

Original Indexes
113 East View
Wideopen
Tyne & Wear NE13 6EF
0191 236 6416
www.original-indexes.demon.co.uk

S&N Genealogy Supplies
Manor Farm
Chilmark
Salisbury SP3 5AF
01722 716121
www.sandn.net

Stepping Stones
PO Box 295
York Y032 9WQ
01904 400 503
www.stepping-stones.co.uk

Your Old Books & Maps
2 Temple Rd
Dewsbury WF13 3QE
01924 452987
Sales@youroldbooksandmaps.co.uk

Index

D

E

F

G

O

P

Q

R

S

T